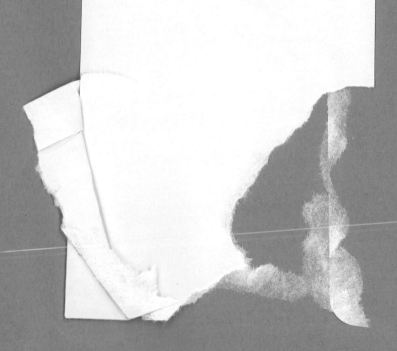

CHRISTIAN WORD BOOK

CHRISTIAN WORD BOOK

J. SHERRELL HENDRICKS
GENE E. SEASE
ERIC LANE TITUS
JAMES BRYAN WIGGINS

ABINGDON
PRESS
Nashville
New York

CHRISTIAN WORD BOOK

Copyright © 1968 by Graded Press

Standard Book Number: 687-07649-8
Library of Congress Catalog Card Number: 69-19739

SET UP, PRINTED, AND BOUND BY THE
PARTHENON PRESS, AT NASHVILLE,
TENNESSEE, UNITED STATES OF AMERICA

DEDICATED TO THE SPIRIT OF CHRISTIAN INQUIRY

introduction

This CHRISTIAN WORD BOOK was created to support serious study. It is intended as a basic source of information for biblical, theological, and ethical studies, as well as for the study of the general area of religion.

Students and young people particularly will find the book useful in explaining complicated concepts, theories, principles, ideas, and many terms they may encounter in curriculum resources. The CHRISTIAN WORD BOOK is meant to provide a fairly comprehensive review of terms from the Christian tradition to supplement and support the student's normal resources for study.

This book may also stimulate thinking that goes beyond the immediate content of the study resources. For example, any study of faith in God may lead to a number of questions, depending on the interests and concerns of the students involved in the class. When a class departs from the specific text of the regular resources, they may very well require information in a compact and accessible form, the form in which it may readily be found in the CHRISTIAN WORD BOOK.

On the other hand, the book has also been designed with the needs of the adult in mind. While the writing is clear and easy to understand, it is pithy and provocative enough to provide the kind of detailed information adult use requires. In the opinion of those who prepared the book there is less reason today than ever before to sacrifice content or detail in a book to be used both by young people and adults.

Today's young person is required every day to read complex, demanding, and sophisticated material for his schoolwork. He prepares detailed scientific reports and explores the nuances of subtle poetry. He also reads many of the same magazines and novels that adults read. He sees the same television shows and movies. In the opinion of the writers of this book, the need is not for a book directed to young people specifically, or to adults specifically, but to reasonably intelligent persons interested in broadening their understanding of some of the more important concepts of Christianity.

The words embodying these concepts were selected for this book only after a long process of elimination. In a survey of the word books now available, it was found that no single standard seems to have been used in their preparation. In some, an obvious word such as "salvation" had been included, but an equally important word such as "existential" had been neglected. Some seemed to lavish several hundred words on a favorite concept and to devote only a few lines to one in which they obviously had less interest. It has been the aim of this book to avoid such omissions.

There are no such things as "Christian words," of course. There are, however, many words that Christians in particular use. The selection of many of these will be unavoidably arbitrary, but an effort has been made to maintain a balanced approach.

Five major areas are included in this book: terms from (1) theology, (2) ethics, (3) biblical studies, (4) ecclesiology, and (5) worship. Terms from comparative religion and Christian education are omitted.

Since readers are inclined to pursue their search for a word in a variety of individual ways, we have tried to include many cross references to help lead the reader to the term he seeks. Since space is limited, we have often included several related terms in one cluster, rather than as separate entries. For instance, "natural theology" includes attention to "liberalism," since they are usually considered a part of the same theological tradition.

In case we do omit a term a reader has an interest in, we refer him to the several major reference works below that are both comprehensive and intellectually responsible.

Encyclopedia of Religion and Ethics, edited by James Hasting (12 vols.; Charles Scribner's Sons, 1910). Includes many terms from comparative religion and historical theology.

The Interpreter's Dictionary of the Bible (4 vols.; Abingdon Press, 1963). Includes basic biblical terms as well as some that might be considered theological.

Dictionary of Christian Ethics, edited by John Macquarrie (Westminster Press, 1967). A recent one-volume treatment of ethical terms.

The Oxford Dictionary of the Christian Church, edited by F. L. Cross (Oxford University Press, 1957). Has a definite English flavor, but does include information on historical figures up to recent times and also information about many liturgical terms.

How to Use This Book

(1) Terms are listed alphabetically.

(2) Each entry includes (a) the most pertinent information on the term; (b) relevant cross references; and (c) the initials of the author.

(3) The longest and most complex entries include an introductory

8

paragraph which serves to summarize the article so that the reader can see at a glance what the article contains.

(4) Some of the words most difficult to pronounce are accompanied by a guide to pronunciation. Only an elaborate and sophisticated guide can instruct readers on proper pronunciation of all the sounds of the English tongue. This guide is a rough and simple one, but perhaps it will enable persons to have some idea about the pronunciation of certain terms. The guide follows these conventions:

a is a short a, as in "atom"
ah is a long a, as in "hurrah"
eh is a short e, as in "get"
ee is a long e, as in "knee"
i is a short i, as in "rig"
igh is a long i, as in "fight"
yu is a short o, as in "cookie"
oo is a long o, as in "moose"
uh is a short u, as in "cup"
ew is a long u, as in "you"

For more extensive treatment of the pronunciation of biblical and religious terms, see *The Vocabulary of the Church: A Pronunciation Guide* by Richard C. White (Macmillan, 1960).

Abbreviations

A.D. Anno Domini, meaning "in the year of our Lord." Unless otherwise noted, dates are A.D.
B.C. Before Christ
c. *circa*, meaning "about," and used for approximate dates
e.g. exempli gratia, "for example"
etc. et cetera, "and so forth"
ff. "following," usually used in quotations from Scripture to indicate the verses immediately following the one cited
(which see) This insertion in the body of articles means that the reader is advised to look up the term immediately preceding.

authors

The Rev. J. SHERRELL HENDRICKS is a minister in the North Texas Annual Conference of The United Methodist Church. He is a native of Dallas, Texas, and has served as pastor of Methodist churches in Celina, Wichita Falls, and Dallas. At the time of this book's publication, he is pastor of First Methodist Church, Terrell, and Elmo Methodist Church.

Mr. Hendricks holds the B.B.A. degree from Southern Methodist University and a Bachelor of Divinity degree, plus 24 hours of advanced study, from Perkins School of Theology. He spent one summer studying at Union Theological Seminary in New York City.

Mr. Hendricks would like to acknowledge the "immeasurable help" of his wife, Anne, who has typed all his manuscripts for this book; Becky Warlick, a perceptive ninth grade student in Terrell; and the Rev. Fred Mooring, a Methodist pastor and writer who has read the articles and made suggestions during the composition.

The articles contributed by Mr. Hendricks are denoted by "J.S.H."

Dr. GENE E. SEASE, a minister in The United Methodist Church, is Administrative Assistant to the President, Indiana Central College, Indianapolis, Indiana. He received his formal education at Juniata College, Huntingdon, Pennsylvania (B.A.), Pittsburgh Theological Seminary (B.D., Th.M.), and the University of Pittsburgh (E. Ed., Ph.D.).

At the time of writing for this book, he was serving as a Conference Superintendent of the Western Pennsylvania Conference of The Evangelical United Brethren Church. Previously he had served for three years as Conference Director of Christian Education and Evangelism and fourteen years as a pastor. He has also been a member of the Gradutae Faculty of the University of Pittsburgh.

11

His great interests, professionally, lie in Christian education, practical theology, church administration, and history.

The articles contributed by Dr. Sease are denoted by "G.E.S."

Dr. ERIC LANE TITUS is Professor of New Testament at the School of Theology at Claremont, in Claremont, California.

Dr. Titus is a native of Freeport, Nova Scotia, and traveled to California by way of Acadia University in Canada, where he received an A.B.; Colgate Rochester Divinity School, where he received a B.D.; and the University of Chicago, where he received a Ph.D.

He has been pastor of churches in Canada and in New York State and also of First Baptist Church of Chicago.

His professional interests include studies in the Gospels, particularly the Fourth Gospel. He is the author of *The Message of the Fourth Gospel* (Abingdon Press, 1957) and *Essentials of New Testament Study* (Ronald Press, 1958). He is especially concerned with textual criticism, the field in which he studied while working on his Ph.D.

Dr. Titus' articles are denoted "E.L.T."

Dr. JAMES BRYAN WIGGINS is Associate Professor in the Department of Religion, Syracuse University, Syracuse, New York. A native of Mexia, Texas, Dr. Wiggins holds a B.A. degree from Texas Wesleyan College in Fort Worth; a B.D. from Perkins School of Theology, S.M.U., Dallas; and a Ph.D. from Drew University Graduate School.

First subject of concern for him among the intellectual disciplines is historical theology, although he also continues to study contemporary theology and philosophy of history.

Articles written by Dr. Wiggins are denoted "J.B.W."

Note:
Articles without initials were staff contributed.

A.D. It is customary in the western world to make the birth of Christ the point of reference for temporal events. The abbreviation A.D. is from the Latin *Anno Domini*, which means "in the year of our Lord." Events before that time are indicated by the abbreviation B.C., "before Christ." The date of Jesus' birth is uncertain. Scholars believe, however, that it took place prior to the death of Herod the Great, who died in 4 B.C. The difference in date is due to an error made in the reckoning of the date of Jesus' birth in the sixth century. At that time the year 1 of the Christian era was determined as the year 754 of Rome. This is the point to which events before and since have come to be referred. (*see* B.C.) E.L.T.

AARONIC PRIESTHOOD (*see Priest*)

Absolute In ordinary language, absolute refers to what is perfect, complete, and free from fault. It is easy to see why theologians and philosophers have so often been drawn to use the idea in relation to the ultimate. For theologians God has been said to be absolute. For philosophers (*e.g.*, Hegel), reason or mind has sometimes been referred to as Absolute Idea. It is remarkable how frequently the notion of God as absolute appears in the history of Christian theology. Thus, by use and tradition "the absolute" frequently refers to ultimate being or reality. When used in this way, the commitment to a particular metaphysic is always present. Two instances may make the problem clearer.

In the early Christian alliance between theology and Greek philosophy, the idea of God came to be a primary problem. Throughout the third century B.C. Christian theologians debated about how to speak most appropriately of God. The problems of monotheism and trinitarianism became acute. Increasingly those theologians sought to affirm both the Christian faithfulness to Jewish monotheism *and* to the divinity of both the Son and the Holy Spirit. One of the biggest questions was how to avoid speaking of the suffering and death of Jesus, the Christ, in such a way that it would seem that God himself had suffered and died. Those who believed God suffered were accused of advocating *patripassianism* (which see). The Council of Nicaea (325 B.C.) was convened to secure agreement between these theologians about how best to speak of God. The result was the offering of a creed that seemed to the popular mind to affirm God as absolute or ultimate. Later orthodox theologians kept the idea in one form or another, depending upon which philosophy they adhered to. No clearer example of this could be cited than Thomas Aquinas' (c. 1225-74) *On the Truth of God* (*Summa Contra Gentiles*) and *Summa Theologicae*.

Among modern theologians, Paul Tillich (1886-1965) was the most concerned about the problem of the absolute. Tillich raised the epistemological question of absolutism versus relativism. This cast his concern for God into terms contrasting God as absolute with God as relative. The issue so conceived, Tillich felt he must affirm God as absolute. God in Jesus Christ reveals that which is absolute, namely, his love which can never be other than it is. Tillich's discussions have thus relocated the problem surrounding the absolute. But problems, nevertheless, remain.

Schubert Ogden (1928-   ), following the lead of the philosopher Charles Hartshorne (1897-   ), has severely criticized the adequacy of any view of God as absolute. Traditional defenses of God as absolute have drawn the conclusion that in order to be perfect God must only be externally related to men and the world. For, if he were inwardly related, changes in men and in the world would change the unchangeable God. But Ogden argues that the Scriptures bear witness to God's creative and sustaining relationship with the world. The defender of God as absolute is forced into a logical inconsistency, since such theologians have traditionally defended their position by reference to Scripture. Ogden proposes an alternative way of viewing theism. He suggests that God must be thought of as at once absolute *and* relative. Put another way, God's absoluteness lies precisely in his perfect and unchanging relation to his creation. Ogden does not hesitate to affirm the consequence: God is constantly and eternally changing—absolute change. (*see Attributes of God, Omnipotence, Omniscience, Process, Relativism, Theism*) J.B.W.

Absolution From the word, *absolvere*, which means "free from," absolution is the act of forgiving sins. In Roman Catholic theology, absolution is the final step in the sacrament of penance. The church serves as the channel of God's grace. The priest, as an agent of the church, hears confessions of penitent sinners and declares forgiveness. Protestants vary in their views of whether confession is necessary, but in general they hold that absolution occurs directly between God and a

14

repentant person or people. (*see Forgiveness, Prayer, Repentance*) G.E.S.

ABSTINENCE (*see Ascetic, Moderation*)

Acceptance Acceptance is used in the Bible in three different ways. It refers to man's affirmative reception of God or His Word. As used here it indicates that man finds God trustworthy or dependable. The Scripture also refers to God's approval or disapproval of man's worship and service. Certain deeds are acceptable to God while certain other deeds are not. God rejoices in certain actions of Israel, but he is provoked to anger by others. Man also faces the question: shall I be receptive toward other men, or what must a man do before I will approve of him? Many passages of Scripture suggest that we should be receptive only to the man who is morally upright. Other passages of Scripture suggests that the Christian is to receive all men with open arms regardless of what they have done.

The deontological (study of essence) school of thought understands acceptance to be bound up with a person's relation to what is right. If man acts to tear down or destroy community life, he should be rejected for it. A man and his actions are viewed here as inseparable, and if a man acts irresponsibly he breaks agreements, or the covenant that binds him to the community. He is responsible for his own rejection.

The ontological (study of being) school stresses the value of being as such. Nicolas Berdyaev (1874-1948) sees the Christian as being one who "discovers the image of God in every man, even in the wicked criminal." Life is more important than law. The affirmation of life is more important than upholding the law; therefore, Christianity is opposed to any approach insisting on obedience to the law at any price.

Psychoanalysis has made a significant contribution to man's understanding of acceptance. This science is dedicated to the observation of and understanding of human life. It tries to stay away from such terms as "good" and "bad." Psychoanalysis tries to examine deeds and persons from an objective (in the sense of non-judgmental) point of view. This is an attempt to view human relations by accepting them for what they are and seeking to understand them. Condemning the man because of his unfortunate behavior is seen as being of little value.

Paul Tillich (1886-1965), in his now famous sermon, "You Are Accepted," interprets the gospel as saying God accepts all men. No matter how great man's sin, God's grace abounds all the more. Man's sin separates him from God, from others, and from himself, but God's love for man is able to overcome this separation. Frequently, man feels guilty about his wrong deeds, and this guilt causes him to reject himself. In effect, man concludes that no one could possibly love a person who sins.

15

Accordingly, he finds himself unable to accept himself. Grace calls man to accept himself and therefore to accept God's acceptance of him. (*see Justification by faith, Self-understanding*) J.S.H.

ACCIDENT (*see Essence, Substance*)

ACT (BY GOD) (*see Covenant, History, Revelation*)

ACTUS PURUS (*see Potentiality*)

ADONAI (*see Name*)

Adoptionism (uh-*dahp*-shun-ism) This belief, which appears in the late second century in the teaching of Theodotus and was expanded by Paul of Samosata, Bishop of Antioch, in the third century, taught that though Jesus was superior in goodness because of the virgin birth, at baptism God promoted him to divine status. Jesus' divinity was confirmed by his resurrection. Adoptionism has since been applied to any view that regards Jesus as born human and as elevated to divinity at some later point in his life. (*see Christology*) G.E.S.

Advent From the Latin word, *adventus*, Advent means "arrival" or "coming" and marks the coming of Jesus as man into the world. The Advent Season begins four Sundays before Christmas as a time of preparation for the coming of the Son of God to earth. From about the middle of the sixth century, Advent has marked the beginning of the church year and is the first season in the Christian calendar. While our calendar begins with January 1, the church year actually starts with Advent. The expected return of Jesus Christ is referred to as the "Second Advent." (*see Incarnation*, PAROUSIA) G.E.S.

AEON (*see Eternal*)

Aesthetics (es-*thet*-iks) Aesthetics is the branch of philosophy that deals with the question of beauty. What is beautiful? Is there any standard for judging art? If so, what is it? What is in good taste, and what is not? How can man tell what is good poetry and what is bad poetry? This same question is asked about music, literature, dancing, decoration, and design. Aesthetics is an attempt to use reason to discover in nature and taste the actual rules and principles of art. It tries to answer the question: what is artistic? It may be defined simply as the philosophy of art. Aesthetics is also concerned with style and taste. Style has to do with the mode or form of an expression. Taste deals with the question: is a particular manner of expression pleasing?

The concept of beauty played a significant role in the thought of Plato (*c.* 427-347 B.C.) Man is the kind of creature who may crawl in degradation or soar to great heights. Society can be structured so that it encourages man to seek corruption. Man may be controlled by animal impulses alone. But reason may take precedence over "wants and impulses." Man's creative imagination (such as in poetry) may change abstract ideas into living realities and help man to fall in love with these realities. According to Plato, love is actually the quest for the beautiful. All forms of beauty in this world are derived from and refer back to the true ideal beauty. Plato's criticism was both rational and moral. He believed that art should both inform people about what is going on and help to reform people by suggesting in what direction man should move. Aristotle (384-322 B.C.) saw the poet as imitating life. The poet's role is to please man. The poet arouses man's emotions and enables man to go away from the experience having been relieved of pent-up emotions that might otherwise have been damaging to him.

G. W. F. Hegel (1770-1831) taught that beauty is essentially spiritual. The inner life of man, that is, man's relation to the eternal or to value, finds expression in art. Man encounters the eternal and makes his own reaction to this reality. In art he expresses this experience in sensuous form. This is a part of man's way of understanding his encounter with God. Anywhere man encounters genuine beauty he encounters the beauty of God. Plato had first taught that beauty lures, charms, and inspires. Christian theology talks of God as truly beautiful. In union with God all reality is opened up before man, and man is at one with all that is. Some philosophers of art view art as pure intuition. In art the mind beholds a vision of reality. This does not include a judgment about reality, for art only reflects what is there. John Dewey (1859-1952) saw art as valuable in that it helps man to integrate and enjoy immediate experience. Art helps man to better understand the things that are going on about him. With this increased understanding comes increased enjoyment.

Paul Tillich (1886-1965) views art as a picture mirroring reality. The role of works of art (poetry, literature, painting, dancing) is best understood by looking at its power to express what concerns man ultimately. Art can reflect more powerfully than the written word the value-struggle man is involved in. In the written word man uses concepts to communicate his understandings and feelings about life. In art he uses images to communicate. Thus, man takes art seriously in order to understand its "vision of the world." J.S.H.

AFFECTION (*see Love*)

AFFUSION (*see Baptism*)

17

AGAPE (*see Love*)

AGENT (*in ethics*) (*see Consciousness, Decision, Self*)

Aggiornamento (aj-ohr-nah-*men*-toh) This Italian term comes from a word whose basic meaning is "to adjourn" or "to become daylight." *Aggiornamento* was used to describe the task of the Vatican II Council of Roman Catholics. Many Roman Catholic scholars and religious leaders saw the task as one of "bringing the church up to date." Thus *aggiornamento* continues as the Roman Catholic church explores the relation of the church to the world, a modern understanding of its dogmas, and the meaning of ecumenicity.

Agnostic (ag-*nahs*-tik) The word derives from the Greek *gnosis*—knowledge—and *a*—no. Thus it literally means "no knowledge." As such, it can be applied when someone refuses to accept or reject any assertion that others claim to "know." Christians believe in God's reality. Agnostics deny that men can attain such knowledge and argue that it is meaningless to debate the issue. In the modern era, agnosticism has often gone hand in hand with the scientific enterprise. Only those realities can be known that are capable of scientific description and proof; all else is unknown, *i.e.*, about such matters one must be an agnostic. In theology, agnosticism often accompanies faith. For example, one may have faith in the reality of God and at the same time be an agnostic about God's innermost quality and attributes. (*see Atheism, Skeptic*) J.B.W.

Agnus Dei (*ag*-noos *day*-ee, or *dee*-igh) This Latin translation for "Lamb of God" has its origin in John 1:29, " 'Behold, the Lamb of God, who takes away the sin of the world!' " The Agnus Dei is part of the Mass or the Holy Communion. In its liturgical form, it is spoken, "O Lamb of God, who takest away the sins of the world, have mercy upon us." G.E.S.

ALETHEIA (*see Truth*)

Alienation (ail-yuh-*nay*-shun) Alienation means being estranged, separated, cut off, or withdrawn. It implies a hostile or indifferent relationship. The word "alien" or "stranger," used in the Old Testament, refers to one who is away from his home. An alien is one who has turned aside from his own people and is in the midst of strangers. After Cain killed Abel he is told " 'you shall be a fugitive and a wanderer on the earth.' " (Genesis 4:12) This is a punishment placed on Cain because he did not recognize his responsibility to be his brother's keeper.

The New Testament story of the prodigal son (Luke 15:11-24) is a story of alienation and reunion.

G. W. F. Hegel (1770-1831) taught that entities have qualities, which in turn are entities external to the entities which have them. Man as man includes the quality of being able to reason and have ideals. He may possess the quality we call freedom. Freedom is a reality outside of man, and it has independent being. Freedom is an ideal, and ideals are real. Freedom is of the essence of man—if man is to be fully a man he must be free. Freedom is a reality as a table or car is. This teaching that ideals are real leads to the conclusion that alienation occurs when man fails to pattern his life after the ideal. For example, man has a picture of the ideal of freedom. When man fails to live in accordance with this ideal his life and the lives of others suffer. To be alienated is to be cut off from the ideal. Man is to overcome alienation by using his mind to discover ideals and then pattern his life after the ideal.

Karl Marx (1818-83) understood alienation to be a social disease. Men are estranged from one another because they have used privately owned property for selfish gain to the damage of other human lives. The basis of alienation does not lie in ideals but in the material world. Man is to overcome hostilities, nature's challenges, and be happy by securing the proper distribution of material goods. Walter Rauschenbusch (1861-1918) taught that man's inhumanity to man has led to a sick society (including war, poverty, and injustice). He sees in the teaching of Jesus of Nazareth the way man can overcome all of these problems. If man follows Jesus' example and teaching, the kingdom of God will be established on earth. Man will overcome all his enemies, and all men will live together on earth. Alienation is the result of man's failure to relate to his fellow man as God would have him to do. Alienation is man's enmity with other men, and man's failure to establish the kind of society on earth that God wants him to.

Paul Tillich (1886-1965) defines alienation as man's situation of being cut off from the center of meaning and of purpose for his own life. Man has lost contact with the basis for his life. Man is alienated when he is not being true to what it means to be a man. In this situation he is at odds (the opposite of being at one) with himself, with his neighbor, and with God. Man experiences alienation when he exists and yet remains a stranger to himself. (*see Sin, Soteriology*) J.S.H.

Allegory The classic example of an allegory in literature is *Pilgrim's Progress*, by John Bunyan (1628-88). A good biblical illustration of allegory is found in John 15. In that chapter, Jesus is represented as the vine, the disciples are the branches of the vine, and God is the vinedresser. It can be seen from this that each element of an allegory possesses its own distinct meaning.

Allegory has played an important part in the history of biblical interpretation. The tendency was to allegorize the Old Testament so as to find references to Christ throughout. But with the rise of the critical and scientific approach to the Bible, allegory ceased to play a central role in the study of the Bible. It should be said, however, that where the literature is allegorical in intention, the interpreter should treat it as such. (*see Analogy*) E.L.T.

ALTRUISM (*see Idealism, Virtue*)

Amen The Greek word *amēn* is a transliteration of the Hebrew equivalent, which is related to the root word meaning "to make firm" or "establish." The idea of "truth" is a part of its meaning. Translation into English is difficult, if not impossible, but its force in use is strongly felt. Four uses of the "amen" have been distinguished: (a) the initial amen, where it marks a weighty saying to follow; (b) the final amen, where it means solemn confirmation of what has been said; (c) the responsive amen, where it expresses assent to the words of another; and (d) what might be called the subscriptional amen, where it closes a writing. (e) the use of Amen as a title for Jesus in the Johannine Apocalypse. This is found in Revelation 3:14, and as a title it is peculiar to the Apocalypse and to this passage; (f) John's Gospel uses the double amen at the beginning of utterances of Jesus. This use occurs twenty-five times in John, but nowhere else. (*see Faith, Truth*) E.L.T.

AMORAL (*see Morality*)

Analogy (an-*al*-oh-jee) An analogy is a form of reasoning that begins with the recognition of similarity between two or more objects (*e.g.*, these four tables each have four legs) or relationships (*e.g.*, this father loves each of his three children). From the original similarity, analogical thought assumes that there are further similarities between the objects or relationships, even if such similarities are not observable, or even if the words describing the similarities do not mean the same in reference to both objects or relationships.

Inheriting the idea of analogy from Greek philosophers, the medieval scholastic Christian theologians developed analogical thinking to a fine point. Thomas Aquinas (*c.* 1225-74) was an outstanding example. Aquinas distinguished between two kinds of analogy: (1) the analogy of proportion, and (2) the analogy of proportionality. By an analogy of *proportion*, Thomas meant that because of a similarity between two subjects, a quality used in description of one of them could be applied in a related but slightly different way to the other. By the analogy of *proportionality*, Thomas meant that if the relationship between the subjects of one pair of things in an analogy exists, that same relationship may exist between the subjects of another pair. "Seeing" is the relationship that exists analogously between the eye and vision, on the one hand, and the mind and intellectual understanding, on the other hand. Such a mode of thought is particularly relevant in regard to the attributes of God (which see). To say that God is merciful or that God exists presupposes enough likeness between men and God to make such an analogy meaningful. In man mercy is imperfect; in God mercy is perfected and unlimited. But by analogous thinking it is nonetheless meaningful to speak of mercy in reference both to God and man. Such an analogy is technically called "analogy of being" (*analogia entis*). Such a method of thought also presupposes that such analogies are based upon the use of natural reason.

The use of analogy has been debated among non-Roman Catholic theologians and philosophers of religion since the Reformation. Some philosophers of religion, following Immanuel Kant (1724-1804), have argued that since God is infinite and absolute, it is impossible for men with finite minds to know anything about God. Such thinkers have rejected metaphysics as an aid to theology and have been skeptics regarding epistemology. Others, following Friedrich Hegel (1770-1831), have argued that the mind of man is the only means of knowing God, who by analogy is supremely Mind.

In the twentieth century the debate has continued vigorously. Karl Barth (1884-   ) has denied that Christianity has anything to do with natural reason. Instead he has insisted that revelation, which must be received by faith, is the only means a Christian will have for knowing God. He has proposed an "analogy of faith" (*analogia fidei*) based on revelation to replace the "analogy of being" based on reason. Thus, Barth admits that analogy is a helpful way to make meaningful statements about God, but only an analogy of faith that will be meaningful to those who share the faith, or who at least accept the reality of revelation. Paul Tillich (1886-1965) denies the radical separation that Barth wants to maintain between the analogy of being and the analogy of faith. For Tillich, revelation is not the contradiction or disruption of reason but is rather its fulfillment. Thus, the two types of analogy will not produce such radically differing statements as Barth seems to imply.

Schubert Ogden (1928-   ) is a theologian for whom the problem of analogy represents a serious issue. (*see Epistemology, Faith, Ontology, Reason, Revelation, Theism, Verification*) J.B.W.

ANALYTIC PHILOSOPHY (*see Language*)

ANAMNESIS (*see Communion*)

Anathema (an-*ath*-uh-muh)   This Greek word is now used freely in English and means, "a thing devoted to evil" or "a curse." Used by Paul in Galatians 1:8,9 and in 1 Corinthians 12:3 and 16:22, it marks one who has been rejected by God. It refers to something polluted or cursed and to persons excommunicated from the church. (*see Apostasy, Heresy*) G.E.S.

ANGST (*see Anxiety*)

Anthem   Originally called "antiphon" (responsive music), it was a passage of Scripture sung by two opposing choral groups. During the thirteenth through the sixteenth centuries, the motet came into prominent use. It was a liturgical choral composition using a Latin text. During the Elizabethan period, the anthem came into use in the Anglican and Protestant services. Now a form of sacred music without liturgical words, it uses solo as well as mixed voices. G.E.S.

ANTHROPOLOGY (*see Archaeology, Man*)

Anthropomorphism (An-throh-po-*mor*-fizm)   The term "anthropomorphism" is composed of two Greek words, *anthropos* and *morphe*, meaning "man" and "form" respectively. It signifies qualities of God or a god in human terms. An extreme example of anthropomorphism is found in Genesis 3:8, where God is described as "walking in the garden in the cool of the day," presumably to escape the heat. Anthropomorphism can also appear as personal qualities, such as the pleasure or anger of the deity. The gods of Greek mythology present us with examples of this type of anthropomorphism, nor is it absent from the biblical records. (*see Analogy, Incarnation*) E.L.T.

Antichrist   Apocalyptic literature not in the Bible speaks of a being who will oppose the messiah. The New Testament speaks of "antichrist" who denies the Father and Son (see 1 John 2 and 2 John 7). The antichrist really belongs to the period of the Second Coming, when he will challenge Christ; thus he is the opposite of Christ, not Jesus. Christians later accused their opponents, such as Nero, of being antichrist. They also accused each other. The Reformers called the pope antichrist and the followers of the pope replied in kind. (*For a lengthy and informative article, see "Antichrist" in* THE INTERPRETER'S DICTIONARY OF THE BIBLE.)

Antinomian (ant-uh-*noh*-mee-un)   In Greek *nomos* means law: hence antinomian literally means anti-legalistic. In Christian theology, God's grace is universally seen as the source of salvation. This inevitably raises the question of the relation of a saved person to the law. Those who have held that the saved man is completely freed from moral law are traditionally called antinomians. In the area of theological reflection called "ethics," antinomianism is almost always discussed. Few theologians are willing to accept the antinomian conclusion. (*see Ethics, Law*) J.B.W.

ANTITHESIS (*see Dialectic*)

Anxiety   Anxiety is the uneasiness man experiences when he is aware of both the limitations and his freedom that are his as a human being. Man is by nature one who will die, make mistakes (and thus feel guilty), and lose sight of the meaning of his life. These are facts of life that cannot be effectively avoided. In the Old Testament man is pictured as disturbed because he is uncertain about his own future. The fear of famine (Jeremiah 17:8), fear of not having a child (1 Samuel 1:16), and fear about what the future in general may hold (Daniel 7:15). Thus anxiety is directly related to historical conditions. The answer to anxiety is for man to call upon God to deliver him. The New Testament concept of anxiety (*merimna*) reflects the same problems as does the Old Testament. Jesus' teaching on anxiety is that anxiety is the result of a bad relationship to God. God's providential care and concern makes anxiety unnecessary.

German theologians have used the word *angst* to indicate anxiety in contrast to *sorge*, which means worry or fear about a particular thing happening. Paul Tillich (1886-1965), in *Courage to Be*, asserted that ancient man was primarily anxious about the contingent nature of his life. He realized he was not necessary and that soon he would die (*ontic* anxiety). Thus, he was primarily anxious about the temporary and limited role he played in life. In the Middle Ages man was predominantly disturbed by *moral* anxiety. Man was aware of his own misuse of freedom. He knew he had sinned and deserved to be punished. He suffered from strong guilt feelings. In the modern period of history man is suffering primarily from a third type of anxiety, *spiritual* anxiety. This third type of anxiety is that in which man loses contact with the meaning of his life. He feels life is meaningless; it has no purpose. Every man in every period of history experiences all three of these types of anxiety. Every man is in some way disturbed about the fact that he must die, that he is a sinner, and that he loses contact with the meaning of his life. Thus, anxiety is ontological anxiety; *i.e.*, it is a part of human life by virtue of human life being what it is.

There is a kind of neurotic anxiety, which is quite different from the anxiety described above. Man tries to keep from dealing with any and all of these three types of ontological anxiety. He does this by developing

23

neurotic (or abnormal) anxiety. Neurotic anxiety occurs where man agrees to settle down to a fixed and limited life. Man sets some rather limited goals for himself, such as to make passing grades, to be popular, or to follow fairly closely the moral rules accepted by society. Thus, the predominant concerns of his life are within his control. Anxiety is different from fear in that it has no definite object. Man is anxious about his life in that he may fail to be fully human. In neurotic anxiety he turns this into a more limited situation so that he can deal with it. Now he is afraid people will not like him, or he is afraid he will make bad grades. But these are fears that he can deal with. He can study and secure good grades for himself. He can work at being well-liked and accomplish this. The only problem here is that life itself reminds him that he has settled for something less than a full life.

Religion deals with ontological anxiety. The problems of death, guilt, and meaninglessness can be faced by a human being. He can in faith accept that this is who he is. If he does this he does not exclude anxiety from his life. He is willing to acknowledge the anxious feelings he has about his own limitations, his own mistakes, and the loss of meaning in his life. But in courage he will not run away from nor pretend that he does not have these problems. The man of faith gives of his life in a free and creative attempt to deal openly and honestly with life's problems. (*see Courage, Fear*) J.S.H.

Apocalypse (uh-*pok*-uh-lips) The term "apocalypse" comes from the Greek *apokalupsis*, which means "a revelation" or "disclosure." It is applied to a type of literature that appeared among the Hebrews during the Exile (sixth and fifth centuries B.C.) and found later expressions in both biblical and apocryphal writings of the Jews. It found expression in early Christianity as well, although only one book of the New Testament is a thoroughgoing apocalypse. This kind of literature is the product of a movement, the apocalyptic movement, which tended to replace the older prophetic element. It is sometimes said that prophecy, apocalyptic, and the later Christian martyrology all acted as means of social control, *i.e.*, to maintain group loyalty and solidarity in the face of external threats. An element of truth is certainly to be found in this view, but it fails to exhaust the intention of these movements. Behind the apocalyptic position is the conviction that God is in control of the world and that he will vindicate his people. Another way of saying this is that the apocalypse affirms the sovereignty of God. The apocalyptist would say that, in spite of evidence to the contrary, God is in control and this will be made evident in the future. Presumed supernatural knowledge of that future is what gives the apocalyptist his special authority; the veil of ignorance is lifted, and the faithful are allowed to see the unfolding of the cosmic drama of their own vindication.

The apocalypse differs from both prophecy and eschatology. Prophecy, which is not to be equated with mere prediction, finds its classical expression in the eighth century B.C. and following. The prophet is literally God's spokesman; he is frequently a poet, a man who is in close contact with the great movements of his times, and foresees the consequences of what is taking place. While he speaks for God and from the context of the power of God's Spirit, which is upon him, the prophet looks for the fruition of God's purposes *from within history.* The apocalyptist, on the other hand, looks for a supernatural inbreaking of God, who will sit in judgment over the world and vindicate his righteous purposes. Usually the apocalyptist advances a timetable of this act of God. It is this feature that marks the essential distinction between apocalypse and eschatology. The latter is a feature of apocalyptic literature, but it may stand by itself without the elaborate imagery and specific statement of future events that characterize apocalyptic. Thus Jesus had an eschatology, because he believed in the early end of the age. But he was not an apocalyptist, for he refused to specify "the day or the hour" when the end would come.

In the Old Testament, apocalyptic elements appear in Ezekiel, a book written during the Exile. However, the major apocalypse of the Hebrew scriptures is the Book of Daniel, written against the background of the persecution of Antiochus Epiphanes (168-165 B.C.). The New Testament reflects apocalyptic tendencies, notably in Mark 13 (sometimes called "The Little Apocalypse"), but the great New Testament apocalypse is Revelation, or the Apocalypse of John. The extent of the apocalyptic movement, however, may be understood only as one goes beyond the biblical writings to the so-called apocryphal works, both Jewish and Christian. Non-biblical apocalypses include 1 Enoch, 2 Esdras, Baruch, the Shepherd of Hermas, and the Apocalypse of Peter.

The main characteristics of an apocalypse are: (a) It is usually pseudonymous. Writings are attributed to outstanding heroes of the faith who are supposed to be predicting future events. (b) By the use of spectacular imagery the writer paints a picture of the power and majesty of God. (c) Mysterious symbols are often used, presumably clear to the recipients of the apocalypse but not to outsiders. (d) Apocalyptic is the literature of crisis; it grows out of crisis and speaks to it. (e) It is generally pessimistic about man's ability to right social wrongs, but it is optimistic about God's ability to do this.

Apocalyptic literature may be divided into two types, Jewish and Gentile. The Jewish apocalyptic is concerned with the *group,* whether the nation or an elect community. The Revelation of John, while of Christian origin, is a Jewish-type apocalypse. Its concern is with the Christian group. The Apocalypse of Peter, on the other hand, is a Gentile-type apocalypse, and its concern is with the *individual.* In either

25

case, however, an apocalypse is a tract for the times. In the case of Daniel, the book was written to encourage Jews to resist the persecution by Antiochus Epiphanes. That persecution was the "crisis" that prompted the writing of the book. In the case of Revelation, the setting seems to have been the persecution of Christians during the reign of Domitian (c. A.D. 95). Domitian's persecution is the "crisis" that gave rise to this Christian apocalypse. The notion that an apocalypse speaks directly to the remote future has no basis in fact. (*see Apocrypha, Eschatology, Number,* PAROUSIA, *Prophet*) E.L.T.

APOCATASTASIS (*see End, Soteriology*)

Apocrypha (uh-*pok*-reh-fa) The term "apocrypha" means "hidden" or "secret," and at the start probably applied to sectarian books thought to be of great importance because they contained the secret teachings of the groups. As it has come to be used, it suggests "inferior." Consequently, certain apocryphal books are either placed in a position by themselves between the Testaments or are omitted altogether from the Christian canon.

The apocryphal literature may be classified as follows: (a) the Old Testament Apocrypha, consisting of fourteen books, of which outstanding examples are 1 Maccabees and Ecclesiasticus; (b) the New Testament Apocrypha, which consists of books similar in form to New Testament books, *i.e.,* it contains gospels, acts literature, and apocalypses. Notable examples are the Protevangelium of James, the Acts of Thomas, and the Apocalypse of Peter.

The Protestant Bible has generally abandoned the Old Testament apocryphal books, although they came into the early Christian Bible by way of the Septuagint. In recent times the Smith-Goodspeed *Complete Bible* was an attempt to restore the ancient usage. The Roman Catholic Bible contains the Apocrypha as a result of the action of the Council of Trent in the sixteenth century. (*see Canon, Pseudepigrapha*) E.L.T.

APOLLINARIANISM (*see Christology*)

APOLOGETIC (*see Natural theology, Theology*)

Apostasy (uh-*pas*-tuh-see) From the Greek, *apostasia,* which literally means, "standing firm" or "to revolt," it refers to one who has been loyal to the faith, but who has defected from it. The term is restricted to one who has accepted the faith, and who has been baptized in it, but who has now renounced it. Apostates have been formally excommunicated by the church, usually for heresy. (*see Anathema, Heresy, Pagan*) G.E.S.

Apostle "Apostle" is the English translation of the Greek *apostolos,* which means one who is sent. This general meaning appears in the New Testament, but in the church's use has become overshadowed by a more limited application to an official group, "the twelve apostles." According to the Gospels, Jesus selected and sent out twelve disciples (Matthew 10:1 *ff.;* Mark 3:14 *ff.;* Luke 6:13 *ff.).* The Lucan passage says that Jesus gave the name "apostles" to the twelve disciples. The importance of the number "twelve" for the writer of the Acts of the Apostles is indicated by its account of the choosing of Matthias to take the place of Judas (Acts 1:15-26). Matthias' place in the group is justified by the fact that he had been with Jesus and the disciples from the time of "John's baptism" until Jesus' ascension into heaven (verses 21-22), and becomes, along with the eleven, a witness to the Resurrection. The basic core of the official apostolic office grew naturally out of those who had been with Jesus.

It is of note, however, that Paul, who had not been a member of the original twelve, becomes classified as an apostle in the official sense. The fact that he had not been with Jesus may have been in part responsible for opposition to Paul's claim to apostleship on the part of some. Paul based his claim on the fact that he had seen the Lord (1 Corinthians 9:1; 15:8; Galatians 1:16). As an apostle, *i.e.,* as one sent, he considered his mission to be the Gentiles (Galatians 1:16). In spite of the fact that Paul had not been one of the original twelve, his apostleship became recognized by the church at large.

It should be pointed out that the lists of disciples vary, so that the exact constitution of "the twelve" is a matter of debate. It is of interest that the twelve disciples parallel the twelve tribes of Israel. It has been argued that since the early Christians considered themselves to be the new Israel, there must be coincidence in number with the old Israel (compare Revelation 21:12-14). This argument suggests that the number "twelve" was but a creation of the church. The usage is extremely old, however, as 1 Corinthians 15:5 clearly shows, a fact that argues against this view. (*see Orders, Succession*) E.L.T.

APOSTLES' CREED (*see Creed*)

APOTHEOSIS (*see Anthropomorphism, Theism*)

Appetite Appetite is a recurring desire for something by a bodily organism. In its most basic sense appetite refers to the desire for the satisfaction of certain natural needs (hunger, thirst, rest, sex). Appetite is thus sometimes associated only with physical needs of the individual. It may also refer to the irrational desire of the individual for satisfaction or pleasure. In this regard man's appetites pose a problem for him. An appetite is neither good nor bad in itself, and in one respect appetites are good for they cause a man to seek out the things (food, drink, sleep) necessary to his physical health. Plato (*c.* 427-347 B.C.) taught that appetites need to be controlled by reason. A man needs to control or curb his desire for food or else he will become a glutton. A normal appetite is the desire for food when hungry. When a hungry man eats he naturally experiences pleasure. But if man who is no longer hungry continues to seek the pleasure that eating brings, he is seeking food in an abnormal and harmful way. Here appetites are lifted out of their normal role (of sustaining life) and made an end in themselves.

In the Old Testament appetite is used to mean the experience of being attracted to something. The appetite is the desire for what brings the good life. For example, the good life includes not being hungry; thus man has an appetite for food. Only if man misuses this appetite will it hurt him (gluttony).

The term "appetite" does not appear in the New Testament. Here the term "flesh" is used to refer to man's giving of himself solely to the pursuit of satisfying his own desires. A man who constantly tries to feed his bodily appetites fully is a slave to the flesh. He is a slave to his own desires, and he is in need of help.

Thomas Aquinas (*c.* 1225-74) and the Roman Catholic Church after him, divides appetites into two kinds. (1) There is the desire for sensual or irrational pleasure. This is simply animal appetite, and it is the lowest kind. This lower appetite should be fed only to the extent that is necessary for sustaining life. All unnecessary feeding of this appetite is bad. (2) Man has a higher appetite that may be satisfied by "rational contemplation of the divine." As man thinks about God and His law he is raised up to a new level of life. His lower appetites are controlled. He gives of his time and energy in pursuit of sacred things as opposed to animal things.

Martin Luther (1483-1546) reacted against this understanding of appetite. Creation as such is good. Therefore, bodily appetite is not bad. The body is sacred as is the mind. Man is not to allow his appetite for good to prevent him from being faithful to the will of God. The crucial question is: is man doing what God is calling him to do now? The curbing of his appetite is a secondary concern. Man should control his desire for food if it gets in the way of his service to God. Man does not practice control of his appetites for the sake of making himself a better person. One's making of himself a better person is not the purpose of Christian ethics. Christian ethics calls man to lose himself in concern for the neighbor. (*see Ascetic, Epicurean, Flesh, Sin*) J.S.H.

APPROPRIATE (*see Calculation*)

Aramaic (air-uh-*may*-ik)   Aramaic is a Semitic language, closely related to Hebrew. It was the language of Palestine in the time of Jesus. Hebrew remained only as the language of the sacred literature. When the Torah was read in the Synagogue it had to be accompanied by a translation into Aramaic. Through the policies of Alexander the Great and others the Greek language was widespread in the period, but there is no reason to think that Jesus was acquainted with any language other than Aramaic.

The New Testament was written in Greek. This means that authentic words of Jesus or teachings of the early Aramaic-speaking community had to be translated into Greek. Some have held that our Gospels were first written in Aramaic and then translated into Greek, a theory which has not won wide acceptance. The Gospels show evidence of being composition Greek. Nonetheless, as we should expect, the New Testament shows some evidence of its Aramaic background in remaining words and phrases (Mark 5:41; 7:34; Matthew 27:46; 1 Corinthians 16:22). Beyond this, scholars find many "semitisms" in the New Testament, a clue to the Semitic part of its background. (*see* KOINE) E.L.T.

Archaeology   Archaeology is the scientific study of ancient cultures on the basis of their material remains. It is sometimes divided into prehistoric and historic; the former has to do with the remains of civilizations of which there survive no other records. The latter deals with the period from which written records survive. When dealing with the historical period, archaeology supplements the written records, and the two together offer strong historical evidence.

Archaeology has become an important scientific tool in the study of the biblical period, especially with reference to the Old Testament. A distinction should be made between archaeology and closely related disciplines such as paleontology, which deals with forms of life existing in earlier geological periods; ethnology, which is concerned with distinctive groupings of mankind; and anthropology, which deals with the origin and development of mankind. Ethnology and anthropology interact with the science of archaeology. E.L.T.

Ascension   The fortieth day after Easter is Ascension Day in the Christian calendar. It marks the conclusion of the post-Easter period and signals the approach of Pentecost (Whitsunday) ten days later. The biblical account of the ascension of Jesus is found in Acts 1:9-11. A principle basic to the understanding of the ascension is that God and his Kingdom are above the earth. Satan and forces of evil are thought of as "down" and heaven and God as "up." (See Genesis 28:12; Judges 13:20; Psalms 24:3 and 139:8; Proverbs 30:4; Isaiah 14:13; John 3:13; Romans 10:6,7 and 1 Thessalonians 4:16,17.)

The ascension of Jesus followed various post-resurrection appearances. While the ascension itself is regarded by some New Testament writers as but one of those appearances, it is of the utmost importance to Luke, who gives an impressive record of the final parting (Luke 24:36-51). Among the appearances following his resurrection were those on the road to Emmaus, in the upper room, and beside the Sea of Galilee. Though certain biblical passages do not seem to distinguish between the resurrection and ascension (Acts 2:31-33; Romans 8:34; 1 Peter 3:21-22), there is no doubt about the change in relationship with his followers. Prior to the ascension Jesus was their companion and teacher, but following it he moved beyond time and space to share in God's rule, or sovereignty.

The theme of Ascension Day is that the transcendent Christ is not only risen from the dead but that he has again taken up his divine life at the "right hand of God" to reign over heaven and earth. At the ascension, the spokesman in white said, " 'This Jesus, who was taken up from you into heaven, will come in the same way as you saw him go into heaven.' " (Acts 1:11) First-century Christians anticipated his early return. The faithful continue to await the fulfillment of his promise to return in a second coming, or second advent.

Jesus' sovereignty plays a crucial role in Christian thought. As King, the ascended Christ is Lord over all creation and the church, and all believers are subjects. The ascension confirms his lordship and sovereignty. Yet, he is not only a sovereign ruler but a compassionate savior. The Son serves as advocate (like a defense attorney) and he intercedes for all repentant followers, thus climaxing his life, suffering, death, and resurrection. (see Resurrection) G.E.S.

Ascetic (uh-*set*-ik) An ascetic is a person who views physical pleasures (eating, drinking, *etc.*) as bad. Therefore, man is better off if he practices abstinence, *i.e.*, voluntarily refrains from indulging in these pleasures. Pleasurable experiences, at least, must be kept under strict control. The common or natural pleasures are rejected in order to give of oneself to the higher values. A group of Christians called Montanists (A.D. 150) may be viewed as representative of the ascetic. This group taught that every person should follow strict moral disciplines. Marriage should be entered into but once. Fasting is a good thing. It is good to suffer for a good cause. (see Moderation) J.S.H.

Aseity (uh-*see*-eh-tee) If something exists for which there is no explanation besides itself, it is said to have the quality of aseity. In theology that depends upon classical Greek philosophy, only God exhibits aseity. God exists only because of God, whereas everything else that exists is created by God. Everything for which causes and explanations can be offered is not God. Put differently, only the existence of God is necessary, whereas the existence of all else is contingent—it was not necessary for anything else to exist. "In the begining God created the heavens and the earth." (Genesis 1:1) God is necessary; the world is contingent. (*see Contingent, Creation* EX NIHILO) J.B.W.

Ash Wednesday The first day of Lent, determined by counting back forty days from Easter Sunday, not including Sundays. (Easter is the first Sunday after the first full moon after the vernal equinox [first day of spring].) The name for the day is derived from the use of ashes on the foreheads of penitent believers, placed there by the priest. More recently all the faithful in the Roman Catholic Church receive the ashes as a sign of penitence. (*see Lent*) G.E.S.

ASPERSION (*see Baptism*)

ASSENSUS (*see Faith*)

Atheism From the Greek *a* and *theos*, atheism literally means "no diety." In common use it refers to a belief in the non-existence of a divine being. It is, therefore, meaningless to discuss atheism apart from a study of theism. None of the forms that atheism takes is really understandable apart from the particular conception of deity that is being rejected by the atheist. This point is dramatically clear when one remembers that the name "atheist" was applied to the opponents of Socrates, as well as to the enemies of Christians, Jews, and Marxists. Christianity, for example, faced the polytheism and emperor worship of the Roman Empire, in which there were many ideas of the divine. Christianity, by contrast, insisted that there is only one God, the creator, savior, and sustainer of the world. Since the Christian understanding of God did not allow for ony other God, Christians denied the emperor was a god. Christians refused to offer sacrifices and prayers in the shrines of the imperial cult. Thus, by the standard of the imperial cult advocates, Christians were "atheists" because they denied imperial divinity. Often the charge of "atheism" results when what a person or a people deny about the divine is examined without equally examining what such a person or people affirm.

Within the Judeo-Christian religious tradition atheism has an interesting history. In principle the Bible denies that atheism is even a possibility for the thoughtful person. "The fool says in his heart, 'There is no God.'" (Psalms 14:1) But Christianity can distinguish between practical and theoretical atheism. When faith is construed in terms of intellectual assent to theological propositions, then one can be a theoretical theist while at the same time living one's life as if such assent made no difference. This results in so-called practical atheism in spite of theoretical theism. Similarly, one may theoretically reject dogma about God and be a theoretical atheist while at the same time living a life of love and hope and thus being a practical theist.

It is clear that such confusion or difficulty can arise only if faith is construed in terms of "belief in doctrine." If faith, on the other hand, is viewed in terms of ultimate concern and trust, then atheism must be re-evaluated. The existence of large numbers of men who do not accept Christian theological doctrines about God does not require calling them atheists. Paul Tillich (1886-1965), among others, has argued that all men have faith, *i.e.*, are ultimately concerned.

Debate between men should not center, then, upon why some have faith and others do not. Rather, the question is how adequate any given expression of faith is. Further, the introduction of some commonly shared goal may help. For example, Christians, Communists, and humanists may agree that an ultimate goal of human existence is the achievement of full humanity. The discussion between thoughtful men representing each of these faiths may then focus upon the concept of reality underlying them, and how participating in these expressions of faith can lead to full humanity.

In the 1960's younger American theologians have discussed "Christian atheism." This discussion has enlivened the theological scene, forced more traditional theologians to re-examine their most cherished doctrines, and awakened an interest in theology among large numbers of laymen. It is precarious, if not impossible, to suggest where such discussions will ultimately lead. But it is clear that this discussion has contributed toward a re-thinking of the problem of atheism for twentieth century Christian thinkers. (*see Deus Absconditus, Faith, Theism*) J.B.W.

Atonement   *Atonement in Christian theology means the mending of the broken relationship between God and man caused by sin. It incorporates the idea of reconciliation (at-one-ment), satisfaction for sin, and the release of man from his state of bondage to freedom through the grace of God. Many doctrines of the atonement emphasize, "Christ died for sin," but some see the entire life of Christ as an atoning act. Atonement assumes that man's relationship to his Creator was broken by man's disobedience. Atonement makes possible the restoration of man's fellowship with his Creator and brings God and man together again. Various theories of the atonement recognize that Christ's suffering and death on the cross provided the divine act that redeems from sin.*

Two words used in connection with the divine sacrifice are *expiation* and *propitiation*. *Expiation* (ek-spe-*ay*-shun) is to provide an offering as a means of making right some wrong. *Propitiation* (pro-pish-ee-*ay*-

shun) is the payment offered to appease the deity. The Hebrew word for "atone" is *kaphar* (Genesis 32:20; Leviticus 16:10 and 17:11). The holiest festival of the Jewish year is called Yom Kippur, meaning "Day of Atonement."

There are several theories of the atonement: (1) The *ransom* (or classical) *theory* was prominent in the ancient church. Paul's view could be described in this way, as well as the views of Irenaeus (*c.* 115-*c.* 200), Origen (*c.* 185-*c.* 254), Athanasius (*c.* 295-373), Augustine (354-430), and Martin Luther (1483-1546). This theory regards man as having been enslaved by the powers of sin and death, symbolized by the devil. The death of Christ was interpreted as a ransom paid to the devil. God defeated these satanic powers by offering Christ's life. This theory has been criticized because it implies that the power of the devil can be bought off by God. However, it does recognize victory over death and triumph over evil. (2) The *objective* (or satisfaction) *theory* sometimes carries the name of Anselm (*c.* 1033-1109), Archbishop of Canterbury, and is also known as the Anselmic theory. Man's disobedience violates the trust God had put in him and mars the honor and majesty of God; thus retribution is demanded. Since the affront to God is of such an extreme nature, no earthly creature can offer an acceptable sacrifice. God offered the sacrifice in Jesus Christ, thus affirming an important principle of theology—that loyalty is owed to God, and God alone. Critics of this theory claim that God would not demand the death of an innocent person simply to uphold His own honor and justice. (3) The *subjective* (or moral influence) *theory* is identified with Abelard (1079-1142) and frequently carries his name. Medieval scholastics favored this theory. The Creator's sacrificial love in the cross moves man to respond to God's love rather than to be frightened of his wrath. The believer recognizes the transforming power of God, repents of his sins, and seeks henceforth for himself a life of sacrifice and love.

Horace Bushnell (1802-81) viewed love as more important than penalty and saw the whole life of Jesus, not merely his death, as the redeeming act: ". . . the real gospel is the Incarnate Biography itself . . . ," he wrote.

Recent theologians have varying views of the atonement. Karl Barth (1886-   ) does not believe that Christ suffered punishment in order to satisfy the wrath of God, but that he is the Judge being judged in our place. He believes that God does not *represent* man but *replaces* him. Emil Brunner (1889-1967) holds that the doctrine of the atonement must begin with a serious view of sin, guilt, the vicarious nature of Christ's propitiation, and the penalty involved in his death. Reinhold Niebuhr (1892-   ) believes that the cross represents the paradox of the wrath and mercy of God and that all attempts to understand the mystery of the atonement fail. He maintains that God takes man's sinfulness into himself and suffers for man so that justice and forgiveness may be experienced. Paul Tillich (1886-1965) views the atonement as an event in which God and man both participate. He believes that man's estrangement in sin brings continuous suffering to God and that in the death of Christ, this suffering is vividly displayed. He does not believe that the suffering of God in Jesus Christ was substitutional. (*see* Christology, Forgiveness, Incarnation, Sin) G.E.S.

Attributes (*of God*) The term "attributes" of God means simply the adjectives that have been variously classified and listed by theologians in their attempts to speak meaningfully about God. Before one can adequately deal with the question of God's attributes, however, several prior convictions have to be established. First, since the issue of the attributes of God can only arise for theism, the *kind* of theism being advocated must be established. Second, the way in which men may legitimately lay claim to know God must be established. In this connection the relationship between reason and revelation is crucial. If, for example, one follows Karl Barth (1886-   ), then revelation is the sole ground for one's assertions about God, and the form of discourse is an analogy of faith. But, by contrast, if one follows Thomas Aquinas (*c.* 1225-74), then reason and revelation are harmonious in principle, and the assertions about God's attributes are analogies of being. Third, however one disposes of the first two matters, it must be clearly acknowledged that all talk of the attributes of God is *symbolic*. That is, whether one works out an analogy of being, the language is one of analogy. Analogy always uses *equivocal* language, *i.e.*, words about human life do not simply mean exactly the same as they do when one uses the words to refer to God. The attributes as concepts interact in many ways in an overall theological scheme.

It is important to note that the attributes of God symbolize the experience of man's relationship with God. Further, experiences as such have to be reflected upon and conceptually arranged. But then the process of conceptualization requires that attention be given to the tradition and history within which such reflection is carried on. In the case of Christian theology the contextual possibilities have primarily included Hebrew and Greek thought patterns. This context includes an emphasis on monotheism inherited from Judaism and confidence in man's rational capacities inherited from Greek thought. From the larger context of human existence this context has also meant a profound sense of holiness attached to the divine. The result of these combinations has been a consistent Christian witness to the one, holy God who is both immanent (known through reason) and transcendent (knowable through revelation).

John Macquarrie (1919-   ), in his *Principles of Christian Theology* (1966), has suggested four categories for listing the attributes of God. First, God as mystery means he is incomparable. God's transcendence cannot be compared to any other. Second, God as overwhelming means he is unlimited in the way that man is limited. Under this head fall God's immensity or immeasurability, infinity, eternality, omnipotence, omnipresence, and omniscience. Third, God's dynamism means he is immutable or faithful, which is part of God's relation to time and history. Fourth, the holiness of God emphasizes that the attributes of God are all dialectically rather than statically related. (*see Absolute, Eternal, Immutable, Impossible, Infinite, Omnipotence, Omnipresence, Omniscience, and Symbol*) J.B.W.

Authority For Christian theology, the issue revolves upon this proposition: God is the ultimate, but not necessarily the immediate, source of authority. As it is put in Romans 13:1, "For there is no authority except from God. . . ." When the Gospels referred to the authority of Jesus, Christians easily identified Jesus and God. (Matthew 7:29; John 5:27; compare John 5:30) Subsequently, theologians have been self-conscious about the authority for their assertions. And, until the authority can be established, few Christians will be swayed.

For Christianity the powerful authority of Jesus Christ is accepted as the revelation of God's authority. But after the Crucifixion, the source of authority became a serious problem. Challenged by irregular interpretations of the faith, the church in the second century developed a test for what it would regard as authoritative. It was the test of apostolicity, *i.e.*, a teaching that could be traced to the apostles of Jesus was authoritative. The apostles, it was argued, had known Jesus intimately and had received his teachings directly. They had, in turn, handed on those teachings by word of mouth and by writings that were collected into the New Testament. Inspired as they were by the presence of the Holy Spirit, the apostolic teachings came to be regarded as having authority second only to those of Jesus himself.

Beyond the teaching of Jesus and the apostles, authority has been passed on basically by one of two means. Roman Catholics have emphasized tradition and Scripture, as interpreted by ecumenical councils and papal pronouncements, both led by the Holy Spirit. For most Protestant churches authority has been thought to reside in Scripture alone (*sola scriptura*, as Luther put it), interpreted in the individual man's conscience under the guidance of the Holy Spirit. It is clear that in both instances, God himself, through the work of the Holy Spirit, is the continuing *source* of this authority. Further the issue of who has power to exercise authority is a crucial issue. The church has used inquisition and ex-

35

communication because of the conviction that the church, not the individual believer, had this power.

The issue of authority raises critical problems. First, why is authority necessary? Second, how are conflicting claims to authority to be reconciled? To the first question, Christian theology has traditionally answered that, although man is created in the image of God and should naturally accept God's ways as his own, man is a sinner. Therefore, God has given his authority to the Holy Spirit to exercise in calling man back to his responsibility toward God. To the second and more difficult question, the answer is that there is no answer. Because men are sinners, and because all human institutions are sinful—even the church—faith is God's gift to overcome sin. But faith must be free, and all men are free in faith. Certainty is not consistent with faith, and any effort to compel other men to accept what one man or one institution discerns in faith is a violation of faith and authority. This kind of compulsion is authoritarianism, which means proper authority gone bad. True authority, by contrast, makes no claim other than itself. To discern God's truth under the guidance of the Holy Spirit, *i.e.*, to receive revelation, is to be confronted with a revolution in the conception of power. If the power underlying the authority of God's revelation in Jesus Christ was manifest only in death upon a cross, it is a power whose authority can only be discerned in faith. Thus, "the just shall live by faith" might be paraphrased, "those who perceive God's revelation of powerful authority shall live by faith." (*see Faith, Power, Sanction, Truth*) J.B.W.

AUTONOMY (*see Freedom*)

AWARENESS (*see Consciousness*)

B.C. (B.C.E.) B.C. is a customary abbreviation in the western world for "Before Christ." Modern Jewish scholars often use the abbreviation B.C.E. ("before the common era") to signify the same period of time. The abbreviation B.C. points to the period before the birth of Christ in the same way that A.D. (Anno Domini, "in the year of our Lord") indicates the period after his birth. (*see* A.D.) E.L.T.

Baptism   One of the two sacraments of the Protestant churches and one of the seven sacraments of the Roman Catholic Church, *baptism* comes from the Greek word, *baptizein*, which means to "plunge under" or "dip." Historically, it has been the rite through which one is initiated into the community of Christians. In the old covenant, circumcision was the initiatory rite, but circumcision was soon replaced in Christianity by baptism. Jesus, and likely his disciples, received baptism from John the Baptist, but it seems to have been used much more widely following Jesus' death.

Paul spoke of the transition from circumcision to baptism with reference to a "circumcision made without hands" (Colossians 2:11), meaning that Christ brought about a spiritual circumcision for the believer. To be buried with Christ in baptism (Romans 6:4) becomes the spiritual experience by which one participates in the death, burial, and resurrection of Christ. Water is used as the symbol, and God's Spirit accompanies baptism (see Acts 19:1-6).

One of the issues that separates churches is the mode (method) of baptism. Immersion seems to have been the accepted mode in apostolic times. There is no positive evidence that babies were included, though some may have been in household baptisms (Acts 16:25-34; 1 Corinthians 7:14). Baptists and Anabaptists restrict the mode to immersion and practice only "believers' baptism," excluding the baptism of children. In churches that practice infant baptism, the vow is taken by the parents, who promise "to bring up the child in the nurture and admonition of the Lord," until the child will confirm what his parents have earlier done on his behalf. Some traditions, however, view infant baptism as a means of including the child into the fellowship of the church. "Confirmation" does not supplement, but only permits the believer to acknowledge, his baptism.

Two other modes of baptism are practiced: aspersion, commonly called sprinkling, and affusion or pouring. In immersion, done either in a church baptistry or in an outdoor body of water, the one seeking baptism and the officiating minister both go into the water and the candidate is put into the water by the pastor, usually three times. In aspersion, a baptismal font or water receptacle is used; into it the pastor dips his hand and sprinkles the head of the candidate. In affusion, the shoulders are draped, and water is poured over the candidate's head. Though the earliest baptisms appear to have been in the name of Jesus Christ only, the trinitarian formula developed very early (Matthew 28:19) and is used almost exclusively today.

Regarded as a symbol of an inner cleansing and the mark of a new life, baptism is usually performed only once. In cases where babies are baptized, the rite is usually followed by confirmation at a later age. One of the early problems raised with regard to baptism was its administration by

37

unauthorized ministers. It is now generally agreed that the human agent is not the significant part of the administration. Baptisms are usually recognized as valid among churches of differing theologies regardless of the person who administers the rite. (*see Confirmation, Redemption, Sacraments, Trinity*) G.E.S.

BASAR (*see Body, Flesh*)

BECOMING (*see History, Process, Righteousness, Self*)

BEGOTTEN (*see Christology, Creed, Trinity, Virgin Birth*)

BEING (*see Ontology*)

BELIEF (*see Doctrine, Dogmatics, Faith*)

BENEDICTION (*see Prayer*)

BERITH (*see Covenant*)

Biblical criticism *Biblical criticism began about four hundred years ago. It became very important during the 1800's. Science and the study of history influenced it. It assumes that the methods used to study ancient documents may be applied to the study of the Bible as well. This type of criticism is divided into two parts, textual or lower criticism, and higher criticism. Textual criticism tries to discover the original text of a given book. Higher criticism seeks to understand a book by examining the situation at the time it was written; the kind of literature it is; the men, books, and ideas the author relied on; and the history of the traditions within it. It is concerned with matters of authorship, date, purpose, place of writing, to whom it was written, and the occasion that prompted its writing.*

The term "biblical criticism" applies to the study of the Bible in modern times, when it became possible to apply to it, as to other documents, the various methods of scientific inquiry. It may be said with accuracy that biblical criticism roots back into the Renaissance, when the minds of men became liberated from the shackles of tradition. But it was shaped by two great forces of later times, by the scientific revolution of the sixteenth and seventeenth centuries and by the nineteenth century changes in historical method. Indeed it may be said that, in a clearly defined sense, biblical criticism was a nineteenth century achievement. This achievement was made possible because of a new outlook on the Bible as the product not only of superhuman, divine activity but also as the product of men in history, who were subject to the strengths and weaknesses of human beings generally. The assumption of biblical criticism, therefore, is that the Bible can be approached the same way that any ancient book can be approached, and that linguistic, textual, literary, and historical tools appropriate to the one are appropriate to the other also.

Traditionally, biblical criticism has been divided into two parts, (1) *textual criticism* (sometimes called *lower criticism*) and (2) *higher criticism*. These two forms of criticism seek to recover, insofar as it is possible, the original or intended meaning of a given document. This means that the investigation is concerned not only with the book to be investigated but also with the complex setting in which it had its origin. The assumption is that the setting throws light upon the meaning of the book, that it cannot be understood in isolation. Moreover, each book has had a history, extending from the time it was written (and, where sources are involved, even before) to its present existence in a particular translation. That history includes its textual transmission, for we must remember that manuscripts were copied by hand until the invention of printing in the fifteenth century, and the story of the canon (authoritative list) of Christian Scriptures.

(1) Textual criticism has as its main goal the reconstruction, to the degree that this is possible, of the original text of a given document. To use Mark's Gospel as an example, the textual critic seeks to establish the text of this Gospel exactly as it left its author's hand. This would be the original text. The attempt, however, is admittedly only relatively successful. The long history of the transmission of manuscripts by hand on the part of scribes or copyists has left its mark in terms of error. Sometimes error crept in through accidental slips due to carelessness, fatigue, and the like. At other times, changes were intentionally introduced into the text: the scribe believed that he could improve the style, or that he must correct false teaching that had been introduced at an earlier time, perhaps by heretics. The textual critic must take these factors into account. The end result of his work is a Greek text of Mark close to the original. On the basis of this Greek text it is then possible to make a translation into the English language. Any good translation of the Gospel of Mark (or any other New Testament book) is made from such a reconstructed text. This is why, in part, some modern translations of the New Testament are to be preferred over the King James Version. The King James Version did not have the advantage either of many of the good manuscripts now available, or of the critical process now used by textual scholars.

What has been said for New Testament textual criticism applies in a a more limited way to the Old Testament as well. It is true that the problem of Old Testament textual criticism is somewhat different because of fewer witnesses to the text. But in recent times added incentive has been given to this discipline as a result of the monumental discovery of the Dead Sea Scrolls, which include several biblical documents, notably the Isaiah scroll. The fact that the official or Masoretic text dominated the work of Jewish scribes for centuries, and that no Hebrew manuscripts of the Old Testament survive that are older than the ninth century of the Christian era, highlights the importance for Old Testament textual criticism of the Dead Sea Scrolls.

The phrase "higher criticism" refers to a method of investigation that goes "up the stream" to the source of a given book. Its aim is better understanding of the book by attention to the total situation that gave it birth. It deals with questions of authorship, date, purpose, occasion, destination, literary relationships, and the like. Books that deal with these problems are called *introductions*.

To establish matters such as authorship, date of writing, and place of writing two kinds of evidence are used: (a) *internal evidence* and (b) *external evidence.*

Internal evidence is information supplied by the book itself. It may be that the name of the writer is included, or that some reference provides information regarding date or place. Yet it is always necessary to treat such items critically. For instance pseudonymity (use of a pen name) was a common convention in ancient times. It was the practice of the time to give authority to a work by attributing it to outstanding persons of the past. Thus, the Pastorals (1 and 2 Timothy and Titus) are attributed to Paul, although they certainly were not written by the great apostle. Nevertheless, great weight must be given this kind of evidence when critically evaluated.

External evidence is evidence supplied by documents outside the book itself. The date of writing may be determined, at least approximately, by how much the writing is used in other writings whose dates are known. This use may be in the form of direct quotations or by more general allusions. Sometimes the allusions may be too vague to make a very confident judgment. Again, as in the case of internal evidence, critical judgment must be brought to bear upon this kind of evidence.

(2) Subsumed under the heading, higher criticism, are various methods of approach. (a) *Literary criticism* is concerned with the literary structure of a document and with the way the author (or authors) uses it to express his purpose. One may begin with the simple identification of a writing as a poem, a letter, a homily, an apocalypse, a gospel, a historical writing, and so forth. This identification of the *kind* of material being dealt with is important, for it is essential to deal with a given document in its own terms. But beyond this, literary criticism analyzes the structure of a document, pays attention to its style, the kinds of literary units within it, its sources, possible interpolations (insertions) or introduction into the text of elements later than those of the original writer, and the possibility of its being a composite. It is well known that the

Book of Isaiah is made up of at least two major documents, composed by different authors, and usually designated by the terms, the First and Second Isaiahs. In the New Testament, the "Corinthian Correspondence," 1 and 2 Corinthians, is generally considered to be made up of at least four documents. With regard to sources, the so-called synoptic problem offers a good example. The synoptic problem is the problem of the interrelationship of Matthew, Mark, and Luke. A prominent solution to this problem asserts that Matthew and Luke depend upon Mark and a second source, usually called Q (from the German word *Quelle*, which means "source"). These are matters with which the literary method deals.

(b) *Historical criticism*, like literary criticism, builds on textual criticism, and deals with a document in terms of its setting in history. Consequently it is necessary to know about the forces that were at work in relation to the production of biblical books. For an understanding of certain books of the Old Testament, for example, it is important to know not only the religion of Israel but also the Canaanite religion with which it came in contact. Certain books of the New Testament require on the part of the reader a knowledge of the colorful religious life of the Hellenistic world. The Dead Sea Scrolls open to us a picture of a vital element in first century Judaism, and at the same time throw light upon emerging Christianity and its literature. To the extent that the time and place of writing of a book can be pinpointed, to that extent its context in history aids in an understanding of its content.

(c) *Form criticism* was first applied to the study of the Old Testament. Hermann Gunkel (1862-1932) was the first scholar to apply it seriously to the Old Testament, and Karl Ludwig Schmidt (1891-   ) one of the first to apply it to the New Testament. Another name for this method might be "tradition criticism." Here stress is placed on the *oral* history of tradition before it became reduced to writing. This method holds that traditions were formed according to certain laws governing their growth, and that these traditional units (forms) may be isolated and classified, as, for example, into historical narratives, sagas, parables, miracle stories, and legends. It holds, further, that these units of tradition arose under certain historical conditions; each unit has a definite *Sitz im Leben* (zitz-im-*lay*-ben) or "setting in life." Form criticism attempts, therefore, to go back of the written document to determine both the form of a given unit of tradition within it and to isolate the life situation that gave it birth. Coming into prominence around the turn of the century, this method continues to have prominence in both Old and New Testament studies. (*see Form criticism, Literary criticism, Source criticism*) E.L.T.

BIBLICAL THEOLOGY (*see Theology*)

BIRTH NARRATIVES (see Legend)

BISHOP (see Diocese, Episcopal, Order)

Blasphemy Blasphemy technically means "to curse" and comes from the Greek word, *blasphemia*,—"to revile or use abusive language toward persons." (It is translated "slander" in Mark 7:22; 1 Corinthians 4:13; Ephesians 4:31.) Its current meaning is to dishonor the name of God. A strong use of the word is found in Mark 3:29, with the warning that there is forgiveness for all sins except blasphemy against the Holy Spirit. One interpretation of this passage is that those who consistently ignore God's voice will soon become insensitive to it. In John 10:33, it was regarded as blasphemous when the Messiah announced himself as God: " 'We stone you for no good work but for blasphemy; because you, being a man, make yourself God.' " G.E.S.

BLOOD (see Atonement, Sacrifice)

Body The ancient Israelites did not speculate about the nature of man enough to develop a theory of human nature. The Old Testament gives us no word that might be translated precisely "body." The word *basar* (ba-*sahr*) is perhaps the closest to this, although it is commonly translated "flesh." It is only secondarily "the body," and even in this instance applies to the general state or condition of man as a creature of flesh. This lack of a word for "body" reflects the Hebrew view of the unity of the human person; there is no dualism of body and soul as found in Greek thought. Where dualism occurs in Hebrew literature, it is the result of the impact of Greek ideas. According to Genesis 2:7, God made man of the dust, breathed into his nostrils the breath of life, and man became a living soul (*nephesh*) (*nef*-ish). The Old Testament speaks, therefore, of the creation of *man* and not of the creation of the body.

In non-Jewish thought the idea developed that the body is itself evil, the prison and tomb of the soul. But this idea is foreign to the Old Testament. For the Hebrews, sin was not the result of the possession of an evil body; sin was rather rooted in the heart or mind (Jeremiah 7:24; 9:14; Psalms 14:1). In a similar fashion the bowels are the seat of the emotions. The belief that matter is evil and that the soul, imprisoned in the body, is good, is a view quite foreign to ancient Jewish thought, except in instances where Judaism had come under the influence of Greek ideas. The dominant thought that emerges from a consideration of the Jewish doctrine of man is that he is a unity. It is this legacy from Judaism that made it possible for the New Testament to speak of the church as the body of Christ.

42

The New Testament word for body is *soma*. It must be clearly distinguished from *sarx*, flesh, which itself means more than the substance of the bodies of animals or of men. Paul can speak of a spiritual body as well as of a physical body (1 Corinthians 15:44). In this connection he is discussing the question, " 'With what kind of body do they come?' " *i.e.*, those raised from the dead. His reply assumes the death of the physical body, but since the term "body" is for him not equivalent to the material substance that can be seen and touched, "body" can also mean "body of spirit." On the basis of this passage, Paul rejects the notion of the resurrection of the flesh but accepts the idea of a bodily resurrection of the spirit. The Pauline use of the word "body" in connection with the resurrection has the value of retaining the idea of the unity of the human person after death. There is no concession to the view that after death the individual soul of a man is reabsorbed into a universal soul; it is *Christ* who arose from the dead; it is the *believer* who will arise from death.

But the Corinthian passage does not exhaust Paul's use of *soma*. When Paul speaks of believers giving their bodies as a living sacrifice (Romans 12:1) he means that they shall give themselves totally to God's service. The body can also be abused, so as to become a body of sin and of death (Romans 6:6; 7:24). But it can also be a temple of the Holy Spirit (1 Corinthians 6:19).

The term "body" is used to designate the church (1 Corinthians 12: 12 *ff.*). Paul argues that just as many parts of the body have different functions, and yet make up one body, so the church, composed of many members with differing functions (apostles, prophets, teachers), is a unity. The value of the metaphor is that it illustrates the principle of unity in diversity. An extension of this idea of the church as "body" is found in its identification as "the body of Christ" (1 Corinthians 12:27; Ephesians 1:23; 4:12; 5:30). As in the case of the simple analogy of the body, so here the principle of unity is expressed, but it has the additional element of unity *in Christ*. (*see Church, Flesh, Heart, Image of Man, Self*) E.L.T.

BODY OF CHRIST (*see Church*)

BOWELS (*see Heart*)

BREAD (*see Communion, Elements*)

BROTHER (*see Neighbor*)

BURNT OFFERING (*see Sacrifice*)

C

Calculation Calculation is the art of weighing the factors involved in a situation and arriving at a conclusion. It is a process of reckoning or computing. Plato (*c.* 427-347 B.C.) gives a clear picture of the place of calculation in man's attempts to know and do what is right. In life, things are not always what they appear to be. An action may appear to be the right action when it is not. Man can use his reason to examine the facts closely and avoid some mistakes. As man weighs and measures the size of objects he will come to know the actual facts about them and their relation to other objects. If man considers carefully the different possible courses of action open to him and their consequences, he will at least come closer to knowing the truth about what he should do. It is the better part of man's soul that inclines him to trust in calculation.

During the Middle Ages most ethical thinkers depended on a theory of revelation. They assumed that God had shown to man through Jesus Christ what was right. The church had preserved this teaching in a pure and undefiled form; thus, man could go to the church and there find out exactly what he should do. Calculation was not needed in order to discover the right. However, calculation still played an important role. Calculation was needed in order to adopt means to an end. Man is to use his reason, helped by revelation, to discover the best possible way of accomplishing a task. Man is committed to absolute obedience to the Word of God. He should use prudence in carrying out this commitment. He is to be careful in his actions. He should use his very best skill and "know how" in serving this purpose. For example, man knows from God's law that it is right to preserve life and wrong to destroy it. It is fitting for him to use the best of medical science in order to accomplish this task.

Reinhold Niebuhr (1892-   ) points out that man does not always know what is right. The Christian is called upon to be a loving person at all times. This love shows itself in man's search for justice in society. In man's search for justice sometimes he has to choose between courses of action of which all are bad. He is called upon to calculate which course of action would be "more or less" evil than the other. The Christian comes to every situation committed to the absolute demand of love. But, he still has to decide what is "fitting" or appropriate in the given situation. Man is guided by the absolute norm of love and he calculates what method is to be used. (*see Contextual, Deontological*) J.S.H.

CALL (*see Vocation*)

Calvary Matthew 27:33 uses the Aramaic word *golgotha* (*gahl*-go-tha) as the name for the place where Jesus was crucified, explaining that it was called the place of the skull (Greek *kranion*). The King James Version translators changed the *kranion* of Matthew 27:33 into plain English: "a place of a skull." But when they came to Luke 23:33, which uses *kranion* only and not *golgotha*, they translated it "Calvary," perhaps because they were using a Latin text. In Latin *calvaria* means "a bare skull." Thus popular religious thought has used "calvary" to mean the same thing as Jesus' crucifixion. Tradition says the actual location of the crucifixion is a place just outside Jerusalem, where the landscape seems to resemble a skull. G.E.S.

CALVINISM (*see Freedom, Grace, Providence, Predestination, Theocracy*)

Canon The term "canon" originally applied to a reed used for measuring. The idea of a standard of measurement naturally passed over into a metaphor to signify books that were held to be authoritative. So we speak of the canon of scripture, *i.e.*, the books considered authoritative by a religious group.

The Christian canon consists of the two historic divisions—the Old Testament and the New Testament. These, in turn, may be divided into distinct parts, each of which has its own historical development. The Old Testament canon is divided into three parts: the Torah or Law, consisting of the Pentateuch or the so-called five books of Moses; the Prophets, consisting of the Former Prophets and the Later Prophets; the Writings or Hagiographa, headed by the book of Psalms. It is generally recognized that all three sections of the canon had come to be accepted by the Jews by A.D. 90, although the first two groupings had received recognition much earlier than that.

The New Testament canon consists of two divisions: the Gospel section, composed of Matthew, Mark, Luke, and John, the division to which the church has always attached paramount importance; the Apostle section, in which the letters of Paul play an important, though not an exclusive role. It is generally recognized that use, rather than action by councils, determined what books should be included in the canonical list. Many factors played in upon the selection, however, not the least of which was the pressures from heretical groups. The list of books that we have in our Bibles was fairly well established by the close of the fourth century. (*see Apocrypha, Inspiration, Pseudepigrapha*) E.L.T.

Canticle (*cant*-eh-kul) From the Latin word, *cantus,* which means "to sing." Canticle refers to biblical texts placed in the liturgy as musical compositions. These liturgical songs use biblical passages other than the Psalms. Best known among the canticles are the *Magnificat* (Luke 1:46-55), the *Benedictus* (Luke 1:68-79), the *Nunc Dimittis* (Luke 2:29-32). (*see* V*espers*) G.E.S.

Cardinal Called "a prince" in the Roman Catholic Church, the cardinal is next in rank to the Pope and is a member of the College of Cardinals (or Sacred College), an important advisory and administrative group to the Pope. The College of Cardinals was increased by Pope John XXIII in 1959 to seventy-nine, then again in 1962 to eighty-seven members. In 1967 the College was increased to a record 120 members, nine of whom are citizens of the United States. The symbols of the office are a red cap (biretta), a sapphire ring, a red cassock, a red mantle, and a red hat. Though a red hat is placed on the candidate's head by the Pope at his consecration, he does not wear it after that. The College of Cardinals is responsible for the administration of the affairs of the Church. Upon the death of a Pope, it elects the next Pope. G.E.S.

Casuistry (*kaz*-yew-uh-stree) Casuistry in its most basic sense means the application of general rules to specific circumstances. It is used in Christian theology mainly to refer to the application of general laws to indicate what is right and proper. Casuistry answers in advance what ought to be done in particular cases. For example, if a Christian studies Ephesians 5:25-33 he may learn in specific terms something of what it means to be a husband. This Scripture gives us some general rules about what it means to be a husband. From these a man can learn what he should do in specific cases if he is to be a Christian husband. Casuistry attempts to give clear descriptions, in terms of specifics, of right and wrong. For this reason it is legalistic, though not necessarily in a narrow or undesirable sense.

Martin Luther (1483-1546) rejected casuistry primarily on two counts. (1) It violates Christian freedom. (2) It assumes that sin is a violation of particular laws. Sin is unfaith. According to Luther faith needs no detailed list of rules to guide it. Casuistry assumes faith does need a detailed list of rules to follow. The term is sometimes used to refer to dispute over unimportant matters or man's attempt to give a good reason for doing the wrong deed. (*see Legalism*) J.S.H.

Catechism Usually taught in question-answer form, catechism is a systematic study of religion as old as the church itself. Among better known catechisms have been the *Didache,* and those of John Wyclif (*c.* 1320-84), the Moravian Brethren, and the Waldenses.

Martin Luther (1483-1546) introduced a new era in catechism with his *Small Catechism.*

While Roman Catholics and Lutherans have traditionally practiced catechetical instruction, other denominations have become more concerned about this phase of Christian education during the twentieth century. Most denominations now provide some kind of church membership instructions either as catechism or a pastor's class. The person receiving catechism in the early centuries was instructed before receiving baptism. G.E.S.

CATEGORICAL (*see Absolute, Deontological*)

Catholic This word has both a general and specific meaning. It is used generally to describe the universal nature of the church. This use is employed in the Apostles' Creed: "I believe in . . . the holy catholic Church." The term also refers to the Roman Catholic Church. In order to distinguish, some use a small "c" to refer to the universal nature of the church and a capital "C" for the Roman Catholic Church. All members of the Christian church are considered catholic in the sense of the undivided or whole Christian family. (*see Church*) G.E.S.

Celebrate Though this word is used generally in English to refer to festive acts, it has been used by recent theologians to refer to the act of worship. As celebration, worship is the full and active response of the people of God. It particularly refers to the sense of the holy: life, created by God, is holy. Celebration thus underscores the holiness of all of life, though it can also include confession as man's admission that he has abused the goodness of creation. G.E.S.

CEREAL OFFERING (*see Sacrifice*)

Certitude (*sir*-teh-tewd) When a person is firmly convinced of the reality of something, of the correctness of a belief, or the rightness of an action, he is demonstrating certitude. Certitude is the psychological condition within which a person is unshakeably settled or fixed in his perception of what is real or true or right. Certitude is the result of being persuaded by experience or argument and is the condition that is entered by deciding to accept one's own perception. When Paul was converted on the road to Damascus, his certitude regarding Jesus as the Messiah was thereafter unshakeable. Certitude should be distinguished from certainty, which depends upon demonstration and proof observable by others. Certitude can exist even if nobody else ever shares it. Certainty is public; certitude is private. J.B.W.

CHANCE (*see Destiny, Possibility, Providence*)

Character Character refers to the distinctive qualities of a person. If a person has good qualities (for example, honesty and benevolence) he is said to have a good character. If he has bad qualities (for example, selfishness and rudeness) he is said to have a bad character or no character at all. Man is a creature of choice. There are many options open to man at any time. Man is able to rationally examine and criticize his own choices. He can compare his life to the ideal life (or the supreme good). And he can try to reshape his own life in accordance with the supreme good. Aristotle (384-322 B.C.) said that character expresses itself in actions and passions. A man can be taught to use his reason to control his passions and actions. A man can be taught to live the reasonable life (avoiding extremes). (*see Habit, Virtue*) J.S.H.

Charisma (kuh-*riz*-mah) *Charisma* is a Greek word meaning "free gift." The word had special relevance to the religious life of the Pauline communities. In 1 Corinthians 12–14 Paul speaks of problems that had arisen in the church at Corinth because of the "varieties of gifts" (12:4) bestowed upon the people there. He lists these "gifts" in 12:8-10: wisdom, knowledge (*gnosis*), faith, healing, miracles, prophecy, the ability to distinguish between spirits, tongues, the interpretation of tongues. The possession of these abilities was evidence of the possession of the divine Spirit on the part of the individual involved. (*see Glossolalia, Inspiration, Orders, Prophet*) E.L.T.

CHARITY (*see Love*)

CHILIASM (*see End*)

CHOICE (*see Decision, Freedom*)

CHOSEN PEOPLE (*see Elect*, Laos)

CHRISTIAN SOCIALISM (*see Social Gospel*)

Christmas It is unclear how the date of December 25 was chosen to mark the anniversary of Christ's birth or Incarnation. There is no biblical information. It was set following the fourth century, after various days had been used. January 6 is the date used by Orthodox Christians.

Christmastide, also known as Yuletide, extends from Christmas Eve until New Year's Day, or until Epiphany, which begins January 6. "Christ's Mass" is the celebration of God's sending his Son to man in human flesh. (*see Advent, Incarnation*) G.E.S.

Christology (kris-*tahl*-o-jee)   *Christology is the study of the person and work of Christ, the historical Jesus, the centrality of Christ to the Christian message, and of his divine and human natures.*

Soteriology *is more specifically defined as the doctrine of Jesus Christ as Savior while Christology has been more concerned with his natures. The Hebrew word* mashiach, *which also means "anointed," becomes* Christos *in the Greek version of the Old Testament and is translated into English in the word "messiah," which means "an anointed one."*

Though there is no finally developed doctrine of christology or of the Incarnation in the New Testament, the theological ideas of the first century included concepts of the life and the work of Jesus Christ. Names used for Jesus in early Christian writings include "Messiah," "Son of Man," "Son of God," "Son of David," "Christ," "Lord," "Lamb of God," and "Savior." The suffering servant of Isaiah 53 and messianic passages were used to explain his mission. In Paul's thought, Christ's crucifixion and resurrection were the critical points at which God entered history to make possible a "new creation" for man. The Gospel of John, on the other hand, portrays Jesus as the "word made flesh," so that God's grace is at work in the whole life of Jesus. As the Christian community grew, and especially as it moved into the Greco-Roman world, which did not have the background of the Jewish religion, it was necessary to have clearer interpretations of the symbols that describe the person and work of Jesus Christ.

A variety of doctrines grew as such words as "Son of Man," "Lord," and "Savior," began to be interpreted within the context of varying backgrounds and ideas. *Philo*, the Jewish philosopher and contemporary of Paul, saw Christ as the Logos ("word") or the Divine Principle of creation and rational world order. *Monarchianism*, current in the second and third centuries, argued against any distinctions within God and affirmed that Christ had been elevated to become the Son of God but did not possess equality with God. The *Apologists* explained the Logos Christology in philosophical terms without identifying the details of Christ's person and his life, thus slighting interest in the historical Jesus while emphasizing the Incarnation of the Word. *Sabellianism*, or modalism, was the view that Father, Son, and Holy Spirit are the same being, but with different names.

Arius, in the late third century and early fourth century, insisted that the Logos became flesh in Christ but that this new creation was produced out of nothing and did not possess a human soul. His view set off the Arian controversy, which lasted from 318 until 381. A decisive statement was made at the Council of Nicaea (325) that "Christ had come as God from God and was not made but was begun." The Nicene Creed condemned the views of Arius and used the phrase, "being of one substance with the Father." The teaching of the Trinity set forth at the Council of

Nicaea was confirmed in 381 by the Council of Constantinople, which affirmed "Consubstantiality" (the sameness of being of the Father and the Logos). Three heresies arose following this declaration. (1) *Nestorianism* (nes-*tow*-ree-an-ism) so stressed the differences between the human and divine natures of Christ that it made Christ seem two persons instead of one; (2) *monophysitism* (muh-*nof*-eh-seh-tism) so emphasized the divine nature that it neglected the human nature; and (3) *apollinarianism* (uh-*pohl*-eh-*nair*-yuh-nism) asserted that the body and soul of Jesus were human but that his reason was the divine, thus indicating that he was not truly human. (The term used to describe views of the Trinity in which the second and third persons are inferior to the first is *Subordination*.)

The Council of Chalcedon (451) stated that Jesus Christ was one person in two natures. It affirmed that he was both divine and human; that he was one individual not parted or divided into two; and that his natures were inseparable. The phrase coined by Origen (*c.* 185-*c.* 254), *theanthropism* (God-man), defined the person of Christ as one person with two natures that could neither be mixed nor separated.

Succeeding generations emphasized the life, work, and death of Christ with limited discussion on christology. The Reformers did not question the Chalcedon doctrine. Luther (1483-1546) indicated that he was not interested in the philosophical aspects of christology but rather in the saving nature of Christ. The other reformers seem to have adopted Luther's view that the atoning death of Christ was a penalty for human sin.

Friedrich Schleiermacher (1768-1834) rejected the language about the "natures" of Christ and viewed him as a person who gradually developed a consciousness of God. The perfection of Christ becomes then his awareness of God in every moment. As a redeemer, Christ in turn makes man aware of his need for God, until religious consciousness turns into full-fledged God-consciousness.

Albrecht Ritschl (1822-89) also called for a break with the ancient language, indicating that to say Jesus was divine is not objective but is rather a value statement indicating that one has found in Jesus and his Kingdom his own relationship to God. Ritschl's teachings encouraged interest in the historical Jesus. Adolf von Harnack (1851-1930) wrote a book in 1904 (*What is Christianity?*), in which he reduced Jesus' gospel to a proclamation of God's Fatherhood and the value of the human soul. His distinction centered on the gospel *of* Jesus in contrast to the gospel preached *about* him. This work created an interest in other books that dealt with the historical life of Jesus and Jesus as a human person, among them *The Quest of the Historical Jesus* (1910), by Albert Schweitzer (1875-1966).

Strong reaction against this movement was registered by Karl Barth (1886-   ) and Emil Brunner (1889-1967), who argue for the revelation of God in Christ as over against the historical person of Jesus. They place their emphasis on the Christ who is seen through the eye of faith and not as a human personality. Brunner has also been critical of the statements from Chalcedon. He insists that believers can affirm the divinity and humanity of Christ, but that it is beyond man's ability to try to define the two natures in human language. (*see* Atonement, Incarnation, Name) G.E.S.

CHRONOS (*see* Time)

Church The word church is the English form of the Scottish *kirk*, derived from the Greek, *kuriakon*, which is designated as a building for worship and may be translated, "The Lord's House." This word does not appear in this context in the Bible but came into use after the Christians began having church buildings. The word translated "church" in the New Testament is the Greek, *ekklesia* (ek-lay-*see*-ah), which does not mean a building but an assembly (Acts 19:32), a local congregation (Matthew 18:17), or the church universal (16:18).

Another word used for church members is *koinonia* (koy-noh-*nee*-ah), which means "fellowship" or "sharing" and employs the idea of Christians sharing together with Christ. (Acts 2:42; Romans 15:26; 1 Corinthians 10:16; 2 Corinthians 9:13) The earlier view of the church is the community of God's people who believe in Jesus Christ. The idea of the church as an institution to perform the work of Christ among men comes later. In this sense, the Bible does not distinguish between the visible and invisible churches.

With the development of bishops, liturgy, and sacraments, the emphasis on the institution increased. During medieval years the church became a hierarchy, ruling for God and mediating grace to people in a fixed order. The Protestant Reformation was a rebellion against medieval life, as well as against the elaborate organization of the church.

Though he respected church authority and the special role of priests, Martin Luther (1483-1546) emphasized the priesthood of all believers and taught that man's response to the Word of God must be a matter of conscience. The Reformers felt the Bible alone (*Sola Scriptura*) should be the authority for faith—not the canons, decisions of councils, nor papal decrees.

The concerns of the Reformation have continued to distinguish between denominations to this day. Among such concerns are: (1) The place of the sacraments in the church and their relationships to the believer (in this regard, Anabaptists differ with others on both the form and meaning of baptism); (2) organization of the church and whether it should be episcopal, presbyterian, or congregational; (3) the authority of the Bible as related to the authority of the church; (4)

51

the relationship of the visible or institutional church among men to the invisible church. The church to which members belong is frequently referred to as "militant," and the invisible church is spoken of as the church "triumphant." Actually the church triumphant refers to the eschatological or the future church, while the church militant describes the church at work in the world preaching the gospel, providing for the administration of the sacraments, and witnessing among men by helping meet their physical and spiritual needs.

Some critics of the church, such as Stephen Rose and Albert van den Heuvel, call on the church to abandon its traditional organization and reshape its life in a radical way. Others, such Martin Marty (1928-   ), hold that the local congregation can still be useful and meaningful. Gibson Winter (1916-   ) has pointed out that the institution may continue to grow, but by increasing the number and quality of professional religious workers, rather than by gaining members and adding buildings.

Liberal thinkers today normally emphasize the "church in the world." By this they mean that moral action is more important than spiritual or verbal activity. Conservative thinkers continue to emphasize personal salvation and personal ethics. However, some conservatives, such as Carl Henry (1913-   ), have called on those who think of the church in spiritual terms to be more responsible in meeting moral problems like racism and war. (*see* EKKLESIA, *Elect, Institutional,* KOINONIA) G.E.S.

Church fathers Theologians and church leaders who made outstanding contributions in the early centuries through their preaching and writings are called *church fathers.* The name given to the study of their life, thought, and writings is *Patristics* (puh-*tris*-tix). They lived, for the most part, from the first to the eighth centuries. They wrote in response to attacks upon Christianity from both philosophy and other religions. Systems of doctrine were constructed in order to combat heresies. The traditional groupings are: the Apostolic Fathers (*c.* 95-150): Clement of Rome, Hermas, Barnabas, Ignatius, Polycarp; the Apologists (*c.* 150-200): Quadratus, Aristides, Justin, Tatian, Melito; the Ante-Nicene Fathers (*c.* 185-325): Clement of Alexandria, Origen, Tertullian, Cyprian, Irenaeus, Hippolytus; the Post-Nicene Fathers (after *c.* 325): Arius, Athanasius, Basil, Gregory of Nyssa, Cyril of Alexandria, Theodore of Mopsuestia, Jerome, John of Damascus, and Augustine of Hippo. (*see* Christology, Reason, Theology) G.E.S.

CHURCH IN THE WORLD (*see* EKKLESIA, *Institutional church, Mission, Secularization*)

CODEX (*see Manuscript*)

Collect (*kah*-lekt)   Collect is short for *Oratio ad Collectam*, which means, "a prayer upon assembly," and is a short prayer offered in worship. It usually includes an invocation, petition, and conclusion and sums up the devotions of the people. In the Roman Mass, the collect preceding the Epistle is called the *Oratio*, and varies with the day on which it is offered. Perhaps the best known collect is, "Almighty God, unto whom all hearts are open, all desires known, and from whom no secrets are hid; cleanse the thoughts of our hearts by the inspiration of thy Holy Spirit; that we may perfectly love thee and worthily magnify thy Holy name; through Jesus Christ, our Lord, Amen." This collect illustrates the fact that the prayer is addressed to God, not to the congregation, then mentions a Divine attribute and a brief petition, and ends with the ascription, "in the name of Christ." In collects, verbs abound, but adjectives are few. (*see Prayer*) G.E.S.

Communication   Used in the liturgical sense, communication is the act of taking bread and wine. This symbol of God's relation to man undergirds the more general use of the term to refer to personal dialogue and to the use of electronic media. G.E.S.

Communion (Holy)   The word *communion* is used to designate one of the two sacraments of the Protestant churches—the Holy Communion, or the Lord's Supper.

This sacrament stood at the center of worship in the early church and is based upon the final meal that Jesus ate with his disciples before his crucifixion. Though some have questioned whether or not the supper occurred, all the Synoptic Gospels include an account: Matthew 26:17-29; Mark 14:12-25; Luke 22:7-20. Was it a Passover meal or simply a weekly Kiddush? The Gospel accounts use the word "Passover," but the connection between the Passover and the Last Supper is unclear. If Jesus was crucified on Friday, that day itself would have been the Passover; a meal held the previous night would not have been a Passover celebration. However, the timing of the supper would not have prevented Jesus from relating his approaching death to the sacrifice of the Passover lamb.

The Kiddush was a weekly meal of a rabbi and his disciples. It was commonly observed in circles where belief in an approaching messiah was strong. Unlike the Passover, leavened bread was used. The meal may have been a symbol of the heavenly feast, in which the messiah would celebrate his victory over the forces of evil with his faithful believers.

The Lord's Supper was observed as a meal in the early church. Paul told the Corinthians that they ate and drank in excess and were "guilty of profaning the body and blood of the Lord." (1 Corinthians 11:17-29) Second century writings indicate that the supper idea was lost in favor of a ceremonial rite. The *Eucharist* carries with it the idea of gratitude, thanks for favors, rejoicing. The feast was not restricted to the Apostles or Jewish Christians but was also celebrated by gentile churches. Unleavened bread was used, and the cup of wine was called variously "the cup of blessing" and "the cup of the Lord."

Several different views of communion have divided the church in its observance. *Transubstantiation* means that the bread and wine actually become the body and blood of Christ. In *consubstantiation*, the elements do not necessarily change into the body and blood but Christ lives in them. Another view of the sacrament is the Lutheran view of the *real presence*, in which a mystical change occurs within the life of the believer who seriously receives the elements. Others hold a *symbolic view*, in which the bread and the cup represent the broken body and shed blood of our Lord and serve as a symbol.

When communion is received, the communicant approaches the act with a contrite heart, confesses his sins and receives the sacrament in faith. Through the sacrament, the worshiper remembers what was done for him through God's mercy in Jesus Christ. This remembrance is known as *anamnesis* (an-uhm-*nee*-suhs), which means "to remember." The rite unites Christians in worship as members of various church families participate in this unique fellowship affirming their hope. (*see Kiddush, Sacraments*) G.E.S.

Communion (of the saints) Taken from the Apostles' Creed, "I believe in . . . the communion of saints," the idea of *koinonia* (fellowship) is conveyed and identifies the peculiar fellowship of Christians. The word "saints" as used in the New Testament means simply "the holy ones," or Christians. The communion of saints is a mystical concept, embracing the dead and the unborn of the faith in relation to the living church. (*see* KOINONIA, *Saints*) G.E.S.

COMPLINE (*see Office*)

Conference The administrative work of The United Methodist Church is organized into a chain of conferences. The *General Conference* is the highest legislative body. Meeting each four years, its membership consists of an equal number of ministerial and lay delegates elected by annual conferences. The number of delegates is decided by: (1) the number of ministerial members of the annual conference and (2) the number of church members in the annual conference. *Jurisdictional conferences* are composed of delegates from several annual conferences within their bounds and have such authority as the General Conference confers upon them. There are five jurisdictions within The United Methodist Church: Northeastern, Southeastern, North Central, South Central, and Western. Bishops are elected and assigned, conference boundaries determined, and members of general boards and agencies elected by jurisdictional conference, which meets each four years.

Annual conferences meet each year and are considered the basic body of the church. They vote on all constitutional amendments, elect delegates to Jurisdictional and General Conferences, and vote on orders of the ministry. The president, who is the bishop, announces appointments of pastors to serve local churches (and other ministers) at the yearly meeting, though appointments can be made at any time. *District conferences* are held upon the call of the district superintendent. All ministers and selected local church officials are members and vote on licensing of preachers and other matters. A *charge conference* is organized in every pastoral charge, with certain elected officials constituting its membership and is presided over by the district superintendent. It fosters the spiritual and temporal interests of the church and carries out the program of the church according to the *Discipline* of The United Methodist Church. The charge conference must meet annually and is the final authority in the local church. The annual *Church Conference* is an optional, congregational meeting. (*see Bishop, District superintendent, Synod*) G.E.S.

CONFESSION (*see Prayer*)

Confirmation The act of confirmation completes baptism as a rite for reception into the church. In the early church, baptism required a period of study that sometimes took several years. Following the second century, only bishops baptized and confirmed. As the church grew, it was not always possible for bishops to be present, so parish pastors baptized. The rite of confirmation was reserved for the visit of the bishop. In the western church, a bishop presided at confirmation, but in the eastern church, confirmation also was administered by parish pastors. In the Roman Catholic Church, confirmation is a sacrament. The word *confirmation* really means "to ratify" or agree to the vows that were made by one's parents at the time of baptism. A candidate publicly promises to seek to grow as a Christian and be a faithful disciple of Jesus Christ. In most churches, confirmation includes the laying on of hands and prayer. In other churches, communicant members are received by the ministers or deacons extending the "right hand of Christian fellowship" to the candidate as a symbol of reception into church membership. (*see Baptism, Sacrament*) G.E.S.

CONGREGATION (*see Church, KOINONIA*)

CONSCIENCE (see Consciousness)

Consciousness Consciousness is awareness. A man is said to be conscious when his facilities (reasoning capacities and feelings) are ready to register any experience. Man is conscious of something when he knows that it exists. Knowledge or awareness as used here refers to intellectual activity. This activity may be broken down into four stages. It begins with a vague shadow-like awareness that something is there. The individual moves out from this vague realization to seek more information. The third stage is one in which man tries to evaluate or judge the present experience. He does this by relating it to certain past experiences. The fourth stage of consciousness is to make a decision.

A consideration of consciousness has always been a part of Judeo-Christian ethical thought. In the beginning "conscience" was used to mean the same as consciousness. In the Old Testament there is no word for conscience, but its meaning is implied. In Romans 2:15 conscience is used to refer to natural man's knowledge of God's law. In the New Testament there is a close connection between conscience and loyalty to the faith (1 Timothy 1:5). Roman Catholic theology developed its thinking about conscience in relation to natural law. Conscience came to be thought of as the voice of God in man, telling man what is right and what is wrong. For some this came to mean that man always knows what is wrong and right. When man is faced with a decision a voice inside tells him what he should do. If he will follow this he will be a good man. The Roman Catholic Church in the sixteenth century used conscience in this way with one important exception, namely, the conviction that the conscience can err. Therefore, the church is needed to train the conscience.

The Reformers, Martin Luther (1483-1546) in particular, were much more skeptical of the value of conscience. Luther lumps together satan, law, God's wrath, despair, and conscience. All of these are opposed to the gospel. Men cannot be taught to have a good conscience (to know what is right and what is wrong). Man cannot develop the ability to do the will of God. The good news is that God gives the Christian this ability through Jesus of Nazareth.

Sigmund Freud (1856-1939) described man's subconscious desires and thoughts. Man learns from the group in which he lives that certain desires and thoughts are wrong. Man inwardly consents to these ideas. This internal authority is man's superego or conscience. It serves the purpose of keeping man from both doing and thinking certain things. This understanding of conscience has been strengthened by the study of the different forms conscience takes in different cultures. One thing may be considered wrong in some societies and right in others. A person's conscience is shaped, at least in part, by the society in which he lives. Yet, man is a free moral agent, *i.e.*, he has the power to decide for or against certain alternative courses of action.

How is man to know if he has a good conscience? Man's ability to use his imagination is of significant help here. Man can place himself figuratively in the shoes of the other. He can experience feelings vicariously. Man is also able to examine his own acts and thoughts. He can ask how he would like it if he were treated as he is now treating this other man. He can become conscious of himself (self-consciousness) in relation to the actual world. (*see Self, Self-understanding*) J.S.H.

CONSERVATIO (*see Providence*)

Conservative Though this word means to "save" or "preserve," it may be used in many different ways. (1) A conservative may be a person who keeps the present order of things, at least until very good reason is shown for changing. (2) A conservative may be one who seeks to conserve human values rather than tradition. (3) A conservative in spirit may be one who operates on the principle of taking the least action necessary.

In religion, conservative often means a person who believes that Scripture, church tradition, and personal piety are more important than social action or the merely useful. Often, too, a conservative tries to conserve what is fairly recent. For example, Protestants who hold revivals are returning to a practice only one or two centuries old.

"Conservative" is different from "fundamentalist," which is also a particular school of thought among Protestants. Its most famous doctrine is that the Scriptures are inerrant, but it has other doctrines as well. "Reactionary" is also different from "conservative." A reactionary, as the word implies, reacts strongly against an idea or movement and usually wishes to reinstate an older method or idea. For example, a Christian who tried to retain the exact form of the church during the Reformation would probably be considered reactionary. "Radical," which means "root," has still another meaning. A radical is one who wishes to bring about change, usually rapidly, by "getting at the root of things." For example, a Christian who proposed doing away with the church so that God's spirit would be free to work among men would be a radical. "Orthodox" means "right thinking" and usually refers to religion that emphasizes the standards of the community of faith, rather than individual conscience or the relation of the church to the world. One can be "orthodox" in any religion; the proper noun refers to the Greek or Russian Orthodox Church.

"Left" and "right" are sometimes names for liberal and conservative, respectively. However, these terms are not very precise in religion. During the Reformation, for example, the free churches were on the left because they wished to abolish many church traditions. Today, however, many free churches are conservative, such as those denominations that emphasize revivals.

There may be no relation between a political conservative and a religious conservative. The term conservative has to be related to what is being conserved. A person may be conservative in religion but liberal in politics, and vice-versa. (*see Fundamentalism, Natural theology*)

CONSUBSTANTIAL (*see Christology*)

CONSUBSTANTIATION (*see Communion [Holy]*)

Contextual (kon-*teks*-tew-uhl) Contextual l i t e r a l l y means having reference to the context. In ethical thought contextual is closely related to yet distinguishable from the words "milieu" and "situational." Contextual ethics affirms that man's decisions belong to and are dependent on the actual parts or factors (physical, psychological, and sociological) of his life. Thus, each decision is arrived at as a direct result of all the factors that make up the actual conditions in which the decision is made. Milieu ethics affirms that a person is strongly influenced, as opposed to determined, by his environment or surroundings. A group of intelligent and cultured people can help to bring about the kind of society that in turn will encourage more people to become intelligent and cultured. The individual lot of man can be improved by upgrading the environment in which man lives. Milieu ethics is a vital part of the Renaissance. The Renaissance may be understood as man's confidence in what he can accomplish by shaping and improving his own future. "Situational" literally means the place occupied. Contextual suggests a close identification of man's decision with the factors of his life. All the factors involved in the present are woven together as yarn is woven together to make a piece of material. "Situational" recognizes the importance of the various factors involved in each decision. A decision occurs in a particular time and place in history. This means that specific persons with particular needs and problems are involved in each decision. This fact is important for understanding what decisions a man does or should make.

Thomas Hobbes (1588-1679) taught that good and bad are relative to human desires and aversions. Friedrich Nietzsche (1844-1900) understood all men to be driven by a basic "will to power." Good and bad are to be determined by whether or not they help the individual to become a fully developed (powerful) individual. Man can become master of his own situation if he fully develops his capacity for power. A strong man shapes his own life. A weak man allows forces outside of him to mold his life. Thus, both Hobbes and Nietzsche represent a rejection of the idea that there is an absolute standard outside of man that should be used as the pattern for shaping the individual's life. Rather, the individual is free to participate in and react to the historical situation in which he finds himself.

Present day ethical thought uses both of the terms "situational" and "contextual" to describe Christian ethics. Emil Brunner (1889-1967) concludes that all of man's decisions are relative to the absolute demand of God. Reinhold Niebuhr (1892-   ) views man's decisions as relative to the social environment in which he lives. The concepts of both these men serve as the foundation for developing a Christian ethic of love. Principles, laws, and standards are not binding in any and all situations. Christian ethics is built on the conclusion that man ought always to be loving. How man is to be a loving person is something that each man must decide for himself. Only love is constant. (*see Calculation, Deontological, Law, Love*) J.S.H.

Contingent (kahn-*tin*-juhnt) By contrast with "necessity," something may be said to be contingent when its reality is neither impossible nor necessary. Reality must allow something to be or to happen in order to avoid its impossibility. Something else must have been possible rather than this event or this object in order to avoid its necessity. In theology, God is generally seen as the *only* necessary reality (see Aseity). All else is contingent since all else, other than God, might have been other than it is experienced or thought to be. (*see Unconditional*) J.B.W.

Conversion This term received its modern meaning from the age of the revivals. To be converted was to be saved. The sinner had to be convicted of his sin, repent, and be baptized. Conversion did not always mean church membership, however. The idea is rooted in the biblical notion of repentance. During the liberal era, nurture was substituted for the sudden, emotional experience. The revivalists often emphasized the very hour of conversion. The liberals spoke of a gradual development of faith in the individual. (*see Redemption, Repentance, Soteriology*)

COOPERATION (*see Providence*)

COOPERATIVE GRACE (*see Grace*)

Cosmogony (kahz-*mah*-juh-nee) *There are several crea-*
tion accounts in the Old Testament. The Genesis story, while relatively
late in assuming its final form, roots back into very early times. It is
priestly doctrine and the result of centuries of careful reflection. The
story relates how God brought cosmos out of chaos. In its emphasis on
the watery chaos, the account is probably influenced by the Babylonian
creation epic. The story of creation is in the Hebrew Bible, not as
scientific statement, but because of its importance for faith. The early
Christians accepted the Hebrew Bible, and so the concept of God as
creator. To this they added other ideas of creation, such as the creative
Wisdom and the Hellenistic Logos or Word. The heretic Marcion (sec-
ond century) rejected the Old Testament, claiming that the God of Je-
sus was not the God of the Old Testament. Current speculative ideas in-
fluenced his view that the Demiurge created the world. The early Chris-
tians brought the creation idea into the personal realm and spoke of the
man in Christ as a new creation. Modern views of creation have been
dominated by the scientific interest. From the time of Isaac Newton
(1642-1727) in particular, various views have been advanced, most of
them including the notion of an expanding universe, so that in a sense
creation is considered to be still in progress.

"Cosmogony" comes from the combination of two Greek words, the
word for "world," and the word meaning "to be born." It has to do,
therefore, with the whole question of the origin of the world (or universe). In Hebrew and early Christian history we think naturally of the
Old Testament creation stories and of Wisdom, of the creative Logos
(Word), and of certain non-biblical views such as that held by the
heretic Marcion in the second century of the Christian era.

Some scholars believe that the earliest Old Testament account of
God's creation of the world is in the Book of Job (9:8 ff.; 12:7-10; 26:7-
12; 28:25 ff.; 38:1-38). This book may be dated at about 600 B.C. Psalms
104 contains a relatively early story of creation in poetic form also. But
the account to which the mind inevitably turns has been preserved in the
book of Genesis (1:1-2:3). The final form of this material probably dates
from the Exile, but it is now known to root back into very early times.
It is Priestly doctrine, the result of centuries of careful reflection. To date
it in the period of the Exile is only to recognize its final form. During the
long period of its history prior to that time the material seems to have
undergone an amazing refinement, until the result was the familiar account, powerful in its unadorned simplicity, and free from the cosmological details so characteristic of ancient views of creation.

The story of Genesis 1 gives us ancient Hebrew views regarding the
creation of the world. According to that view, God brought cosmos out
of chaos. By chaos is meant the notion of a primeval watery waste over-

laid by darkness and characterized by formlessness. The cosmos, with its order, is the result of God's action upon this primeval deep. In this account, one starts with the watery chaos, and passes through the various acts of creation: light, the firmament, the dry land, the seas, vegetation, the sun, the moon and the stars, animal life, and finally man. It is probable that the thought of this story is influenced by Babylonian mythology and especially by its view of the cosmos. According to the Babylonian creation epic, Marduk, the Babylonian god, is victorious over the primeval watery chaos. Out of this chaos emerges the seasonal order of nature. Thus there are similarities betwen the two accounts, although perhaps the differences are more striking than the similarities. Nevertheless, the world assumed by the Old Testament is that of the Babylonian cosmology. This is true not only for the Genesis account, but for the entire Old Testament: a flat earth, above which rises the vault or firmament of the heavens; in the firmament are fixed the heavenly bodies, while above the firmament are the waters, held back only by the solid nature of the firmament; the earth is spread over a watery abyss, supported by pillars of the earth.

It would, however, be incorrect to view the Genesis creation story as cosmogony *for its own sake*. Its inclusion in the biblical narrative, as well as its strategic position at the beginning of the Hebrew canon, is due to its importance for faith. It says, in effect, that the God who made a covenant with Abraham and Moses is also the creator of the world. Thus there is drawn a line, so to speak, from creation itself through the history of God's people, a history of the saving acts of God. Behind the covenant relationship with Abraham and the formation of the community was the work of God in the creation of the world. The Genesis creation story, therefore, is foundational for faith.

The early Christians naturally accepted the Hebrew Scriptures as their Bible. Consequently they inherited the Hebrew view of creation. But they added ideas popular in late Judaism and in non-Jewish, Hellenistic, society. In the eighth chapter of Proverbs, for example, Wisdom is personified and described as a "master workman" who was with God at the creation of the world (8:30). This must mean that Wisdom is an agent, or at least an associate, of God in the formation of the world. It is of interest to note, however, that the role of Wisdom in the Proverbs account does not jeopardize the monotheistic position of Judaism, since the account places major stress on the primary work of God himself; at most, Wisdom is but an attendant of God in the work of creation. In fact it can be safely said that Wisdom is nothing more than the action of God himself.

The New Testament at a few points reflects tendencies to embrace Hellenistic ideas of creation, especially that of the Logos or Word. The Logos idea is present in Colossians 1:15 *ff.*, Hebrews 1:2-3, and especially in John 1:1-18. In Stoic thought, Logos was the rational principle of the universe, and it was the duty of men to live in accordance with that principle. But Logos in Hellenistic time possessed many meanings stemming from a variety of sources. With regard to the creative function of the Logos, with which we are concerned here, it is likely that its meaning has been influenced by the creative utterance of God in the Genesis account, and, possibly, by the creative Wisdom such as that set forth in Proverbs 8. It is important to note that New Testament references to the creative Logos never pass over into an extended and detailed cosmogony. It is simply pointed out that the Logos (specifically stated or implied) was God's agent in the creation of the world; and, of course, in these writings the Logos is the Christ of the Christian church.

In the second Christian century (*c.* A.D. 140), a Christian by the name of Marcion held a different view regarding the creation of the world. Born in Pontus, Marcion went to Rome, where he became a member of the Christian church. His views regarding the Old Testament and its God, Judaism, as well as his radical dualism, in which matter was held to be intrinsically evil, caused him to be looked upon as a heretic by the developing catholic Christianity. Marcion could not equate the God of Jesus and the church, a God who was essentially loving and gentle, with the God of the Old Testament. Moreover, his emphasis upon matter as evil prevented him from affirming the Christian God as the creator of an evil universe. This led him to identify the creator God of the Old Testament with the Demiurge of current speculative thought and to discard the Old Testament. This inferior deity could have been the world-creator, but was not the good God of Paul (Marcion's hero) and the Christian church. We may see in this approach that the origin of evil and the origin of the world itself comes together. On the assumption that matter is evil, the question becomes: How could a good God create an evil world? Marcion's answer was that he did not. And while his view may have provided an immediate answer to his problem, it raises other serious problems, such as the relationship between God and the natural order and the continuity of Hebrew and Christian religion.

The concept of a God who created the world easily passed over in early Christianity to the thought of the man in Christ as a new creation. In 2 Corinthians 5:17, Paul writes: "Therefore, if any one is in Christ, he is a new creation. . . ." In the same letter he relates the creator God of Genesis 1 to knowledge of God that has been mediated through Christ: "For it is the God who said, 'Let light shine out of darkness,' who has shone in our hearts to give the light of the knowledge of the glory of God in the face of Christ" (4:6). Here we have the conviction that in Christ there is, so to speak, a recapitulation of the original act of creation, only this time in personal terms. Here we become aware of the close connection in the Hebrew-Christian tradition between God as the creator of the natural world on the one hand and his creative role in the spiritual life of man on the other.

In modern times, cosmogony has been dominated by scientific views concerning the origin of the world. From the time of Isaac Newton in the seventeenth century various theories have been advanced. Newton applied the law of gravitation to particles of matter, which he supposed in the beginning were distributed through limitless space. By gravitational attraction these particles eventually grew into the sun and other stars. In the eighteenth century, the philosopher Immanuel Kant advanced the theory that the universe developed from a spinning nebula. This idea was later developed independently by de LaPlace (1749-1827), a French astronomer and mathematician. A view receiving considerable attention today is one that has been called the tidal theory. According to this view, the planetary system was caused by the gravitational pull of a star moving through space on our sun. This pull caused gaseous "bulges" on the bodies of both stars, and these separated to become our planets. Another view advanced by some is the so-called "Big Bang" theory. The idea is that our universe was the result of an initial vast explosion; this happened billions of years ago, and from it stems the evolution of our present universe. Most modern scientific theories incorporate the view that our universe is in a process of expansion; that, in effect, creation is still going on.

It should be pointed out that these scientific theories differ from the biblical creation story in that they do not stem from a religious concern characteristic of the latter. Yet the modern views of cosmic evolution, under whatever form, have profound religious implications. (*see Cosmology, Creation* EX NIHILO, *Word, World view*) E.L.T.

Cosmology (kahz-*mah*-luh-jee)   From the Greek words *cosmos* and *logos*, cosmology means a doctrine of the world formulated in ordered discourse. Cosmology should be distinguished from *cosmogony*, which is the study of the mythological aspects of accounts of the origins of the world. Whereas cosmology deals primarily with the structures of the world, a cosmogony is a story of the origins of the world.

Cosmology is traditionally one of the divisions of metaphysics. Two of the earliest and most influential cosmologies are those of Plato (*c.* 427-347 B.C.) and Aristotle (384-322 B.C.) These philosophers reflected on the problems with which cosmologies were traditionally concerned: the relationship between time and eternity, the beginnings and sources of matter, and the laws of nature. With the rise of modern science and the empirical method, by contrast to the speculative basis of metaphysics, many of these problems have come under the domain of the special sciences such as astronomy, physics, and geology. As a result, many philosophers have given up pursuit of these matters as being inappropriate to them with their methodologies. Often in the process philosophers have shifted to ontology, *i.e.*, to a concern for the underlying structures of all reality, the world being only a special case of a more basic problem. Martin Heidegger (1889-   ), a contemporary German philosopher, has thought and written much about this matter, as has Alfred N. Whitehead (1861-1947), the noted British-American.

Theologians, early attracted to this issue in the history of Christianity, have not been either willing or able to leave it to anyone else. So long as cosmology was primarily a concern of philosophers who by the nature of their work were speculating upon the nature of the world, Christian theologians could engage them at the level of revelation and reason. Sometimes theologians would claim triumphantly that revelation gave them access to truth not available to speculative reason. Other theologians, convinced that there could be no final conflict between revelation and reason, incorporated great portions of philosophical cosmology into their theologies. Thomas Aquinas' (*c.* 1225-74) reliance on Aristotle is a most remarkable instance of this attitude. In either case certain theological doctrines were inseparably connected with such discussions. For example, the sovereignty and providence of God, or creation *ex nihilo*, were inevitably considered as a basic conviction of faith.

With the rise of modern science in the seventeenth century, theology was put on the defensive. The smoldering warfare between theology and science broke into actual conflict during the eighteenth and nineteenth centuries. Theologians had uncritically thought it literally true that the world was created in six days, and that its age was dated from 4004 B.C. They were threatened by such hypotheses as evolution, which made creation a process unaccessible to man and placed the age of the earth at millions of years. Gradually, however, many theologians have come to hold that the Bible was never intended to be a scientific handbook. Further, they argue that Christian theology is not dependent upon any particular scientific view.

Problems, however, have remained. Spokesmen for Christianity have insisted that even if, for example, a picture of a three-storied universe (heaven above, earth in the middle, and hell below) is no longer defensible or necessary, certain religious insights are, nonetheless, valid. Men do experience bliss and torment, heaven and hell, and if they cannot be spatially pictured, their realities are no less. These realities must be spoken of in such a fashion that even the most specific modern man will be made aware of them. Though other examples could be cited, it is clear that the basic convictions of Christianity cannot be conceded to others, no matter what new forms of speech emerge. (*see Cosmogony, Creation* EX NIHILO, *Metaphysics, Natural theology, Prime mover, Theology*) J.B.W.

Courage The outstanding example of the classical use of the word "courage" is the soldier. The soldier does not hide from danger. This picture views courage as man's accepting danger and fate and being a strong person in their midst. In this way of thinking courage is one value alongside of other virtues. For example, in Plato's *Republic* courage is presented alongside of wisdom and virtue as the three significant values in the life of man.

Paul Tillich's *The Courage to Be* expands the definition of courage to include faith. Courage is not simply a way of meeting danger; it is a way of life. Man is given the opportunity to be a part of the creative work of God in this world. But man must accept the restrictions society places on him and work inside the actual given structures of society. This is called the courage *to be a part*. It involves taking the risk of failing to be oneself. Another form that courage takes is the courage *to be oneself*. This is the decision to be true to oneself, to make one's own decisions. This involves taking the risk of failing to be a part of the group. Faith in God transcends the "courage to be a part" and "the courage to be oneself." In faith man can accept all his own individual questions and doubts about the world he lives in. "*The courage to be is rooted in the God who appears when God has disappeared in the anxiety of doubt.*" (THE COURAGE TO BE, *by Paul Tillich, page 190. Yale University Press, 1952*) J.S.H.

Covenant The idea of covenant is one of the most important and profound elements in the biblical tradition. It unifies both the Old and New Testaments. The Old Testament word for covenant is *berith*, and that of the New Testament *diatheke*. Though the Old Testament contains accounts of covenants between individuals, as in the case of that between Jacob and Laban (Genesis 31:44), the more important idea of covenant relates to the compact made between God and Israel. The traditions of the covenant, as they are related to Moses, are found in Exodus 19–24.

To understand and appreciate the covenant idea, one must grasp the serious relationship between the two parties of a covenant, for a covenant was in no sense entered into casually or lightly. The solemn character of the covenantal relationship is indicated by the fact that it was ordinarily sealed in blood. In early times, this was accomplished by the cutting of the wrists so that the blood of the two parties could be intermingled. Sometimes sacrificial animals were employed to suggest the same idea. The mutual and binding character of the contractual relationship was thus indicated. The eucharistic words of Jesus may be compared with this: " 'This is my blood of the covenant, which is poured out for many.' " (Mark 14:24; compare 1 Corinthians 11:25)

Of paramount importance in the history of the covenant is the Hebrew tradition of Moses' role. This tradition is embodied in Exodus 19–24. The covenant account set forth in those chapters tells of God's gracious act in taking as his own people those whom he had delivered from the Egyptians. The Decalogue, which figures in the account (20:1-17; see Deuteronomy 5:7 ff. and Exodus 34:11-28 for variant forms) represents the terms of the contract. A covenant may be between equals (1 Samuel 20; Genesis 34), or it may be between a dominant party and one who is weaker (1 Kings 20:33-34). In the case of God's covenant with Moses, it is of course the latter. Nevertheless, the assuming of mutual responsibility was of the essence of this covenant. This covenant, richly associated with Moses, Sinai, the deliverance from Egypt, and the giving of the Law, was through the centuries basic to Hebrew life and thought. This memory again and again called the nation back from disobedience.

So far covenant has been treated as an outside, or external, act. Yet it later came to have an inside, or internal, meaning. Jeremiah later spoke of a new covenant that God will make with his people: " 'Behold, the days are coming, says the LORD, when I will make a new covenant with the house of Israel and the house of Judah, not like the covenant which I made with their fathers when I took them by the hand to bring them out of the land of Egypt, my covenant which they broke. . . . But this is the covenant which I will make with the house of Israel after those days, says the LORD: I will put my law within them, and I will write it upon their hearts; and I will be their God, and they shall be my people." (Jeremiah 31:31-33) This is a most important step in the history of the covenant idea. It becomes the basis of the concept of the new covenant that we find in the New Testament and early Christianity.

The older view of "covenant" is still found in the New Testament. Acts 7:8, for instance, speaks of the covenant God made with Abraham, confirmed by the rite of circumcision (compare Acts 3:25; Romans 9:4), but the dominant view of the New Testament is that of the new covenant. It goes beyond Jeremiah's thought in that now the life and death of Jesus are seen as the event which makes the new relationship possible (Matthew 26:28; Mark 14:24; Luke 22:20; 1 Corinthians 11:25; 2 Corinthians 3:6). The Letter to the Hebrews, which is constantly contrasting the superiority of the new revelation in Christ over the old, fittingly employs the covenant idea to reinforce its thesis (Hebrews 7:22; 8:6; 12:24). The concept of covenant had the value of maintaining continuity between the religion of the Old Testament and that of the New. To put it another way, the early Christians saw themselves and the church as the continuation of the main line of descent of the people of God. The God who had made covenant with Moses on Sinai had now established a new relationship with his people, a covenant ratified by the death of Christ. Indeed, the New Testament witnesses to a "Moses motif," as, for example, in Matthew's account of the Sermon on the Mount, where Jesus is in effect a new and greater Moses bringing forth a new "law" upon a new mountain. (*see* LAOS, *Law*) E.L.T.

CREATION (*see* Cosmogony)

Creation ex nihilo (eks *nee*-hee-loh) From the Latin *ex* (from) and *nihilo* (nothing), hence "creation from (or out of) nothing." This concept may be traced to the second century A.D. The idea originated in conflict with other thinkers who believed that God used material that already existed before God created it. Such matter would then be not contingent, but necessary. Christian theology has generally affirmed creation *ex nihilo* in order to ascribe the creation of everything to God. Recent religious, rather philosophical, interpretations have focused upon creation *ex nihilo* as a way of confessing faith in God as the source of everything. He who knows God as creator will know himself as a creature. (*see* Cosmogony) J.B.W.

Creed This word comes from *credo*, the Latin word meaning, "I believe," which stands at the beginning of the Apostles' and the Nicene Creeds. The earliest confession was, " 'Jesus is Lord.' " (1 Corinthians 12:3) The early church developed more elaborate confessions as a test of faith. One major motive was to combat heresies.

The Apostles' Creed grew out of the Roman *symbolon*, or Old Roman Creed, used by the church at Rome. It dates from sometime in the second century and was a confession used at the time of baptism. Though it began with a phrase about God, the all powerful Father, it was mainly a confession about Jesus. The phrases that now stand at the end of the Apostles' Creed after the Holy Spirit phrase were added in the years after 200.

The Nicene Creed was the product of a long theological debate in the fourth century, complicated by political intrigues. The dispute began when Arius (256-336), an aging presbyter of a church in Egypt, apparently challenged the views of his bishop, Alexander. Arius believed that Christ, the Son, was a created being. To affirm a member of the Trinity as part of creation was to say that God was not one, since God himself was the Creator and not a creature. As a result of the argument, the Emperor Constantine summoned a council of the church, which met in Nicaea in 325. It finally reached an agreement, under pressure from Constantine, who wanted unity in the church. The most crucial phrase was that Christ was "begotten, not made," and that he was "of one essence with the Father." Thus Arius' view became a heresy.

The dispute did not end, however. Alexander's secretary, Athanasius (c. 295-373) later rose to become a bishop of the church. He defended the Nicene statement against Arian attacks. Not until 381, when another general council was held, did the church agree on the exact form what we today call the Nicene Creed.

The creed usually called "A Modern Affirmation" was written by Edwin Lewis (1881-1959), a theologian at Drew Theological Seminary, at the request of the Methodist Episcopal Commission on Worship and Music, whose chairman was Bishop Wilbur P. Thirkield (1854-1936).

The Korean Creed grew out of a meeting of Methodist bishops in Singapore in 1922. The bishops became concerned at the lack of a creed speaking to the special needs of the Orient. Bishop Herbert Welch (1862-) eventually drew up the creed, which received its name because it was adopted by the Korean Methodist churches in 1930.

Both the Korean Creed and A Modern Affirmation were included in *The Methodist Hymnal* of 1935. (*see Doctrine*) G.E.S.

CRUCIFIXION (*see Atonement, Calvary, Christology,* Kenosis, Kerygma, *Scandal*)

Culture Some thinkers define culture as everything that man makes, including ideas and values. H. Richard Niebuhr (1894-1962) wrote that culture "comprises language, habits, ideas, beliefs, customs, social organization, inherited artifacts, technical processes, and values." (*Christ and Culture,* page 33)

Some thinkers, however, distinguish between culture and civilization. The latter is the world of technology. Culture is more primitive and includes art and religion. Thinkers who make this distinction include Oswald Spengler (1880-1936), the German historian, and Bronislaw Malinowski (1884-1942), the Polish anthropologist.

Niebuhr described five different ways Christians have related to culture: (1) Christ against culture (1 John, Leo Tolstoi); (2) the Christ of culture (Abelard, Adolf Ritschl); (3) Christ above culture (Clement of Alexandria, Thomas Aquinas); (4) Christ and culture in paradox (Paul, Martin Luther); and (5) Christ transforming culture (John, Augustine, F. D. Maurice). (*see Church in the world, Natural law, Natural theology*)

Curate (*cure-*ut) Its root is found in the phrase "cure of souls" and is the title used for a parish priest whose responsibility includes visiting, administering the sacraments, and shepherding the flock. A curate may be the pastor in charge of the parish or a priest who assists the parish rector. (*see Rector*) G.E.S.

Cynic (*sin-*ek) A cynic is one who mistrusts the moral motives of men. Usually cynicism is connected with skepticism, which is the mistrust of human knowledge. Because one doubts that certain knowledge is possible, he also often doubts that there is any defensible basis for moral action. Often a cynic concludes that self-interest underlies all human actions. From such an outlook, a cynic may offer to others who think their motives to be clear and unselfish a reminder that moral decisions are extremely difficult and complex, and that self-interest is seldom ever unimportant in making moral decisions. (*see Skeptic*) J.B.W.

D SOURCE (*see Source criticism*)

DAY OF THE LORD (*see Apocalypse, Eschatology,* Parousia)

De Profundis (dee or day pro-*fun*-dis) From the first two words of Psalm 130 (Psalm 129 in the Vulgate), meaning "out of the depths," this is an agonized expression of despair. It is a chant used to reflect upon man's misery apart from God's presence and power. G.E.S.

DEACON, DEACONESS (*see* Diakonia, *Orders*)

DEAD SEA SCROLLS (*see Manuscript*)

Death In the Old Testament death is considered both as the normal end of life and as the negation of life. In Genesis 15:15 and Job 5:26 death is the normal end to earthly life. It does not here seem to be a threat or problem to man. It is simply one experience set alongside of the other experiences of man. Death is also pictured as the opposite of life. The spirit is what makes man a living being (Genesis 2:7). At death the spirit returns to God and the body turns back into dust (Ecclesiastes 12:7). Life is a good gift, and death, being the opposite of life, is bad or undesirable. A dead person is unclean and therefore should not be touched (Numbers 19:16). Death is also viewed as a destructive force in the world. Man is made of perishable or temporal

69

material. Man had the opportunity of becoming immortal if he had not sinned. Man disobeyed the command of God and now cannot be immortal. Death may be considered a result of man's sin. Death is the punishment man receives because he has broken God's command. Likewise, if a man has broken the law of the community the community may punish him by putting him to death (Deuteronomy 24:16). At death man goes to Sheol, the place of shadowy existence in which praise of God is impossible (Isaiah 38:18). In the Old Testament there is a growing interest in the status of the dead (Job 14:10-12; Ecclesiastes 3:16-22).

The New Testament does not consider death a natural occurrence. Death is an evil thing and a source of terror (Luke 12:16-21). Death is an enemy of man (Romans 8) because man has sinned (Romans 7:9).

Paul interprets Adam as a symbol of a cosmic force of destruction. The world is the battleground in which the opposing forces of life and death fight out their battle for man. Still, man is responsible for the choices he makes. He can give himself over to the powers of sin and destruction or be obedient to the Word of God. Man can be at one and the same time physically alive and spiritually dead. This "spiritual death" is the result of man's failure to live the faithful life. Spiritual life, or full life, only comes through open and honest communion with God and neighbor. If a man is closed up in himself he is dead. He may be alive biologically, but if he is not aware of others he is dead.

Scientifically considered, death is the cessation of life. The biological organism is considered dead when a man stops breathing or his heart stops beating. Death is the natural end of a human life. Yet, modern day medicine is pledged and organized to fight against death. And generally today Western man considers it a good thing to avoid death. Some ancient Greek thinkers pictured death as a desirable experience. At death the soul is liberated from the body and set free for higher forms of life.

Death has been surrounded with many taboos. Any contact with a dead body makes it necessary that a man be cleansed through a ritual ceremony. In general man should avoid contact with the dead. The idea has been widely circulated in the past that death is an unnatural event caused by witchcraft. (See Arthur Miller's *The Crucible*). Medical science seeks to understand death in terms of natural causes. Disposal of the dead body has been handled in many different ways. The body has been left above the ground, put in caves, buried under the ground, and cremated. Funeral ceremonies conducted at the time of death have varied greatly both in length and content. In ancient times it was the custom to bury at least some of a man's belongings with him.

Martin Heidegger (1889-   ) understands death as the unavoidable end of man's life. Man has a beginning and an end. Man knows this! His knowledge of death helps him to see himself as who he is. He is

70

aware of his utter isolation. He must die his own death alone. Biological death is viewed as helping man to see what it means to be alive. This approach to death has at least one point in common with Christian theology. Christianity is not an attempt to avoid death but rather a way of living and dying. Thus, Christian theology seeks to understand the attitude of a Christian toward death, as well as the way he dies. (*see Anxiety, Cosmology, Eternal, Immortality, Resurrection, Sheol*) J.S.H.

DEATH OF GOD (*see Atheism*)

Decalogue (*deck-uh-log*) This term means "ten words" and refers to the Ten Commandments, which may have originally been oral words preceded by "not." The Decalogue is a part of the tradition of God's dealing with Moses on Sinai. Scholars see in the code of the Decalogue an important part of the covenant tradition of Moses. From this point of view, they make up the terms of the contract between the two parties of the covenant, namely, God and Israel. In this case, the covenant is between two parties, of which one, namely, God, is superior to the other, Israel. And so it is God who sets the terms of the covenant relationship.

There are, in fact, two editions of the Decalogue. One is found in Exodus 20:2-17; the other in Deuteronomy 5:6-21. Some scholars feel that the Deuteronomic code is earlier than that found in Exodus 20. But the two are very similar. Earlier, scholars tended to rule out the possibility that these collections of laws could stem from the time of Moses. More recently, however, criticism has tended to see strands of very old tradition embodied in the Decalogue, perhaps going as far back as the time of Moses himself. This, of course, does not prove that Moses wrote the Decalogue. (*see Covenant, Law*) E.L.T.

Decision The Bible pictures man as faced with many possible courses of action. Any concrete course of action involves rejecting certain historical possibilities while choosing others. This of necessity involves man in the task of interpreting what is happening in history, distinguishing the good from the bad, or choosing the right from the wrong. (Matthew 16:3; 1 Corinthians 6:5) To make the right choice is to be obedient to God. Man is a free moral agent in that he has the power of choice, *i.e.*, to choose between different possible courses of action and thus shape his own future.

Man's actions are significant because of the different concrete choices open to him. But, how, according to the Bible, does man make the right decision? According to Paul Minear in *Eyes of Faith*, "obedience" in the New Testament is a concrete historical act. It is not a quality or attribute that can be learned, neither is it a habit that can be developed. The crucial question for man is: will I be obedient? This question must be answered anew in each given moment. It is not a virtue to be cultivated. It is an opportunity contained in each present moment; thus, life is a matter of decision. Life becomes actualized in and through more choices.

In pre-New Testament times Stoic thought presented the idea of a scale of values. The values range from the highest good to lowest possible act (bad). Man is armed with a conscience that urges him to be true to the highest value (good). Man's decision is primarily one of either being true or untrue to the virtues he knows beforehand. Decisions viewed thus are an occasion for character building.

Traditional Christian thought has been deeply influenced by this understanding of what is involved in decision making. Christian man is concerned not only with building his own character, but he is also concerned to preserve the unity of the church. Therefore, the church is given the authority (through its officers) to decide what is right and what is wrong. The individual is then to be obedient to the decisions of the church. He uses his decisions as an occasion to develop his own character by doing what the church tells him. Thus, he simultaneously strengthens the church.

Socrates (c. 470-399 B.C.) may be used to illustrate how one might go about the process of making a decision. Socrates had lived his life in an attempt to do what he understood to be his duty. Some persons considered his actions harmful to society. Socrates was tried and sentenced to death. His friends were ready to help him escape from prison. He decided to stay in prison and accept the punishment (his death) the authorities of the community had placed on him. How did Socrates make this decision? He first set out three conclusions that he used as a basis for approaching the decision. (1) Man ought to decide by asking what is the reasonable (or rational) thing to do. Emotions should not be allowed to affect the decision. (2) The answer to any question cannot be found simply by appealing to what people think. (3) Man should not do what is morally wrong. Having laid down this foundation, Socrates then gave the threefold reason for his refusal to break the law by escaping from prison: (1) Man should never harm anyone. If one breaks the law of the state he will harm the state. Therefore, man should never break the law of the state. (2) Socrates, by continuing to live in the state, had consented to obey the law of the state. He could have left the state and gone to another, but he did not. (3) Socrates considered the state as virtually the citizens' parent. Man ought always to obey his parents. (see Calculation, Duty, Freedom) J.S.H.

DEISM (see Immanent, Natural theology, Theism)

Demonic (deh-*mah*-nik) This term has fallen into disuse by many theologians since the eighteenth century because of the scientific reaction against superstition. Paul Tillich (1886-1965), however, has insisted upon the significance of the term for understanding the history of Christianity. Jesus, Paul, Augustine, and Luther are but a few of the most famous Christians for whom the demonic was real and important. Tillich regarded the demonic as the symbol of the structural and inescapable power of evil. Upon the symbol of the demonic turn such other symbols as the fall of man and original sin. The power of the demonic is plainly seen in the tragedies of individuals and societies. Even good intentions may lead to evil results. The power of the demonic is then seen to be real. (*see Myth, Theodicy*) J.B.W.

DEMYTHOLOGIZE (*see Myth*)

Denomination This term refers to the religious body that administratively and legally unites like-minded congregations. A denomination is a church family and may be congregations forming an association (Baptist, for example), or churches of one organization (like The United Methodist), administered by both conference and local church officials. Denominational churches cherish tradition, doctrine, sacraments, and an official clergy, while sects rely on personal experience, an uneducated clergy, and spontaneity in worship. (*see Conference, Sect*) G.E.S.

Deontological (dee-*ahn*-toh-*loj*-ik-uhl) *Deontological is a name given to a particular method of dealing with ethics. It begins with the question of what "ought" man to do. The deontological school of thought teaches that doing what is right is an end in itself. Classical deontological theories are of two different types: act-deontological and rule-deontological.*

Immanuel Kant, a rule-deontologist, concludes that any man who makes a free choice to act in a certain way uses rules. A man is basing his actions on the right rules if he would be willing to have all men's actions guided by the same rules.

Present day ethical thought is raising serious questions about dividing ethical thought into teleological and deontological categories. Deontological ethics may be best understood in contrast to teleological ethics. Teleological ethics says that man is to seek to realize fully his own humanity. Thus, teleological ethics is founded on consequences or the end accomplished. Deontological ethics deals with man's obligation or duty rather than seeking the good. Ethics is not a question of seeking to fully develop one's potential self-realization, but rather doing what one "ought"

73

to do in the present situation. Deontology may be defined as simply "the science of duty."

The word "deontological" includes two words, *deon* and *logos*. *Deon* means what is binding or proper. It is taken from *dein*, which means to bind. *Logos* means description or word picture. The two words put together literally mean "a description of that which is binding." That which is binding is to be discovered by asking what should one do in the present situation. No reference need be made to what will be accomplished as a result of one's present act. The question of right and wrong is an end in itself. Man is not concerned with right or wrong as a means to some "good end." A concern for what is right or wrong is the primary business with which man should be occupied.

Classical deontological theories are basically of two different types: act-deontology and rule-deontology. Act-deontological theories teach that man is always to decide what is the right thing to do on the basis of the particular situation. General judgments about right and wrong are of little help. Some act-deontologists would say that some general rules about what is right or wrong are of help, but these rules should not take the place of the particular judgments. The rule "do not lie" may be of some help to man in deciding what is right. However, this rule does not relieve man from deciding anew each time he acts whether or not on this occasion he should tell the truth or a lie. Present day "situation ethics" or "the new morality" are in close agreement with this understanding of the importance of each particular "act" as including a new and unique decision.

Rule-deontology places a considerable stress on the value of rules (sometimes called "standards" or "principles"). There are standards of right and wrong. Certain principles should always be followed. Some of the rules are very specific, such as "do not cheat." Other rules are abstract, such as "one man should not treat another man in a way he would not want the other man to treat him." Rule-deontology teaches that these rules are to be followed in any and every situation. What is right or wrong is determined by reference to rules and principles. One major problem for rule-deontology is what one does in a situation in which any act will break some rule or principle. How does man decide which rule to break? Assuming that man has been taught (1) not to tell a lie and (2) never to hurt anyone's feelings, what does he do when he has to answer a question which, if answered honestly, will hurt another person's feelings?

Immanuel Kant (1724-1804) is an excellent example of a rule-deontologist. Kant teaches that everyone who makes a free choice to act in a certain way is actually using rules. These rules may be formulated or described in a systematic way. Man is making the right decisions only if he would be willing to set up the rules he is following as universal rules for all men to follow. A rule is morally right only if it can be consistently willed that everyone base his action on it in every situation. Obviously it is wrong to act on the basis that it is good to break promises. If everyone broke promises when it was convenient to do so, then there would in reality be no promises at all. When man breaks promises to suit his own purposes he is acting in an immoral way. Kant proposes to solve the problem of conflicting principles by the use of "pure reason." Reasoning through what one ought to do man arrives at a "categorical imperative," which stands above rules and places them in the proper relation to one another. The first form of this categorical imperative is to "act only on that maxim which you can at the same time will to be a universal law." The major criticism of Kant is the same that has been offered against all rule-deontologists. Kant is unable to put forward one basic principle that eliminates or solves the conflicts arising between different principles. Emil Brunner (1889-1967) makes considerable use of Kant's "categorical imperative" in coming up with his understanding of man's duty. Brunner teaches that man is faced in every decision to act with the "divine imperative." In every situation man has a claim laid on his life. Man is not on his own. He is under orders to act in accordance with the divine command.

Paul Ramsey (1913-) understands his own ethical thought as a movement away from teleological thinking and in the direction of deontological thinking. Teleological thinking, according to Ramsey, is motivated from within. Thus, the Christian is to stay clear of humanistic ethics that pushes for the self-realization or self-development of each man. The Christian is not to seek the good. Christian ethics begins from beyond itself. It begins with God's righteousness. Man is to live in the image of God and in this way he will reflect the right. The Christian doctrine of right is thus derived from man's service to God. Man forgets all claims to having or seeking a good life and becomes a Christ (a loving servant) to his neighbor. He asks: what is God calling me to do for this man? He acts according to his understanding of the answer to this question.

Present day ethical thinking is calling into question the division of ethical thought into teleological and deontological categories. The question is being raised: Is it not misleading to contrast "the good" and "the right" as opposite alternatives? Are the motives for "self-realization," or pursuits of the good, contrary to the motives for "doing one's duty," or the "right"? (see Good, Principle, Righteousness, Teleology) J.S.H.

DEPRAVITY (see Sin)

DESCENT INTO HELL (see Kenosis)

DESPAIR (*see Courage, Hope*)

Destiny From the Latin *destinare*, the word means what is ordained or determined beforehand. It may be used in a fairly loose and general fashion to refer to what will happen in the future, *e.g.*, "He is destined to become king." Or, it may refer to what has happened in the past, *e.g.*, "It was his destiny to remain poor." Often there is an implied necessity of the course of events. Thus, by extension "destiny" is often a reference to whatever or whoever is the agent that determines those events.

The ancient Greeks, as early as Homer's *Iliad* and *Odyssey*, were conscious of a force or a reality that defined the limits human activity was unable to cross. They called it *moira* (*moy*-rah), and it may be translated in many ways—destiny or fate, but also chance or luck. Eventually as men became more sophisticated, *moira* became an instrument of the gods, ultimately of Zeus alone. The challenge to man is to discern and submit to the divine order. If man tries to do more than destiny allows, he will only break himself in the process. The Greek tragedians and classical philosophers all wrestled with this problem.

The Israelites also were confronted by the awesome power of the will of their God, Yahweh. Though they sometimes were faithful to it and gave themselves over to that will, they also often departed from it and were judged and chastised by it. The psalmists and the prophets bear eloquent testimony to the demand of faithfulness laid upon the chosen people.

Christianity fell heir to the Greek notion of destiny and to the Hebrew faith in the providence of God. Some decision was laid upon early Christians. They had either to admit to the existence of an independent "power," destiny, alongside their God, or they had to affirm the basic monotheism of their Israelite heritage. They, of course, chose the latter. The only power they acknowledged was God. This was of fundamental significance in the conflict with all dualistic systems, *e.g.*, second century gnosticism. It was this decision that made destiny as an independent force play such an insignificant role in early Christian thought. Where earlier men had faced concrete limitations and possibilities and proposed destiny as their answer, Christians, facing the same concrete human problems, answered with the love of God revealed in Jesus Christ. This has been typical of the classical history of Christian thought.

In modern theology one Protestant, Paul Tillich (1886-1965), has provocatively analyzed this matter. In his significant *Systematic Theology*, Tillich observes that only within the context of the question of human freedom does destiny make any sense. He writes, "Our destiny is that out of which our decisions arise; . . . My destiny is the basis of my freedom; my freedom participates in shaping my destiny." (Volume I, pages 184-85) Tillich goes on to observe that only he who has freedom has a destiny. Obviously this concept of destiny, any more than in classical Christianity, is not understandable apart from God. In Tillich's usage, destiny becomes one aspect of the human situation in which God has placed man.

Such doctrines as the sovereignty and governance of God and predestination represent particular attempts on the part of Christian theologians to speak to the issues raised by destiny. (*see Freedom, Predestination, Providence*) J.B.W.

DETERMINISM (*see Freedom*)

Deus absconditus (*day*-us ab-*skahn*-deh-tus) This Latin phrase, which means "the hidden God," was made notable by Martin Luther (1483-1546). In the Bible, the prophet Isaiah wrote, "Truly, thou art a God who hidest thyself. . . ." (Isaiah 45:15) When Luther reflected upon the history of theology that tried to discover what God really is, the result, he argued, was unsuccessful: God hides from those who presume to know too much. Man may truly know God only as *Deus revelatus,* (rev-eh-*lah*-tus), *i.e.*, as God wills to reveal himself. The *Deus absconditus* term has recently been re-emphasized in the "death of God" controversy because of the assertions of William Hamilton and Thomas J. J. Altizer. (*see Atheism, Revelation*) J.B.W.

DEUTERONOMIC SOURCE (*see Source criticism*)

DEVIL (*see Theodicy*)

Diakonia (dee-*ak*-oh-*nee*-ah) *Diakonia* means practical service to the poor, orphans, widows, and others in need of food or other physical needs. In the New Testament *diakonia* is used in three different ways. (1) It is used to refer to waiting on tables and is thus closely connected with the idea of providing food that sustains the body (see Luke 10:40). (2) It may be used to refer to any service rendered in love. (3) It also refers to the carrying out of certain duties in the community. In this sense the word includes the idea that each man does his job in the community.

In Christian thought the word "deacon" is closely related to the word *diakonia*. In the New Testament there are only two offices with a specific designation in the Christian church (Philippians 1:1, 1 Timothy 3:8, 12). These were deacons and bishops. Deaconesses (females) are also mentioned in the New Testament (Romans 16:1), but this is the same office as deacon. We do not know the duties of the bishop and deacon from

77

the New Testament. Both a deacon and a bishop are to be blameless in character. The deacon assists the bishop. The bishop's office is administrative. The deacon's office is practical service. Sometimes the office of deacon is defined as the lowest degree of holy orders. In Greek thought man is presented as being unhappy when he has to serve some one. Thus, to serve is to do something that takes away from the dignity of man. Within the Jewish faith service is exalted as an honor (Isaiah 52:13–53:12). In the New Testament service is presented as being the key to being a follower of Jesus Christ. Within this way of thinking there is a complete reversal of the idea of greatness and rank: " '. . . let the greatest among you become as the youngest, and the leader as one who serves. For which is the greater, one who sits at table, or one who serves? Is it not the one who sits at table? But I [Jesus] am among you as one who serves.' " (Luke 22:26-27) The Christian is called to share in this service (doing the will of God). The fact that this may include suffering is not to keep the Christian from being faithful to his task.

Throughout its life, the church has been concerned to help meet bodily needs. In the fifth, sixth, and ninth centuries the popes seemed to have taken charge of feeding the poor. In the third century the records show the church caring for five hundred persons who had special needs (widows, *etc.*). The church called upon the rich to make provision for the poor by donating to a fund in the church used for this purpose. In this period a *diakonia* was a church where the poor gathered for religious service and received food. In the medieval period of history the church conducted most of the welfare work. (*see Orders*) J.S.H.

Dialectic (digh-uh-*lek*-tek) This term derives from its use in logic. It stems from the Greek word *dialektike*, which means "art of debate." In a formal sense Aristotle (384-322 B.C.) attributed the beginning of dialectic to Zeno of Elea (fifth century B.C.) who used it in discussions with his intellectual opponents. He would hypothetically accept the opponent's assertions and proceed to demonstrate how they led to contradictory conclusions. As Socrates (*c.* 470-399 B.C.) used dialectic, it became the means of evolving a satisfactory definition or solution to a problem by a systematic sequence of questions and answers. In the dialogues of Plato (*c.* 427-347 B.C.), dialectic was the underlying form of the dramatic conversations. From these related uses, dialectic finally came to mean something like "logical development" in Aristotle's analysis. Subsequently, the Stoic philosophers divided logic into its form (rhetoric) and its method (dialectic) and "logic" became virtually synonymous with "dialectic." This was its meaning throughout the Middle Ages.

Medieval theologians of scholasticism often adopted the dialectical method. They began by posing a question. Then they stated the opinion of some recognized authority, such as the Bible or a church father; this was then countered by an equally trustworthy authority. Finally, they then reasoned to a position that reconciled the contradiction. Theology could be undertaken in this fashion so long as authority, revelation, reason, and truth were regarded as non-contradictory.

The eighteenth century German philosopher Hegel (1770-1831) argued that the very nature of reason lies in positing a thesis (*thee*-sus) (an assertion claiming to be true) that generates its own antithesis (an-*tith*-uh-sus) (a contrary assertion also claiming to be true) and these lead, in turn, to a synthesis (a new assertion that reconciles the contradictory thesis and antithesis). Hegel believed this logical process to be a clue to the very nature of reality. He then proposed a remarkable philosophy of history upon this basis. Hegel's influence upon Karl Marx is well known.

Hegel was himself countered in his own time by Soren Kierkegaard, the Danish theologian (1813-55). Kierkegaard sought to show the limits of reason rather than its unlimited power to discern reality. For him the use of dialectic did not produce a synthesis of contradictions but rather brought man squarely against two truth claims that could never be reconciled. For example, Kierkegaard would posit man's freedom, on the one hand, and necessity, on the other hand. He argued that neither can be understood apart from the other, but that neither could be reconciled logically with the other. Paradox rather than synthesis was the defeat of reason's access to ultimate reality.

Neo-orthodox (see Dogmatics) theologians have sometimes been committed to Kierkegaard's defense of dialectical paradox. Karl Barth (1886-   ) was the first twentieth century theologian to see merit in Kierkegaard's efforts to demonstrate the limits of human reason. Barth's own arguments were aimed against the liberal theology (see Natural theology) of the nineteenth and early twentieth centuries, in which great confidence was placed in man's ability to know ultimate reality, even God himself. As Barth wrote in his famous *Commentary on Romans* (1919), the testimony of the Bible is that man is bound in sin to the degree that he is incapable of reaching God, least of all by reason. Rather, thinks Barth, God must come to man, which He did supremely in Jesus Christ. Thus, Barth uses dialectics by posing on the one hand what human reason takes to be true, and then contrasting this with what the gospel proclaims. These he believes to be paradoxical, *i.e.*, irreconcilable. To be in the process of being saved one must both use reason *and* receive revelation and accept the consequent logical contradiction in faith.

Paul Tillich (1886-1965), depending much more on philosophy than Barth, has argued strenuously against the Kierkegaardian, neo-orthdox use of the idea of dialectic and in favor of the traditional view in which dialectic leads to clarity, not the confusion he sees in Barth's use.

Finally, dialectic, when taken traditionally relates directly to the issue of epistemology. In its connection with logic, dialectical forms of discourse may be said to be discursive, *i.e.*, they attempt to communicate knowledge by carefully moving deductively from step to step. Discursive language should be contrasted with other forms of language, such as description, which does not depend upon man's ability to reason logically so much as upon man's ability to perceive. The debate is whether theology is descriptive of perceptions of experience, or discursively rationalistic. At various times it has been both. (*see Authority, Paradox, Reason, Revelation, Truth*) J.B.W.

Diaspora (digh-*as*-poh-rah) The word *Diaspora* applies to the Jews scattered abroad outside Palestine, the Dispersion. Paul, for example, was a Jew of the *Diaspora*. The *Diaspora* was considerable in number and extent. During the Old Testament period Jews were exiled to Babylonia in considerable numbers. Alexandria in Egypt had a large community of Jews with their own Temple. Jews were common in Rome and in Asia Minor in the New Testament period. To all of these the term *Diaspora* applies.

The *Diaspora* was historically of great significance, both for Judaism and Christianity. The Babylonian Jews produced their own Talmudic literature. In Alexandria the work of Jews living there resulted in the production of the Septuagint. The work of Philo constitutes an important element in the history of the Jewish people; and Philo was a *Diaspora* (Alexandrian) Jew.

Christianity probably spread much faster because of the *Diaspora*. Individual Christians, such as Paul and Apollos, were themselves Hellenistic Jews. The Book of Acts, at least, represents the synagogue, located in towns and cities of the *Diaspora*, as significant in the westward spread of the Christian movement. E.L.T.

DIATHEKE (*see Covenant*)

Didactic (digh-*dak*-tik) From the Greek word, *didaktikos*, meaning "to teach," it refers to systematic instruction. Catechism is a form of didactic. The teaching of the Apostles was collected in the *Didache*. Written about A.D. 150, the *Didache* is a manual of how church members should live and gives instruction regarding baptism, the Lord's Supper, and the disciplined Christian life. (*see Catechism,* Kerygma) G.E.S.

Diocese (*digh*-oh-sees) From the Greek word, *dioikesis*, it literally means the district or jurisdiction given to one in authority.

Traditionally, this is the territorial jurisdiction for the administrative and spiritual supervision of a bishop. (*see Bishop, Orders*) G.E.S.

Discipline In The United Methodist Church, the set of rules that serves as a standard for conduct and polity (organization) of the church, the church's book of government, is called the *Discipline*. It is also that training that helps mold the intellect and moral fiber by cultivating the mind and body.

The word "discipline" is derived from the Latin, *disciplina*, which means "learning" or "teaching," and from *discipulus*, which is derived from *discere*, "to learn." A disciple is a scholar, learner, or pupil, a follower of a teacher or teachers. While the word "disciple" appears frequently in the Bible (more than 250 times), the word "discipline" appears fewer than thirty times. The books of Proverbs and Hebrews contain the most frequent references. Proverbs uses it as the training of a child through the demand of obedience and punishment for disobedience. (See Proverbs 13:24; 22:15; and 23:13.)

Hebrews 12:5-11 is an appeal to discipline comparing the discipline of earthly parents to their children to the discipline God seeks of his children. It suggests, "For the moment all discipline seems painful rather than pleasant; later it yields the peaceful fruit of righteousness to those who have been trained by it." (Hebrews 12:11)

Voluntary poverty, celibacy (abstention from marriage and sexual relations), and fasting were among the practices considered marks of Christian discipline. *Asceticism* is one name given to these rigorous practices. The earlier ascetic organization within Judaism was the Essenes. Though not all Christians chose to be ascetics, there were many celibates who denied themselves all but necessities and exalted hard work. The early ascetics seem much like Essenes, but there is no proof of Essene influence upon the Christian faith. Asceticism provided the foundation for monasticism, which arose in the latter part of the third century and is traced through the Medieval monasteries. Famous among the monastics were Origen (*c.* 185-*c.* 254), Anthony (*c.* 251-*c.* 356), Simeon Stylites (?-459), Basil of Caesarea (*c.* 330-79), Gregory of Nazianzus (*c.* 329-*c.* 389), Martin of Tours (*c.* 316-*c.* 399), and Jerome (*c.* 340-420). The history of monasticism is a long and detailed movement the interested reader might explore in church history volumes such as *A History of Christianity*, by Kenneth Scott Latourette.

One test of discipleship is discipline. Obedience to the Christian faith includes the belief and practice of Jesus' teachings. Currently there is renewed interest in the discipline of fasting. Small-depth Bible study groups are experiencing spiritual growth through disciplined Bible reading and prayer. While the practice of these disciplines is increasing,

DISCURSIVE

churches that have historically required celibacy as a discipline for priests now find it difficult to maintain this tradition. (*see Ascetic*) G.E.S.

DISCURSIVE (*see Dialectic, Epistemology, Methodology*)

District Superintendent The administrative officer responsible to the bishop and the annual conference for the supervision of pastors and churches of a district within the conference is the district superintendent. Appointed by the bishop each year, he cannot serve more than six consecutive years on a district. He is responsible for traveling through the district to oversee the spiritual and temporal affairs of the church. He supervises the work of pastors, including counseling with pastors and their families. He presides over the charge conferences, promotes the interests of the churches within the bounds of his district, assists in the assignment of ministers to churches, and administers the work of the conference within his assigned district. These statements apply to The United Methodist Church. (*see Conference*) G.E.S.

DIVINE (*see Holy, Theism, Transcendent*)

Docetic (doh-*set*-ik) Derived from the Greek, *dokeo*, which means "to seem," docetism arose in the early third century as a belief that Christ did not really suffer but only seemed to. Docetics had much in common with gnostics. Their belief was in part based on the cry of Christ from the cross, " 'My God, my God, why hast thou forsaken me?' " The term is now more generally used for those who emphasize the divinity of Christ as over against his humanity. (*see Flesh, Gnostic*) G.E.S.

Doctrine Doctrine is a set of teachings accepted by a group of persons who are followers of a particular ideology or philosophy. Akin to doctrine is *dogma*, which also basically means "teaching," except that dogma carries with it the implication that what is set forth is beyond dispute. Doctrine is teaching about a certain religious truth that may be agreed on by scholars and church leaders, then taught to other Christians.

Christian doctrine has traditionally considered such concepts as: the Trinity (God, Christ, the Holy Spirit), creation, sin, the Kingdom of God, Scriptures, the church, grace, and the age to come (eschatology).

In the Great Commission (Matthew 28:19-20), Jesus commanded his followers to make disciples of others through teaching and baptism. The New Testament, especially the four Gospels, contains many references to teaching. Jesus is frequently called Rabbi; they were astonished at his teaching; he taught with authority; he taught daily in the Temple;

82

his teaching was "of God"; history has called him the "Great Teacher." In the Acts of the Apostles, teaching and fellowship are joined together; teaching and preaching are part of a single command to the disciples; teaching took place from house to house; Paul's visits among the churches are marked by "teaching the word of God." (Acts 18:11) Creeds were soon formulated to express the nature of Christ and the central beliefs of the church. The creed, or affirmation of faith, was used in the rite of baptism with the ritual stating that it is this faith into which the candidate seeks to be baptized. Schools were used to instruct candidates in the catechism prior to baptism and church membership.

As controversy over doctrines arose, councils were called to clarify particular beliefs. The councils themselves became authorities, in addition to Scripture and reason, for the truth of faith. Doubtless history's most outstanding revolt to the established doctrine of the church was the Protestant Reformation. In 1517 Martin Luther (1483-1546) nailed ninety-five theses to the church door at Wittenberg. This act triggered the rejection of established dogma. Luther argued that church councils had departed from the Bible in their interpretation of dogma. He based his understanding on the Bible alone. His initial disagreement followed his reading of Romans 5 and a newfound interpretation of justification by faith. Since that time, with the establishment of various churches without central authority, a myriad of doctrines has arisen.

No established dogma or doctrine is universally acceptable to all Christians. Theological students align themselves with particular theologians whose writings and teachings are most acceptable to them. Ministers ordained by particular denominations find their doctrinal position most closely akin to that church, but there are wide differences. The era of emphasis on systematic theology now seems to be giving way to revived interest in biblical theology. Though many theologians and practicing Christians agree on broad principles of theology, many differences on details continue. Among important theological issues upon which there is considerable discussion and little agreement are the sacraments; office and authority of the clergy; the being of God; the nature of the church; the place of the Bible; the relation of revelation, reason, and faith; the nature of Jesus; and the nature of man. Honest inquiry into those problems is a wholesome sign. (*see Catechism, Creed, Dogma*) G.E.S.

Dogmatics *Dogmatics is the organization of the dogmas of the Christian church. A dogma is a teaching of the church drawn up by church leaders. If a member of the church does not believe the dogma to be true, he can be cut off from the church. Some teachings, called "doctrines," are not considered so important. "Orthodox" means that one believes in the teachings and creeds of the churches. A "heretic" is one who does not accept these right beliefs. Early Christians believed* *that God's truth lay in Jesus Christ. In later years the bishops had authority to interpret that truth. Also, the writings of the apostles were authorities. When the bishops came together, their councils drew up and defended dogmas. For centuries Christians thought of truth as unchanging. Then Martin Luther argued that what was true depended on its acceptance in the heart of the believer. In the 1800's, thinkers known as "liberals" said truth was known in nature, as well as in Scripture and dogma. The Danish thinker Kierkegaard disagreed: only a "leap of faith" can save man, he said. Karl Barth (1886-   ) followed him in saying that God reveals his truth in preaching, the Bible, and in Jesus Christ. Dogmatics is a science, said Barth, but can still make errors.*

In the most general sense dogmatics may be defined as the organized presentation of the dogmas of the Christian church. Already, however, such a definition requires drawing careful distinctions between dogma in contrast with doctrine. A dogma is a doctrine that is formulated for the church by its duly accepted authorities and promulgated as normative church members. "Normative" means that if a member denies the dogma, he can be expelled from membership. There are fewer dogmas than doctrines, since not all doctrines are of dogmatic status. Only dogma is regarded as established by legitimate authority. Thus, Roman Catholicism accepts as dogma the pronouncements of the twenty ecumenical councils and the pronouncements of the pope on faith and morals. Eastern Orthodoxy and Anglicanism regard only the first seven ecumenical councils as authoritative. Protestantism, for the most part speaks little of dogma, preferring instead to regard their doctrinal statements as "confessions of faith," and regarding the decisions of only the first four ecumenical councils as having anything approaching dogmatic status.

The subject of dogmatics has been treated in theological studies during the past century by both Protestants and Catholics. During that period it has become increasingly clear that the particular idea of revelation one holds is inseparably related to one's attitude toward dogmatics. If one regards revelation as having been given by God to man in relatively fixed propositions the task of dogmatics is mainly to show that the church's dogmas are correct in relation to Scripture and to the statements of previous theologians. Critics of dogma (heretics) are then to be refuted on the same grounds.

If, however, one regards such a concept of revelation as inadequate, then the concept of dogmatics is greatly altered. Also, when the philosophical presuppositions upon which a dogmatics is built comes under criticism, then dogmatics must also be reconceived. Both the ideas of revelation and the philosophical supports for traditional dogmatics were challenged by the rise of science and the new philosophy in the seventeenth and eighteenth centuries. In such a situation dogmatics became a salvage operation. Some serious thinkers even denied any role for dogmatics. When a revision of both the concept of revelation and of dogmatics was begun with the work of F. D. Schleiermacher (1768-1834), the path of liberal theology was charted.

Orthodoxy: If used as a title, "orthodoxy" refers to the large bodies of Eastern Christians who have been faithful through the centuries to those dogmas proclaimed by the first seven ecumenical councils. Or the word may refer to the body of teachings or creeds claiming the loyalty of the vast majority of Christians, at least until fairly recent centuries. It is in this second sense that the concept is discussed here. As such, it will be clear that orthodoxy connotes "right belief" in contrast to error or heresy (heterodoxy). What are its sources and what is its view of dogmatics?

The New Testament is an obvious place to pursue the issue. The testimony of many of its books is that the earliest Christians had no orthodoxy as dogmatic formulations. Witness to a common faith, however, rested on the basic conviction that in the life, teachings, crucifixion, and resurrection of Christ, God had mightily revealed himself to man. Christians interpreted the meaning of God's act in Christ in several directions in later centuries. Without a formulated dogmatics, there was no means to refute interpretations of Christ offered by any and all. But first the seat of authority had to be established in the church. In the second century the office of bishop became more and more highly regarded. The doctrine of the apostolic succession of the bishops meant that bishops stood in a direct and unbroken chain of succession. Since Jesus had delegated authority to his apostles, the bishops, as apostolic successors, had received authority. (see Succession) The bishops then were authoritatively able to certify a creed, the Old Roman Symbol, as an authoritative formula of Christian experience. (see Creed) Further, writings that were thought to be written either by apostles or by their students were eventually accepted as part of the New Testament. (see Canon) Finally, beginning at the Council of Nicaea (A.D. 325) the bishops together made certain pronouncements that became dogmas. Later ecumenical councils also produced dogma. When the bishop of Rome eventually secured his position as primary bishop, his pronouncements *ex cathedra* (which see) on faith and morals came to have dogmatic status, as well.

The collection of these dogmas and their arrangement into orderly systems became the task of orthodox dogmatic theologians. The arrangement and defense of these dogmas against those who denied them was inevitably connected with particular views of reason, revelation, faith, truth, and authority. Scholasticism in the twelfth and thirteenth centuries may be taken as the high point of Roman Catholic orthodox dogmatics. Protestant orthodox theologians, particularly Lutheran and Reformed, in the seventeenth century demonstrate the same for Protestantism. Truth was thought to be absolute and static. God was regarded as the super-natural revealer. Generally it was argued that in the matter of reason and revelation there could be no final contradiction, since God was both the creator of reason and also the giver of revelation. Thomas Aquinas (*c.* 1225-74) held this view. Others, however, denied that reason was adequate to understand revelation, and gave priority to revelation as authoritatively preserved in the church's dogmas. William of Ockham (*c.* 1300-*c.* 1349) held this view. In either case revelation was embodied in dogma, and to be a Christian meant to assent to the dogmas of the church.

With Luther (1483-1546) the emphasis upon faith as the only means of receiving God's revelation threatened for a time the very notion of orthodoxy. Faith, awakened and sustained by the indwelling of the Holy Spirit, was located in the heart-conscience of man. It might or might not assent to propositional dogmas as traditionally formulated. In principle the only dogma Luther advocated was "justification by faith alone." Even Luther himself was not always consistent in this view. And by the seventeenth century, the Protestant theologians were as severely dogmatic as their Catholic counterparts. Thus Protestant orthodoxy coupled with Catholic orthodoxy. With the challenges of secularity, both were equally on the defensive. It was rigidly maintained by Catholicism, but liberalism superseded it in Protestantism in the nineteenth century. Not until the twentieth century was orthodox thought revived among protestants.

Neo-orthodoxy (*nee*-oh-or-thuh-*dak*-see) This name was coined by opponents of the movement and rejected by its advocates. "Neo" implies the new and different. "Orthodoxy" as just described implies the old and fixed. Even so, the name seems appropriate. Negatively, neo-orthodoxy has denied any value for Christianity of natural theology (which see).

Kierkegaard (1813-55), the Danish philosopher, is popularly regarded as the father of modern existentialism. It is not so well known that in his philosophical work he was fighting theological liberalism in his own time. In his view of Christianity, it was absolutely necessary to recognize that by himself man cannot be saved. God in his grace must awaken faith in man, who must "leap" into a trust in God's grace.

Kierkegaard went largely unheeded in his own time. But later he sparked the remarkable rediscovery of orthodoxy, most notably in the work of Karl Barth (1886-   ), the twentieth century's most renowned dogmatic theologian. Barth is not, however, since he is a highly intelligent and alert modern man, just a repeater of the old orthodoxy. The differences are, in fact, quite remarkable. His view of revelation is not that God issues fixed truths. Rather, revelation is dynamic. It occurs in relationship between God and a particular man in a particular time and place. It is an experience of God, not in natural expected ways, but rather in a transcendent way. Natural reason and natural theology, just because they are natural, can never reach God. Further, when God reveals himself it is not a total revelation, but rather is both a revealing and a hiddenness. Sin is what separates man from the "wholly other" God. Salvation is never a possession of revelation but rather is a continuing opening of man to hear God's ever new revelation. When a man is encountered by God's revealing Word, supremely in the proclamation of the Christ in the church, he is forced to decide on a course of action, to adopt a life style in the world of sinful men.

From the brief foregoing description it will be obvious that Barth is not just a sophisticated fundamentalist. But it will be equally clear that, by re-emphasizing such doctrines as original sin, God's gift of grace that saves, revelation, and the centrality and authority of Scripture, Barth has much in common with orthodoxy. As a careful student of the history of theology, Barth is seeking to proclaim the pure gospel without falling into what he believes to have been the pitfalls that ensnared previous dogmatists.

If it can be called a movement at all, neo-orthodoxy is surely different from the old orthodoxy in that the theologians whose names are sometimes associated with it disagree with each other. Emil Brunner (1889-1967), another Swiss, and Reinhold Niebuhr (1892-   ), the American theologian, have many points of connection with Barth, but also many differences from him and from each other.

Barth has written extensively on the subject of dogmatics. Beginning with the assertion, "Dogmatics is a science," Barth affirms that dogmatics is done for and by the Christian church—the place where the gospel is proclaimed. Thus, Barth is the champion of ecclesiastical dogmatics. Given his view of the humanness of the church, perhaps Barth's greatness is nowhere clearer than when he writes: " . . . Christian dogmatics will always be a thinking, an investigation and an exposition which are relative and liable to error." This is surely neo-dogmatics appropriate to neo-orthodoxy. (see *Authority, Faith, Fundamentalism, Natural theology, Revelation, Truth*) J.B.W.

DOING (see *Works*)

DONATISTS (see *Freedom*)

DOSSAL (see *Reredos*)

DOXOLOGY (see *Glory*)

Dualism This is a metaphysical theory that reality is composed of two independent and mutually exclusive substances. Some religions have drawn religious consequences from dualism. Christianity has been influenced by some such attempts at various times in its history. For example, in the second century A.D. Christian gnosticism flourished. According to some typical representatives of that position, God is supremely transcendent and good. The world is evil and all material reality, e.g., the human body, is evil. The Gnostics denied that God was the creator of the world. Rather, the powerful force of evil was the creator of it. In this view salvation meant freedom from the contamination of the world. God and the forces of evil battle for man's soul. These two forces that cannot be reconciled are the realities with which man must contend. Gnosticism was rejected by orthodox Christianity as heretical. Monotheism has been a consistent bulwark of defense for Christianity.

Dualism has another connotation in epistemology (which see). If one says there is an ontological (which see) independence between what is known (the object) and the knower (the subject), his view is dualist. The problem is clear in theology when man's knowledge of God is considered. For God to be God, it is generally argued that he must be beyond human thought. But, if he is entirely unknowable, what does revelation mean? Thus, there is actually a denial of the dualism that is formally suggested.

Except for this latter case, there is scarcely any dualism in the mainstream of Christian theology. (*see Cosmology, Flesh, Monism, Theodicy*) J.B.W.

Duty Duty refers to what a man is obligated to do. Some of these obligations are enforced by law and others are moral, but in both cases a man is called upon to follow a prescribed line of conduct. Duty calls man to act in a certain way. Frequently duty is considered a limit on man's desires in that man may want to do one thing while duty beckons him to do another. Duty in its most basic sense grows out of an attempt to be faithful to trust or confidence existing in human relationships. A man wants to be loyal to the one he loves. This loyalty shows itself in terms of devotion to duty. Socrates (*c.* 470-399 B.C.) taught that man is to discover and evaluate his duty by use of his reason. Man can know and follow the "ideal" course of action. For example, man ought never to disobey the state.

The Socratic approach to duty is too simple. Many times one's obligations to the state may be in direct contradiction to one's obligation to himself or his family. What is a man to do when he finds himself in the midst of conflicting duties? No set of rules is free from conflicts. It has been suggested that a set of "prima facie duties" can be drawn up that tell what man should do if no other moral considerations intervene. ("Prima facie" is pronounced *pry*-ma *fay*-she and means "on first appearance.") One "prima facie duty" is to keep promises, for to do so is something that man should always try to do. Man should break a promise willfully only if not to do so would mean the failure to carry out a more important obligation.

Man needs help in deciding what duties are the right ones to be followed in a given situation. Leo Tolstoi (1828-1910) suggests that man is to decide on his duties by "unenlightened unselfishness." Man goes into each new situation with a desire to help the other. The rights or needs of others that come to his attention are to be his concern. Man simply asks what he can do to help the other and then does it. Augustine of Hippo (354-430) goes a step beyond Tolstoi by recognizing the fact that man goes into each new situation with a permanent set of relationships. Therefore, a man may refuse to give money to a beggar in order to meet another obligation.

Josiah Royce (1855-1916) conceives of man's duty in terms of loyalty. Loyalty is the central value (or virtue) around which man is to organize his life. The problem is that loyalty to loyalty seems to be an empty idea. Loyalty to the wrong cause may be an evil thing. The crucial question for loyalty is, loyalty to what?

The concept of "obedience" is an attempt to answer the question: What is the Christian's duty? The law tells man to what he is to be loyal. It is man's duty always to do what the law demands of him. One problem with the idea of obedience to the law as man's duty is that it does not go far enough. This is an idealistic understanding of duty.

Emil Brunner's (1889-1967) concept of the "imperative" is an attempt to move beyond the idealistic understanding of duty. Man is a free agent who goes into each new situation with the responsibility of deciding what he is to do. Man's course of action has not been decided in advance for him. In life man is constantly under obligation to do the right thing. But what is the right thing for him to do is not always the same. Man is to respond anew to the demands of each new situation. (*see* Contextual, Deontological, Law) J.S.H.

DYNAMIS (*see* Power)

E SOURCE (*see* Name, Source criticism)

Easter Known early as the celebration of the Feast of the Resurrection, Easter is one of the oldest festivals of the Christian church. The date was not fixed until the Council of Nicaea (A.D. 325) when the first Sunday after the first full moon following the vernal equinox (first day of spring) was established. There is an attempt at the present time to establish a particular calendar day for Easter. (*see Lent, Resurrection*) G.E.S.

Eclectic (ehk-*lek*-tik)   The word is from Greek and literally suggests "pick out," "selecting," or "choosing." When applied to theology or philosophy, therefore, it refers to those thinkers who pick and choose what is thought to be the best from a broad range of ideas. The total systems or religions from which ideas or practices are selected may not be compatible at all, but parts of them may cohere in some pattern. Such an attitude is characteristic of the Bahai religion in modern times. Usually, the term eclectic is used as a label by critics. They protest on the grounds that such a procedure violates the integrity of the systems and religions from which the ideas and practices are taken. In practice, however, most philosophers and theologians are eclectic in their work. J.B.W.

Ecumenical (*ehk*-yew-*men*-eh-kuhl)   From the Greek word, *oikoumene*, which means "the things relating to the inhabited world," this word has become important in the last decade. Ancient church councils, called ecumenical councils, were brought together with representatives from the entire Roman Empire on the assumption that their decisions would be based on representation from the total church. Following the split between the eastern and western churches, non-Roman communions contend that there have been no ecumenical councils since the Second Council of Nicaea in 787. The Roman Catholics consider a council to be ecumenical if it has been called by the Pope, so they record twenty-one, including the Vatican II Council (October 11, 1962-December 8, 1965) called by Pope John XXIII. By definition, the word "ecumenical" means to represent the whole body of churches, to have world-wide influence, and to move toward Christian cooperation of Christian unity for the entire human creation.

What is assumed to be a modern movement can actually be traced to the early centuries of the church. Three World Conferences on Faith and Order (Lausanne, 1927; Edinburgh, 1937; Lund, 1952) and four assemblies of the World Council of Churches (Amsterdam, 1948; Evanston, 1954; New Delhi, 1961; Uppsala, 1968), along with various Conferences on Faith and Order, have moved toward this end. The most recent attempt to bring churches together is that of nine denominations (African Methodist Episcopal, African Methodist Episcopal Zion, Disciples of Christ, Christian Methodist Episcopal, United Methodist, Presbyterian U. S., Protestant Episcopal, United Church of Christ, and

United Presbyterian), to explore together the possibility of union. Known as the Consultation on Church Union (COCU), meetings have been held each spring since 1962. Believing that the Christian family should not be so fractured, COCU is studying the establishment of a united church, "truly catholic, truly evangelical, and truly reformed."

Ecumenics is a science of the world community of Christians. It occupies an important place in graduate schools and seminaries as a specialized study. Interest has steadily increased since the mid-thirties, but especially during the last decade. Among organizations, in addition to councils of churches, that have aided dialogue among Christians have been the YMCA and YWCA, the Religious Education Association, and the National Conference of Christians and Jews. The ecumenical movement has been referred to as a "laboratory" more than a "conference hall," since churches meet together to try to analyze their problems and needs and find help from one another. More recent emphasis has been placed on renewal than on organic unity. Thus a more accurate definition of the ecumenical movement today might be that it is a movement toward the renewal of the church and the manifestation of its unity.

Problems that face churches in the movement toward renewal and unity are: differences in structure, ministerial orders, sacraments, and problems created by maintaining traditions of particular denominations. Some noteworthy accomplishments have been in areas of social relations, missions, education, and curriculum development and research. (*see Church, Institutional church, Mission*) G.E.S.

EGO (*see Self*)

Eisegesis (igh-suh-*jee*-suhs) The interpretation of a text always runs the risk that the interpreter's personal views may be read into it. This practice of reading into the text meanings that are intrinsically foreign to it is sometimes called *eisegesis*. The word means literally "a leading in." Eisegesis is the counterpart to exegesis ("a leading out"), which is the proper method for the exposition of a text.

Involved in eisegesis is one of the fundamental problems of the historian, namely, the subjective-objective dilemma. To what extent is it possible for the interpreter of a document to lay hold upon the past, to understand the motivations and intentions of an ancient (or modern) writer? Reduction of eisegesis to a minimum can be achieved only by the mastery of relevant critical skills such as linguistic competence and competence in the various aspects of critical methodology. (*see Exegesis*) E.L.T.

EKKLESIA (*see Church*, KOINONIA)

91

EL SHADDAI (*see Name*)

ELDER (*see Orders*)

Elect As used in the Bible, the elect are those whom God chooses. Thus, we say God elected Israel to be his people, though the word "elect" is not used in the Old Testament. The elect in the New Testament are those destined for a place in the Kingdom. John Calvin, and those who followed his theology, preferred "the elect" as a name for Christians. Some Christians believe that God elects only certain persons to be chosen but others hold that God elects all, but some refuse his choice. (*see Predestination, Redemption*) G.E.S.

Elements In communion, the bread and the wine are called *elements*. Some use unleavened bread, some wafers, others break bread into small pieces, and still others use a full loaf of bread. Grape juice is used by some, and others prefer fermented wine, as the symbol of Christ's shed blood. (*see Communion, Sacraments*) G.E.S.

ELOHIM (*see Name, Source criticism*)

Emanation (em-uh-*nay*-shuhn) The opposite of creation, emanation holds that all things in existence have flowed or issued from the substance of absolute Reality or Being. Creation out of nothing does not take place; rather the finite is derived from the infinite. Gnosticism taught that Jesus Christ was such an emanation. Neoplatonism believed that the finite order was a series of emanations differing in greatness, and that soul was among the highest. (*see Gnostic*) G.E.S.

EMPIRICISM (*see Existential, Experience*)

'EMUNAH (*see Faith*)

End End may be used to refer to the conclusion of an act or person. "End" has been used by the Christian church in a much broader sense to include purpose or ultimate meaning. Thus, conversation about the end of a man's life includes an understanding of the purpose and value of his life. Eschatology (the study of last things) includes a consideration not only of the last thing that will happen to man but also the goal of life.

In the Exodus story God's final victories are understood to be closely related to history. God is presently working in history for the purpose of freeing Israel from slavery. God is using Israel for the accomplishment of His purpose in history. God is judge of history, and thus he both judges the acts of men and gives his merciful judgments in history. These judgments may be defeat or victory, depending on the acts of Israel, but they are God's judgments. In the Book of Daniel there is a movement in a different direction. God's victories are accomplished by God's independent activity, which goes beyond history.

Christians have offered many different interpretations concerning Jesus' teaching about "the end of man's life." The Roman Catholic Church traditionally has understood the end of man in relation to the destiny of man's soul. Man by nature was created for fellowship with God. This nature was determined by God. Man does not choose the end of his life. The "end" or "purpose" of man's life is given. If man is faithful to God his soul will go to be with God in heaven forever. If he has been unfaithful his soul either will go to an eternal hell (no hope left for the man), or purgatory (where he still has hope of gaining heaven). Protestants traditionally have talked of the end of man in much the same terms (with the exception of purgatory).

In the medieval church many talked of the end of man as being "the unhindered and immediate vision of God." This type of experience is the ultimate destiny of human life, and only a few ever accomplish it. Millennialism (or chiliasm) believed that only one thousand persons would accomplish the final end of life. Apocatastasis affirmed a belief in the final and complete salvation of all beings (universal redemption).

The Greek word *teleos* is usually translated by the English word "end." Rudolf Bultmann (1884-   ) views Jesus' message about the *teleos* of life as a proclamation of the nature of the reign of God. The Kingdom of God is at hand. Today is the day of decision. Jesus (his life and his message) comes anew each day calling man to respond in faithful obedience to the demand of God. When man responds in faithful obedience, the actual *teleos* or "end" of life is being served.

For Bultmann, the meaning of history lies always in the present moment and when man's eyes are opened to see the possibility for serving God here and now, he sees the purpose of his life. Man serves God when he responds to the present needs of his neighbor. In doing this he fulfills the meaning and purpose of his life. The "end" of man does not depend upon the continued existence of some part or all of man after death. The question of how long a man lives is a secondary question. The primary question for man is what he will do with this moment. The moment is to be used in free and open service to the neighbor.

The end of man's life is of considerable importance for the ethical life. Is man to use his life in an effort to gain some reward in the future? Or is man to give of himself fully in a simple concern to be faithful in the present moment? (*see* Eschatology, Existential, Teleology) J.S.H.

ENLIGHTENMENT (*see* Deism, Rationalism, Reason)

EPICLESIS (see Prayer)

Epicurean (*ep*-uh-kyu-*ree*-uhn) The Epicurean school of thought was founded by Epicurus (*c.* 342-270 B.C.) He taught that pleasure is the highest good. Pleasure of the mind is superior to bodily pleasure. Aesthetic values are important. The long range effect of one's actions is to be taken into account. Overeating or excessive drinking are viewed as causes of displeasure. Happiness is a kind of tranquility (peace), which is unshaken by danger, pain, or fear. This peace cannot be arrived at by "ignoble self-indulgence." Happiness is gained by using one's head (mind) and practicing self-control (not doing those things that cause more bad than good). This school of thought tries to deliver man from his fears, especially his fear of the "gods." (*see Appetite, Aesthetic, Happiness, Hedonism*) J.S.H.

Epiphany (ee-*pif*-uh-nee) From the Greek, *epiphaneia*, which means "manifestation" or "appearance," the Festival of Epiphany begins on January 6 and commemorates the appearance of God to men in the human form of his Son, Jesus Christ. The account of the visit of the Wise Men or Magi who followed the star seeking the promised Messiah has traditionally been associated with this day. It also marks the disclosure of Christ to the Gentile people. (*see Advent, Christmas, Incarnation, Theophany*) G.E.S.

Episcopal Derived from *episcopos*, it is the type of church administration that uses a bishop as its chief officer. Three primary types of church government are: episcopal, presbyterian, and congregational. In the episcopal form, ministers are consecrated or ordained bishops, who are given responsibility for the ordination of other ministers and the supervision of churches in an area or diocese. In the presbyterian form, though it is connectional, no power is placed in a chief administrator, but a unit of churches is administered by a presbytery official who is considered "one among equals." In congregational government, local autonomy is respected, and no authority is held by individuals or organizations beyond the local church. (*see Presbytery, Diocese*) G.E.S.

Epistemology (ee-*pis*-toh-*mahl*-oh-jee) *Epistemology means a study of knowledge. Is knowledge possible? How? Are there limits to knowledge? Does knowledge come through reason or the senses? These are the questions of epistemology. Christians are interested because the answers to the questions affect man's knowledge of God. One major problem is how faith is related to knowledge. Some thinkers say men can know some things about God by reason. Some say men can know of God only through his revelation—through the Bible, the* *teachings of the church, and religious experience. Today science says any statements about knowledge have to be tested by experiments. Christian thinkers reply that not all knowledge can be tested. Paul Tillich was a Christian who said questions were raised by reason and answered by faith.*

From the Greek words *episteme* (knowledge) and *logos* (discourse), epistemology literally means "discourse about knowledge." The more usual definition is "theory of knowledge." The subject itself is as old as Western philosophy. But the term "epistemology" as a name for a specific branch of philosophical investigation was first used in 1854 by J. F. Ferrier in his *Institute of Metaphysics*. The basic problem is: what does it really mean when someone says, "I know"? Since Plato (*c*. 427-347 b.c.) first distinguished between knowledge and belief or opinion, the issue has been joined. Is knowledge possible only on the basis of sense experience, only by a proper use of pure reason, or by some combination of these?

Usually philosophy's task was to provide men with knowledge of reality. In spite of a distinction between philosophy and the sciences drawn since the seventeenth century, it is only in the twentieth century that philosophy has largely conceded to the sciences the task of providing new knowledge. Even so, philosophers have insisted that theirs is still the task of proposing theories of knowledge to enable men to understand what they are claiming when they say they *know* anything. In the process logic has been clearly separated from epistemology. Logic is the science of the principles of valid reasoning. Epistemology is the inquiry into the problem of validity itself. Further, epistemology is both connected to and different from the science of psychology. Both study perception, memory, imagination, conception, and reasoning. Psychology is, however, interested in describing these processes, whereas epistemology examines the claims to knowledge resulting from them.

Because philosophy and theology have been closely related, the status of epistemology at any given time has directly influenced theology. Ever since theology first used Plato's epistemology the problems of "revealed," as compared with "natural," knowledge has been a vital concern.

Problems: In epistemology certain problems arise again and again. Before examining the relationship between theology and epistemology, a few illustrations will show what is at stake.

1. Is knowledge possible at all? To the unthoughtful mind it often seems self-evident that knowledge is possible. But when the skeptic points out that often different people perceive the same thing in different ways, what then? Or, what of the skeptics' observation that reason often leads to contradictions? Must one simply assume knowledge is possible without understanding? Or must one take an extreme skeptical view that no knowledge is possible at all? Alternatives have been offered by Rene

Descartes (1596-1650), John Locke (1632-1704), and Immanuel Kant (1724-1804).

2. Are there limits to knowledge? Admitting that the skeptics demonstrate that there are limits to the knowable, some philosophers insist that some knowledge is certain, and that beyond prescribed limits, knowledge is impossible.

Kant, for example, argues that only a person's perception, not the thing perceived, is knowable. Man knows, for example, that he perceives a tree to be brown and green. He can never know whether the tree in and of itself is brown and green.

3. Does knowledge come through the rational intellect or through man's senses? Divisions between modern philosophers have arisen over this question. Some, like Descartes, have relied primarily on reason as the source of knowledge. Others like Locke and David Hume (1711-76) have relied mainly on sense impressions. Kant and others have tried to assign a place to both reason and the senses.

Theological attitudes: Christian faith has a great stake in epistemology. The proclamation of the gospel and its intellectual defense in theology depend upon presupposing that knowledge is possible. Further, theology must suppose that even if there are limits of knowledge, God is either able to overcome those limits or to make himself known within such limits. For revelation must be in some sense or other known if it is to be meaningful to man. Is knowledge given in revelation received through the intellect or the senses? Theology has taken different courses. Some have accepted reason as the means for receiving revelation, but others have sought to relocate revelation in other faculties, such as the will or the imagination. In contrast with this procedure, however, there are some theologians who refuse to accept the notion that revelation produced knowledge at all. Rather, they argue that revelation awakens faith, and that faith is only a faint analogy to knowledge.

So long as men generally believed truth to be fixed and eternal, and knowledge of it to be certain, theologians assumed that revelation made plain that truth. If philosophy could show that through reason knowledge could also be certain, then the problem was the relationship between revelation and reason. Thomas Aquinas (*c.* 1225-74) made a distinction between natural and revealed theology. Natural theology is all that man can learn about such matters as God and immortality through the use of unaided reason. Revealed theology is the way God makes himself known directly. Because he presupposed the unity of truth, Aquinas concluded that the truths of reason could never contradict those of revelation. For Aquinas both were knowledge.

With the emergence of modern rationalism assertions about the truth of revelation were subjected to the same tests as those of natural revelation. Descartes insisted that unless an assertion satisfied the demands of reason, he would not accept its truth claims. With the rising tides of rationalism in the Enlightenment of the eighteenth century, many dogmatic theological claims were swept away because they seemed so unreasonable, *i.e.*, they did not satisfy the demands necessary to establish knowledge.

Today science claims to be the only legitimate means for establishing knowledge, so that theology has a great problem in the realm of epistemology. If the method of science dictates that knowledge must be verifiable in order to be knowledge at all, and if theological assertions cannot be verified, then is theology in any sense knowledge? (see Verification)

Paul Tillich (1886-1965) has tried to recover a view of truth as a unity. Then theology and philosophy can take part in dialogues; reason and revelation can be correlated. But Tillich's thought is meaningful only if his effort to recover the unity of truth is meaningful. Otherwise, it was inevitable that Friedrich Nietzsche (1844-1900) would say: "God is dead and we have killed him." If men limit the means by which they accept the assertions that make up knowledge, then God who can only be known through revelation can no longer be reached. (*see Metaphysics, Natural theology, Rationalism, Reason, Revelation*) J.B.W.

EQUIVOCAL (*see Analogy, Attributes*)

EROS (*see Love*)

Eschatology (es-kuh-*tah*-loh-jee) *Eschatology is the doctrine of the last things or of the end of the age. It was a view current in late Judaism and in early Christianity. A type of eschatology is found as early as the eighth century prophet Amos. He speaks of the Day of the Lord, which will be a day of judgment upon the nation. During the Exile new features, apocalyptic in character, enter in, so that by the time of the New Testament the eschatological and apocalyptic have assumed a common pattern of thought. Jesus and most of the New Testament writers, assume an early end of the age. This pattern is broken somewhat by the Fourth Gospel, which stresses a higher and a lower world. The Son of Man idea, with which Jesus is identified, appears commonly in the Gospels. The Son of Man is an eschatological figure who comes on the clouds to exercise judgment. A distinction should be made between eschatology and apocalyptic; the latter, in contrast with eschatology, has a complete time-table of events. This is one of its notable traits. Eschatology is important for a biblical concept of time, for ethics, and for a view of salvation. In current theological thought it remains as a most important concept, though often reinterpreted in terms of modern views of history and of man.*

The term "eschatology" is derived from the Greek *eschatos*, meaning "last." Eschatology is, therefore, the doctrine of the last things. In connection with biblical thought it refers to the end of the present evil age. Both Jews and early Christians viewed time in linear fashion. Both looked forward to a consummation of history. Therefore, eschatological (es-*kat*-oh-*lah*-jeh-kul) elements are to be found in the religion and literature of both groups.

An early form of eschatology is expressed in the Book of Amos in the eighth century B.C. In that book Amos rebukes the people who desire the coming of the Day of the Lord (Yahweh). Since they are God's chosen people, they expect the day to come when God will intervene in history and defeat Israel's enemies. Amos' rebuke to these people consisted of an entirely different concept of the Day of the Lord: it would be a day of darkness and not of light (Amos 5:18-20). This emphasis on judgment as a dominant feature of the end times was to have a profound effect on later Jewish and Christian eschatology. This Day of Yahweh eschatology is found in Isaiah also. There sin is seen as pride and arrogance on the part of man, against which God will send Assyria to be the agent of his judgment (Isaiah 2:12, 10:5 ff.).

With the Exile (586 B.C.), eschatology took on new elements. This was largely due to the experience of oppression in the Exile itself. There was both a looking back and a looking forward. The ideal Davidic kingdom of the past became the hope for the future. So side by side with eschatological expectations we find the hope of a messianic Ruler of the house of David (*e.g.*, Isaiah 9:2 ff.; 11:1 ff.). Amos' Day of the Lord, with its note of judgment on Israel, while not entirely forgotten, becomes a time of divine vengeance on the nation's enemies. The day of crisis is foreshadowed by various signs, such as the swarm of locusts in the Book of Joel (1:4-6). With the Exile, too, there came into the literature of Israel the whole apocalyptic strain of thought. Ezekiel, sometimes called the Father of Apocalyptic, illustrates the bizarre character of the movement. It has been pointed out that apocalyptic exists where the end of history is envisaged (eschatology), and where it is anticipated that there will be a transformation of the world into another. The myth of the end in Ezekiel 38–39 corresponds to the myth of the beginning in Genesis 1. The marriage of eschatology and apocalyptic is further illustrated in the Book of Daniel, a work belonging to the second century B.C., after the desecration of the temple by Antiochus Epiphanes.

In late Judaism, as part of the apocalyptic development, there appears the concept of the Son of man. The title in this connection does not refer to a human being but rather to an exalted Being. The Son of man appears in Daniel 7:13 ff., and in the Similitudes of Enoch. He appears very frequently in the Gospels, and in the Christian mind of the period is identified with Jesus. It would seem that in late Judaism two hopes ran parallel: the first affirmed the coming of the Messiah and the inauguration of the Davidic kingdom; the second looked for the Son of man, a supernatural agent, to come on the clouds of heaven and to inaugurate the new age. This two-age view of history is what we find in the New Testament period, except perhaps in the Gospel of John, where it has been largely replaced by a special view of two orders of reality, the world above and the world below. The old idea of judgment is still associated with the Last Day, when the Son of man appears. But the New Testament eschatology displays a more personal and individualistic interest than was true of the earlier period. Repentance is called for in the light of the imminent coming of the new age, but it is a call to personal, not only group or national, repentance.

It seems likely, on the basis of an analysis of Gospel tradition, that Jesus used the term Son of man in an eschatological manner. It is not likely, on the same basis, that Jesus used the term of himself, but rather of the exalted Son of man who would soon come in judgment and to establish God's Kingdom. According to the earliest Gospel, Mark, Jesus' central message was a call to repentance in view of the imminent coming of the Kingdom of God: "Now after John was arrested, Jesus came into Galilee, preaching the gospel of God, and saying, 'The time is fulfilled, and the Kingdom of God is at hand; repent, and believe in the gospel.' " (Mark 1:14-15) It would seem that the coming of the Kingdom of God assumed the work of the supernatural Son of man as the inaugurator of that Kingdom on God's behalf.

While it is highly probable that Jesus did not identify himself as the eschatological Son of man, it is clear that the early church soon made the identification. The earliest strata of Synoptic tradition indicates this. The Synoptic tradition regarding the Son of man may be classified under three headings: (a) sayings regarding the exalted Son of man; (b) sayings concerning the suffering Son of man; (c) sayings about the earthly ministry of the Son of man. It is likely that the sayings in (a) are the most primitive. In these sayings, Jesus is looked upon by the church as at the right hand of God, but soon to come on the clouds in judgment. The suffering passages seem to reflect the idea of the suffering servant and are applied to the suffering of Jesus. Group (a) bears directly on the eschatological hopes of the early Christians. The concept of the two ages is taken over from Judaism and the function of the eschatological judge is given to Jesus. Salvation, in its fullest sense, is related to this final Day, *i.e.*, it is deliverance from this present evil age and entrance into the new age in which God is in complete control.

It has been observed above that the Day of the Lord eschatology came under the influence of apocalyptic at the time of the Exile. But a real distinction may be made between eschatology and apocalyptic. In the teachings of Jesus, for example, there is the full acceptance of an imminent eschatology, but his teachings (those considered genuine) are free of the usual characteristics of apocalyptic. The apocalyptist normally resorts to elaborate and often bizarre imagery, and, most important, possesses a rather complete time-table of events that are to take place. It is quite possible for one to possess an eschatology without the elaborate imagery and the precise schedule of events. Mark 13:32, for instance, represents Jesus as saying: " 'But of that day or that hour no one knows, not even the angels in heaven, nor the Son, but only the Father.' " Here, eschatology is accepted, but the time-table of apocalypse is rejected. It is well, therefore, to make a clear distinction between eschatology and apocalyptic.

The ancient biblical eschatology has raised the whole question of its relevance to modern times. From one point of view, it may seen as an outworn theory of history. Jesus and the early Christians, as men of their times, accepted the current view. One could say knowledge of Jewish eschatology is important only as it provides the frame of reference for an understanding of the biblical situation. But this response almost certainly represents an oversimplification of the eschatological point of view. If we have a proper understanding of the word "myth," we may say that Jewish eschatology was mythological. The Genesis myth looks to the past and speaks symbolically of unknown origins; the eschatological myth looks to the unknown future. Myth gathers up the experience of value and expresses it symbolically. Not that it is merely symbol, for it is undoubtedly the case that early Christian eschatology looked for the transformation of this world. But behind the hope for world transformation—behind the mythological expression—was the conviction, based on experience, that God will act to transform the things that are into the Kingdom of his will. Other theories of history are equally mythological, whether they are the Greek cyclical view or modern ideas of change and development.

It is undoubtedly true that the early church thought of itself as the eschatological fellowship, a community of God's people and the fulfillment of God's purposes. In this regard, the church was not an accidental or isolated group in history, but rather the fulfillment of the covenant relationship instituted by God himself. From one point of view, the eschatological event in Christ might be considered the end of history, for history in one sense of the word is ended. But from another point of view, Christ may be considered the center of history, for a new and better age is to be inaugurated. In any case, eschatology has to do with a concept of time: "But when the time had fully come, God sent forth his Son . . ." (Galatians 4:4).

The relation between eschatology and ethics, especially as it concerns the New Testament, has long been a subject of debate. It has been suggested, for example, that the ethical teachings of Jesus constitute an "interim ethic," *i.e.*, their high ethical demands are for the brief period before the end. This view has largely been abandoned. It is now seen that the final authority for the attitude and behavior that Jesus demands lies in his experience and conception of God. This being the case, the ethical element in the teachings of Jesus holds true whether or not an imminent eschatology dominates one's view of history. In the case of Paul the situation is somewhat different. While Paul, like Jesus, held to an eschatological position, he conceived of the ethical life as the result of being in Christ. In Galatians 5:22-23, for example, he provides a long list of Christian attributes, headed by love, which he describes as "fruit of the Spirit." This fruition in terms of love is quite in keeping with Paul's aversion to "works," but it provides a basis for the ethical life of Christians in the present life.

Paul, too, provides us with a good example of the relationship between eschatology and salvation. For him, salvation is primarily, if not exclusively, eschatological. Even the state of reconciliation (with God), which is the condition of the man who has been justified by faith, is not identical with salvation. The present experience of reconciliation is the ground of hope of the future eschatological salvation. This looking to the future is the general New Testament (and, in its own terms, Old Testament) view of salvation. The Gospel of John provides the great exception. In that Gospel, salvation is a present experience, made possible by a knowledge of God through Christ. Eternal life (John's expression for salvation) is an experience *now*: " 'And this is eternal life, that they know thee the only true God, and Jesus Christ whom thou hast sent.' " (John 17:3) While John has some remnants of a futuristic eschatology, his view of salvation is not determined by that fact. (*see Apocalypse, End, History, Judgment, Kingdom, Messiah,* Parousia, *Prophet, Salvation, Time*) E.L.T.

Essence Literally the word is from the Latin *essens*, a participle of the verb *esse*, which means "to be." Thus, in classical philosophy the essence of anything is what is necessary in order for anything to belong to its particular class. In thought about a particular dog, for example, one may think of the particular dog named Lassie. If the dog's color and other qualities were listed, they would describe the dog's *actuality*. If the description were of the dog's actions, it would be of its *existence*. But if the discussion were aimed at showing that Lassie fulfills the necessary qualifications to be called a dog, it would be a discussion of its *essence*. In general usage essence is synonymous with *substance*.

The concept of essence played an important role in classical philosophy and later in classical forms of Christian theology. Plato (*c.* 427-347 B.C.) and Aristotle (384-322 B.C.) believed it to be the aim of all thought to apprehend the eternal structures of reality, *i.e.*, to discern the essence of reality. In Plato's thought the essence of the whole of reality is grounded in the eternal mind (*nous*) of God. The essence of man in his view lies in his rational mind, with which he can discern the essence of reality by participating in the mind of God.

Christian theology based itself upon the same formal distinctions. This is shown in the way in which Augustine of Hippo (A.D. 354-430) explained the doctrine of creation. God, in whose mind is found the essence of reality, translated these essences into concrete existences. Thus, knowing what a mountain was in essence, God could create an existent mountain. But every particular mountain has its own characteristics, or accidents, which are peculiar to it and which mark it as unique. Between the essence of "mountainness" and the accidents of a particular mountain, obviously, there is a profound difference. The point is clear, however, that essentialist thought could be employed fruitfully by a Christian theologian.

In the Middle Ages the discussion of essence was altered somewhat. By then "substance" was often used instead of "essence." Then the distinction would be drawn between the substance of some material object and its accidents.

The theological use of essence is also intimately connected with the discussion of "being." The being of God and of man continue to be points of theological arguments, as are the "nature" of God and of man. Thus, a whole complex of crucial concepts turns around the idea of essence. Aside from Roman Catholic use, which has traditionally seen great theological significance in "essence," Paul Tillich (1886-1965) is one Protestant theologian who gives considerable attention to the idea of God as "being itself." (see Idealism, Nominalism, Ontology, Realism, Substance, Transubstantiation) J.B.W.

Eternal This is an adjective derived from the word "eternity," whose meaning may be traced from portions of the Old Testament. The Hebrew word 'olam originally meant a period of time, in which one boundary—beginning or end—was not fixed. It would change in duration depending upon the object described. For example, the length of a man's life can simply mean "lifelong." Though the birth date of a man is known, the time of his death is not known; it is unfixed until it occurs. Eternal in this context refers to a quantity. But when one reads of the "everlasting hills" in Psalms, it is clear that a quality is meant. This is undeniably the case when one reads ". . . from everlasting to everlasting thou art God." (Psalm 90:2c) The contrast between hills and God explodes the time limits of God. This latter sense asserts profoundly the meaning of God's eternity. "Everlasting" is a common translation of 'olam for this meaning. The interaction between the eternal God, who is timeless, and the events of history, which are timebound, was the basis for Israel's faith in the "mighty acts of God." In the New

Testament Greek word *aion* (aeon) the Hebrew connotation is apparently what was meant. Thus, the Old Testament witnesses to acts of God that are fulfilled by His supreme act in Jesus Christ.

In Greek philosophy the word "aeon" meant ages. Characteristically two aeons were described as eternal: (1) the infinite extent of time before the present (the past) and (2) the infinite extent of time after the present (the future). In this sense, eternity means the indefinite extension of time, whereas the Hebrew concept of eternity meant timelessness. These are radically contrasting notions.

As Christianity emerged in the Roman empire it was heir to both the Hebrew and the Greek concepts of eternity. Almost all Christian thinkers spoke of the eternal God. Eternity was held to be God's unique mode of existence. But was this to be understood in its Greek or its Hebrew connotations?

Augustine, bishop of Hippo (354-430), was the most thorough investigator of this issue. He accepted the view that fundamental to the Christian faith is the belief in God as creator. He argued from that position that God is the creator of all that is, including time. Time is the agent of change, and all created things experience change. God, however, embraces as perfect knowledge what men experience as past, present, and future; for God does not change, and he is not surprised by events. One of the implications of this view, from which Augustine did not shrink, was a theory of predeterminism. It is no accident that those later theologians who accepted Augustine's view gave great weight to theological predestination.

Critics of Augustine's position have abounded. They have taken two different thrusts. First, there is the profound difficulty, inherent in the biblical view as well, of how the eternal God can involve himself in temporal affairs, or even why he should, since he already knows of them ahead of time. Second, if God unchangeably foreknows all that is and will be, how can the idea of human freedom have any meaning at all?

The attitude taken by theologians to the issue of the meaning of eternal is a good index to the state of theology in any given period of history. Karl Barth (1886-   ) and Paul Tillich (1886-1965) are among those modern theologians who have given considerable attention to this matter in quite creative ways. (*see History, Infinite, Omniscient*) J.B.W.

Ethics   *Ethics is that branch of philosophy dealing with the science of human conduct. Teleological ethics tries to give a definition of good or value. Deontological ethics is the science of moral obligation and thus tries to give a definition of right and wrong. Comparative ethics is an attempt to understand and relate the ethics of different societies. Ancient Greek philosophy was a basic attempt to understand human behavior. In the Old and New Testaments ethics is rooted in and grows* *out of religious faith. Moral theology has played a predominant role in Roman Catholic thought. Idealistic ethical thought is personalistic; it appeals to individual men one at a time calling them to pattern their lives after the "ideal man." Social ethics is more concerned with the structures of society. Present day ethical thought debates the role and relationship of rules and individual decision.*

Ethics includes an investigation of both the right and the good. It tries to understand what actions are right and what actions are wrong. The right is man's duty. The right is discovered by pursuing the question: What is in accordance with truth, or what is the correct thing to be done? Virtue and justice are important concepts used in defining the right. Ethics seeks to define the good, investigating the intrinsic qualities in different acts. The good is what has excellent qualities. The good is beneficial and useful. The good is what brings fullness of life.

All forms of ethics lead to an examination of underlying principles. Christian ethics is built on theological presuppositions and of necessity includes a consideration of the "will of God." Ethics is sometimes divided into "social" and "individual" ethics. "Social ethics" is concerned to understand and evaluate social relationships. "Individual ethics" is concerned with what a man ought to do, and how what he does can help him to be truly a man.

Old Testament ethics is based on tradition, the needs of the society, and the religious experiences of Jewish leaders (see Deuteronomy). What their ancestors had done and said before them became directives for the human conduct of the day. The particular needs of the day also helped to modify the Israelite understanding of what was right. People in slavery in Egypt needed at least a slightly different set of rules from a people wandering in the wilderness. The individual experiences of the leaders of Israel helped to shape the Israelites' understanding of ethics. The books of Job and Ecclesiastes reflect experiences of leaders *calling* into question what the Israelites had been teaching.

Greek philosophy reflects a rational understanding of ethics. For Socrates (c. 470-399 B.C.) virtue is knowledge. A man should rationally examine and analyze his situation. He is to decide what is the most reasonable thing to do in a situation. Then man is simply to do what he has decided is the reasonable thing. Plato (c. 427-347 B.C.) develops this understanding of ethics and spells out what would be involved in a happy (or good) life. A happy life is based on justice, temperance, and a genuine knowledge of the good. For Aristotle (384-322 B.C.), reason is the guide to a happy life. It shows man the right course to follow. Man's mistake is to be an extremist. A coward is one who is excessively afraid. A fool is one who does not show the proper regard for danger and lives recklessly. Courage is "the golden mean" between these two extremes. A courageous man is cautious or careful, but he is not afraid to act. Man's life is damaged when his emotions overrule his reason and cause him to lose control of himself. The good man is one who leads a well-balanced life.

The Old and New Testaments emphasize the fact that ethics is grounded in religion (Matthew 22:37-40; John 13:34). A man's actions are the outgrowth of faith. What a Christian should do is made clear in the gospel (the Christian understanding of life). Moral demands are conclusions drawn from or implicit in God's grace. The ethics of Jesus may be set in context by Mark 1:15: " 'The time is fulfilled, and the kingdom of God is at hand; repent, and believe in the gospel.' " Man is to have fulness of life by accepting God's love. If he accepts this love he will respond to it by doing the will of God. How does man discover what is the will of God? The early church gave a threefold answer to that question. The Christian's understanding of the will of God is closely connected to the life and teachings of Jesus. In Jesus, God is showing man what is required of him. The laws that God gave to Israel help to make clear what is expected of the Christian. The living Lord (Holy Spirit) will encounter man in each new situation. Thus, the Christian needs to keep his eyes open and pay close attention to the needs of men. God is showing the Christian what is expected of him in the needs of the neighbor. If a man is hungry, then this is a message from God calling the Christian to do something about it.

Roman Catholic ethics, which is sometimes called moral theology, is developed on the basis of the naturalistic thinking of Thomas Aquinas (A.D. c. 1225-74). In human nature man finds the basis of the good. Originally man could, by developing his natural abilities, achieve the good, but man's sin has so affected his life that it is no longer possible for him to do the good. Man needs "supernatural" help. Ecclesiastical moral theology describes the "supernatural" help available to man only through the church. Through the sacraments and deeds of penance man can become good.

Martin Luther (1483-1546) reacted strongly against this system of ethics. He challenged it at two main points. Roman Catholic ethics fails to take seriously (1) the corrupt nature of all men (even the church is sinful), and (2) it does not place complete trust in God's grace for salvation. It still assumes man can become good by doing certain deeds rather than by risking oneself in a relationship.

Idealistic ethics has a strong individualistic emphasis. It begins with an idea of what it means to be a person. Then it calls man to give of himself to this ideal. The individual, as he patterns after the ideal, realizes fullness of life and helps others to do the same. The naturalist sees the good life as being achieved by the development of man's natural abilities and the satisfying of man's natural desires. The good life is

105

free from anything resembling evil by doing and being "what comes naturally."

The Social Gospel began as a formal movement in the nineteenth century. This movement tries to judge all of the relationships of society by principles found in the Christian faith. Society is to be reshaped according to the will of God, and when this job is completed the Kingdom of God will have come on earth. War and all the other enemies of God can be eliminated from history if man will but work at the task. The two world wars in the twentieth century have raised one big question of the Social Gospel: Is it not naive to assume that man can develop a perfect society on earth?

Contemporary Christian ethics is trying to evaluate the role of rules and theories about the good in Christian ethics. Contextual ethics rejects the idea that man is to have and follow a set of rules regardless of the circumstances. It also rejects the idea that man does not need any rules. Man needs moral teachings, but these must be evaluated and followed or not followed in the light of each new set of circumstances. This is an attempt to get a "love centered" or "person centered" ethic as opposed to a "law centered" ethic. Thinkers who defend the use of principles insist that only law can lead to justice, that contextualists use principles whether they admit so or not, and that love can work through principles to restrain evil and accomplish good. (*see Contextual, Deontological, Law, Morality*) J.S.H.

ETHNOLOGY (*see Archaeology*)

Etiology (*ee*-tee-*ahl*-oh-jee) The term "etiology" is derived from the Greek word *aitia*, meaning "cause" or "reason." "Etiology," therefore, in the study of tradition, applies to those elements that attempt to account for existing practices and institutions. So we may speak of an etiological myth or story.

Etiological elements occur in both the Old and New Testaments. Sometimes the material deals with the origin of sacred places (Genesis 28:10-12), or of circumcision (Genesis 17; Exodus 4:24 *ff.*; Joshua 5:2 *ff.*). Sometimes the origin of certain facts and events is explained: why the snake goes upon its belly (Genesis 3:14-15); why women suffer in child-bearing (3:16); why men have to toil (3:17). From one point of view the creation story is etiological in character, since it explains the origin of creation in God. So far as the New Testament is concerned, some scholars have found etiological meaning in the Passion story, since it sets forth the death of Jesus in such a manner as to show that it was the expression of God's will and that Christians should respond accordingly. E.L.T.

EUCHARIST (*see Communion*)

Evangelism   Evangelism is derived from the Greek, *euangelion*, which means "gospel," "good news," or "good tidings." Evangelism is the proclamation or telling of the message of good tidings of the gospel.

Related to the word evangelism is *kerygma* (keh-*rig*-mah, keh-*rewg*-muh), a noun derived from the Greek verb meaning "to proclaim." The message proclaimed was that the promised Messiah had come and that in the life, death, and especially the resurrection of Christ, the age of fulfillment had arrived. Rudolph Bultmann (1884-   ) raised the question of whether one can actually say that Jesus preached the *kerygma*, since he did not preach about his own death and resurrection. Existential theologians indicate that *kerygma* is the call to the new life rather than an agreement to a set of facts.

Evangelism has been variously defined. George Sweazy defined it as all the ways Christians reach outside the church to bring persons to faith in Christ and to membership in the church. Toyohiko Kagawa (1888-1960) said, "Evangelism means the conversion of people from worldliness to Christlike Godliness." Archbishop William Temple (1881-1944) described it as, "The winning of men to acknowledge Christ as their Savior and King so that they may give themselves to His service in the fellowship of His church." Such definitions specify one of the duties of the church to be reaching outside of itself to bring people to faith in Christ and membership in the church.

Many people think of evangelism as the use of high-pressure tactics to get people to join the church. Albert Outler (1908-   ) deplores these "Madison Avenue" methods. He also criticizes what he calls "non-interventive evangelism," the view that the church simply preaches and teaches the gospel, and lets persons respond as they will. Evangelism is more than simply hearing the Word and then saying that one will be a Christian. True faith involves actions, as well as words. The church must help Christians grow in thinking and acting, as well as enlisting them in the faith, according to Outler. (*see Atonement, Conversion,* KERYGMA, *Redemption, Repentance*) G.E.S.

EVIL (*see Theodicy*)

Ex Cathedra   A Latin term which literally means "from the chair," it refers to statements made by the Pope from the chair in St. Peter's Cathedral in Rome. Declarations made by the Pontiff with regard to doctrine are infallible (without error) when he speaks *ex cathedra*. Only decrees of doctrine, not *all* statements of the Pope, are regarded as infallible. The Vatican Council ruling is: "When in the

107

discharge of his office as pastor and teacher of all Christians, by virtue of his Supreme apostolic authority, he defines a doctrine regarding faith or morals, to be held by the universal church," such teaching is infallible. G.E.S.

Ex opere operato (eks *ah*-peh-ray ah-peh-*ray*-to) The phrase is Latin and refers to the Roman Catholic understanding of the process by which the sacraments confer grace to those who receive them. According to Catholic sacramental theology, a sacrament "works" when it is intended by the person (priest or bishop usually) administering the sacrament to do what the Church says the sacraments do—namely, to grant grace to the person who receives it. Such a view is aimed at under-scoring God's priority in sacramentalism. Sometimes when *ex opere operato* is overemphasized, it results in superstition rather than piety. (*see Sacrament*) J.B.W.

Exegesis (eks-eh-*jee*-sus) Exegesis is the critical ex-planation or interpretation of a text. Biblical exegesis has to do with the interpretation of a text of Scripture, either Old or New Testaments. In the accomplishment of his task, the *exegete* must use the appropriate methods of scientific investigation. He must know the document as a whole, the historical situation out of which it emerged, the language in which it was written. He must be relatively sure that the text before him is a good one, *i.e.*, that it has not been unduly changed in the course of its transmission through the centuries. The object of exegesis is (as the word suggests) to "lead out" of the text the meaning in-tended by its author. (*see Eisegesis, Hermeneutics*) E.L.T.

EXISTENCE (*see Existential, Ontology*)

Existential (egs-eh-*stehn*-chul) This is an adjective from "the philosophy of existence," or existentialism, the belief that the understanding most worth having is not objective knowledge or carefully worked out ideas but rather an understanding of one's self as existing. Scientists and many philosophers teach that truth is known by detached observation of external reality. Existentialists say that truth is only known by one's experience as a living, existing human. This knowledge is nowhere more forcefully apparent than in the issue of death. A medical scientist, for example, can view death from a detached point of view that allows him to divide his definition of death into neat parts. A person may be taught about death by such a scientific description. But, say the existentialists, a man only really knows death when he faces the reality that he, himself, as an existing human will die. Thus, it is sometimes said that existentialism means that nobody can die someone else's death for him.

It is clear that existentialism would end traditional philosophy, if it were universally accepted. It takes its modern origin from Soren Kierkegaard (1813-55), the Danish thinker. Because his writings were not translated into German until early in this century or into English until just before World War II, the impact of his work was received in the twentieth century. Among notable existentialists are the Germans Martin Heidegger (1889-   ) and Karl Jaspers (1883-   ) and the Frenchmen Jean Paul Sartre (1905-   ) and Albert Camus (1913-1960).

In insisting upon the concrete rather than the abstract, the existentialist will reject the question "What is man?" and ask the question instead, "Who am I?" That question, of course, can only be answered in concrete, living terms, not abstract concepts. Dramatic categories are appropriate means of expression for existentialists. The use of personal and dramatic language implies that man is radically limited by space and, more importantly, by time. Man has but a short time to discover and accept his salvation. Such urgency is in radical contrast with the traditional notion that God has eternally decreed a single means of salvation. In its most complete form, this latter view has been fully developed in those who have held to a predestinarian view of the man-God relationship.

The theological relevance of existential thought is obvious in this discussion of salvation. Some of the Christian theologians who have employed existentialist thought are the Russian Nicholas Berdyaev (1874-1948), Rudolf Bultmann (1884-   ) and Paul Tillich (1886-1965). One typical view of most existentialist theologians is their view of faith. The self is a unity of limitedness (finitude) and freedom. Faith is the acceptance of this paradoxical reality. Faith does not mean the acceptance of a creed or of a particular theological foundation. Rather, faith means the decision to be the person one is—free and finite—not in some once-and-for-all fashion, but in each new moment. This decision can only be made, they hold, because God gives the grace and unlimited acceptance to man to enable him to so decide.

According to such a view of faith by the grace of God, the Bible requires to be radically re-interpreted. Bultmann has led the way in what he calls "demythologizing" the Scriptures, by which he means, "existentially interpreting." For example, when the Bible talks about God's creative action (Genesis 1), the decision to be made is whether or not one acknowledges his creaturely dependence upon God.

Existence and decision within the limitations of existence are the basic concerns of existentialists, including theological existentialists. (see Dialectic, Empirical, Experience, Faith, Freedom, Myth, Salvation, Self) J.B.W.

EXORCISM (*see Name*)

EXOUSIA (*see Power*)

Experience Experience in its broadest sense refers to everything that happens to man. Every moment man is having experiences. Man evaluates the events of his life through one or more of the five senses (seeing, hearing, tasting, feeling, and smelling). The term "experience" is used sparingly in the Bible. The Greek word *pascho* is used in a few places to refer to everything that befalls a person. It came to be primarily associated with bad events or illness. It is used in the latter sense to refer to painful experiences such as suffering persecution (2 Corinthians 1:6).

In philosophy "experience" is most closely associated with "empiricism" (em-*peer*-eh-sism), that school of thought that leans heavily on sense data. Man learns by the direct use of his five senses. He develops his knowledge through observation, which he then in turn evaluates. The entire scientific method of experimentation, learning by trial and error, is closely related to this school of philosophy. Theories are accepted as true only after being tested through actual experience. Empiricism insists on a practical acquaintance with things. Abstract ideas are of questionable value and are regarded as likely to be false until proven by experience.

Theology uses experience differently from science. The theological use is based on the assumption that not everything that man experiences can be seen, heard, touched, tasted, or smelled. William James (1842-1910), whose view is sometimes labelled "pragmatism," describes man's experience of God in two ways. (1) Man is uneasy about himself. He has a sense of inadequacy and thus is looking for help. (2) Man finds the solution to his problem by discovering the proper relationship to higher powers, powers that transcend his own life. The empirical school of religious thought emphasizes man's practical everyday life. Man in his activities encounters certain basic realities. He experiences limits to his life. He experiences help from forces that transcend his life. Through such experience man gains his primary knowledge of God.

Friedrich Schleiermacher (1768-1834) taught that man can be immediately aware of what transcends "intellect and will," subject and object. When man becomes aware of this reality he experiences a "feeling of absolute dependence." Man experiences his own relationship to God and thus comes to know something of the nature of both God and man. Paul Tillich (1886-1965) points out that experiences are the means through which we learn of the sources of theology. Our experiences are not the sources of theology, so theology is never concerned with "experience" in and of itself. It is concerned with the reality lying in and

110

beyond the experience that gives meaning to it. This point is important in understanding Protestantism; for in Protestantism every form of experience is to be kept in its rightful place. God is primary. Man's experience of God is secondary. Man's experience of God is imperfect and at least partly in error. At the same time Tillich concludes that theology cannot be shown apart from experience. A person cannot be sure that his knowledge of God is correct apart from risking himself in service to God.

"Religious experience" has been used in the church in two very different ways. (1) The phrase "religious experience" is used in a restricted sense to refer to man's experiences in religious meetings. Here the term usually refers to a peculiar or unusual happenings ("ecstatic feelings") in the life of a man of faith. (2) The phrase "religious experience" is also used in a much broader sense. It is used to refer to the sense of a greater power, which all men experience. (*see Epistemology, Existential*) J.S.H.

EXPIATION (*see Atonement, Redemption, Sacrifice*)

Faith *Faith comes from the Latin word* fide, *which is a translation of the Greek word* pistis. *It can be used in two senses. In the first, faith is a quality or attitude that characterizes human existence. This may be meant in such a statement as, "He is a man of faith." In the second use, faith may mean the contents or set of beliefs a person holds. Such use is implied in saying, "He believes in the Christian faith." The first use is the most proper. In this case faith means confidence or trust in God rather than belief in certain doctrines. Faith is necessary for any particular beliefs. Faith always has its ground in some being or power, and in Christianity faith has its ground in God.*

Christian thinkers inherited two highly significant connotations of "faith" from the Jewish tradition. In the Old Testament and the Talmud, the Hebrew word 'Emunah (eh-moo-*nah*) refers to the quality of faithfulness. This is evident in Deuteronomy 32:4, where Yahweh is referred to as a "God of faithfulness," and Proverbs 20:6, where reference is made

111

to a "man of faithfulness." *'Emunah* also refers to confidence in or trust in Yahweh. The Jewish rabbis found great virtue in this latter sense of faith. The world's decline, argued the rabbis, is in large measure brought about by the disappearance of men of faith. Clearly, however, the concept of faith is not a central one in the Old Testament. Only under the pressure of continued interaction with Christians and Muslims did Jewish thinkers in the Middle Ages develop a notion of faith that linked it with "belief in" a set of propositions.

Jesus seems to have shared the view of the relative insignificance of the idea. He often proclaimed the faithfulness of God in good rabbinic fashion. The Apostle Paul, although an outstanding student of some rabbis of his time, launched the effective career of the word "faith" (Greek *pistis*) for Christian theology. Paul wrote about faith in many of his letters, but one of the most influential of his statements was: "For in it the righteousness of God is revealed through faith for faith; as it is written, 'He who through faith is righteous shall live.' " (Romans 1:17) Further, the faith to which Paul refers is symbolized by the confession "Jesus Christ is Lord and Savior." According to this view, faith in Jesus as Lord is more important for salvation than the works which one does. But there is a basic ambiguity here. Faith would appear to mean either "belief in" Jesus as Lord or "complete trust and confidence" in the power of God in Christ. The great debates in Christian history over this word have focused upon which of these alternatives is followed. In the Bible the tension between the meanings is clear when one reads John 8:43-47. The implication of faith is clearly "to believe in" the teaching of Jesus. Such a view makes faith mean "to give intellectual assent" to certain propositions. On the other hand, one reads in the Hebrews 11:1: "Now faith is the assurance of things hoped for, the conviction of things not seen." In this instance the view of faith as trust and confidence clearly is the emphasis, as the remainder of the chapter seeks to make clear.

The development of scholastic theology led to Thomas Aquinas' (*c.* 1225-74) view that faith meant both intellectual agreement (*assensus*) and trust and confidence (*fiducia*). But the weight of the argument goes to the assent view. Since the layman was often untrained in theology, the definition of faith as agreement meant in reality agreeing to accept the teachings of the church as authoritative. In this sense, a Christian is described as one who has faith in the church as the authoritative teacher of God's truth.

When Martin Luther (1483-1546) began to reflect upon the meaning of faith, he was convinced that the church had too severely restricted its understanding of faith. Luther wished to recover the notion of faith as trust or confidence in God's saving gift of Christ. Confidence was ranged against agreement in the contest between the views. From the

Catholic perspective it was Luther who was restricting his notion of faith. For he was proposing that God himself, not the church, was to be trusted. And this seemed, in principle, to devalue the dogmas and doctrines of the Roman Catholic Church. As Luther liked to put the matter, there is a profound difference between agreeing to some particular formation of the doctrine of the Incarnation and in trusting one's eternal well-being to God's activity in Christ.

The creeds of the church become a pertinent case study within this context. When one joins a congregation in saying the Apostles' Creed, does that mean that one is giving intellectual assent to the articles of the creed? The answer is "yes" if one takes faith to mean agreement with propositions. But if one takes faith to mean giving trust or confidence to God, then the creeds may be thought of as models or symbols that give *expression* to the more fundamental *experience* of faith. By such a view the expression of faith never is equal to the experience of faith. All theology is symbolic, according to such a view.

The view of faith that Luther defended did not remain typical for Protestantism. In the contest between Catholicism and Protestantism, the view of faith as agreement with propositions became most common. The emergence of rationalism and science also tempted religious thinkers to think that religion should be rational and believable in the same fashion as science. The eighteenth and nineteenth centuries, however, provided ample evidence that so long as religious faith is so regarded, it will be challenged and often defeated by science.

Some theologians of the nineteenth century, most notably Friedrich Schleiermacher (1768-1834), sought to reestablish the confidence-trust view of faith. And in the twentieth century, many Protestants and an increasing number of Catholic theologians have come to such a view. Not only the liberal and neo-liberal, but also the neo-orthodox, theologians, such as Karl Barth (1886-   ), have emphasized the encounter with God's grace as the focus of faith. There are, to be sure, still numerous evidences of the intellectualistic view. John Dillenberger (1918-   ) has written that faith is the dynamic center of a relation to God and man, but faith is anchored in the mercy of God, which only God can give and which always remains a mystery to man. Whether this is regarded as fully adequate may be debated, but that such a view is at least a vital aspect of faith would receive widespread agreement among theologians today. (*see Doctrine, Dogmatics*) J.B.W.

Fall From the story of Adam and Eve in Genesis 3, theologians have developed two crucial conceptions. The first is the passage from innocence into sin—"the fall" of Adam. The second is a term related to the passage itself—"original sin." Thus, there is a very intimate connection between the two conceptions. Although most discussions of these two doctrines refer to the story in Genesis the meaning to be attached to them varies greatly.

Regardless of how literally or mythologically the account in Genesis is read, the reasons for sin are finally a mystery. No satisfactory single explanation for the presence of the tempter in the garden can be offered. What is important for any theologian who takes the fall seriously is the reality and universality of sin. From this common denominator the differences in meaning become clearer.

In the New Testament the writings of Paul devote greatest attention to the fall. In 1 Corinthians 15:22 Paul wrote "As in Adam all die, so also in Christ shall all be made alive." There is no suggestion to indicate that Paul regarded the story in Genesis as non-historical. It is clear that Paul viewed Adam as the ancestor of the human race. The very name "Adam" means "the man." Thus, Adam is for Paul the "type" of the race. Adam's action in the story represents what the entire human race is, i.e., alienated from God. From Paul's perspective, every individual man "typifies" this calamity of Adam. The hope for man in this state of fallenness is Christ, in whom men can be reconciled with God by faith, just as with Adam they are alienated from God in sin.

Although other theologians after Paul gave attention to this doctrine, it was Augustine, bishop of Hippo (354-430), who treated the doctrine of the fall more thoroughly than anyone before or since. He reflected upon Adam as the father of the whole human race, who by his own original sin and fall had contaminated God's perfect creation. Later generations inherited this contamination. The effects of the fall are physical, mental, and spiritual degeneration. Further, Augustine emphasizes that the horror of the first sin also includes guilt. This is truly fallenness with a vengeance.

Theologians have traditionally employed the doctrine of the fall in their doctrines of man. For example, some theologians would say that man's will was corrupted by the fall, but that his reason is less contaminated. Others will take the view that reason is fallen, but that the will is relatively able to respond to God's saving revelations. However it may be used, the traditional view of Christian salvation requires that man be *in need of salvation*. To assert the universality of sin through the fall is one common way of making the salvation offered in Christ a universal possibility.

In modern theology the doctrine of the fall has been forced to new ways of expression. Under the impact of biological evolution and psychology, the doctrine of man has been reassessed. With such reassessments have gone readjustments of the view of salvation. Thus, the doctrine of the fall is a good illustration of how intricately interwoven is the whole system of doctrines in Christian theology. (*see Image of God, Methodology, Sin, Soteriology*) J.B.W.

FALLING FROM GRACE (*see Sanctification*)

FATALISM (*see Destiny*)

FATHER (*see Trinity*)

Fear of God   The English word "fear" usually carries the meaning of "apprehension." The biblical concept of fear, however, has a dual meaning. It may indeed mean "apprehension," but it often denotes a feeling of awe, wonder, and reverence in the presence of the majesty of God or of a manifestation of God. So Moses says, " 'And now, Israel, what does the LORD our God require of you, but to fear the LORD your God . . . ?' " (Deuteronomy 10:12) Proverbs 1:7 speaks of the "fear of the Lord" as "the beginning of knowledge" or wisdom.

The fear of the disciples at the Transfiguration (Matthew 17:6) and at the Resurrection (Mark 16:8) may be a sort of reverence. In both instances it results from a special manifestation of God or of his mighty acts. It is of interest that certain Jews, who, according to Acts, attached themselves to the Christian movement, were called "God-fearers." (Acts 10:2) (*see Anxiety, Holy, Religion*) E.L.T.

FEELING (*see Existential, Experience, Happiness*)

FEELING OF ABSOLUTE DEPENDENCE (*see Religion*)

FELLOWSHIP (*see Church, KOINONIA*)

FIDUCIA (*see Faith, Revelation*)

FINITE (*see Contingent, Infinite*)

Flesh   The term "flesh" (Hebrew *basar*; Greek *sarx*) expresses a variety of meanings in biblical literature. It may refer (a) to the material of the body, whether of animal or man (Isaiah 31:3: "The Egyptians are men, and not God;/and their horses are flesh, and not spirit."); (b) also to living things, including men (Genesis 6:13; 7:15-16; 1 Corinthians 15:39); (c) it may denote kinship (Genesis 37:27; 2 Samuel 19:12-13); (d) it may stand for human nature in its frailty and imperfection (Isaiah 40:6; 2 Corinthians 4:11); (e) it may convey the idea of earthly descent (Romans 9:8); (f) it often signifies the external part of life (1 Corinthians 1:26; 2 Corinthians 5:16; John 8:15); (g) in Paul's thought flesh is often thought of as the instrument of sin (Romans 7:25; Galatians 5:16). These are but some of the more common or important uses of the term.

The Pauline use of the term *sarx* is of particular importance. It is one aspect of his anthropology, or doctrine of man, and it has an important bearing on his whole doctrine of sin and salvation. In the Hellenistic period, in which Paul lived, there were groups who stressed the radical difference between flesh and spirit (dualism). A movement known as Gnosticism (from the Greek word *gnosis,* meaning "knowledge") held to this radical dualism that believed matter as such was evil and only spirit was good. Man, who originally was spirit, had become imprisoned in evil matter, so that the fleshly body was looked upon as "the tomb of the soul." Man could find salvation only as he gained knowledge of his true self as spirit, a knowledge which the Gnostics believed could come only by supernatural revelation, by a Redeemer, who would bring this enlightenment to men. In the New Testament period, then, there was current a view of the flesh that was one pole of this radical dualism.

Paul, it should be noted, does not go to this extreme; there is no evidence that he believed matter per se to be evil. On the other hand, "flesh" does denote for him man's lower nature, his tendency to sensuality and the like. It is for this reason that Paul could hardly have spoken of the resurrection of the flesh, for to him that would mean the continued struggle with sinful human nature. But he can and does speak of the resurrection of the body, although, significantly, it is body of spirit that is raised and not body of flesh (1 Corinthians 15:44). It is evident, too, that Paul's view of flesh as the instrument of sin has a direct bearing on his doctrine of salvation. While man is in the flesh, salvation in its most complete sense is impossible. The present condition of the believer is life in the Spirit or in Christ, a condition in which knowledge of God's love has been made known in Christ. But this knowledge or experience of the love of God is but the guarantee of that which is still in the future, namely, the inbreaking of the new age, when men will be set free from the limits of the present age (Romans 8:18-25).

This sharp contrast between being "in the flesh" and "in the Spirit" has a bearing on the ethical life of men. In Galatians 5:19-21 he gives a long list of what he calls the "works of the flesh." It is a dark list, evidently reflecting his observation of a level of life of the day. On the other hand, those who possess the Spirit give evidence of a quality of life that transcends the requirements of the law itself (5:22-23). Paul calls this kind of life the "fruit of the Spirit." It is notable that love stands at the head of the list.

The other New Testament area where the concept of flesh is prominent is the Gospel of John, as well as the related 1 John. The Gospel presents us with the most forthright statement on the Incarnation found in the New Testament: "And the Word became flesh and dwelt among us. . . ." (John 1:14) This the Gnostics could never say. John obviously does not have the view that matter as such is evil. Nevertheless, in John there is a contrast between flesh and spirit. And this comes out in its view of the new birth: " 'That which is born of the flesh is flesh, and that which is born of the Spirit is spirit.' " (3:6) Rebirth, which results from belief in Jesus as God's Son, elevates one above the level of flesh to the level of divine Spirit, from sin (unbelief) and death to eternal life.

In 1 John, which bears some relation to the Gospel, one of the dominant concerns is a heresy known as docetism. This was a view that held that matter is evil, and that consequently Jesus could not have come in the flesh. His body therefore was not a real body of flesh; it was an appearance, an apparition. The writer of the epistle, convinced of the reality of the Incarnation, refutes this position (1 John 4:2 ff.). (see *Body, Docetic, Dualism, Gnostic, Heart, Incarnation, Spirit*) E.L.T.

FOREKNOWLEDGE (see *Omniscience*)

Forgiveness Forgiveness is presented in the Bible as being God's way of removing the barriers that separate man from God, self, and others. According to the Old Testament God is a holy God who expects holiness of Israel (Leviticus 11:44-45). God loves Israel, and this love includes the expectation that Israel obey the law, thus keeping the covenant made with God (Deuteronomy 4:9-14). Israel does not uphold the covenant and by failing so to do erects barriers between herself and God. An unrighteous people are separated by their own unrighteousness from a righteous God (Hosea 5:4). The wrath of God is now to be poured out on Israel, since God is a just God (Amos 8). Yet, because of God's mercy, there is still hope for the barriers to be overcome and the right relationship between God and Israel to be restored (Amos 9:14-15). In the Old Testament Israel is never without this hope (Psalms 86:5). At the same time there is a significant interest in the Old Testament to preserve God's justice. God will by no means "clear the guilty" (Exodus 34:7). Forgiveness then is the removing of the barriers of sin and guilt while not violating God's righteousness; justice is to be maintained. Forgiveness gives to man an opportunity to turn from his wrong deeds and give himself obediently to the law. This opportunity may become a reality only if man repents of his evil deeds (Hosea 5:15).

In the New Testament the Greek words *aphiami* (translated "forgiveness") and *hilaskomai* (translated "to be merciful") describe the basis for God's relation to man. God through Christ (Mark 2:5-12) brings man into an at-oneness with himself (see Atonement). Paul views forgiveness as the means by which man is released from the power of sin (Romans 6:15-19). Man has been assuming the wrong relationship to God. In Christ man has been shown a new way of relating to God, self, and others (Romans 8:31-39). Forgiveness in the New Testament becomes a dynamic term opening up a new way of life (see Righteousness).

117

There is still a concern for justice in the New Testament. The absolute priority in the New Testament is on God's reconciling activity (Romans 5:1, 10). Man, having received forgiveness, forgives others (Matthew 6: 12, 14-15; 18:21-22; Luke 17:3; Mark 11:25).

Baptism is a rite of initiation into the Christian church. As a rite it assumes that man is to repent and be baptized for forgiveness of sins (Acts 22:16). Baptism is a purification from sin (1 Corinthians 6:11; 1 Peter 3:17–4:6). Man in baptism shares in the death of Christ, putting to death his old way of life. After baptism man is now to walk in a new way of life (Romans 6:1-4). (see Baptism)

After the first century, forgiveness comes more and more to be associated with the sacraments of the church. The sacrament of penance was substituted for the more dynamic concept of forgiveness as found in Paul. Sin comes more and more to be understood as violation of the law of the church. Sins were graded according to the degree of their severity. The bishop is able to forgive sins a man commits after being baptized. Deeds of penance can be required of the offender as a requirement for the bishop's forgiveness. This understanding of forgiveness was further constructed into the granting of indulgences, in which a man could secure forgiveness in advance from the church for evil deeds he planned to do. Augustine (354-430) understood forgiveness as God "sweeping away" man's sin. He was close to the idea that forgiveness is an external and magical act. Thomas Aquinas (c. 1225-74) understood forgiveness as being inserted into man (see Infused grace). Martin Luther (1483-1546) stressed more the certainty of God's forgiveness as that in which man trusts. Forgiveness is not a formal act of the church but rather a living experience.

Paul Ramsey (1913-   ) describes Christian forgiveness as a way of relating to people. The Christian is one whose willingness to forgive is not numbered (i.e., it is unlimited). It is unlimited because the Christian abandons all claim on the neighbor; he accepts the neighbor as who he is and is only concerned to help the neighbor. J.S.H.

Form criticism   This is a type of criticism first applied to the Old Testament and in that connection associated with the name of Hermann Gunkel (1862-1932). The application of the method to the New Testament was prepared by the work of Karl Ludwig Schmidt (1891-   ), who saw that the framework of the Gospel of Mark was the work of the author, but that the material of the Gospel apart from this could be analyzed into independent units of tradition. Building on the work of Schmidt, scholars such as Martin Dibelius (1883-1947), Rudolf Bultmann (1884-   ), Vincent Taylor (1887-   ), and F. C. Grant (1891-   ) have applied the method to the synoptic materials.

The method has further been applied to other New Testament writings and has resulted in the isolation of early traditional form.

Form criticism, as applied to the Gospels, is concerned with the tradition in its pre-literary form. Basically, two areas of concern are present: The "form" in which the tradition circulated before it became embedded in a Gospel, and the *Sitz im Leben* (zitz im *lay*-ben) or "setting in life" which it reflects. Dibelius, whose book, *From Tradition to Gospel*, is an English translation of a German pioneering work in this field, sets forth the theory that "the history of literature is the history of its various forms." This theory did not originate with him, but he used it with reference to the study of New Testament, or more strictly Gospel, literary forms. Dibelius felt that the theory has special significance when applied to materials where, as in the case of the Gospel tradition, no significance is attached to authorship. The handing down of the material is the work of many unknown persons, not of a single author. Usage and practical necessity dictate the form that the tradition assumes. Gospel writers are authors only in a minor way; they are principally collectors and editors, passing on tradition that they group and edit. This is true for Dibelius at least of the Synoptics; it is less true of the Fourth Gospel, where the author is more of a composer. "Forms" develop according to certain "laws," which apply to a certain "non-literary" level of tradition. The tradition lying behind the Gospels was not intended for publication; it is not only pre-literary (before the Gospels themselves) but also sub-literary, *i.e.*, belonging to circles "not touched by literature proper."

Perhaps the more important part of form criticism is its attention to the *Sitz im Leben* of the pre-Gospel tradition. "The ultimate origin of the Form is primitive Christian life itself," wrote Dibelius. Worship was one of the settings for the development of form, the missionary enterprise was another, preaching was another, and so forth. In other words, the various customs and concerns of the life of the church shaped, and in some instances originated, the traditions that we find in our Gospels. When the various units of tradition have been isolated from the present literary setting, these are classified under certain descriptive headings, such as tales, paradigms, legends, and exhortations. Various scholars offer somewhat different categories, although it must be said that there is a striking similarity in the various lists.

Form criticism has been applied not only to the Gospels but also to other parts of the New Testament. For instance certain elements in the letters of Paul are now seen to be pre-Pauline in origin. Primary examples of such passages are 1 Corinthians 15:3 *ff.*; Philippians 2:6-11; Romans 1:3-4. A good example from the non-Pauline Pastoral Epistles is 1 Timothy 3:16.

While form criticism is a valuable tool, certain limitations are inherent in the method. Since it involves a working back from the written to the oral period, it is open to the criticism of subjectivity. Moreover, attention to the parts of the Gospel tradition often tends to overlook the "wholistic" functions of the Gospels themselves.

Each Gospel presents us with a christology of its own. Granted that Mark, for example, is composed of what were independent units of tradition and that the author supplied the framework for his account, it still remains true that the finished product is so arranged that it presents a view of Jesus that is more than the sum total of its parts.

A fear has often been expressed that form criticism leads to the conclusion that nothing can be known of the historical Jesus. Bultmann's deemphasizing of the Jesus of history as unnecessary for faith may have contributed to this fear. It is true that great attention is paid to the life of the church in relation to the growth of tradition, but the problem of the historical Jesus does not grow from the method of investigation, form criticism or any other; it is inherent in the nature of the sources themselves. (see *Biblical criticism, Literary criticism, Oral tradition, Source criticism*) E.L.T.

FORTY (see *Number*)

Fraction Meaning "broken" or "to break off," fraction refers to the priestly act in the Mass or service of communion when the celebrant breaks the bread, signifying the broken body of Jesus Christ. (see *Communion*) G.E.S.

FREE WILL (see *Freedom*)

FREEDOM (of God) (see *Providence*)

Freedom (of man) *Freedom is release from outside control. It is the liberty to live one's own life. In the Old Testament freedom is understood specifically as freedom from slavery. In the New Testament freedom is the new relationship to God that Christ gives to man. In Christ man is set free from bondage to sin and death. In the teaching of the church man's freedom may be used to oppose God. The power of God has been understood as a limit to man's freedom. However, God's power is more properly understood as that which makes man truly free. Existentialism sees in freedom the key to human existence. Man is a creature of choice. Man is true to himself when he makes his own choices. Choice is the ability to shape the future by deciding between different possible alternatives. Martin Buber views freedom as essential to genuine human relationships. Reinhold Niebuhr interprets human freedom as being rooted in man's ability to transcend nature. Emil Brunner sees freedom as man's constant task of dealing with the demands God makes on his life.*

Freedom is sometimes used to mean that man can do anything he pleases. The New Testament concept of freedom refers to man's opportunity to live his life as it was created to be lived. The Christian understanding of freedom includes the fact that freedom and responsibility are always interrelated.

Freedom in early Greek thought was understood in terms of man's mastery of himself. No one, no thing, and no set of circumstances cause him to do what he does. He is master of his life in that he is deciding where he will go and what he will do.

Freedom in the Old Testament is understood as freedom from slavery. Israel was held as captive in Egypt. Freedom is deliverance from this captivity. The Exodus story is an excellent example of what it means to be set free. Freedom includes a reference to what God is doing in history; that is, working in history to set his people (Israel) free. When God's final victories are accomplished Israel will be completely free. No other nation will be able to make them a slave people.

In the New Testament freedom is used to describe the ultimate relationship between the Christian and Christ. Freedom (as opposed to slavery) is one possibility open to man. Paul interprets Christ's ministry as setting man free from sin, law, and death. These three forces prevent man from having a full life. Sin is man's failure to be obedient to God. Man places self, desire, nation, or religion at the center of his life. His life is controlled by these forces rather than by God. To be made a new creation is to be made free by surrender to the God who has made himself known in Jesus Christ. Man uses the law as a means of establishing his own life. He thinks that by following the law he will make of himself a righteous man. Christ sets man free from any attempt to prove his own righteousness. The fear of death has haunted man and paralyzed him. Christ sets man free from this fear.

Pelagianism (puh-*lay*-juh-nism) says that man always has had and still does have the ability to choose between good and evil. Man can will to do the good or he can will to do the evil. To be a man is to have this kind of freedom.

Augustine (354-430) feared that Pelagianism meant that man could make of himself a good man. He insisted that "indwelling grace" alone could make a good man. God makes possible all of man's accomplishments and apart from him man can accomplish nothing. Augustine reasoned that in the "fall" (which see) man lost the ability to choose the good. God in Christ sets man free. Semi-pelagianism takes a stand halfway between Augustine and Pelagianism. Man has the ability to turn toward God and accept God's grace. God's grace supports man in this new life. Actually this controversy is at least partly due to misunderstanding and confusion. God's grace and man's freedom need not be put in opposition to one another. Roman Catholicism has stressed the effectiveness of the sacraments, apart from man's use of his freedom, in shaping human life. Donatists insisted that the effectiveness of the sacraments was impaired when the priest administering the sacraments used his freedom irresponsibly.

Immanuel Kant (1724-1804) understood Christian freedom in terms of man's right of self-government. Man imposes laws on himself. He does not let anyone else impose a law or a rule or a principle on him. Man wills to accept an obligation as his own. He uses his rational ability to decide what he is obligated to do. He is willing to accept for all mankind what he accepts as right for himself.

Calvinism held a doctrine of predestination that God decided in advance what men are to be saved and what men are to be damned. Jacob Arminius (1560-1609) rejected this view, insisting that it made God responsible for sin. Arminius argued that man in his wrong use of his freedom is responsible for sin; it is possible for any man to be saved depending whether or not he in his freedom chooses to believe in Jesus Christ. It is wrong to understand John Calvin (1509-64) as using divine cause in a mechanical sense. Rather, his point was to acknowledge the fact that salvation is a mystery to man.

"Free will" was used often during the seventeenth and eighteenth century debates to emphasize man's ability to choose good or evil. However, Augustine's debates with the Pelagians were enough to show that free will is an unclear concept. One can use it to mean (a) only God is the source of the will's power, (b) God grants man his own control over will, or (c) within the limits of creation man can make free choices. Out of the Calvinist era, however, came the concept of "voluntarism," which was that men are free to make contracts with one another for their welfare. Thus, a "voluntary association" is an organization, unlike a state or a family, that man is free to join as he wishes.

Modern day conversations about Christian freedom have been deeply affected by the psychology of Sigmund Freud (1856-1939) and existential philosophy. Freudian psychology includes within it a kind of deterministic understanding of life. A man acts in a certain way because of a certain experience in his past. Man does not have control of himself. He does try to repress certain feelings and actions he has learned he should not express. But repression creates problems for man. Repressed feelings and drives cause internal turmoil and show up in some external behavior. Involved in this is the often-posed question: Is man what he is as a result of heredity or environment? The question assumes that man's life is determined by something outside of himself. A French existentialist, Jean Paul Sartre (1905-   ), views man as having autonomy, which rejects any and all external authority. He views the nature of human existence as decision. The most important single factor man knows about himself is his ability to make choices. Man not only has the ability but also the duty to choose whom he will be.

Martin Buber (1878-1965) in his book *I and Thou* develops the idea that freedom is a necessary element of genuine human relationships. Human beings are rightly related one to another only when both respect the other's freedom to choose. If one person tries to make choices for another he therewith prevents the possibility of a genuine human relationship occurring. Although this is true, there is reason to believe that man is afraid of freedom. Freedom brings with it ambiguity or confusion. It requires courage to be a free man, for there is more security in slavery than there is in freedom.

Reinhold Niebuhr (1892-   ) presents man's freedom as grounded in man's ability to surpass nature. Man is a part of nature just like every other animal. He has the same basic needs. But man is able to think about what he does and evaluate different possible courses of action. He makes judgments about what is right and what is wrong. Emil Brunner (1889-1967) sees freedom as man's constant task of dealing with the demands on his life. These "demands" are always present. There are certain things that need to be done, and man knows that he should do them.

Freedom is also used to refer to basic social and political rights of man. Man has certain basic rights. No one is to prevent him from exercising these rights. Freedom understood in this way is primarily a safeguard. A problem arises when one person's exercise of his right of freedom violates the rights of another. Out of this basic conflict civil laws are made to protect the rights of all involved.

The Christian church has often understood freedom to be closely connected to duty. A man is not free to do just anything he pleases; he loses his freedom if he uses it as license. Yet man is free to live a full life, and his freedom abounds as he does the will of God. (*see Existential, Predestination, Providence*) J.S.H.

Function   The "function" of a thing is the way it works or the way it is used. The idea of function comes from sociology, which tries to describe how a practice of a society or a community actually works to serve the people in it. For example, the ritual of worship sometimes functions to preserve memory, to give the community an image or idea of itself, or to provide security. Émile Durkheim (1858-1917) did not think it enough merely to show that certain social facts satisfied social needs. To fully explain a social fact, in his view, one must know both its origin and use.

The reverse of functional is "dysfunctional." For example, the use of rattles and charms by a medicine man may become dysfunctional for the community if the tribe comes to believe that scientific medicine heals.

123

Durkheim points out, though, that dysfunction is not the same as obsolescence. Some facts of social life can continue without being useful; indeed, they may have never been useful. That is why knowledge of its origin is important. (*see* Pluralism, Representation, Secularization)

Fundamentalism Although the name "fundamentalism" seems not to have been employed until the 1920's, the origin of the ideas underlying it date from 1912-14 in America. A series of tracts published during that period, titled *The Fundamentals,* was distributed to virtually every clergyman in the land. The thrust of those tracts was a scolding attack on theological liberalism. The essential doctrines of Protestantism, as viewed by these thinkers, were set out and strongly defended. Generally five fundamentals seem to have been regarded as most basic. They are: (1) the inspiration and inerrancy or infallibility of the Bible; (2) the doctrine of the trinity; (3) the virgin birth and deity of Christ; (4) the substitutionary theory of the atonement; and (5) the bodily resurrection and ascension of Christ. It is clear that the first of these fundamentals is the presupposition of the others. Further, it is clear that defense of orthodoxy with the Bible as the major authority was the major thrust of the movement. This was meaningful in contrast with liberalism's growing acceptance of the work of biblical critics who had called many aspects of the Bible into question, so that its basic authority seemed also to be under threat of collapse. Liberals had gone so far in denying the literal meaning of the five listed fundamentals that defense of them seemed required.

Although William Jennings Bryan and his part in the famous Scopes "monkey trial" in Tennessee are the images most closely connected in the popular mind with fundamentalism, there were able, scholarly theologians vitally involved. One such man was the Princeton New Testament scholar, John Gresham Machen (1881-1937). He, along with others in the movement, was displeased with the label. Instead, he preferred "conservative Christianity," or "evangelical Christianity." In his criticism of liberalism, Machen proved himself to be knowledgeable and competent. His basic attack was against what he believed to be liberalism's uncritical acceptance of a scientific closed universe that left no possibility for revelation from outside the universe. He argued that if man is in need of salvation and has only the natural world as his hope, then he is hopeless. Rather, as he believed the Bible to witness, the supernatural God must enter nature and reveal the way of salvation. As a caution against an uncritical acceptance of science by theologians, even if Machen's alternative is unsatisfactory, the point is well taken. Further, so far from the irrationalism often associated with it, fundamentalist attacks upon liberalism have often included the charge that liberalism is really irrational. Another important

124

figure in this movement, E. J. Carnell (1919-   ), in the 1950's exhibited great erudition in philosophy and science and attacked any attempt to shield Christianity from rational reflection. He argued that conservative Christianity explained all the experiences and aspects of reality more cogently than any alternative. One of the favorite attacks was aimed at liberalism's consistent refusal to accept any idea or doctrine of God as exhausting God's reality. Machen, for example, argued that liberals stress doing the will of God, but in effect do not even know the God whose will they claimed to do. Thus, the liberals were the obscurantists, not the conservatives.

The battle between fundamentalism and liberalism ended around 1930. This, of course, does not mean that there are no more fundamentalists to be found. It does mean that since then fundamentalists have often found refuge as relatively small segments of major denominations or in smaller sectarian religious groups where emotion has often replaced reason as its major thrust. Thus, fundamentalism has come to connote fanaticism in the minds of many who are unaware of the earlier history of this movement.

Paul Tillich (1886-1965) has observed that the major impulse behind fundamentalism is a fear of missing God's eternal truth. This forces a choice for some previous theological position and then elevates that particular theology to divine status. Thus it confuses eternal truth with time-bound expressions of truth. This is the trap into which many fundamentalists have fallen. (*see* Ascension, Atonement, Christology, Conservative, Incarnation, Inspiration, Natural theology, Resurrection, Trinity) J.B.W.

FUTURE (*see* Apocalypse, Destiny, History, Hope, PAROUSIA)

GEMATRIA (*see* Number)

Gentile The word "Gentile" refers to non-Jews. In the New Testament, the word translated "Gentiles" may also be translated

125

"nations." Throughout the Old Testament there is a great deal of evidence of conflict between the Hebrews and others, as, for instance, between the Hebrews and the Canaanites, the inhabitants of the land. In later times, tensions are apparent as the Jews come into contact with Greek culture. This is seen in a vivid manner in the Maccabean revolt of the second century B.C. At that time, Antiochus Epiphanes attempted to foist Greek culture on the Jews. The story of the desecration of the Temple by Antiochus and the heroic resistance of the Jews under the leadership of Judas Maccabeus is told in 1 Maccabees.

In the early days of the Christian movement the Gentile question arose. Christianity began as a Jewish movement, so the question was whether Gentiles might become followers of Jesus. More specifically, the question was: Must Gentiles be circumcised? This is the question posed by Paul in his Letter to the Galatians. His answer to the question is that they need not be circumcised; their participation is dependent simply on faith in Jesus Christ. (*see* Elect, Laos) E.L.T.

Genuflect (*jen*-yew-flekt) From the Latin word, *genu*, which means "knee," and *flectere*, which means "to bend," it means to kneel in an act of respect in worship. Worshipers genuflect upon entrance to the nave of any church or before entering the pew. As one approaches or crosses before the altar, it is appropriate to bow. This act also occurs before the sacrament of the Eucharist and during the recitation of the creed. Genuflection is used primarily in churches of a more formal liturgical order like Roman Catholic, Anglican, and Episcopal. G.E.S.

GHOST (Holy) (*see* Spirit)

Gloria in Excelsis Taken from Luke 2:14, " 'Glory to God in the highest, and on earth peace among men with whom he is pleased!' " this hymn of thanksgiving is one of the ancient angelic hymns of the church. In the Roman Catholic Mass, it is used after the "kyrie" (Lord have mercy), except during seasons of penance. In the Anglican Church, it is used following the sacrament of Communion and in the eastern churches, it is used in the morning services. (*see* Kyrie) G.E.S.

Glory "Glory" is a translation of the Greek *doxa*, a word that means "brightness," "splendor," "radiance." In the Old Testament the glory of the Lord is essentially the shining forth of light by which recognition of the divine Presence comes (Exodus 24:16-17; Leviticus 9:23; Numbers 14:10b; 1 Kings 8:10-11; Isaiah 6:1-3; Ezekiel 1:28; 3:23; 8:4). The Old Testament idea of the *Shekinah* is relevant here, the glory or Presence overshadowing the mercy-seat.

In the New Testament the term "glory" expresses the concept of revelation. Paul, for example, says that "the light of the knowledge of the glory of God" was in the face of Christ (2 Corinthians 4:6). And the Fourth Gospel speaks of beholding the glory of the Logos who reveals the Father (John 1:14). Basically, the term refers to the nature of presence of God, or of God as revealed in Christ. E.L.T.

Glossolalia (glaw-soh-*lay*-lya) A term transliterated from the Greek word for "tongue" or "language." The term refers mainly to the so-called "gift of tongues," discussed by Paul, along with other "gifts," in 1 Corinthians 12–14. The event referred to here is undoubtedly the incoherent speech of religious ecstasy. The churches considered it to be a sign the believer was possessed of the Holy Spirit. It caused disorder in the Christian assembly at Corinth. While Paul did not reject glossolalia, he was aware of problems created by this "gift." Speaking in tongues per se is unintelligible, apart from the gift of the interpretation of tongues, and this violates Paul's principle that all must be done for edification. Since edification is the norm, Paul places prophecy above glossolalia in his list of "gifts of the Spirit." (*see* CHARISMA) E.L.T.

GLUTTONY (*see Appetite, Moderation*)

Gnostic (*nahs*-tik) Taking their name from the root *gnosis* (knowledge), Gnostics believed that salvation was accomplished by deliverance of the spirit from its captivity in the world through secret knowledge. Such knowledge, they believed, came from spiritual insight. A divine emancipator comes from his kingdom of light and slips disguised into the evil forces of darkness and provides secret knowledge, thus accomplishing deliverance to the captives. Elaborate mythological systems describing this imprisonment and deliverance were a part of their belief. Revealed knowledge brought salvation, and a person could be saved and achieve Pleroma (paradise) by knowing the secret. The impossibility of harmonizing Christian beliefs with various Oriental philosophies, a reduction of emphasis upon faith, too sharp a distinction between matter and spirit, neglect of affirmation of the divine-human Christ, an overemphasis of the magical, and their internal divisions weakened Gnosticism.

Some see traces of an early Christian gnosticism in the Gospel of John (see 17:6 ff.). Others see the emphasis on preaching as a public act one of the defenses against Gnosticism (see Galatians 3:2, Matthew 5:14-16). Persons who seek to flee from the world to remain pure, and those who view Christ as not fully human, are sometimes referred to as gnostics. (*see Cult, Flesh, Mysticism*) G.E.S.

127

GOD (see Theism, Theology)

Good *The word "good" may be used to indicate that something is pleasant to behold; we say, for example, "she is good looking." It may be used to indicate that a man possesses virtue; for example, "he is a good man." Good may also be used to indicate that something functions as it should, for example, "this is a good car." In Christian theology good has been used as the opposite of bad and the opposite of sin. The good is closely identified with the will of God. The good man is one who does what is right and has the right relationship to self, God and others. In Plato's teaching the "good" is desirable in itself. For Aristotle the "good" is that at which everything by nature aims. In the Judeo-Christian tradition the "good" builds up, rather than destroys, life. Early in the history of Christian thought the idea appeared that the good is "spirit." Summum bonum is a Latin phrase meaning the "highest good."*

Plato (c. 427-347 B.C.) bases his quest for the good on the question: What is desirable in itself apart from any other consideration? The good life is to be arrived at by first discovering the "ideal" ingredients to life. Man can list the ingredients (qualities) that will make up a good life. He can rank these qualities in order of their importance. Then he can include these in his life in accordance with their importance. Plato offers man the following list in his *Philegus*: (1) moderation, (2) proportion or beauty, (3) mind or wisdom, (4) sciences, and (5) painless pleasure of the soul. The good life includes all these in their proper proportion. The followers of Plato have given many lists of actual characteristics or qualities of human life, which they consider to be the guide to a good life. Man is to take the idea and then mold a good life by patterning after the idea. Truth is good; man finds out what truth is, and then he shapes his life accordingly.

Aristotle (384-322 B.C.) defines the good as being that at which everything aims. By nature man has the capacity to acquire the good life. The good life is a happy one. However, this should not be confused with the idea that the good life is the one that seeks first and foremost to have pleasure or fun. The happy life is one in which man realizes his full potential. He develops his native abilities and becomes a whole man. It is always for the sake of some end (see End) that all else is done. A man discovers what he can do in order to realize his full humanity (be what by his nature he should be). He seeks these means in order to secure the happy life. The way man discovers his most distinctive ability is by discovering what is peculiar to him. Man shares physical existence even with the plants. Man and animals both have a life of senses (feelings). Man alone has a life of the reason; thus the good life places a high priority on the life of reason, while also recognizing the importance of the senses and physical existence.

In the Old Testament something is good if it is of service to life; if it builds up life (Genesis 1:1–2:4a). The light is good in that it is helpful to human life. A good land bears enough food to support human life (Joshua 23:14-16). A good man is one who helps his neighbor (Genesis 4:1-16). Sometimes good is used to indicate that something is pleasing to taste (good wine). In the wisdom literature good has more of a moral implication (Proverbs 22:1-16; 31:10). Every Israelite is to seek to do what is right (follow the law) (Joshua 23:14-16). He is to become a good man by seeking wisdom and not gold, by being impartial and slow to anger, and by having a straight or fair mind. In the New Testament the word "good" is used in two significant ways. First, no man is good (Mark 10:17-31; Matthew 19:16-30; Luke 18:18-30; Romans 3:10). When measured by the requirements of the law all men fall short (are sinners); thus, no man has a reason to boast of his own goodness (Romans 3:27-31). Second, the New Testament is delivering to man the message (good news) that will enable man to have the good life (be saved, have the right relationship to self, others, and God). This message brings life to man (John 20:30-31). It heals his sickness.

Origen, a second century Christian theologian, understood "spirit" as being the good. Pure spirit is pure good, sometimes called "transcendent essence," or the image of God. The material world is a place for fallen spirits. The material world is created and as such is the opposite of God. God was not created and has no material form of existence. Goodness is a "spiritual" rejection of the material world. The good man will have as little as possible to do with the material world. The monastic life is a very good life. Other church fathers reacted against Origen's understanding of the good, but Origen's views prevailed throughout the Medieval period. "Good" here becomes closely tied in with the church and its sacraments. The church was considered the final judge of what is good. The traditional position of the church fathers (which see) was that man in his original created form (before the fall) was good, but man sinned and became corrupt. Man in the fall completely lost the image of God; therefore, even man's reason, in this fallen state, is of no value to him. He can discover nothing of the truth by use of his reason. A group of theologians, usually referred to as "natural law" theologians, arose in opposition to this understanding of the fall. Man can discover, by using his reason, at least something of what it means to be redeemed (see Fall).

There are many different understandings of "the good" in the present day. To say that something is good may mean that it is useful, or a means to accomplishing something of value, or that something is of value to someone in and of itself. Emil Brunner (1889-1967) has pointed out that man of necessity makes concrete decisions in regard to what is good. Each day a man has to make decisions, and in so doing he decides to do certain things while leaving others undone. These decisions are in and of themselves value judgments. Each day brings with it its questions about what is good and man, by the life he lives, gives his answers to these questions. According to the Christian understanding "the good" is revealed to man through Jesus Christ as the will of God. The good, or the will of God, actually comes to man as a claim on his life. It comes to him, yanking him out of his own self regard and making him concerned for others. The will of God comes to man as a command. The neighbor has a need. Love will not let him ignore that need. It is a good thing for man to do for the neighbor what needs to be done for him in the present moment. This understanding of the good is arrived at by examining the obligations or duties that are man's. To ask what is the good is to ask what ought man to do.

Paul Tillich (1886-1965) seeks to discover the good by analyzing reality. The good is involved in every encounter with reality. If man examines reality he discovers in it the good. The good is the essential nature of a thing. For a man to live a good life is for him to fulfill the potential implied in his life. The good is the inner aim of creation. Man arrives at the good by discovering secondary or derived values. These are considered valuable because they help man achieve the inner aim of all creation. Justice, righteousness, and virtue are all servants of life. They help man to achieve a fully developed human life. They are not good in and of themselves. Justice is good because it helps man overcome non-being (destructiveness) by serving being (constructive or creative life).

H. Richard Niebuhr (1894-1962) spoke of good as internal and external. Every person or thing has a "good" for itself. It is also good in relation to other things or beings. The difference between good and value is that the latter is concerned with the many ways "goods" are related to one another. "Right," on the other hand, is the relation of beings to each other in such a way that they help one another to develop. Niebuhr said that "everything is good, but not everything is right." By this he meant that all of creation, living and dead, being and non-being, was good, but that disorder was still present. (see *Truth, Value*) J.S.H.

Good Friday Traditionally, the Friday before Easter, on which the crucifixion of Jesus Christ is commemorated is Good Friday. Sometimes referred to as "Black Friday," the word *good* is presumably used to refer to the benefits of Christ's death. Since the Middle Ages, this day has been marked by special observances and has usually been a day of fasting. No paraments (altar and pulpit clothes), except black, and no flowers are used in churches on Good Friday. (see *Calvary, Lent*) G.E.S.

GOSPEL (*see Synoptic*, KERYGMA)

Gothic   A style of church construction developed in the thirteenth and fourteenth centuries, gothic uses pointed arches and cove moldings. This architecture marked the change from placing all of the weight of the roof on the walls and reduced the thickness of the walls by using buttresses and posts. Small windows were now made larger and columns were used to support the roof. Interpreters of the gothic style sometimes symbolize it as hands that are clasped together in prayer, forming an arch pointing heavenward. G.E.S.

GOVERNOR (*see Providence*)

Grace   Grace is used in the Old Testament to refer to someone doing a favor for someone else. God delivers Israel out of bondage in Egypt because of no merit on Israel's part.

The word "grace" is used twice as many times by Paul as by the rest of New Testament writers. The non-Pauline use of the word falls into six different categories: (1) pleasantness, kindness, favor or thanks (Luke); (2) accompaniment to truth (John 1:14); (3) God's loving concern and readiness to help all men who turn to him in need; (4) the privileged state of Christians (2 Peter); (5) growth in grace (2 Peter 3:18) and (6) grace misunderstood as an excuse for lawlessness (Jude 4). In Paul's letters grace is understood as God's work through Jesus Christ (2 Corinthians 8:9), which rescues man from his own self-destruction. Grace is a free gift (Romans 4:4). Pelagius (*c.* 360-*c.* 420) taught that "freedom of will" was the basis for salvation. Man could not be saved apart from God's grace, but in the presence of grace man is still free to choose. Thus, if man is to be saved he must make the right choice. Augustine (354-430) taught that God's grace cannot be resisted by man. In Adam all men fall into sin and in the midst of sin man cannot deliver himself. God through Jesus Christ works man's deliverance. At the same time Augustine does not consider this a violation of man's freedom. Only by grace is man "able freely to choose the good." Grace restores communication with God and gives man liberty.

John Wesley (1703-91) views grace as a supernatural intervention by God endowing man with free will and discernment. Harald Lindström writes of Wesley, "Grace is not irresistible. Man can either cooperate with it or oppose it." (*Wesley and Sanctification*) Some Roman Catholic scholars have taught that the grace of God is objectively present in the sacraments, as a supernatural power, which works the work of God apart from any effort on man's part. The love of God is thus injected into or infused in man. Receptionism locates the presence of Christ in the one who receives the sacraments. Thus, how the sacraments are received—

with or without faith—effects the value of the sacraments. Calvinism stresses the value of the Scripture as a source of revelation and source book for preaching. The preached word is a means through which God's love becomes effective in the world. The role of man, subjectively speaking, in making God's love an effective force in the world, may be viewed in many ways. The term "cooperating grace" is used to say that God's love and man's freedom work together to accomplish God's purposes in this world. Some Protestants have viewed man as a passive recipient of God's love. Man does not act but is acted upon. Even man's love of God is actually God's love of himself through man.

Karl Barth (1886-   ) presents God's inconceivable mercy as that which makes the Christian life possible. In Jesus Christ grace forgives man and pronounces him justified.

According to some Roman Catholics, prevenient grace is the supernatural power that quickens and assists the will to have faith. In Protestantism grace precedes man's decision but is not always identified with a specific quickening power. (see Freedom, Providence, Sacrament) J.S.H.

Ground of being This is a phrase that Paul Tillich (1886-1965) has used as his designation for God. He has insisted that the phrase is the only non-symbolic formula available for expressing God. As used in this context, it means that fundamental reality or basis without which nothing else could exist. For example, when God is thought of as personal, one is really thinking of God as the basis, the first cause, the *ground* of personality. Strictly speaking, God is not *a* person, but rather the possibility of personhood at all. According to Tillich no concept of God is ever exhaustive of God's reality. For anyone to exist and to be able to have a conception of God is already to be dependent upon God. (see Ontology, Providence, Reality) J.B.W.

Guilt In the Old Testament guilt is used to describe man's relation to God. The law has been given by God to Israel. If Israel fails to do what the law requires, she will be held accountable. The law breaker must make some kind of payment or receive some punishment in order to pay for the wrong deed. This payment should both correct the damage done and punish the offender for his past wrong deed. This is a juristic or legal concept of guilt. A man has done a deed that he should not have done. He now comes before the bar of justice (the law of God) and is forced to pay for his misconduct. The above concept of guilt is an objective and external one. In the Old Testament guilt is also considered from an internal point of view. A man is to be held accountable if he has the wrong desires or feelings. Likewise, in the New Testament guilt is considered in regard to man's relation to God. A man's heart, mind, and action are to be determined by man's surrender to the will of God. Man's life gains its value and purpose from the will of God. If man does not give of himself completely to God he then has the wrong relationship to himself, to others, and to God. His life is out of adjustment; he is sick.

Christian thinkers have understood guilt as having both an objective and subjective meaning. Objectively viewed, guilt is the breaking of a law that requires that the guilty party be punished by an external act. The subjective meaning of guilt has to do with the relationship an act has to the inner being of the man. A past act may continue to cause problems in man's life. He may have trouble living with himself because of some past deed.

The puritan understanding of guilt is shaped by the assumption that Christians should have nothing or almost nothing to do with "worldly things." A Christian should keep himself unstained by fighting the desires of the flesh. Christians are to group themselves together and help each other have as little to do with the world as possible. The community draws up a long list of "do's and don'ts" and checks on its members to be sure the list is followed. A man is guilty if he fails to follow the list. He is then to be treated in such a way as to help him remain pure and undefiled by the world in his future decisions.

Augustine (354-430) taught that guilt is not a matter of external obedience. Adam misused his freedom. This mistake has stayed with the human race. Man, since Adam, has an inclination to do the wrong thing. In fact, man cannot set all things right; thus, man is living in a set of wrong relationships. God through Jesus of Nazareth has given man the possibility of having his relationships set right. If man has faith in God through Jesus of Nazareth he will be freed from his past acts and will not be punished.

Soren Kierkegaard (1813-55) affirmed that man is guilty at the center of his being. Man desires the wrong things; his life thus becomes distorted by misplaced values. He refuses to be honest about his mistakes. He assumes he can be his own physician, yet he knows that his whole outlook on life needs to be changed. Man is guilty in that he knows he has been using his life for the wrong purpose. Karl Barth (1886-   ) views man as being caught in a web of wrong decisions. Man has so misused his freedom as to lose it. Man is now unable to respond to present opportunities. He is guilty in that he is "caught" in a "misuse" of life. He is a slave to sin. In this situation man's future is death and eternal punishment. Man brought this on himself and truly deserves what he will get; namely, an eternity of punishment. God in Jesus Christ offers to man forgiveness. If man accepts this forgiveness, he is set free from concern about the past and is then able to respond in a constructive way to the opportunities of the present.

Guilt is an important concept in psychoanalysis. Some analysts have taught that guilt feelings are always damaging to a man's health. Most analysts distinguish between normal and abnormal guilt. Abnormal guilt is disturbance out of proportion to an individual's actions. At the same time man does sometimes act in a way that merits severe disturbance. On these occasions it would be wrong for man not to be upset with himself. Guilt can play a constructive role in man's search for a healthy life. Once man has misused his freedom, his feeling displeasure with himself can become a stimulant to healthy changes in attitudes and actions. (*see Anxiety, Sacrifice, Sin*) J.S.H.

Habit A habit is a stable pattern of acting, talking, or thinking that a person has learned through repetition. The term, as used in connection with virtue, refers to the fact that patterns of behavior may be learned. Virtue is an established disposition to do good deeds. Habits are well-defined patterns of acting or thinking that occur without being consciously initiated. A person's character is made up of the specific qualities that distinguish him as an individual. These specific qualities are shaped by nature or by learned patterns of behavior or habits.

Aristotle (384-322 B.C.) taught that just as the intellect requires teaching, so must man be taught "moral virtue." Moral behavior comes by practice and becomes a habit. Roman Catholic moral theology is developed on Aristotle's understanding of virtue. In this view a habit is a disposition or a tendency to act in a certain way. Habits may become a part of a man's life in one of two ways. A habit may be infused— injected into man—by the grace of God through the church and its sacraments. These habits are supernatural and can only be possessed by an individual as a result of God's action. Faith, hope, and charity are made possible by the power of God. Some virtues (prudence, justice, temperance and fortitude) are attainable by human power. These virtues may be learned as a result of teaching and training (or practice). A disposition to act in a certain way may be either good or bad.

In the Middle Ages, Scholasticism stressed the importance of developing the intellect. Man can learn about the higher things and turn from wallowing in a foolish use of his animal nature. Man can be taught to be a civilized creature. A whole society can develop set patterns of acting and thinking (customs). Men can also arrive at certain agreements on how the persons in a given society are to act (conventions) and help eliminate confusion. The Puritans thought of these customs and conventions as equal to moral habits.

Present day ethical thinking is impressed by the fact that faith is a distinct act. In each new moment man must decide anew what is the right thing for him to do. He cannot make this decision ahead of time. Man's decision to be faithful or unfaithful is always a spontaneous one. Thus, there has been a tendency to play down the role of habit in present day ethical thinking. However, Emil Brunner (1889-1967) points out that man's life includes two aspects, (1) the distinct acts and (2) the settled conditions, *i.e.*, the habitual, the permanent. There is such a thing as Christian character. The difference between Brunner and Roman Catholic moral theology is basic. Brunner understands Christian faith to be a turning away from the self and toward the other. Roman Catholic moral theology begins with the person and tries to raise him up to higher things (self-improvement by means of good habits). (*see Character, Infused grace, Virtue*) J.S.H.

HAGGADA (*see* KERYGMA)

HAGIOGRAPHA (*see Saint*)

HAGIOS (*see Holy*)

HALAKHA (*see* KERYGMA)

Hallelujah The term "hallelujah" is a Hebrew expression meaning "praise Yahweh" or "praise the Lord." It is found many times in certain Psalms, notably in Psalms 146-150, and has particular significance in what the Jews call the Hallel ("praise"), namely Psalms 113-118, which are regarded as a liturgical unit. It is commonly held that the hymn sung at the conclusion of the Last Supper (Matthew 26: 30) was the second part of the Hallel. But this is on the assumption that the Supper is the same as or an analogy to the Passover celebration, since that part of the Hallel was sung at the conclusion of the Paschal meal (see Communion).

The sole use of "hallelujah" in the New Testament is found in Revelation 19:1 *ff.* In that passage it occurs several times. The symbolic and liturgical character of the book gives the term a most fitting setting. E.L.T.

Happiness Happiness is a state of being springing from enjoyment. Happiness is also a feeling of satisfaction, contentment, and peace. Plato (c. 427-347 B.C.) made no substantial use of the term happiness, but Aristotle did. Aristotle (384-322 B.C.) taught that natural law prescribes the good for man. Man is to use his reason to discover the good and exercise self control to attain it. The result will be the experience of the greatest good, happiness. However, happiness is not the same as pleasure. Happiness is a more inclusive term, referring to the condition of the whole man. A man is happy when he has peace with himself, others, and God. Pleasure is used in a more limited sense to indicate gratification of the senses or the mind; pleasure is the experience of an agreeable sensation or feeling. Aristotle teaches that if man lets his bodily hungers and desires wallow freely in self-gratifying pleasure he will destroy himself. Happiness is the excellent activity of the soul and is to be found by living in obedience to the intellect. (see Epicurean, Hedonism) J.S.H.

HARMONY (see Peace)

Heart A full discussion of the term "heart" would call for an explanation of the anthropology and psychology presupposed by the biblical writers. Suffice it here to mention the following points: (a) Thinking, feeling, and remembering are functions of the heart in Hebrew thought (1 Samuel 9:20; 2 Kings 9:15; Ezekiel 11:5). (b) The heart is the seat of morality (Psalms 51:10) and the source of sin (Jeremiah 7:24). (c) The unbelieving heart may lead to atheism: "The fool says in his heart, 'There is no God.'" (Psalms 14:1) In general, it may be said that in Hebrew thought the heart is used to indicate the inner nature of man, his intellectual and moral nature.

The Old Testament view of the heart is carried forward into the New Testament. Jesus speaks of the "pure in heart" (Matthew 5:8); of those whose heart is where their treasure is (Matthew 6:21), of lust in the heart (Matthew 5:28). Similar ideas occur in Paul and elsewhere in the New Testament. Physiological terms, then, are used to denote inner and psychological functions. Just as "heart" becomes the seat of the intellectual and moral life, so the "bowels" become the seat of the emotions. (see Body, Flesh, Image of God, Self, Spirit) E.L.T.

HEATHEN (see Pagan)

HEAVEN (see Cosmology, World view)

Hedonism (hee-doh-nism) Hedonism is the view that pleasure is the goal of life. Bodily pleasure is more important than pleasures of the mind. The right choice for man to make is the one that helps him to feel good by experiencing pleasing sensations through the five basic senses. Every man does act from a desire for pleasure. This is referred to as psychological hedonism. Ethical hedonism emphasizes that it is man's duty to seek pleasure. The purpose and thus obligation of human life is to increase pleasure and decrease pain.

Hedonism is not necessarily a selfish principle. Egoistic hedonism is the view that man should seek his own pleasure. Man should do what he enjoys most. Utilitarian hedonism teaches that man should do that which will bring the greatest amount of pleasure to the largest number of people. John Stuart Mills (1806-73) believed that man should be concerned about the welfare of all men. Man is to seek the "greatest happiness of the greatest number." In opposition to this point of view it is said that man does not directly seek pleasure. Actually pleasure may be either good or bad. Happiness is not to be sought after as a goal in itself. Rather, the greatest happiness comes when man rightly uses his life. (*see Epicurean, Happiness*) J.S.H.

HEILSGESCHICHTE (*see History*)

HELL (*see Cosmology*)

HENOTHEISM (*see Theism*)

Heresy Any belief or doctrine contrary to the accepted truth held by the institution or authority concerned is considered heresy. In the Roman Catholic Church, "material heresy" is an error of ignorance and "formal heresy" is deliberate. Protestants usually recognize as heretical any teachings that depart from the Bible, since the Scriptures form the final authority of faith and practice. However, few churches, Protestant or Roman Catholic, hold actual trials for heresy. (*see Anathema, Dogma*) G.E.S.

Hermeneutics (her-meh-*noo*-tiks) "Hermeneutics" comes from a Greek word meaning "translation" or "interpretation." Sometimes it is used synonymously with "exegesis," but it has come to apply more to the study of the laws and principles of interpretation generally, whereas "exegesis" has to do with the meaning of a particular text. Some of the rules that have been in common use by interpreters may be listed as follows: (1) the methods of investigation used in the study of the biblical literature are not different from these applied to other kinds of literature; (2) the biblical books are historically conditioned, a fact that calls for knowledge of historical background on the part of the interpreter; (3) due consideration must be given to the literary form of a document (whether it is poetry, prose, or apocalyptic, for example); (4) the goal sought is the meaning intended by the original author; (5) an author should be interpreted in terms of consistency of meaning; (6) words used by an author should be interpreted in terms of their meaning at that period of history; (7) matters of authorship, date of writing, place of writing, and to whom the document was written, all have their bearing on interpretation of a document. These are examples of considerations guiding scholars in their interpretation of biblical literature.

In recent years the hermeneutical question has emerged with renewed vigor. A major cause for this new interest derives from the basic question of the meaning of history itself. Philosophers of history such as Wilhelm Dilthey (1833-1911) and R. G. Collingwood (1889-1943) have profoundly influenced biblical interpretation in this respect. As a result, all sorts of questions are being raised: Is there such a thing as "bare historical fact"? Are not all historical events embedded within a complex historical setting? Is a historical event purely objective? What is the relation between the subject under investigation and the interpreter? Can the past ever be transported into the present? What is the relation of "meaning" to a historical event? These are the kinds of questions being raised in connection with hermeneutics. The problem is an abiding one. The question of how to relate the biblical proclamation to each succeeding age will remain so long as the true and inner authority of the Bible is recognized, and so long as the gap between the ancient mythological world view and that of the modern world is understood. The problem of hermeneutics is how creatively and honestly to bridge that gap; it is essentially one of communication. (*see* Exegesis, History, Myth) E.L.T.

HESED (*see* Love)

Heteronomy (*het*-er-*ah*-noh-mee) Heteronomy means "other law"—the laws imposed on man from the outside. An outside authority places obligations on man that man would not place on himself. Immanuel Kant (1724-1804) used heteronomy to mean that man is to live by principles that do not arise from his own rational will. Heteronomy is the opposite of *autonomy*, which means "self-law"—the laws springing from man himself. Heteronomy is based on the conviction that man comes to have a full life only when he subjects himself to an authority outside of himself. Autonomy is based on the conviction that man comes to have a full life by refusing to let any authority be imposed on him from outside himself. *Theonomy* (which see) is an attempt to offer a solution to these two opposing views. J.S.H.

HIGHER CRITICISM (*see Biblical criticism, Literary criticism*)

Historical Jesus   The expression "the historical Jesus" is used to distinguish the Jesus who lived from the theological Christ of the Christian community. Sometimes the expressions "Jesus of history" and "Christ of faith" are used to make the same distinction. It is now generally recognized that the Gospels, which purport to tell of Jesus of Nazareth, his activity and teachings, are in fact theological or christological documents. They were written not to give a factual account of Jesus' life, but to inform the faith of the church. This does not mean that they lack historical information about Jesus, but rather that the traditions that they embody are not included to provide factual data about Jesus. They are edited so that they present Jesus as the consummation of the hopes of Israel, as the Christ, Son of Man, Son of God, *etc.* This understanding of the sources has resulted in skepticism in some quarters about the possibility of gaining real knowledge of the historical Jesus. This skepticism has been balanced in still other quarters by the assertion that knowledge of the historical Jesus is unnecessary for faith, and that the important thing is confrontation with the living Christ of the New Testament and of the church.

The liberal lives of Jesus of the nineteenth and early twentieth centuries assumed that the life of Jesus could be written by attention to the historical background in Judaism and by analyzing the Gospels in a way that would lead to pertinent factual information. Great stress was placed on objectivity in this research. The appearance of Albert Schweitzer's *The Quest of the Historical Jesus* (1910) marks a milestone in the history of the "quest." Schweitzer showed, on the one hand, that Jesus belonged to a time in which the conception of history was quite different from that of the modern period. The view of history in Jesus' time was eschatological, in which the momentary end of the world was expected. On the other hand, historians of the life of Jesus tended to reflect their own world view, so that in the lives, Jesus took on the characteristics and spirit of their age. This raises the whole question of subjectivity and objectivity in the writing of history, and indeed the question of the nature of history itself. What is an historical "fact"? Is there such a thing as a "bare fact"? What is the relation between an event and the meaning of that event? Does not the historian select from an infinite number of possibilities? By what standard does he make his selection? These are some of the questions that now arise in connection with the quest of the historical Jesus.

One of the most difficult aspects of this investigation into the life of Jesus is the nature of the sources with which the historian has to deal. The Gospels, particularly the first three, make up the main sources, but they are now seen to be documents that embody the faith of the church. They are not ancient "lives of Jesus." It is true that they embody traditions much earlier than themselves, some of which originate with Jesus, but in their finished form they are theological or christological interpretations of the faith of the church. We may distinguish here between the Jesus of history and the Christ of faith. The Christ of faith, *i.e.*, the post-Easter Christ of the church, is the controlling concern of each Gospel writer. Since the Gospels were not written as lives of Jesus, some scholars have concluded that it is a poor method to use them in the writing of "scientific" history. Others feel that the difference between the intention of the Evangelists and that of the modern historian does not lead to this skeptical conclusion.

The work of Rudolf Bultmann (1884-   ) has been most influential in this area of New Testament study. Bultmann emphasizes the distinction between the Jesus who lived and the Christ of the *kerygma* (proclamation of the church). The latter, not the former, is the object of faith. The former belongs to the history of Judaism; the latter is the object of faith. This does not deny continuity between the historical Jesus and the Christ of the church. However the continuity lies in the "that" of Jesus' history and not in the "how" of his history. Both Paul and John testify, each in his own way, that it is the *event* of Jesus, the "that" of his history, that is important. Paul emphasizes the crucified and risen Lord, while John fails to present characteristics of Jesus' humanity. Both are concerned with the "that," not with a portrait of the man who lived. Not the Jesus of history, but the Christ who confronts man is important for faith.

The influence of Bultmann has been profound. Nevertheless, a new school has arisen, the so-called post-Bultmann group, which, while taking into account the various problems that have been raised (the nature of the sources, the subjective-objective dilemma, and the nature of history) seeks to continue the quest for the historical Jesus. The extent to which this venture will be more successful than the earlier one remains to be seen. (*see Christology, Exegesis, Hermeneutics, History*) E.L.T.

HISTORICAL THEOLOGY (*see Theology*)

History *History may refer most generally to all the events that have occurred in the past. It may refer only to those events in the past from which some records remain. It may refer to writings that record in a narrative style the events in the past. It may refer to the interpretations of events, known through historical data, that occurred in the past. Unless all these views are accounted for, no consideration of history is complete. For Christian theology the importance of history lies in the conviction that God has revealed himself through "mighty acts"* *in time. Some thinkers see these acts of God, like the Exodus and the death of Jesus, as part of a history of salvation. Other thinkers object: How can you tell "salvation history" from "world history"? Reinhold Niebuhr is a modern thinker who sees history as a drama: man's love and justice are judged by the Kingdom of God. Regardless, history is important for theology. Some thinkers say becoming (or history) is most important; others say being (or nature) is.*

From the Greek *historia*, the word literally means "learning or knowing by inquiry." As it has developed in the course of the intellectual development of the West, history has come to refer to many related but quite distinct ideas. First, in terms of epistemology (which see), history refers to the branch of knowledge dealing with the past. Second, history may refer to a particular kind of literature, a continuous discourse of past events relating to a particular subject, such as "the history of the United States." Third, it may refer to the content of time (whether written about or not) and would therefore mean all the events that have ever occurred in the past. Fourth, in a more technical vein, history may refer only to those events from which records—historical data—of some kind or other have survived.

These different meanings underscore how complex the subject of history really is. Uncritical assertions are often made about history that examination will not support. It will be helpful to observe some of these complexities. Any event, in order to be known at some later time, must be recorded in some fashion. The form that such records may take include art, coins, pottery, furniture, city walls, *etc.* These kinds of historical data have been dramatically increased by the young science of archaeology. Other forms of recording are to be found in various literary types. Legal documents, treaties, pieces of literature, such as epic poems, are but illustrations. In and of themselves, however, such historical data may signify something—or nothing. Thus the data must be interpreted. A clear distinction must be made between the existence of data (a necessary precondition for any historical meaning) and the response or interpretation made by a particular historian to that data. Disagreements between historians may arise, then, for two quite different kinds of reasons. On the one hand, one historian may discover data, literary or otherwise, that another historian has overlooked. The first historian may demonstrate the inadequacy of the second's scholarly labors and thus create a disagreement. On the other hand, historians with equal access to all the known pertinent data related to any particular event in the past may disagree profoundly about the significance or meaning of those data. The recognition of this serious problem has given rise in recent scholarship to the means by which historical judgments can be legitimated, to the kinds of research that really apply in historical scholarship, and to the vastly difficult issue of how the past is ever known.

These problems have come to occupy the attention of not only historians, but also philosophers, psychologists, poets, and theologians.

The connection between Christianity and history is significant. Christianity has long understood itself as a "historical religion." By this is meant that concrete, historical events have been given central prominence in Christianity's view of reality. From the Old Testament heritage has come the faith in a God who acts in space and in time, as, for example in the Exodus and the prophets. For Christianity the supreme instance of God's historical activity is his revealing of himself through the human, historical Jesus of Nazareth. Christianity's high evaluation of time has traditionally been regarded as one of its marked differences from other religions. In some religions the human *psyche* is of crucial significance rather than the "arena of history."

Special attention has been given to the problem of history during the last century or so, especially by Protestant theologians. In the nineteenth century, the study of history became important in western thought. Every aspect of human experience was subjected to historical scrutiny. In that context theologians sought to discern the life of Jesus, the origins of the church, and its development through the centuries. Talk of the "assured results" of historical studies became fairly commonplace. And, as was typical of the nineteenth century, there developed among theologians a widespread acceptance of the notion that progressive movements had been and were being made within Christianity.

Further scholarly investigations contributed to casting doubt on such an interpretation, as did world events in the twentieth century. Two devastating world wars and an economic crisis contributed to a furthering of historical studies. Progressivism seemed to be refuted by such world shaking events. This encouraged the development of the historical disciplines by forcing them to become more self-critical. Theologians tended either to contribute to this critical re-examination or to reject all traditional historical scholarship and to try to propose a theological alternative.

Since the historical discipline seemed so incapable of established "assured results" about such critical issues as the life of Jesus, theologians began to propose *heilsgeschichte* (*highlz-geh-shik-teh*), i.e., "salvation history." The acts of God by which he has revealed his love and grace became the focal issues. Such theological doctrines as Creation, Exodus, covenants, life and death of Jesus, and the *parousia* (which see) were strongly emphasized. These "acts of God" have to be received in faith and are not accessible to ordinary historical scholarship. By affirming this supra-historical quality the faith basis of Christianity can be emphasized, and historical criticism cannot touch these events.

To critics of *heilsgeschichte* the problems were greater than the advantages. Why, they argue, are some events attributed to divine, supernatural causes and others not? Further, if faith is construed as believing reports about past events that can in no manner be legitimated by historical investigation, it seems that faith is equivalent to sacrificing critical intelligence. Finally, why should "events" 2000 years or more ago be taken as having such profound significance for today? Is God not the living God who continues today to reveal himself?

Such searching criticisms of *heilsgeschichte* have stimulated even greater theological interest in the problem of history. Among the most significant contemporary theologians concerned about this question are Reinhold Niebuhr (1892-   ), Paul Tillich (1886-1965), Rudolf Bultmann (1884-   ), and Nicholas Berdyaev (1874-1948). Niebuhr has written on the problem in several places but perhaps most importantly in *Faith and History* (1949). In that book Niebuhr depicts history as a drama. God's will for creation is to be accomplished in time. Man, the rebellious creature, attempts, by misusing his freedom, to achieve his own rather than God's purposes. The Kingdom of God will be realized only when the conditions of history are overcome. But the idea of the Kingdom stands in judgment upon every human undertaking. Human love and justice fall short of the Kingdom.

Time as the arena within which man and God interact is central for any view of history as it relates to the Christian faith. Tied to most views of time is the idea of flux and change, death and birth, destruction and creation. Becoming precedes being in such considerations. Theologies that take history as the most significant realm and those that assume ontology (which see) to be most significant are in conflict with each other. The battle between them continues. (*see Eschatology, Kingdom of God, Salvation, Time*) J.B.W.

Holy The Hebrew word *qodesh*, translated "holiness," suggests a strange, mysterious force abiding in objects, places, and persons. A few examples from the Old Testament make this clear: In 2 Samuel 6:7, when Uzzah touched the ark, "God smote him there because he put forth his hand to the ark. . . ." In Numbers 4:15 the Levites are instructed not to touch the holy objects lest they die. Both Exodus 29:37 and Leviticus 6:27 speak of the transmission of holiness by the mere touch. Both the Hebrew word and its Greek counterpart (*hagios*) seem to convey the idea of separation. Holy men are therefore those who have been separated out and dedicated to the service of God. The meaning is cultic but does not mean that the word did not include the moral element. Probably the root meaning of separation, with its suggestion of power, was either the same as or very much like ideas of holiness in the ancient Near East generally.

The idea of the holy is also applied to God. In Judges 13:22 we read, "And Manoah said to his wife, 'We shall surely die, for we have seen God.'" In the call of Isaiah the threefold stress on the holiness of

143

God appears: " 'Holy, holy, holy is the LORD of hosts;/the whole earth is full of his glory.' " Isaiah's response to his temple experience is one of awe: " 'Woe is me! For I am lost; for I am a man of unclean lips, and I dwell in the midst of a people of unclean lips; for my eyes have seen the King, the LORD of hosts!' " (Isaiah 6:5) The idea of a holy God explains the Hebrew sacrificial system; the offering of sacrifice by the High Priest, in atonement for the sins of the people, made it possible for them to approach God. This concept is used by the New Testament Epistle to the Hebrews, where Jesus becomes the eternal High Priest who has entered the heavenly sanctuary through his death, and thereby makes it possible for men to draw near to God.

The same basic ideas carry into the New Testament. Matthew's Gospel speaks of the holy city (Matthew 4:5; 27:53). In Luke, Zechariah mentions " 'his holy covenant.' " (Luke 1:72) Reference is made to "holy angels" (Mark 8:38; Luke 9:26) and to " 'his holy prophets' " (Luke 1:70). In numerous places the divine Spirit is called the Holy Spirit. In Mark 1:24 the demonic spirit calls Jesus " 'the Holy One of God.' " The Old Testament view is that the people of Israel, chosen by God to be his people, are a holy people. A parallel to this view is found in the concept of the church in the New Testament. From the New Testament point of view, it is more correct to say that the church represents the fulfillment of the notion of the chosen people of God. For the Christians are called "holy ones." The translation of the Greek *hagioi* as "saints," which is the usual practice, obscures the idea of "holiness" the word conveys. The "saints" are Christians, who have been consecrated to God (Acts 9:13; Romans 8:27; 1 Corinthians 6:1 *ff.*; Ephesians 2:19). In Romans 12:1 the offering of Christians' lives to God is described as holy. In 1 Peter 1:15 the holiness of Christians is grounded in the holiness of God, the writer appealing in this regard to Leviticus 11:44-45.

In modern times, the idea of the holy has received fresh attention, due largely to the work of Rudolf Otto (1869-1937) in his book, *The Idea of the Holy*. The book appeared in 1917 under the title, *Das Heilige*. Fully aware of the original connotations of the term in Hebrew, Greek, and Latin, Otto used the idea of the holy to express that religious experience that contains not only the moral and rational but also "the *feeling* which remains where the *concept* fails. . . ." The holy, minus the moral factor, he calls the "numinous," and speaks of a "unique 'numinous' category of value and of a definitely 'numinous' state of mind. . . ." An important element in the numinous is the sense of dependence or "creature-feeling." Over and beyond faith, trust, and love religious experience may be characterized by what Otto calls the *mysterium tremendum*, consisting of a sense of awe, majesty, and energy. He uses the expression "wholly other" in his analysis of the *mysterium*, a term used by other theologians to indicate the complete transcendence of God. But this is not at all the purpose of Otto; his object is rather to emphasize that aspect of deity that lies beyond the rational and before which man responds with a sense of awe. (*see* Fear [*of God*], *Mystic, Sacrifice*) E.L.T.

HOLY COMMONWEALTH (*see* Mission)

HOLY SPIRIT (*see* Spirit)

Homiletics (hahm-oh-*leh*-tiks) Relating to the word, homily, this is a transliteration of the Greek word, *homiletikos*, which means "of conversation" or "to be in company with." It means the art or science of preaching and includes public speaking, sermon building, the history of preaching, examination of sermons, studies of contemporary and outstanding preachers, and practice preaching. (*see Hermeneutics, Kerygma*) G.E.S.

HOMO RELIGIOSUS (*see* Natural theology, Religion)

Hope In the thought of Plato (*c.* 427-347 B.C.) a man's hopes are the images that he forms for himself of his future. He draws mental pictures of what the future will be, and he wishes that the future will be this way. Man creates his own hopes.

The Old Testament concept of hope is rooted in and gains its meaning from God's covenant with Israel. God has made certain agreements with Israel. If Israel remains true to these agreements (is faithful to the law), then the covenant will be kept. As used here hope is closely connected with confidence. The person who is faithful to the covenant *now* is afraid of nothing. This confidence is also a future reality in the sense that man has not yet been delivered from all his troubles.

The messiah is the one who will come and bring about these final and complete victories. The community hopes for the coming of the messiah because he will enable the community to become totally faithful and healthy. In the first century A.D., Philo emphasized hope as expectation. The man of hope is one who expects certain things; thus, the Jew is a man who waits expectantly for the appearance of the deliverer.

The New Testament understanding of hope is rooted in the Old Testament understanding of the word. (1) Hope has to do with expectation more than desire. For man to hope is for him to wait with open arms for the future. He is counting on the future being worth living in, and he goes to meet that future. Hope does not mean that man expects the future to be what he wants it to be. Hope is man's attitude as he moves out to meet a future, the contents of which he cannot know in advance.

145

(2) This moving out to meet the unknown is grounded in faith. Paul emphasizes this when he suggests that to hope in God is to trust in God. It is to risk oneself in love of God, neighbor, and self.

In the nineteenth century hope was used in a still different way. Here hope was understood as belief that man can accomplish almost anything he wants to. God has made man just a little lower than the angels; thus, man is able to overcome all the obstacles that have hindered him in his life. Poverty, sickness, and war can be overcome. This hope was understood in terms of very specific objectives.

Neo-orthodoxy reacted very strongly against this understanding of hope. Neo-orthodoxy said that the nineteenth century's understanding of hope was too simple. One must take seriously the fact that man is a sinner and not assume that man can accomplish more than he can. Existentialism built a concept of hope on this objection. Man's life is brief and much of his work is useless. If hope means that man assumes he is building God's kingdom on earth, then this is a false hope. Hope is not the assumption that certain concrete goals will be accomplished; rather, hope is living in the present in confidence.

In the 1960's a new school of German thinkers has emphasized hope. The "theology of hope" draws on the promises of God to his people in the Old Testament. The concept that God reveals himself as One coming in the future grows out of apocalypse, including the literature of the apocrypha. In the New Testament, Jesus' preaching of the future kingdom of God, and the church's belief in the *parousia* is emphasized. Jurgen Moltmann speaks of "Christ" as past and future. Important to him and other thinkers in this school is history. Their concept of hope explains how God can be acting to redeem man in the world of technological change. (*see* Dogmatics, Existentialism, Parousia) J.S.H.

Host From the Latin word, *hostia*, meaning "victim" or "sacrifice," it is the unleavened bread that is held high in the Eucharist services and offered as the sacrifice of Christ's body. The host is then eaten by the communicants. (*see* Communication, Communion, Elements, Sacraments) G.E.S.

HOURS (*see* Office)

Hubris (*hoo*-bris) This is not a characteristically biblical expression. The Greek words are *hubris, hubristes,* and (the verb) *hubrizein. Hubrizein* means "to treat in an arrogant or spiteful manner." *Hubris* means "insolence" or "arrogance." *Hubristes* is a violent, insolent man. One form or the other of these words appears in the New Testament in the following places and connections: Acts 27:10, 21, where it refers to disaster; Luke 11:45, of insult with words; Romans 1:30, where it describes the sins of the pagan world; Matthew 22:6, Acts 14:5, Luke 18:32, 1 Thessalonians 2:2, and Titus 1:11, where it is used of mistreatment; 2 Corinthians 12:10 lists the things that Paul suffered as the result of *hubris*. These are the major passages, but the idea of *hubris* is often present even when the word is absent.

To grasp the meaning of the term one must explore its usage among the Greeks. In Greek use *hubris* is connected with the notion of man's relation to the gods. Permeating Greek literature from the time of Homer is the idea of the envy of the gods: their envy would be awakened should one overstep, in happiness or success, the bounds of his status as a mortal man. Back of this doctrine of the envy of the gods lies the human tendency for man to forget his finitude, his creatureliness, and to make himself equal with the divine. Consequently *hubris* becomes the great sin of man. It is the insolent and arrogant attitude of pride that sets itself against both man and God. It was a true instinct that led Jesus to see in the *attitude* of pride the great sin of man. While *hubris* does not occur in this connection, Jesus' condemnation of pride, particularly religious pride, illuminates the gravity of man's condition in this regard.

In modern times, certain theologians have seen pride as the chief sin of man. Reinhold Niebuhr (1892-), for example, stresses this in his book, *The Nature and Destiny of Man*. He distinguishes three types of pride: (a) pride of power; (b) pride of knowledge or intellectual pride; (c) pride of virtue. In his discussion of this, Niebuhr sees the sin of pride as relating not only to individuals but also to groups and nations. Group pride has its source in individual attitudes but comes to have an existence of its own with authority over the individual. The egotism of the national state is the most consistent expression of pride in the collective sense. Its tendency is to claim for itself "the final and ultimate value," an expression of human pride and arrogance that reaches its highest form in the pretension that the nation is God. While Niebuhr at this point does not use the term *hubris*, it is clear that in his discussion both of individual and group pride he is close to the Greek concept.

Since Niebuhr's writing, numerous ethical systems have stressed pride as a basic factor in the moral dilemma of man. It may be said that the modern insight in this regard has its roots both in the classical view of *hubris* and in the New Testament identification of pride as sin. In the history of theology and ethics it is represented by a theological strain beginning with the work of Augustine (354-430). (*see Sin*) E.L.T.

Hymn Hymns are part of the traditional worship of the church in which the congregation actively participates. Old Testament Psalms were used in ancient worship and continue to be a part of our worship. A hymn was used at the conclusion of the Last Supper (Matthew 26:30). Not only does the New Testament refer to the use of hymns (Ephesians 5:18-19; Colossians 3:16-17), but it also includes portions of early hymns (Philippians 2:5-11). Hymns are musical compositions expressing the essentials of the Christian faith. They form a part of the rich heritage of Christian worship in praise, thanksgiving, and penitence. Since 1965, the Roman Catholic liturgy includes hymn singing, along with Mass in the vernacular. (*see* Anthem, Liturgy, Vesper) G.E.S.

HYPOSTASES (*see* Trinity)

Icon (*igh*-kahn) From the Greek word, *eikon*, which means "an image" or "a representation," icons usually consist of paintings or mosaics venerated in worship. Some believe it a violation of the commandment that says, " 'You shall not make for yourself a graven image . . . .' " *Iconoclasm* is the practice of using icons. An *iconoclast* is one who opposes the use of religious images and destroys them. G.E.S.

Idealism In a way similar to many basically philosophical terms, idealism has been used in such a variety of ways that no single definition will do. Rather, the use in specific contexts must help establish that particular meaning. Some characteristics generally shared can, however, be noted. In any use one must determine whether the word idealism derives from "idea" or "ideal." Both are common, but the meaning of the term may vary considerably, depending upon which the word derives from.

In what may be regarded as the original form of idealism, Plato (*c.* 427-347 B.C.) said that ultimate reality is found in the mind of God. There in unchanging, perfect, and absolute form reality resides. The corollary of this view is that the material, spatial, corporeal forms that are encountered through sense experience are imperfect representations of God's perfect idea. Man, for example, as he is encountered in his peculiar shapes, with his particular ideas, morals, *etc.*, is only a reflection of what "manness" is in God's conception. Thus, from very early in classical philosophy the problem of reality is acute. Plato raises clearly the conflict between appearance and reality.

Neoplatonic philosophy influenced many of the early Christian theologians. Nowhere, however, is this influence more obvious or thoroughgoing than in the thought of Augustine, bishop of Hippo (A.D. 354-430). In Augustine's epistemology the doctrine of illumination is quite prominent. By this doctrine, Augustine could insist that all knowledge is a result of the insight provided by God to enlighten and penetrate natural darkness. Further, in his view of history Augustine could insist that the meaning of events in time comes only from being given illumination and experiencing faith. Idealism is obviously at work in such doctrines.

In recent philosophy and theology the developments in Germany during the nineteenth century serve to illustrate. A form of idealism often called "absolute idealism" was proposed by G. W. F. Hegel (1770-1830) and in his followers. Their conviction was that, in order to believe in the validity of one's knowledge, man must presuppose the world to be a rational structure, quite apart from any man's perception of its rationality. Only if man's rational faculties correspond with the rational structure of reality that underlies existence can man really know reality. One way of expressing this belief in the rational structure of reality is to say it all originates in the divine reason or mind. All reality is therefore the expression of the divine mind. Although not uncritical of the optimism inherent in absolute idealism, liberal theology often employed this philosophy to express its theology. One of the closest alliances between liberalism and idealism is found in their common emphasis upon the development of theological personalism that many Methodist theologians have found acceptable. (see Alienation, Epistemology, Metaphysics, Ontology, Presupposition, Realism, Reality, Theism, Theology) J.B.W.

Identity Erik Erikson, an American psychoanalyst, uses the term "identity" to mean the individual's awareness of what he believes in, what he can do, and what he can become. Identity is especially important in the late teen-age years, according to Erikson. At that time a person changes his view of himself. This is partly because society changes its view of him. He is no longer a child but an adult. Each person works out a satisfactory way of understanding himself. If he does not, he may remain immature or become neurotic. Identity, or "self identity," does not mean that a person sees himself only in one role. An individual may be able to mix several roles together, but he holds an image of himself that he and society can accept, and that enables him to live as a normal person. (see Consciousness, Self)

Image of God Genesis 1:26-27 presents the idea that man was created in the image of God or after God's likeness. Man is

149

the height or summit of creation. He is ruler over all created things. He has a unique relation to God. God places demands on man, who is able to respond faithfully to these demands. (See also Genesis 5:1-3, 9:1-7 and Psalm 8.) The New Testament uses the term "image of God" in the same sense as the Old Testament. However, the New Testament changes its meaning to include the idea of a mold or pattern after which something is to be formed. Thus, Christ is the image of God; his life and teaching give a picture of God. For Paul the image of God enables man to fulfill his life. In Greek thought the image of God is the light that comes from God to light up the dark world. Jesus Christ, the image of God, then would be the light showing man how to live.

In Roman Catholic theology the image of God is understood in a two-fold way. The image of God is essential to man's natural make-up. Thus, man's reason and his free will are the image of God in man. Man's misuse of freedom has injured his reason and free will. Man is not able to discover all the truth or do all that he needs to do by simply using his natural abilities. The image of God also refers to what is beyond the natural (the supernatural). God's grace through Jesus Christ and his church has given man the help needed for him to have a life in the fullness of God's image. Now man can be like God, in that he can live a life of integrity and have eternal life (life without end). Martin Luther (1483-1546) rejected this division into the natural and supernatural. For Luther, "image of God" meant the freedom to choose obedience to the will of God. In this obedience lies life. Man misused his freedom and lost it. He is now hopelessly trapped in slavery to wrong choices, but the image of God can be restored to man through faith in Christ.

Another meaning of God's image is that it distinguishes man from the animals. Some follow Aristotle (384-322 B.C.) and see man's reason as the image of God. Others follow the romantic spirit and say that man's imagination and his ability to be an artistic creator is the image of God. The liberal theological movement stressed the idea that man was created in the image of God. Man in and of himself is of value. Human life is sacred. Also man is able to do what needs to be done on earth. The term "image of God" is sometimes used as a relational concept. When man is obedient to God his life then reflects (like a mirror) God to other men. Paul Tillich (1886-1965) is opposed to understanding the image of God in a relational way. Rather, he is convinced that the image of God is rooted in man's being as such (not in possibility but in fact). Man's very make-up includes the image of God, which is man's rational structure. This structure is a structure of freedom through which man has the possibility and necessity of being who (or what) he was created to be. (*see Fall, Self*) J.S.H.

Immanent (*ehm*-ah-nuhnt) From the Latin, immanent means "in-dwelling." In its typical theological use it relates to the connection between God and the world and man. The word suggests the concept of space, which places it in contrast with transcendent, which means above or beyond the world. In typical philosophical use these concepts are opposites. Something is either transcendent or immanent. If the meaning of something is entirely self-contained, its meaning is immanent. In a broader sense, immanent may mean simply the presence of something in contrast to its absence.

In theological use the advocates of a totally immanent view of God are called pantheists. Any description of the world and its workings is at once a description of God and his workings. The limit of this view is obvious when it is recognized that the destruction of the world would also mean the destruction of God. If something is more powerful than God, then it may itself more correctly be regarded as God.

The opposite view that sees God as totally transcendent is often called deism. The logical problem is very great here, also. If God is wholly unconnected to the world, how may it be accounted for? Deists have compromised their position generally by advocating a view of the creation of the world by God, but have insisted that after the creation God withdrew from any connection. The difficulties of consistency in such a position are obvious. Traditional theism, as incorporated by Christian orthodox theology, holds that God and world are related in a transcendent-immanent way. This paradox is felt to be very near the center of the Christian revelation. Theism admits to many different interpretations and has many problems inherent within it.

Liberal theology tended toward an immanent view of God. Its representatives hoped to gain rapport with spokesmen for science, whose influence was gaining ever greater followers during the nineteenth and twentieth centuries. Liberals by and large believed that science and theology could not ultimately be in conflict. They accepted the findings of science in order to correct traditional theological doctrines.

Neo-orthodox theology reacted against the liberal defense of the immanence of God and reaffirmed a strong view of his transcendence. (*see Deism, Dogmatics, Natural theology, Theism, Transcendent*) J.B.W.

IMMERSION (*see Baptism*)

Immortality In popular Christian thought, immortality is equal to "eternal life." The fact that this equation persists shows how strong is the influence of Greek philosophical thought upon Christian theology. The Greeks thought of a dualism between the human body and the eternal soul of man. The body is corruptible and decays after death.

151

The soul, by contrast, is not subject to corruption or decay. Thus, immortality of the soul is taken to be a natural human quality.

The Hebrew concept of post-death existence is very different, and it dominates the New Testament passages on the subject, just as it does the Old Testament. Because of the complete conviction that God created the world and that his creation is good, it was impossible to think of the body as evil and dispensable. Rather, as in 1 Corinthians 15, thinkers like Paul could only conceive of life after death as a renewal of the intimate connection between body and spirit. Death was acknowledged as complete death.

Eternal existence belongs to God alone (1 Timothy 6:16). If man is to live after death, it will be only by a creative act of God. It will be by resurrection, as a gift; it is not a natural quality of the human soul. Because God raised Jesus from the dead, man may in faith hope for his own resurrection by God.

Early Christian theology was heir to both the Greek and the Hebrew conceptions. As in so many instances, reconciliation of the two views proved to be difficult. This was done by proposing three theological notions. First, the soul of each individual, rather than being eternal, was held to be created by God. Second, upon death it was held that the soul goes to some intermediate place to await final judgment. This gave rise to the Roman Catholic idea of purgatory. Third, it was held that at the final judgment the soul would be rejoined with the body and assigned to eternal dwelling in heaven or hell. The thrust of this third step was to emphasize the eternal life of man. This, of course, served to reinforce the popular belief in immortality. Although the Reformers of Protestantism did not accept the second idea of purgatory, in general they accept the same view of life after death.

Liberal Protestantism was determined to understand theology in a way that would make it compatible with scientific reasoning. Since any literal meaning of "resurrection of the body" seemed impossible to men who were becoming ever more knowledgeable about physics, chemistry, and biology, liberal theologians tended to drop the idea. They tended to emphasize the moral and psychological interpretation of ideas of heaven and hell. This put them in closer relation to the Greek heritage than the Hebrew in Christianity.

With the rise of neo-orthodoxy, however, the liberal view was regarded as unbiblical. These theologians, notably Karl Barth (1886-   ), emphasized the resurrection of the body as most compatible with the biblical witness. This view seems to be re-emphasizing the Hebrew ideas.

In any consideration of immortality or eternal life it should be emphasized that Christianity attempts to affirm that God is more powerful than death. If death is overcome, it will be by the power of God given by grace to man. The God who loves man in life will love him no less in death. (see Death, Dogmatics, Dualism, Eternal, Judgment, Natural theology, Resurrection) J.B.W.

IMMUTABLE (see Impassible)

Impassible   Literally this word means incapable of suffering harm or pain or incapable of emotion. As such, it is only slightly different from immutable. The same arguments that have been advanced for or against immutability would generally apply to impassibility. Historically, theology became acutely aware of this problem during the third century A.D. when some theologians were advocating a view of God implying that God, the Father, suffered and died when Jesus was crucified. The orthodox position rejected such a notion, labelled *patripassianism* (pah-tree-pas-shun-ism), i.e., literally, "suffering father." The classical Christian concept of God underscored the belief that he was unrelated to creation. Recent theology has re-examined the doctrine of God in order to somehow show that God is related to creation. (see Absolute, Aseity) J.B.W.

IMPERATIVE (see Deontological, Duty)

Incarnation   *From the Latin word,* incarnatio, *which means "to be made flesh," this term refers to a divine being coming to earth in the flesh of a person. In Christian doctrine, it refers to the divine Word (Logos) becoming flesh and dwelling among men, or more especially, God in Christ.*

The use of the word is not restricted to the Christian vocabulary. Whenever any god assumes a human or animal body for its habitat, this act is known as an incarnation. Hindus have a highly systematized caste system of incarnations of deceased humans in various animal forms, according to their faithfulness on earth. Their after-death incarnations in various animals, rodents, insects, or the like is called "reincarnation." Countless stories are told of Vishnu, the Hindu god, who upheld the right and defeated the wrong. Such accounts reveal his incarnation as a turtle, combination man and lion, boar, and fish, among others. Zeus and Apollo stand highest among the Greek gods who came to earth in the form of animals or men. Buddhism similarly teaches the incarnation of goodness in human forms. The Bodhisattva is a Buddha-to-be and is qualified for Nirvana (a state of complete freedom and bliss), and to become a Buddha, but who prefers to continue to be incarnated into various beings to aid distressed men on earth.

Included among reasons given for the role of incarnation in religion are these: divinity and humanity are inclined to be pulled apart, and incarnation brings them together; man needs constant help from God, and God is closer when he is in animal or human form; and messiahs need a credential of divine authority, such as incarnation.

The classic Christian doctrine of the incarnation was formulated at Nicaea in A.D. 325, at which time the problem of christology, linking the concepts of truly God and truly man together, was dealt with. The Nicene Creed attempts to resolve this problem. Eighty-four of its total of 101 Greek words center upon the Son.

Friedrich Schleiermacher (1768-1834) viewed humanity itself as basically god and religious. For the Redeemer to enter in human form was not hard to accept. Schleiermacher, however, did not accept the traditional belief that a supernatural person entered into a natural person. Jesus was a man like other men, but "distinguished from them all by the constant potency of His God-consciousness, which was a veritable existence of God in Him." (*The Christian Faith*, page 385) As early as 1830, then, a major Christian theologian questioned the thousand-year-old settlement of Nicaea.

Soren Kierkegaard (1813-55) was in many ways more radical than Schleiermacher, and yet he pinned the hope of man's salvation on the "God-man" Jesus Christ. Kierkegaard offered no explanation for the Incarnation, but only pointed to him as the figure who overcame the alienation of man from God.

Karl Barth (1886-   ) begins his monumental *Church Dogmatics* with the revelation of God in Jesus Christ. More precisely, Barth views the Trinity as revealed in the Resurrection of Christ. It is quite wrong, Barth argues, to begin with human nature, as did Schleiermacher, and then to try to understand the incarnation in natural or historical terms. Rather, one can only begin with truth as we see it in Christ and then proceed to understand the world. (*see Christology*) G.E.S.

INFALLIBILITY (of the Pope—*see* Ex Cathedra) (of the Bible—*see Fundamentalism*)

INFANT BAPTISM (*see Baptism*)

Infinite   In the Latin the concept meant immeasurably great, *i.e.*, without limits. As such, it is a philosophical concept, which, like so many others, has been borrowed on occasion by theologians. When it is used theologically, "infinite" most often refers to the attributes of God and conveys their unlimited or unbounded implications, *e.g.*, the infinite love, mercy, and grace of God. Historically, the idea of infinity is closely connected with classical Christian theology that has conceived God as *absolute*. Thus, his attributes are infinite. To say that God's power is infinite is to say that it is perfect or absolute. (*see Aseity, Impassible, Omnipotence, Omnipresence, Omniscience*) J.B.W.

Infusion of grace   Infusion of grace means a pouring into man of God's grace. Augustine (354-430) taught this in order to make the point that man is totally dependent upon God for all his life. If man has a healthy or righteous life it is not due to any act or decision of his own. Man, in his use of his freedom, has earned nothing for himself. God, in his infinite wisdom and love, gives to man a "new direction and inclination" toward God. God's grace is understood as being located in the sacrament of the church. When man receives the sacrament of Holy Communion it becomes effective in his life separate and apart from any intentions, desires, or attitude man has. (see *Grace, Sacrament, Virtue*) J.S.H.

Inspiration   The English word "inspiration" may be used in a variety of ways. We speak, for example, of an inspiring or inspired work of art. On the other hand, the term may be used in a more specific sense, as when we speak of the inspiration of the Scriptures. Sometimes this use is subdivided to include the verbal inspiration of the Bible, a view that holds that the human author was simply a mouthpiece of God; God dictated the Bible, so that every word represents the divine mind. This largely mechanical theory of inspiration is rejected by critical scholars, who view the Scriptures as historically conditioned, although they would not rule out the impact of the divine Spirit upon the human agent.

The English word is derived from the Latin *inspiratio* and literally means the act of breathing in. It is interesting to note that both the Hebrew and Greek words for "breath" can also mean "spirit." And the idea of inspiration is closely connected with the concept of the operation of the divine Spirit upon the human spirit. Second Timothy 3:16 states: "All scripture is inspired by God. . . ." The Greek is translated by the Vulgate to read, *omnis Scriptura divinitus inspirata*. This rendering may well lie behind the use of the term "inspiration" to express the notion of the divine element in Scripture.

The term "inspiration" is used only twice in the Bible. The first is in Job 32:8, where the spirit of God is said to give men understanding. The second is in 2 Timothy 3:16 (referred to above). The lack of many biblical references to the word, however, does not do justice to the *idea* of inspiration contained in the Bible. Yet here one must distinguish clearly between the question of inspiration generally and that of the inspiration of the Scriptures in particular. In both the Old Testament and the New, certain persons were convinced that they were directed by a divine power. This was true of the prophets of the Old Testament with their "thus says the Lord." However, the more obvious expression of prophetic inspiration was the ecstatic state. This was particularly true of the earlier prophets. A vivid example of this is found in 1 Samuel 10:5-6,

10, and in 19:24. In the later prophets there is often the sense of an overmastering force that the prophet interprets as God's action upon him (Ezekiel 2:2; 3:24 *ff.*; Jeremiah 4:19; 20:7-9). The great prophets of the eighth and seventh centuries B.C. relate their experience of the divine to the crucial social and political issues of the day.

The belief in the action of the divine Spirit is strong in the New Testament literature. There is the action of God's Spirit on Jesus himself at his baptism (Mark 1:10 and parallels); the descent of the Holy Spirit at Pentecost empowers the church (Acts 2:1 *ff.*); in the Pauline churches the Spirit's presence expressed itself in certain "gifts," among them the gift of speaking in tongues and the gift of prophecy (1 Corinthians 12:1-31; 14:1-33). With regard to the ethical life Paul speaks of the "fruit of the Spirit" (Galatians 5:22).

The Protestant Reformation, with its stress on *sola scriptura*, had to come to grips with the question of the inspiration of the Bible. In general, the great Reformers accepted the verbal inspiration of the Scriptures. But this assertion itself needs some modification, for Luther, who can say that God is in every syllable, still recognized errors and inconsistencies in the Scriptures. For example, he saw the differences between the birth stories in Matthew and Luke. Furthermore, the Reformers recognized a lack of quality and authority within the Bible itself. Luther's statement that the Epistle of James is an epistle of straw is a case in point. While the principle of inspiration was accepted, uniformity of inspiration was not. For both the Reformers and for Catholics, the divine Spirit must provide understanding in the interpretation of the Scriptures. (*see Canon, Fundamentalism, Glossolalia*) E.L.T.

Institutional church The meaning of this term has changed in recent years. Traced to 1894, when The Open and Institutional Church League was formed, it originally meant help for the underprivileged. This organization was short-lived but had a wholesome influence upon churches by making them sensitive to their mission to the world. Today, the institutional church is understood to be the organization by which the Christian church acts. It includes buildings, memberships, pastors, church executives, congregations, budgets, auxiliary organizations, programs, real estate, administrative boards, and councils.

The concept of the institutional church implies a concern for numerical growth, both in membership and finances, as opposed to involvement in mission. The Encyclopaedia Britannica estimates that in 1966 there were nearly 600 million Roman Catholics, 230 million Protestants (including Anglicans), and 145 million Eastern Orthodox, in contrast to 13 million Jews and over 2 billion participants in other religions. While figures in the *American Yearbook of Churches* reveal growth in the institutional church, critics severely attack its effectiveness. Since World War II, there has been increased criticism that the church is more concerned about preserving itself than meeting the spiritual and moral needs of men.

Among the criticisms leveled at today's church is that it is no longer "relevant" to persons' needs. The church is accused of speaking a strange tongue to modern people. Critics complain that the form of worship and the educational institutions, like the Sunday School, are out-of-date. They charge the church with attending only to personal and family needs, and not the larger, social needs of men, such as racial and economic injustice.

Coupled with the frequent use of the word "relevant" is the word "renewal." Critics of the church contend that persons will find renewal outside of the church unless the institutional church is renewed. Fear of involvement in controversial social issues, lack of mission, obsession with building bigger buildings and raising larger budgets, increasingly larger administrative overheard, and theological naïveté, are among criticisms leveled at the church.

There are equally strong defenses. Some contend the church has always had to grapple with the question of relevance. Each generation has faced the problem of how the Word can be made flesh, but the church has continued as the Spirit-filled institution accomplishing God's mission. Even those who criticize institutionalism admit, however, that means are necessary for the task of mission. Without structure, order, and program, purposeless and aimless chaos would result in the church. The test that must be applied to the institutional church is whether the parts of its institution—its buildings, program, organization, and finances—become ends in themselves or means to the real end, mission in the world. (see Church, Mission, Structure) G.E.S.

INTERIM ETHIC (see Eschatology)

INVOCATION (see Prayer)

IRRESISTIBLE GRACE (see Grace)

I-Thou Martin Buber (1878-1965) considered man to have two basic relations. The "I-Thou" relation is one in which the self meets the other, the Thou. In this relation, which is not an experience, the I truly discovers itself. What is the Thou? It is another reality, perhaps a self, but certainly not an object. The I can place no bounds on the Thou, which is free to be its own self. Though the "I-Thou" relation is one between men, Buber said that the Thou was not a "He" or a "She." Apparently he meant that the Thou was a full human being in its own right and had to be regarded as such. "Love is responsibility of an *I* for a *Thou*," he wrote.

Man does use things, however, and Buber called the man-nature relation an "I-It" relation. Man changes, and controls, the It, which may be the raw material of the world, technology, or (wrongly) other people.

One being always remains "Thou," however. God is always beyond man, but He is "addressed, and not expressed." Man addresses God as Thou and in this relation becomes fully human.

Though the pronouns suggest an individual relation, Buber apparently meant "I-Thou" as the constantly changing relation of men to one another in community. Though this relation is deeply personal, I-Thou is not, as so many have tried to make it, a sentimental feeling of one person for another.

Emil Brunner (1889-1967) used the term "thou" for the personal relationships of men apart from official structures. For instance, any chance friendship or personal attachment growing out of human feelings might be a "thou" relation. But a boss and his employee would, in Brunner's thought, have an official relation of duty to one another.

Harvey Cox has criticized a Christian view that makes all human relations either "I-Thou" or "I-It." Helpful human relations may be "I-You" in nature. A business transaction or a contract may be "I-You," in which the self does not allow the other to be totally free, and yet acknowledges the humanity of the other person.

J SOURCE (*see Name, Source criticism*)

JEHOVAH (*see Name*)

JESUS (*see Christology, Historical Jesus, Name*)

Judgment (of God)   In the Bible judgment carries two distinct meanings, both of which appear in the Old Testament. First, there is a plural use, "judgments," which refers to the laws, decisions, and testimonies of God. It is sometimes used interchangeably with law, perhaps the single most important concept in the Old Testament. This use originated from a widespread practice in the ancient Near East. When men needed a ruling on a particular problem, they went to the shrine of their God and sought a word. The cult official or priest would cast lots, or if a prophet he would seek the answer in a vision or a dream. When the answer was given, it became precedent to which future instances of this particular problem could be referred. This was called a judgment of God. Second, there is a singular use in reference to God's evaluation of men. This was sometimes thought of as occurring in time and in other cases it was regarded as something that would happen at the end of time. Isaiah 1:27 says, "Zion shall be redeemed by justice." At a future time the sin and corruption of the city will be removed by the judgment of God. "For the LORD is a God of justice. . . ." (Isaiah 30:18)

By the time the books of the New Testament were written, belief in the resurrection of the body had entered Jewish thought. (Daniel 12:2) Since a notion of judgment was already present, it is easy to see why many passages in the New Testament testify to the early Christian belief in a future, universal judgment by God of the living and the dead. In Matthew 25:31 the Son of man is pictured as coming to judge the living and dead.

The idea of God as judge is directly connected with the view of him as king. Such doctrines as the providence of God, which includes the doctrine of God's sovereignty, has long been popular in Christian theology. In the ancient world a king exercised his control by making judgments. God was thought of as a king by analogy. It was natural that his function of judging would be used as an extension of the idea. His complete and ultimate kingship, when he established it in the future through the last or future judgment, would be the kingdom of God. It was also natural to extend the image backward in time as well as to project it forward. Theologians held that beginning with creation God had acted both as king and judge. In every crisis afterward, in the present, and in the future, he acts in these offices.

Many of the earliest theologians held these views. Augustine, bishop of Hippo (354-430), expressed in his *City of God*, the view of history and God's judgment that dominated Christian thought until well into modern times. And it still exerts very great influence.

Among modern theologians, the doctrine of the judgment of God has received many different treatments. But scarcely any movement has emphasized it as much as neo-orthodoxy. In the many writings of Karl Barth (1886-   ) one finds many pages devoted to this concept. Barth strenuously argues for a view of God's providence that demands that his final judgment be consistent with his revelation in Jesus Christ. For

Barth this means that the final judgment will culminate and make universal the love God has revealed for his creation. In spite of the long history of fear connected with certain theological explanations of the last judgment, Barth strongly witnesses to the power of God's love and mercy.

However it may be explained, it is clear that any Christian concept of the judgment of God is inseparably connected with time and history, and the decisions, actions, and events within history. (*see Analogy, Dogmatics, Providence*) J.B.W.

JUS CIVILIS, JUS GENTIUM (*see Natural law*)

Justice The biblical concept of justice is built on the conviction that God is a righteous or just God (Amos 9; Jeremiah 23:6). God treats men fairly. God's judgments on a human life are never in error. At present it may be that the wicked prosper while the righteous suffer (Psalm 73), but in the end this will not be the case. Justice holds in close connection God's mercy or love and God's wrath. God is a "no-nonsense" God (Amos 5:21-27). He is not to be mocked (Deuteronomy 5:8-11). God has given man his laws so that man may know what is expected of him (Deuteronomy 5:32-33; 6:4-9). Now that he has these laws he can be sure that God holds him accountable when he breaks them (Joshua 23:14-16).

In the Bible God's relation to man is revealed through the law and the prophets. Thus, man discovers his relationship to other people. Genuine religion should show itself in human behavior (James 1:27). God's fair treatment of man is to lead man to treat others fairly (Amos 8:4-5).

Paul continued the Old Testament view that man's righteousness stems from God's righteousness. What, though, if those who believed in God were unrighteous? Would that mean that God is unrighteous? "By no means!" answered Paul. "Let God be true though every man be false . . ." (Romans 3:4). The only way man can become righteous is through God's grace. The concept of justification by faith preserves the initiative of God. Further, it enables Paul to get around the problem of the law and its failure. Since man is set free from sin by God's grace, he can no longer think to improve his moral life by good deeds or obedience to the law. Instead, he is called to love his neighbor. Paul begins this argument in Romans 3, but the conclusion that ethics flows from salvation does not emerge clearly until Chapter 12.

Augustine (354-430) follows Paul in the conviction that God's love calls man to be concerned about the neighbor. Man wrongly desires to possess others and hurt them. He lusts after power over others. A man insults other men in order to make himself feel big. Such acts receive an appropriate reward. Martin Luther (1483-1546) uses the term "justice" primarily as a means of describing God's relation to man. God by his very nature is fair.

Jacques Maritain (1882-   ) develops the idea that justice is a part of nature. It is a part of the moral make-up of the world in which man lives. It is as much a part of his life as the law of gravity. Moral laws are present and will remain regardless of what man does, but a man's life will be hurt if he does not recognize and obey these laws.

Paul Tillich (1886-1965) views justice as the form of being and love as the principle of justice. Tillich assumes that created being is cut off from the ground of Being (God). Love is the attempt of these two to be reunited. Since there has to be order as well as impulse, justice serves to give form to being.

Paul Ramsey (1913-   ) criticizes Tillich's view. Justice is given no real meaning. Unless justice can be spelled out in laws and principles, it will be at the mercy of power. Ramsey himself sees justice as the means used by love to accomplish its purpose. For example, love seeks to prevent harm to a neighbor under attack. To ward off the attacker, love is permitted to use force, such as limited warfare. Justice is the use of right means out of love.

Emil Brunner (1889-1967) views justice as the constant standards by which man lives. Love is spontaneous. In some moments a man is loving but not in all moments. However, a man can constantly and in all minutes treat others fairly. Christian love always includes a concern for justice.

For Reinhold Niebuhr (1892-   ) Christian love is a perfect ideal, never attainable in society. Love drives man to seek justice in complex social relationships. In any form of society some men get less than a fair deal. Laws and customs, though protecting some people's interests, fail to protect the interests of others. The Christian's concern for justice shows itself in two specific ways. First, the Christian is concerned to change the laws and customs of society in order to make them more nearly fair to all men. This is a job that is never completed. In history there is no such thing as a perfect law or a perfect society. Second, the Christian seeks to be of immediate help to those who are suffering (by poverty and oppression, *etc.*) because of the structure of the present social order. (*see Natural law, Righteousness*) J.S.H.

Justification by faith   Justification by faith means that man is brought into a right relationship to God, self, and neighbor through faith. This phrase was used by Martin Luther (1483-1546) in his opposition to the Roman Catholic church's teaching on merit. The medieval church taught that God's grace enables man to do good deeds.

If man does these good deeds he can come to have the right relationship to God. What man does is effective in bringing man into the right relationship. Luther taught that man is to trust in God's acceptance of him. Trusting in God's acceptance man is able then to concern himself with the work a Christian is called upon to do—the will of God. (*see Acceptance, Justice, Law*) J.S.H.

KAIROS (*see Time*)

KAPHAR (*see Atonement*)

Kenosis (keh-*noh*-sehs) This word is derived from the Greek verb meaning "to empty." So we speak of biblical passages that are kenotic, *i.e.*, they contain the concept of "emptying," for example, of divine nature. Or we speak of a "kenosis," *i.e.*, of the act of emptying. The noun *kenosis* does not occur in the New Testament. The verb occurs in Philippians 2:7, translated by the RSV as "emptied himself." This passage is by far the most famous of the so-called kenotic passages in the Scriptures. Although it has been argued that the passage has to do with the earthly life of Jesus only, it is more probable that it deals with three stages: (1) the pre-existent being who could have grasped equality with God, but instead emptied himself of his divinity; (2) he became a man, obedient even unto death on a cross; (3) for his obedience God exalted him to the office of *Kyrios* (Lord). This passage has been identified by Ernst Lohmeyer (1890-1946) as a pre-Pauline hymn, and this identification has received widespread acceptance. Nonetheless, the kenotic idea is expressed elsewhere by Paul, for example, in 2 Corinthians 8:9, so that the passage seems representative of Paul's thought.

It is to be noted that in the Philippians passage Christ's emptying is in terms not only of laying aside his divinity but also in his humility (he becomes a slave), and in his obedience even unto death. In the Letter to the Hebrews a somewhat similar situation occurs. In that book, attention is first paid to the eternal Son, who is in fact the Logos, but who appears in history as Jesus. Great stress is placed on the suffering of Jesus, a fact that enabled him to become the supreme mediator between God and man. Whenever the element of pre-existence appears, the kenotic view is possible; the earthly life of Jesus may then be viewed as an emptying of the divine. This is the situation, at least, if Philippians 2:6-11 is seen as the model.

The prologue to John's Gospel has sometimes been viewed in this manner. There, Jesus is presented as the pre-existent Logos, who was "with God" and "was God." But "the Logos became flesh and dwelt among us," a statement sometimes interpreted to mean that he left his divine nature behind. But this is hardly true of the Jesus of John's Gospel. That is the Gospel in which Jesus says, " 'He who has seen me has seen the Father.' " John's Jesus has come into the world bearing with him all the prerogatives of deity. Even when Jesus washes the disciples' feet (John 13), he does so as their Master and Lord. The servant of John 13 differs radically from the servant of Philippians 2:6-11.

The relation of *kenosis* to Jesus develops out of the contrast between his lowly earthly life on the one hand and the exalted ideas of God on the other. Many of the titles applied to Jesus by the church, such as Son of man, Lord, and Logos, suggested the idea of exaltation and could not easily be reconciled with the church's memory of the historical person. Paramount in that memory was Jesus' death on a cross, a fact that seemed to be at the opposite pole from the exaltation of the divine.

One answer given by the church was to adjust the titles to the historical situation regarding Jesus' humble, sacrificial life; and this Mark does in his view of Jesus as the suffering Son of man. The Old Testament concept of the suffering servant served to support this view. Increasingly, the life of suffering and service is seen to be altogether compatible with the function of the Christ, so that in John's Gospel the cross is viewed more as an ascent to the Father, as glorification, and not as a *kenosis*. Service and obedience are seen to be the sign of Jesus' divine life and not the reverse. Thus we see that the kenotic view of Jesus' life represents the church's attempt to come to terms with the question of his humanity in relation to exalted ideas of divinity. The stronger the split between God and the world, the more difficult it was to resolve the problem. In the New Testament period, the church did not seek to resolve the problem philosophically. It undertook, rather, to present its "solution" through dramatic representations: legend, myth, parable, *etc.* So Christ is represented as leaving his heavenly position and "descending" to earth, becoming man, and then, through death and resurrection, returning to a position of exaltation at the right hand of God. The *kenosis* theory must then be viewed as an aspect of the developing christology of the Christian church. (*see Ascension, Christology, Name*) E.L.T.

163

Kerygma (keh-*rig*-mah, keh-*roog*-mah) *Kerygma* is a Greek word, meaning "proclamation." It is applied to the subject matter of the gospel, to the message of the sermon, or to the preaching itself. The verb "to preach" or "proclaim" is found in connection with Jesus' own basic proclamation of the early coming of the Kingdom of God (Mark 1:14-15).

In the area of present-day New Testament study, however, the term is used more specifically of the content of the early Christian message. C. H. Dodd (1884-   ) considers the early Christian *kerygma* to have included a recounting of the life and work of Christ, his "conflicts, sufferings and death, and his resurrection from the dead." Further, it connected these events with the divinely guided history of Israel, for in them that history had reached its climax. This, says Dodd, is the core of the early Christian preaching.

Dodd distinguishes clearly between *kerygma* and *didache* (*did*-uh-kay). The former confronted men with God's act in Christ, and they consented to or rejected the message. If they consented, placing themselves under the judgment and mercy of God in Christ, they became members of the community, the church. As members of the church, they then received instruction, *didache*. This was instruction in morals as distinct from the proclamation of the gospel, *kerygma*. Dodd stresses the fact that this was the characteristic order of approach: first the *kerygma*, and then the *didache*. He points out that this approach has a real analogy in Jewish tradition, where a clear distinction is made between *haggada*, the declaration of religious truth, and *halakha*, regulations governing conduct. Dodd's ideas are set forth in his books *The Apostolic Preaching and Its Development* (1936) and *Gospel and Law* (1951).

It has become commonplace in New Testament study to accept the kerygmatic proclamation as basic to Christian beginnings. Though scholars differ about the various elements that go to make up the whole, all agree the death and resurrection of Jesus are central, and all see Christ as the eschatological act of God. An early example of the *kerygma* is found in 1 Corinthians 15:1-11, which includes the following items: (1) Christ died for our sins, in accordance with the Scriptures; (2) he was buried; (3) he was raised on the third day according to the Scriptures; (4) he appeared to Cephas and to others. This formula is particularly important for it is dated from a time before Paul himself, as his words in verse 3 indicate: "For I delivered to you as of first importance what I also received. . . ." This is technical language to point out the passage of tradition. Other New Testament passages that seem to include kerygmatic formulations are Romans 1:1-4; Acts 2:22-24; and 1 Timothy 3:16. These passages, however, are but examples of ways in which the proclamation of the gospel became stated in rather precise ways. The fact is that the New Testament as a whole is kerygmatic in the general sense that it presents the Christ event as God's redemptive act. Even *didache* is based on the assumption that the new age has been ushered in by the work of Christ, although its fulfillment is still in the future. (*see Kingdom of God*) E.L.T.

Kiddush (keh-*doosh*) The sabbath was one of the most important institutions of Judaism in biblical times. Consequently, the marking out of the sabbath from the other days of the week was of special importance. The introduction of the sabbath was observed by a ceremony known as the *Kiddush* ("sanctification"). The ceremony consisted of the blessing of a cup of wine by the head of the household, the blessing of the wine and of the sabbath, the drinking from the "cup of blessing," a blessing on the loaves, and the partaking of a meal.

Some scholars have seen in the *Kiddush* a similarity with the Lord's Supper, and have concluded that the latter grew out of the former. There is no real evidence for this conclusion. The Synoptic Gospels view the Supper as a Passover meal, although the absence of the usual elements of the Passover meal, such as the unleavened bread, the lamb, and the bitter herbs, causes problems for this identification. The Synoptics are probably saying that the Lord's Supper takes the place of the Jewish Passover; it celebrates the new covenant introduced through the death of Jesus. (*see Communion*) E.L.T.

Kingdom of God The Synoptic Gospels point to the kingdom of God as a major theme of the preaching and teaching of Jesus. Used interchangeably with the kingdom of Heaven, the term might be more accurately translated, "the reigning of God," affirming that the kingdom is the Lord's. When Jesus began his ministry in Galilee, he announced the " 'kingdom of God is at hand' " (Mark 1:15). There are about 115 other biblical references in which Jesus strongly emphasized the Kingdom, both by statement and example. Notable among these are his petition in the Lord's Prayer, " 'Thy kingdom come' " (Matthew 6: 10); " 'seek first his kingdom' " (Matthew 6:33); descriptions of the Kingdom (Matthew 13:24 *ff*.); riches and the kingdom (Mark 10:23-25); the poor and the Kingdom (Luke 6:20); and the Last Supper and the Kingdom (Luke 22:16-18). The parables of Jesus might be described as the parables of the kingdom of God.

The kingdom of God as Jesus presented it is not man's kingdom but God's. " 'The kingdom of God is in the midst of you' " (Luke 17:21), implies that God sends the kingdom. His reign is not dependent upon man's initiative but allows for man's response to God's offer.

Two New Testament views of the time-span of the Kingdom are present and future. Like the mustard seed, it is now present in a small way but will expand and become greater (Mark 4:30-32). Hearers are advised

165

not to anticipate the arrival of the Kingdom at a later time with visible signs, for it is already in the midst of them (Luke 17:20-21). On the other hand, there is a note of expectancy by which God will manifest himself later to intervene in human history and establish a more spectacular divine rule (Luke 21:5-36). Jesus encouraged his listeners to await cautiously the signs of the approaching Kingdom and be ready for it. Paul seems to say that the Kingdom cannot exist in this world (1 Corinthians 15:50).

In *City of God*, Augustine of Hippo (354-430) seemed to separate the kingdom of God from the kingdom of man. God's kingdom is the realm of pure justice, toward which the church strives. The "earthly city" is the realm of pride, greed, and injustice. A closer examination of *City of God* proves, however, that the author saw both cities present in the other. The church, for example, lives in the earthly city, but it embodies some of the qualities of the heavenly city.

Theologians have, for the most part, selected one or another of these views. Some take still another road and view the Kingdom as the ethical reign in human affairs, as a society of men trying to live up to the love-ethic. C. H. Dodd (1884-   ) has tried to solve the tension between its future and present reality by calling the coming period the "now-period" of the church, thus placing eschatological (or future) truth in operation now. In effect, this view sees the Kingdom as coming again and again. Dodd's view of "realized eschatology" is supported by such texts as Luke 11:20. References to the future, says Dodd, came from the early church, but not from Jesus' teachings. To Albert Schweitzer (1875-1966), Jesus believed the supernatural end of the world would come in his lifetime. Albrecht Ritschl (1822-89) interprets the kingdom as the consummation of human history, the event toward which the whole Creation moves. (*see* Ascension, Eschatology, History, Messiah, PAROUSIA) G.E.S.

KINGDOMTIDE (*see Pentecost*)

KNOWLEDGE (*see Epistemology*)

Koine (koy-*nay*)   *Koine* is a Greek word meaning "common." The English adjective usually refers to the kind of Greek employed in the period of the rise of Christianity. Sometimes the expression "Hellenistic Greek" is used as a synonym of "Koine Greek." However, the latter use is extremely widespread. The New Testament is written in *Koine* Greek, which was the language of the common people of the Hellenistic age. We may say that this kind of Greek is common in two senses: (a) that it was non-literary, differing from the Attic or classical

Greek of the educated people; (b) that it was widespread, and so, common to a great many peoples and regions.

Since this kind of Greek was widespread, it follows that a great many works, in addition to the New Testament, were written in it. This was true of the Septuagint (LXX) (the Greek translation of the Hebrew Old Testament); of the writings of Josephus, the historian; of Philo's writings; and of many others. *Koine* Greek, while not technically "literary," is a strong, vigorous instrument of expression. In the New Testament, quality of Greek ranges from relatively weak to strong. E.L.T.

Koinonia (koy-noh-*nee*-ah) This Greek word is often translated as "fellowship." In the non-biblical Greek of the New Testament period it often has the meaning of (a) business association, (b) the marriage relationship, and (c) a person's relationship to God. It is clear how easily the word could pass over into Christian use to express the meaning of the Christian fellowship. Some of the more notable New Testament uses of the word are: (a) It expresses the fellowship of Christians one with another (Acts 2:42; Galatians 2:9; Philippians 1:5; Philemon 6; 1 John 1:3, 7). (b) It is used of the sharing of material things (Romans 15:26; 2 Corinthians 8:4; 9:13; Hebrews 13:16). (c) It is used of fellowship in the Spirit (2 Corinthians 13:14; Philippians 2:1). (d) It is used of fellowship with God and with Christ (1 John 1:3; 1 Corinthians 1:9). (e) It is used at least once in connection with the Lord's Supper (1 Corinthians 10:16).

At its deeper levels, *koinonia* is far more than good will. Its meaning in the New Testament is determined largely by a view of the nature of the church. The church of the New Testament is more than an assembly of people come together for purposes, however good. For one thing, the church is the eschatological people of God, fulfilling the ancient covenant promise. This makes the fellowship something quite special and distinct, and not at all a casual affair. Paul speaks of the church as the body of Christ (1 Corinthians 12:12 *ff.*), an analogy that underscores the organic unity of the church and the interrelatedness of the various members. The divine nature of the church is strongly set forth in the Gospel of John, where the believer is caught up in the unity of Christ and the Father (John 17:16-26). Christian *koinonia*, therefore, receives its quality from the underlying assumptions about the nature of the church itself.

The New Testament idea of *koinonia* has received fresh attention in modern times, especially in connection with the ecumenical movement. This movement sees the need for a doctrine of the church that will give adequate attention to the concept of *koinonia*, a sense of community in the New Testament sense of the word. The complex character of modern society, the dangers of the atomic age, the deep rifts within the church

167

itself—all give new importance to the idea of fellowship or sharing that is basic to *koinonia*. Some feel that the real ecumenical or universal church will emerge at this level rather than on the level of a super-organization. But this view of *koinonia* must not be seen as mere friendliness. It continues the historic Christian position only if it is related to the nature of the church as the body of Christ. (*see Church, Covenant*, EKKLESIA, LAOS) E.L.T.

Kyrie (also *Kyrie eleison*) (*keh*-ree ee-*lay*-ee-sahn) From the same root as the Greek word, *Kurios* (Lord), these are the Greek words for "Lord have mercy." It is the most common response to prayers in the litanies of the Greek and Syrian churches. It is also used in Anglican, Lutheran, and other Protestant churches. The Roman Catholic Mass uses it as a nine-fold response following the introit. (*see Liturgy*) G.E.S.

LAITY (*see* LAOS)

LAMB OF GOD (*see Agnus Dei, Atonement, Sacrifice*)

Language *The word "language" comes from the Latin lingua, which means "tongue." Christians are interested in language because the Bible says that God acts through language (John 1:1). Non-Christians say that language is important because man of all the animals uses it well. Some thinkers have said that Christians are not very careful users of language. They say you need to use language that proves something. When someone says, "It is raining," you can prove the saying by going outdoors. But how can you prove that "God is love"? In reply, Christians have tried to show the real meaning of the Bible and of the Christian faith. Language means more than the use of words, however; it means the use of skills. Music is a language. In the same way, Christian symbols make up a language of their own. To be a Christian is to understand Christian language. One important fact about Christian language is that it deals with history—man's story that he tells about his life in space and time.*

"In the beginning was the Word, and the Word was with God, and the Word was God . . . . all things were made through him, and without him was not anything made that was made." (John 1:1, 3) One of the most notable characteristics of the Bible is that God's creative action is described as *speaking*. From Genesis to Revelation language is a key to the whole.

Throughout the history of Christianity, language has concerned Christian thinkers. In recent decades theologians, both Protestant and Catholic, have once again given attention to it. It is a problem that challenges us in several ways. The most basic problem of language is the level of simple communication. The form of language that theologians use is an additional problem. Finally, the Bible as a literary document uses language unusually. To translate the Bible from the original languages into some other tongue is obviously a problem.

Theologians are but a few of the thinkers in our contemporary setting who have been forced to re-examine language. Psychologists, philosophers, language teachers, poets—these are some of the participants in this re-examination. R. N. Anshen has written: "Man *is* language." Others have agreed by arguing that language is the most basic form of the *human* experience of reality.

The effect of investigating language, especially by certain philosophers, has created many problems for religion. Some of those philosophers, known as language analysts, have severely criticized Christian theologians and believers for their uncritical use of language. They have turned their attention upon the question, "What do words (language) mean?" In order to answer that question they have argued that tests must be applied to any use of language. The first and most damaging test is that in order for any statement to mean *anything*, one must be able to prove it. For example, the statement, "It is raining," can be proved by getting away from cover, such as a roof or an umbrella, to see if one becomes wet from falling water. Therefore, to say, "It is raining," is a meaningful statement. It is true or false, and it can be tested. But how does one test a religious statement such as "God is love"? There is no test that anyone could use to prove or disprove the statement. These philosophers therefore decided that religious statements are not meaningful. A great debate followed. Few religious people or theologians were willing to accept such a philosophical judgment. But many theologians have become quite aware of the difficulties with their use of language.

One of the results of the general discussion about language has been that some theologians have become critical of traditional religious language. Even the words of the Bible have been criticized. One notable instance of this has been the work of Rudolf Bultmann (1884-   ), the famous German New Testament scholar and theologian. Bultmann has insisted that whatever possibility modern man has for becoming Christian depends on whether modern man can understand the language of the Bible. Man today, as always, has living questions, such as, "What must I do to be saved?" Only by stripping away those outdated forms of language that prevent us from hearing the Bible's response to such a question will the Bible "speak" its word.

Language, however, must not be too severely limited. All symbols created by man as he responds to and participates in life experiences must be understood as language. This, of course, suggests that just as skills must be mastered in order to understand spoken language and other skills to comprehend the meanings of written language, so the ability to understand other languages must be learned. Art, music, architecture, drama—these are but a few of the languages that must be mastered fully to become literate. In religion the language of symbolic actions and forms must be learned. The liturgy—celebrations of thanksgiving, marrying, baptizing, dying—must be viewed as a language that speaks its own powerful testimonies to faith, hope, and love.

The insight that language is the means by which men express their experiences of reality leads to the further conclusion that of all the religions of the world, none is more historical than Christianity. For it is now clear that, as the late Carl Michalson (1915-65), a Methodist theologian, wrote, "At this very moment all history exists either in the living memory of those who know it or in some documentary form—a scroll, a vase, a fossil or a ruin. . . . history is nothing apart from the language through which it survives." ("Language, History, and Meaning," *Theology Today*, Vol. XIX, No. 1 [April, 1962], page 4) The languages of Christianity—its Scriptures, preaching, theology, prayers, church buildings, liturgies—attest to its historical nature. Without these languages, Christianity would not exist, for God's actions as experienced by men in time would not be known. (*see History, Image of God, Meaningful, Symbol, Verification*) J.B.W.

Laos (*lay*-ahs) This term is used of "people" generally in the sense of the "crowd," but also of the populace; it is used of the "people" as a nation; it is used of the "people of God," whether of the people of Israel or of Christians. It is the last use that gives the word its distinctive importance for the church. In order to grasp the significance of the term it is necessary to understand the importance of the concept of the chosen people in the history of Israel, and to recognize the relation of the Christian church to that history.

Growing out of Israel's conviction that it had a covenant relation with God was the far-reaching belief that the nation was God's chosen people. It is along this line that one must approach the church's self-understanding. The church did not consider itself as separate from the sacred history of the people of God, but rather that it continued and fulfilled that history. It is not accidental that the Christian sacred meal, the Eucharist, speaks of a new covenant in the blood of Jesus. Nor is it accidental that the Christian church has as its Scripture the Old Testament. It was perfectly natural for the early followers of Jesus, who were Jews, to maintain the tradition native to them and to see in Jesus the fulfillment of its promises. Jesus and the church, from their point of view, was the event to which the Scriptures pointed. The church was the people of God, the covenant people, and in no sense a new group distinct from the sacred history of the people of God.

The concept of the people of God in the New Testament is given a peculiar character because of eschatology. For the Christians were convinced that in the event of Christ, his life, death and resurrection, God had acted decisively in history and that the end was near. The church was the eschatological fellowship, standing in the last days, and so the people of God in an especially favored sense. All that was past was prelude to this new age of God's decisive act in Christ. The flood tide of God's creative energy is now realized in the church of God. But no longer is it a matter of national identity, for the church is open to Jew or Greek alike. It is for this reason that the writer of 1 Peter can say to a church composed largely of Gentiles: "But you are a chosen race, a royal priesthood, a holy nation, God's own people. . . . Once you were no people but now you are God's people; once you had not received mercy but now you have received mercy." (2:9-10)

The view of the church as the people of God involves a view of the position of the laity and of the clergy within its structure. A layman, in the biblical sense of a member of the "people of God," is a priest and minister of the church of Jesus Christ; and, conversely, all "ministers" are "laymen." This view of the layman as a minister along with the professional minister is being reemphasized in present-day attempts at church renewal. This emphasis takes its strength from the fact that it is a position which is fully biblical, which means, simply, that it is true to the original concept of "church."

Sometimes the view of the church as the people of God has been explained in terms of the doctrine of the priesthood of all believers. But this doctrine, which was asserted in the Reformation to combat notions of a human intermediary between God and man, does not do justice to the full range of possibilities included in the biblical view of the people of God. The church, as the people of God, stands as the responsible mediator of God and the gospel of Christ to the world at large. Thus, the concept includes a motive 'for the world mission of the church. (*see Church, Covenant,* EKKLESIA, KOINONIA, *Mission*) E.L.T.

LAUDS (*see Office*)

Law *Laws may be civil, moral, religious, or natural. In the early period of history different kinds of law are considered together. For example, in the early history of Israel there was no clear-cut distinction beween religious laws and civil laws. The Old Testament law is preserved for us in the first five books of the Bible. These laws are a description of what is required of the people of God. In the New Testament the role of law in the religious life is more critically examined. Today law is considered to play widely varying roles in the different ethical systems. Legalistic thinkers stress man's need to conform strictly to a list of rules or laws. The antinomians evaluate laws as being of no value and suggest that man needs no laws (or almost none) to guide him. Other thinkers evaluate law in a manner somewhere between these two. Lex naturalis, natural law, means those structures inherent in human life that can be discovered by reason.*

The Old Testament understanding of the law is grounded in the idea of a covenant people. God has established Israel as his people, and Israel has certain obligations to God. The law lists what Israel is and is not to do. This list of "do's and don'ts" describes how life's purpose is to be accomplished. The laws serve the one basic purpose of helping maintain human life in community.

Law in the Old Testament is not a burden but a helpmate to man. Law presupposes God's grace and mercy. The Old Testament is not a loveless law book. Laws give content and direction to love. Jesus' summary of the law reflects this basic dependence of the law upon love: he who loves God, neighbor, and self has fulfilled the law.

Before the Exodus, Israel did have laws. These laws influenced and shaped the actual written laws. The oldest code of laws that we know of today is the code of Hammurabi of Babylon (dating from about 1700 B.C.). Some of the basic ideas reflected in this code are also reflected in the Israelite laws. Other law codes discovered in the Near East also reflect similarities to the code of laws preserved and passed down in the Israelite community.

The Torah, Jewish law, is contained in the first five books of the Old Testament, the Pentateuch. Old Testament law is a demand made on man that will bring life and blessing if it is obeyed. This demand is closely connected with religious experience. Law is given or revealed by God. It gives to man the totality of God's will. The law is in accordance with and looks forward to the final victories of God. External or written law will not be necessary when God provides man with the new covenant, for then all that the law calls for will be written on man's heart.

Law in the New Testament usually refers to the law contained in the Old Testament. In the New Testament Jesus is presented as replacing the law. Jesus now becomes the mediator between man and God.

Jesus is presented in the New Testament as affirming the law and not canceling it.

Karl Barth (1886-   ), in *The Epistle to the Romans* (pages 77-91), interprets Paul as presenting Christ as the end (or death) of the law. Man as sinner is unable by use of the law to set right the bad relationships that are his. In fact, if man tries to use the law in order to establish the right relationship to God he makes his relationship to God even worse. Man is called upon to recognize the fact that he has no possibility of developing or establishing his own righteousness. If man is to have a life that is rightly related to self, God and others, he will receive the possibility of new life in faith as a gift from God. Through faith in Jesus Christ man is restored to the right relationship to God.

In early Greek thought obedience to the law is viewed as righteousness. Here law meant the civic law or the law of the land. Socrates' (*c.* 470-399 B.C.) devotion to the law of the land is symbolic of the high reverence Greek thought has for law and order. Socrates' decision that it is better for him to be put to death rather than break the law of the land is grounded in the conviction that life must be orderly.

Law is sometimes used in a general way to indicate "every observed regularity." Not until the eighteenth century were laws of nature distinguished from other laws. Today "law" is used to refer to facts of nature. "The law of the land" is a phrase used to refer to our constitution, which lays down the general principles of community life in America. Law is also used to refer to the national, state, and city rules. Moral laws describe facts of life with regard to human relationships. "Religious laws" are the rules describing man's right relation to God, neighbor, and self. Religious laws overlap the other categories since they include ethical rules and ritual rules that describe how certain religious practices are to be conducted.

Present day discussions reflect basically three different attitudes with regard to the laws. One understanding of law places rules and regulation at the center of man's decision making. Man needs a specific set of rules to guide him in life. Legalism indicates complete devotion and unswerving loyalty to the law. Paul Ramsey (1913-   ) suggests that Christian love is the means of arriving at an answer to the problem of absolutism versus relativism. An absolute list of rigid, specific rules will become totally irrelevant over a short period of time. A completely relative approach to ethics, which omits rules, fails to give man any of the stability he needs. Christian ethics is grounded in love. Out of this love grow some general rules or principles that are always valid. In each period of history the community of faith is faced with the obligation of pointing out what ought to be done in specific cases; however, rules can be relied on until the need to make an exception is clear.

A second evaluation of the law is known as antinomianism (which see)
This position holds that man does not need any principles or rules to
help him make decisions. Man goes into the moment armed with his
faith; that is all he needs. A third evaluation of law has been called situation ethics. The Christian needs ethical rules to help him make decisions.
He needs his reason; he needs revelation; he needs to learn from his own
past experiences and the past experiences of his community. The Christian is to use all the help he can find from these resources. They are to
be used to help man meet human needs. They are not to be obeyed if
obeying them will be more destructive of human life than breaking them
would be. Rules may need to be broken on occasions. No set of rules will
be right for any and all situations. In any given situation there are many
factors involved. For example, a man may be faced with the decision to
tell a lie or refuse to tell a lie. But this is not the only question confronting him. What will be the result of his either lying or not lying? Perhaps
telling the truth, which is morally good, generally speaking, will be more
destructive of human life than a lie would be. Each decision is made in
a context and the whole context has an effect on the outcome of the
decision. Thus, man should take into consideration the context (or the
whole situation) in which his decision is made. Likewise, the effects
of any decision are actually varied. As man weighs the different factors
involved in a decision, he cannot know in advance all the factors involved. Neither can he be sure in advance of the total effect of his decision. Man is called upon to weigh the factors involved, examine the
different possibilities open to him, and then calculate which one of the
possible courses open to him will be the best one. Reinhold Niebuhr
(1892-   ) coined the phrase "neatly calculated less and more" to
refer to this complex decision making process. Man's decisions are "more
or less" right and "more or less" wrong.

Some Christians think this third position does not give sinful man
the support he needs. Sinful man is looking for an excuse for breaking
the law. The third position could be misused in this way; however, it
should be remembered that it is not an attempt to free man from his
responsibilities; rather, this position lays upon man the same radical responsibility that the New Testament describes as the fulfilling of the law
(Matthew 22:37-40). (see Antinomian, Deontological, Grace, Legalism,
Principle) J.S.H.

Lectionary   A book that contains a listing of the liturgical readings to be used in the worship of the church, it includes passages from the Scriptures (Epistles and Gospels), writings of the fathers
and saints, and lessons to be read. (see Liturgy) G.E.S.

LEFT (see Conservative)

Legalism   Legalism is concerned that the law be followed in any and all circumstances. If man is to be either moral or religious or both, he needs a set of laws. If man is strictly obedient to the law, then he is a good man. Legalism assumes there is never a reason for not obeying the law. The opponents of legalism sometimes use the term in a derogatory sense to mean outward conformity to the law, a conformity that misses the inner meeting and purpose of the law.

The Old Testament emphasizes the importance of the law and recognizes as severe the consequences of breaking the law (Deuteronomy 28: 58-68). There are many passages in the Old Testament that support legalism as the proper approach to life (Deuteronomy 22-26, especially 26:16-19). However, it would be wrong to assume that in the Old Testament life is considered to be strictly a matter of following rules (Hosea 1-2). Love and mercy, as is law, are necessary ingredients to the moral life. In the New Testament it is even more obvious that the law is not the final authority for man. Jesus' attitude toward the law was one of neither complete acceptance nor complete rejection (Matthew 5:17-48; Mark 2:23-28). He viewed the law as being of service to man. However, in the New Testament there are passages that seem to indicate that man should never break the law (Matthew 5:18).

Legalism has been more or less present as a live influence throughout the history of the Christian church. When the Christian church has decided to break free from a certain law, it has usually replaced that law with another one. The scribes are the legalists in the New Testament. The Puritans are examples of legalists in the Christian church. They assume that the Scripture is a legal code to be followed. Beginning with the Scripture they develop a list of "do's and don'ts" that are to be followed in all cases. This sometimes is referred to as ʼbiblical legalism. Roman Catholic legalists begin with an examination of nature. The mind is to be used to discover in nature certain principles and laws. These laws of nature are to be followed in all cases.

In another sense, legalism is the view that the contents of right and wrong actions can and should be specific. Some ethical thinkers are formalists, which means they are willing to spell out theories and principles of ethics without declaring particular actions to be right or wrong. Formalists insist that Christian ethics has the responsibility for enlightening persons to make decisions, but that the individual has the final responsibility for making the decision.

Legalists, however, are unwilling to leave the law as an abstraction. They believe that particular actions are more nearly right or wrong, depending on their agreement with the law. Christian legalists, for example, may declare abstinence from alcoholic beverages to be right, and racial integration also. Though Christians in favor of abstinence are usually classified as "conservatives," and Christians in favor of integra-

175

tion as "liberals," in both cases a particular action is judged to be right.

Thus, legalism may or may not be considered a negative word, depending on its use. The problems facing legalism are many, but a case can be made for it. (*see Antinomian, Casuistry*) J.S.H.

Legend "Legend" is a literary form and, contrary to popular thought, does not in itself deny that an event really happened. It is to be distinguished from "myth," which deals with the gods as the main characters. Legend has to do with man rather than with the gods. This is a general point of distinction, although at times the lines may be blurred. Sometimes a distinction is made within the definition of legend itself, namely, between etiological (which see) and hero or personal legends. The former relate to the origin of things, such as cult practices, shrines, names, and customs. Hero or personal legends have to do with the exploits of a great person or in some way carry on the memory of his greatness. Though legend does not deny the possibility of a historical core residing in or lying behind the story, it is also true that the historical cannot be established by the standards of historical writing. Modern students of history have seen that all history is pervaded by the legendary, and that in all probability these elements have survived because of the core of historicity they contain.

With the advent of form criticism and its application to the biblical materials, formal structures such as the legend have been studied at length by scholars. As a result, legends have been identified in the Old Testament at Genesis 19 (an etiological legend) and Genesis 12–15; Exodus 1–14; Judges 13–16 (legends of the heroic variety).

The leading thinkers of form criticism have also found examples of legendary materials in the New Testament. Martin Dibelius (1883-1947), for example, speaks of Luke 2:41 *ff.* as the story of Jesus that reveals most closely the marks of legend. He identifies many more illustrations of this type of material, including the birth stories of Matthew and Luke, although Dibelius identifies four independent legends in Luke's story of Jesus' childhood (apart from the story of the twelve-year-old Jesus).

Dibelius feels that the legends of the Gospels served a double need: the desire on the part of early Christians (1) to know something about the men and women around Jesus, and (2) to know Jesus himself in the same way. The story of Jesus in the Temple at the age of twelve illustrates the first type; the account of Peter walking on the sea would be an example of the second type (Matthew 14:28-33).

The Gospel writers tend not to be preoccupied with the protection of Jesus that is characteristic of stories in the apocryphal Infancy Gospels. In the so-called infancy Gospel of Thomas, Jesus is presented as one who creates birds from clay and gives them life. He calls a dead playmate back to life in order that he may testify to Jesus. Similarly, in the apocryphal Acts, Peter and other disciples do fantastic things, such as making a dog talk and a smoked fish swim. The synoptic Gospels are not entirely free of this tendency, to be sure (compare Luke 4:29-30; Mark 11:14, 21; Matthew 17:27), but it is the exception rather than the rule.

In view of the prominence sometimes attached to the birth stories of the Gospels, it might be said that, while the stories are made up of legendary materials, the stories are literary monuments to the church's estimate of Jesus. It is unfortunate that the stories have been made to bear a historical weight that, in terms of their literary character, they are unable to bear. They should be read not as history but more as poetry and as an expression of piety. This is a principle that might apply to other examples of legend in the biblical materials. (*see Form criticism, History, Myth*) E.L.T.

Lent This is the forty day period between Ash Wednesday and Easter Sunday (excluding Sundays) marked as a period of preparation and penitence. In the early days of the church, it was a time to prepare for baptism, which took place on Easter Eve. It is now used as a time for study, personal and congregational worship, and spiritual renewal. (*see Ash Wednesday, Good Friday, Maundy Thursday, Shrove Tuesday, Easter*) G.E.S.

LEVITE (*see Priest*)

LIBERALISM (*see Natural theology*)

LIBIDO (*see Love*)

Life In the Old Testament the word "life" is used to indicate concrete existence. It does not refer to some vague principle. It is used to indicate man's actual physical existence. This existence is a gift from God. Man is to use his life in service to the one who has given it to him. Life is a good gift that, if man uses it properly, will prove to be a blessing. Life after death is not mentioned in the early history of Israel. Israel believed that God's final judgment will set right the injustice in life. The wicked seem to prosper but in the last judgment wickedness will be punished. Faithful obedience to God reaps the reward of an abundant life.

Paul's use of "life" includes the possibility of new life that God offers man in Jesus. This new life is both present and future for the believer. Now he is free from the obstacles that prevent "living love." In love he finds newness of life. The Christian is freed from all his fears and sin. He is a forgiven man. He is free to live in the present moment.

177

The Gospel of John begins with the Old Testament concept of God as life. Since God has made himself known in Jesus, life is found by trusting Jesus. Life is a gift for man. Man's life is affected by his decisions (what he does makes a difference). Man's decisions can either affirm or destroy life.

Gnostic thinkers (first and second century A.D.) taught that genuine life is a completely spiritual reality; thus, bodily existence is true death. To be fully alive is to have nothing to do with the physical world. Traditional Christianity has opposed this view of life.

Augustine (354-430) makes three points in discussing the hideous slaughter of some Christians. (1) The main issue is not how long you live. (2) Man should not worry about how he dies. (3) More important than how I will die, or when I will die, is the question of freedom from my fear of death. Only a life set free from death is truly worth having. Life is sometimes understood as awareness. This idea is related to contemporary depth psychology. Man has all kinds of forces in his life (some constructive and some destructive), and he needs to learn to deal with these forces on a conscious level. By doing this he may be able to channel even his frustrations in a creative way.

Vitalism as a theory is the undifferentiated conception of life based on itself. Life is an end in itself. Man and all other forms of life are joined in a sacred union. Albert Schweitzer's (1875-1966) concept of "reverence for life" is based on this approach. Duration of life is important; thus, man is never to destroy any form of life.

Existentialism (see Existential) sees life as present opportunity for man. Man is confronted with a choice. He may allow all kinds of things to prevent him from making his own decisions. When he does this he chooses death. Life is available only to the man who is willing to take upon himself the responsibility for being himself. (*see Immortality, Self, Spirit*) J.S.H.

Limbo In Roman Catholic theology, "limbo" is considered the abode for souls who are not yet permitted to enter heaven but whose exclusion is not their own fault. It comes from the Latin word, *limbus*, which means "border," and was named thus because it was believed that the location of limbo was near the border of hell. Theologians of the Roman Catholic Church distinguish between two states of limbo: (1) unbaptized children still in the state of original sin and (2) those who died before Christ's ascension into heaven. (*see Purgatory*) G.E.S.

Litany Originally a prayer, litany is now used as a response in which the officiating clergyman or priest reads a line and the congregation responds. Originally composed of intercessory prayers and ancient responses traced to the early centuries of the church, current use of litanies includes invocations, supplications, and intercessions. (*see* *Prayer*) G.E.S.

Literary criticism Literary criticism falls under the heading of higher criticism, as distinct from lower, or textual, criticism. Sometimes a distinction is made between literary criticism and historical criticism, the latter having to do with the historical circumstances surrounding the writing of a document. Actually, the various types of criticism tend to overlap, although the main lines of each method remain clear. Higher criticism in its various aspects is built upon textual criticism, a discipline that seeks to provide a text as close as possible to the original. Literary criticism attempts to assess the literary structure of a document and through it the purpose or purposes of the author. In doing so, the critic must pay attention to such matters as literary style, use of sources, and the possibility of interpolations (later insertions or changes). In other words, all considerations that contribute to an understanding of a document *as a document* must be included under this heading. We can see how difficult it is to exclude from this certain elements, usually associated with historical criticism, such as authorship and the place and date of writing. Furthermore, textual criticism may provide help in determining whether or not a passage is an interpolation. This is true, for example, with the famous *pericope adulterae* ("section on the adulteress") of John 7:53–8:11 (see Pericope). Furthermore, though form critiicsm is concerned mainly with the oral character of tradition, it contributes to literary criticism by distinguishing formal structures within the document itself. An example is Philippians 2:6-11 (*see* KENOSIS, *Pre-existence*). The various types of criticism, then, depend on each other. Literary criticism is a phrase applying to a document in terms of its strictly literary character.

With regard to the Old Testament, perhaps the best examples of literary criticism are to be found (a) in its application to the Pentateuch (Genesis through Deuteronomy) and (b) in its identification of at least two great blocks of material in the Book of Isaiah. The former has resulted in the identification of four strands of tradition, usually known as J, E, D, and P, each letter standing for a distinct type (see Source criticism). The Book of Isaiah is now known to consist not only of material from Isaiah of Jerusalem but also of material from the Exilic period (chapters 40-55). This knowledge, of course, makes more understandable the message of that part of the book. These are but two examples of the results of the application of the method to Old Testament books. The results of its application to other books of the Old Testament may be found in any good Old Testament introduction.

179

Examples of the application of literary criticism to the New Testament are found in the various approaches to the synoptic problem of the Gospels and in the distinguishing of elements of the Pauline body literature. The synoptic problem is the relation of Matthew, Mark, and Luke to each other. It is obvious that there are both agreements and disagreements among the first three Gospels. On what basis can these best be accounted for? The solution to this problem is sometimes called the "Two Document Hypothesis." According to this view, Matthew and Luke are dependent on Mark, and a "document" made up of sayings of Jesus, usually designated by the symbol "Q" (from the German *Quelle*, meaning "source"). This is a partial solution only, since material unique to Matthew and unique to Luke still remains. This has given rise to a so-called "Four Document Hypothesis": Mark and Q, together with M (Matthean material) and L (Lucan material) form the basis of Matthew and Luke. Perhaps it may be said that a "Multiple Source Hypothesis," in which Mark and Q are basic, best suits the situation.

Another New Testament example of literary criticism is found in connection with Corinthian letters of Paul. We usually speak of 1 and 2 Corinthians, and of course this is the way in which the materials appear in our Bibles. But scholars feel that these two letters contain several letters or fragments of letters. According to one reconstruction they are made up of four parts: the letter on immorality (2 Corinthians 6:14–7:1); 1 Corinthians; a "bitter letter" (2 Corinthians 10–13); and a peaceful letter (2 Corinthians 1–6:13; 7:2–9:15). While scholars are not all agreed that this exhausts the possibilities of reconstruction, this analysis suggests the kind of concern involved in literary criticism.

The current interest in form criticism does not lessen the importance of this kind of method in critical investigation of the biblical materials. The investigation of documents as a whole, and not only of the parts, makes up a major concern of biblical scholarship. Literary analysis has a major part to play in that investigation. (*see Biblical criticism, Form criticism, Source criticism*) E.L.T.

Liturgy Liturgy consists of the acts of worship or ceremony that occur in the church. From the Greek word, *leitourgia*, it means "public or common work" or "duty." There are a few uses of the word in the New Testament (Luke 1:23; Hebrews 10:11; Romans 15:16) that refer to the ministry in the Temple and to services conducted there. Worshipers speak of what happens in worship as the church "service" or the "service" of worship. This is very close to the meaning of liturgy, for it involves the idea of service or work. Some whose worship is less formal rebel at the use of this word in connection with worship, but in a real sense, all that a congregation says and does during its worship is liturgical. Even informality may be liturgical.

In the Eastern Orthodox Church, the term is restricted to use with the service of Eucharist (communion). It is actually called the "liturgy," usually takes several hours, and includes dramatic ritual. In the Roman Catholic Church, the term is used for any formal service and includes the Divine Office, Mass, the Litanies, the Sacraments, and other corporate worship. Since Vatican II, there has been a new emphasis on liturgy in the Roman Church. The Mass is now being spoken in the vernacular, rather than Latin. Hymns and layreaders have led to greater participation of the part of the laity. Intensive education in the Roman Catholic Church assists communicants in understanding the Mass.

Within Protestantism there is wide difference in the use of liturgy. The Anglican and Lutheran services have traditionally been more formal, but there has been considerable variety between high and low services. In evangelical churches, there has been less emphasis on worship and more on preaching. Historic prayers, collects, litanies, and the liturgical calendar are being used more widely in recent years. Congregations that formerly used the center pulpit now have a center altar or communion table with a pulpit and lectern on either side of the chancel. Choirs and ministers are making greater use of vestments, and a hymnal and book of prayer are more generally used.

Liturgy emerged sometime late in the third century, and binding forms of the Eucharistic liturgy were used in the fourth century. The liturgies of the ancient church are classified as Antiochene or Syrian, and Alexandrian or Egyptian. These two were used in the Greek church, and the Antiochene became the predecessor for the Byzantine rite. The Latin Church used the Gallican, which gave way to the Roman Mass in the early Middle Ages. Early liturgies were of two parts: the Liturgy of the Catechumens and the Liturgy of the Faithful (or the Service of the Word, followed by the Service of the Upper Room). During the first part, the Scriptures and Psalms were read and services were open, but during the Liturgy of the Faithful only the baptized members were permitted to participate in the communion service. The Roman liturgy changed only slowly from 500 to 1500. Following the Reformation, the Reformed and Wesleyan traditions made far greater use of preaching and singing in worship. The period of revivalism that followed placed even greater emphasis upon preaching and interpretation of the Bible, and interest in historic collects and litanies declined.

Contemporary experimentation in liturgy includes the use of jazz music in the observance of the Mass and other services of worship. While the clergy and laity were once clearly separated during worship, many churches now make frequent use of laymen in the ritual. Greater understanding and participation by worshipers continues to be a need in liturgy. Some view worship as a performance by the minister and choir,

181

but properly speaking, liturgy demands that every worshiper become involved in the service. (*see* Lent, Pentecost, Ritual, Worship) G.E.S.

LOGIC (*see* Epistemology)

LORD (*see* Name)

LORD'S PRAYER (*see* Prayer)

LORD'S SUPPER (*see* Communion [Holy])

Love *Love is used to indicate many different forms of concern one person may have for another. The one English word "love" is used to translate four Greek words* (eros, philos, charis, *and* agape) *which point to different forms love takes. The Latin word "libido" is also sometimes translated by the word "love." Paul Tillich has pointed out that there is only one kind of love, but with four qualities* (eros, libido, philos, *and* agape). *Love is understood in the Old Testament primarily in terms of the covenant relationship between God and Israel. The New Testament concept of love is built on the Old Testament foundation and is interpreted in terms of its power to overcome hostile relationships. Modern day psychological thought has rendered valuable help in analyzing the meaning and risks of love.*

The English word "love" is used in many different ways. It is used to indicate the romantic relationship of a boy and girl. Love means that the persons desire one another and get satisfaction out of being with the other person. Love is also used to indicate the relationship friends have to each other; thus love can mean the desire persons have for the other's company. Here love includes affection, *i.e.*, the exciting or touching of the emotions. The Christian church uses the term "love" to indicate man's right relationship to God and men. Seen in this way love means a concern to help other men build up their lives. It is a constructive spirit that seeks to create and encourage human life.

The Greek language uses four different words, all of which are sometimes translated by the English word "love." All four of these words have different shades of meaning. The meanings of love overlap and all share in one basic characteristic, namely, union of the loved and the lover. *Eros* is a striving of one person for union with another person; it is born out of a desire for value or values within the other. A man longs for the beautiful in the woman. The woman desires the strength she finds in the man. Thus, the man and woman come together out of a search for the valuable. This has been described as transpersonal love, *i.e.*, love rises above a concern with persons and seeks the valuable. *Eros* has come to be associated strongly with the physical attraction between the two sexes. It is used in this sense to describe the passion man and woman have for one another. *Charis* (*kah*-ris) is usually translated by the English word "grace." It is used to describe the kindness that God shows to man even though he does not deserve it. This whole element of love is best described by the word "charity." Love here takes on the form of benevolence; *i.e.*, freely giving to those who are in need. *Agape* (ah-guh-*pay*) is love in response to God's love for man. Man is shown by God what it means to live. *Agape* is man's response in which he gives of himself in building up life. *Agape* refuses to tear down human life.

The Latin word "libido" is used to indicate the desire of one person for another person or thing. This is a form of love that seeks for self-fulfillment through union with the wanted object or person. However, libido is more basic than a longing for pleasure. Man feels incomplete, unsatisfied, and in need of the other person or thing. With the desired object or person he becomes complete and satisfied.

In the Old Testament love is used frequently to describe the joy a man and a woman find in their sexual relationship. Here love means romance in the sense that two lovers are fascinated with each other. Love is also used to describe family ties. Romantic love is exclusive. It is in regard to this quality of love that jealousy becomes an important and disruptive factor. Love is used to indicate the reciprocal relationship existing between friends. A distinctive quality of Old Testament love can best be seen in relationship to the covenant idea. God has chosen Israel to be his people. God's steadfast love (*hesed*) of Israel is shown by His faithfulness to the covenant (Psalms 106:45). God's care of Israel and Israel's faithful response make up the two sides of the covenant. Israel's acts of love cannot be separated from God's mercy, which has been shown to Israel.

The New Testament concept of love is in large measure derived from the Old Testament. God's love for man is revealed in the death of Jesus of Nazareth. Thus, God's love is willing to pay any price in order to bring man into complete or whole life. Man makes mistakes. Man erects barriers between himself and others. Love takes down these barriers and makes man whole again. Christian love is openness to the demands of the day. It is willingness to help the neighbor simply because the neighbor needs help. Christian love does not ask: Do I like the neighbor? Even if man does not like his neighbor he is concerned to help him. The idea (found in both the Old and New Testaments) of love of enemy is a very practical idea. It assumes that men do have bad relationships with one another. It asks: How can these be improved?

183

These hostile relationships can be improved if man will be forgiving and help the neighbor in whatever way he can.

In the Middle Ages love and good works were viewed as being the heart of the gospel. Love shows itself by obeying the law. Man becomes righteous by doing the law. Two problems arise in connection with this understanding of love. (1) Love under the law tends to make of man a means to an end. (2) This concept of love tends to become self-centered. If man is primarily concerned to establish his own righteousness he is using his neighbor for a selfish purpose.

Erich Fromm (1900-   ) understands love as an art that man can learn. Love is the overcoming of separation. Union takes place through communion. Man fears union for one reason: that he will lose his own individuality. But man can maintain his own individuality and at the same time be a genuine part of the community. Only false community would cost man his individuality. Karl Menninger (1893-   ) views love as the force that draws two persons together in a desire to be helpful and to be helped (such as doctor-patient, husband-wife). The work of love is to transform the impulse to fight into a constructive or helpful impulse. In this viewpoint "like" and "love" differ only in degree.

Paul Tillich (1886-1965), in *Love, Power and Justice*, analyzes Christian love as that which unites life. Man is drawn toward physical pleasure for its own sake (*eros*). He is drawn toward the beautiful, which he encounters in many forms (libido). He is drawn toward certain persons and things because he sees his union with them as the fulfillment of himself (*philos*). All three of these are qualities of love. They, at least in a partial way, overcome estrangement by uniting certain parts of creation with certain other parts. These three qualities of love are grounded in a fourth quality that transcends or goes beyond these three and unites them. Man is drawn out of his self-centered preferences as the basis for union with others when he comes to know that he and all other men ultimately belong to the same Creator. Thus all men belong to the same creative process and find fulfillment in working together in this one process. Out of this sense of belonging man is united with all that is (*agape*). In *agape* all estrangement is overcome by reunion of the whole. (*see Neighbor*) J.S.H.

LOWER CRITICISM (*see Biblical criticism, Literary criticism*)

LOYALTY (*see Duty*)

LXX (*see Septuagint*)

MAKING (see Works)

Man A Christian understanding of man may involve several disciplines. Today, few Christian thinkers use the phrase "doctrine of man." Instead, they include their understanding of man under the doctrines of Christ, creation, or redemption.

(1) The Bible has no single view of man. In various places the Bible speaks of man as (a) an appetite, (b) a spirit, (c) a sinner, (d) a son of God. Taken as a whole, however, the Bible pictures man as part of God's creation. Man has both dignity and low status (Psalm 8). The fact that "grace and truth" appeared in the form of a man (John 1:17) emphasizes the importance of man. The term "son of God" appears to mean a destiny promised man (Romans 8:23; Galatians 4:5). Though man experiences God's saving presence, he does not become his true self until (presumably) the Kingdom of God becomes real.

(2) The meaning of Jesus Christ becomes, in the work of many thinkers, the meaning of man. If Jesus is seen as the Christ because he fully obeys God's will, then man is himself only when he obeys God's will. If Jesus is the Christ because of faith, man is man only in faith. Similarly, the way thinkers define sin is the negative side of man. If sin is disobedience, man "loses" his true self by rebellion. If sin is separation from God, man can only become himself through reconciliation with God. The meaning of creation and of redemption usually implies a view of man, also.

(3) Anthropology, the scientific study of man, has cast light on the Christian understanding of man. In fact, biblical scholars sometimes become anthropologists as they study religion, society, and individual man in Hebrew and early Christian history. Today the work of anthropologists helps Christian thinkers in at least two important ways. (a) Anthropologists usually study man in one culture and then compare the view of man in another culture. Thus the differences are noted. Since there are many different views of man in various cultures, Christian thinkers have learned to be careful in making generalizations about "the nature of man" or "the essence of man." (b) Anthropologists have pointed out the amazing creativity and vitality of man. Christian thinkers

take account of this information as they try to assess man's abilities and limits. No matter how evil man may be, for instance, he always seems to act with a reason or purpose. (*see Fall, Image of God*)

Manuscript The word "manuscript" applies to a hand-written document. Before the invention of printing in the fifteenth century, all books were written by hand. This has a bearing on the way documents of the biblical tradition were passed down, since each document had to be copied, a process that often led to errors. Original manuscripts of the biblical books have never been found so that textual critics depend on copies of copies. With such evidence the critics can try to establish a text close to the original.

The earliest manuscripts of the New Testament books were written on papyrus, a plant that in antiquity grew in the marshes of the Nile. The pith of the plant was cut longitudinally into thin strips. These strips were laid side by side; then a second series of strips was placed at right angles to these and pressed together forming a sheet. A sheet might measure from six to fifteen inches high, and from three to nine inches wide. Several of these sheets might be joined together to form a roll, the maximum length of which might be thirty feet, although it was often much less. The papyrus codex or book form, as distinct from the roll, apparently was in use as early as the second century A.D. Some scholars believe that it was a product of the Christian church, although it may have had an earlier form in wax tablets, used as notebooks by Greeks and Romans.

The great manuscripts of the fourth and fifth centuries, however, were not written on papyrus but on vellum. Apparently the Hebrew Scriptures had long been written on skins. By the fourth century A.D. vellum succeeded papyrus although there was a period in which both materials were used. This fact, together with the development of the book or codex form, made it possible to make complete copies of the New Testament. For the fragile character of papyrus put severe limits on what could be included, limits that were greatly improved by the advent of vellum. Hence, we find emerging from the fourth and following centuries outstanding examples of manuscript production, such as Codex Sinaiticus and Codex Vaticanus.

Manuscripts made of vellum are usually classified according to the style of writing they exemplify. Writing on papyrus had been in the non-literary hand of everyday life. But with the introduction of vellum, in combination with the codex form, larger letters could be used. From the first use of vellum in the fourth century until the invention of printing, the formal book hand held sway. This had two basic forms, the capital or *uncial*, and the *minuscule* or smaller, letter forms. The use of the former extended from the fourth to the tenth century. The latter, probably due to the need for the conservation of space and the need for speed in transcribing, came to the fore in the ninth century. Some of the important uncial manuscripts are Sinaiticus (fourth century); Vaticanus (fourth century); Alexandrinus (fifth century); Bezae (sixth century); Ephraemi (fifth century).

Textual critics classify manuscripts according to natural groupings. In the long history of the copying of manuscripts, error has crept in. Some copyists were professional scribes and took great care in their work, while others were less competent. Some changes in the text were accidental, due to fatigue and carelessness, but others were intentional, such as "improvement" in doctrine and style. Textual scholars have grouped these manuscripts by judging their qualities in various ways. One classification speaks of the Neutral Text, the Western Text, and the Byzantine Text. The New Testament presents the textual critic with an amazingly long and varied manuscript tradition; by comparison the Old Testament tradition is fairly simple.

In recent years, the discovery of the Dead Sea Scrolls has provided a whole new source of manuscript study, especially for the Old Testament. Non-biblical manuscripts of recent discovery bearing on the New Testament and the history of the church are the Gnostic documents found in 1945 in Nag Hammadi in Egypt. The study of both of these groups of manuscripts is still going on. (*see Literary criticism*) E.L.T.

MARCIONISM (*see Cosmogony*)

MARTYR (*see Witness*)

Materialism As a metaphysical theory, materialism contends only *matter* is existent or real. The implication is that the universe is not governed by intelligence or for a purpose. Since reality is matter in motion, all human actions can be explained without appealing to mind or spirit. Materialists generally are antireligious, since most religions do appeal to the spiritual. Materialists regard religion, because of its spirituality, as superstitious and often accuse religious people of adolescent ideas. One response of Christian theology is sacramentalism as a belief that material realities—bread, wine, and water—can be the bearers of spiritual gifts. Further, Christianity has traditionally proclaimed the goodness of the material world because God created it. Only when Christians fail to celebrate material good do they give grounds for materialists to criticize and reject Christianity. Teilhard de Chardin (1881-1955), Catholic theologian, has done a great deal of writing in this area. (*see Cosmogony, Sacrament*) J.B.W.

Maundy Thursday Derived from *mandatum* (command), its origin is found in the footwashing ceremony that John's Gospel describes as part of the passion of Christ. Maundy Thursday is observed the Thursday before Easter and usually includes the celebration of communion. In churches where footwashing is practiced, this is also observed on Maundy Thursday, as is the "love feast." (*see Lent*) G.E.S.

MEAL OFFERING (*see Sacrifice*)

Meaningful Paul Tillich (1886-1965), depending on Jean Paul Sartre (1905-   ), called "meaninglessness" the "destruction of the structure of being." He meant that when man feels the order and values of his life disappearing, he no longer finds them meaningful. For example, a father who finds his children hateful and disobedient may find his family becoming "meaningless." Where he used to find joy, love, and satisfaction he now finds only the opposite. In this sense, "meaningful" is the constructive order that upholds life and makes it worthwhile. In itself, the idea of meaningful is not moral. An honest student may find it worthwhile to avoid cheating. But it may be "meaningful," at least temporarily, for another student to cheat. (*see Anxiety, Language*)

Means A means is the medium through which a thing is done, a purpose accomplished, or an end attained. Every act may be divided into three parts. (1) Every act begins with an interest or want. This may be a strong desire with a clear purpose in mind or a vague concern to do something. (2) Every act includes an end that will satisfy, or at least is assumed will satisfy, the original want or need. (3) The third ingredient of every act is the means or way to get from the original interest to the desired goal.

An end or desired goal for one act may become the starting point or means to a new act with a more remote goal. Likewise, means to an end become intermediate ends having their own value. So means and ends are not to be thought of as radically different.

The entire role of means in ethical thinking can best be understood by contrasting two categories of ethical thinkers, the deontological and the teleological. Teleological thinkers believe that the ultimate standard for deciding that something is either good or evil is the balance of good over evil that the act produces. No act is either good or bad in itself without regard to the effect it has. If man desires to know whether an act is good or bad he simply asks: Will it produce more good and less evil than the other courses of action? A "means" gains its value from the result it accomplishes. Deontological thinkers say that whether an act is good or evil is not entirely determined by the end it serves. Rather, certain factors involved in the act itself make it good or evil. Man does not need to ask any questions about the result of the act. Some good may come from an evil deed. Still the deed remains an evil one.

The phrase "the end justifies the means" is carelessly used in our society. Sometimes it is suggested that "communists" or "bad guys" believe that the end justifies the means, while "Americans" or "good guys" reject the idea. Actually all men sometimes use bad or questionable means of accomplishing a good end. Joseph Fletcher (1905-   ) writes that only if the end justifies the means can an act have any meaning at all. The Christian is committed to act in a certain way out of love for the neighbor. He acts so that the neighbor's needs may be met.

Thomas Aquinas (c. 1225-74) pointed out that means are proximate ends. They enter into the ends. A person making a cake puts flour, sugar, and milk into the bowl and mixes them as the means to making a good cake. How much flour he includes will affect the end result. The same is true of daily acts. The means affect the end accomplished and cannot be considered as isolated facts. H. Richard Niebuhr (1894-1962) builds on the above way of thinking and concludes that man needs to find means that fit the end he is seeking; *i.e.*, means that are appropriate and faithful to the goal. (*see End*) J.S.H.

MERCY (*see Forgiveness*)

Messiah   The Hebrew term *Mashiach* means "anointed one." Its Greek equivalent is *Christos*. Messiah refers to the ancient practice of anointing the king who is considered to be God's representative in a special sense. In 2 Samuel 7:12 *ff.*, God promises David that his kingdom will be eternal. This is an important passage, for it reveals the tendency on the part of the nation to present the kingdom of David as the ideal. This emphasis on the reestablishment of the kingdom of David is extremely important in connection with the developing messianic (mes-ee-*an*-ik) hope. For Jewish messianism was always conceived in this-worldly terms; the Anointed One would be of the line of David and would bring in the new age under God. The political, this-worldly character of this Kingdom cannot be overstressed.

Some messianic passages in the Old Testament are Isaiah 9:2-7 and 11:1-9. Later, Christians came to apply these passages to Jesus, but in their own context they simply express the pre-Christian hope of the people of Israel for the vindication of the nation. It is probable that the messianic hope of the Jews roots back into the idea of covenant. When one national disaster followed another, the hope for the ideal of a new kingdom of David was pushed into the future. The Messiah became more and more an eschatological figure, related to the end times. As late as A.D. 132 a person by the name of Bar Kokhba was hailed as Messiah by certain of his contemporaries and led the people in revolt against Rome.

The Jewish Messiah idea should not be confused with the Son of man concept we meet in the Book of Daniel 7:13 *ff.* and in the apocryphal Book of Enoch. In that case the Son of man is a heavenly figure, entirely without the human characteristics of the Messiah. This Son of man appears in the New Testament, especially in the Gospels, as the agent of God in the establishment of the Kingdom of God. But he is a superhuman being and is not at all to be confused with the Messiah who will enter and redeem history. It is of interest, however, that in the Gospels Jesus is identified by the church as both Messiah and Son of man. It may well be that the Son of man emerged in Judaism as an alternate hope for the nation. Since David's kingdom seemed impossible to be restored in human history there was a tendency to imagine a final victory for God and his people through a superhuman power. God would accomplish in this manner what man failed to do.

Scholars are not unanimous in their judgments about Jesus' claim to be the Jewish Messiah. It is probable, however, that the claim came after Easter and was read back into the time of Jesus. It is quite possible that messianic (political and revolutionary) suspicions were raised about Jesus during his lifetime. The fact that he was crucified by Rome would suggest such suspicions. But the extreme reluctance of Jesus to make the claim for himself suggests that the ascription of the title to him is an expression of the faith of the church. Indeed, the Gospel of Mark shifts the emphasis away from the title "Christ" to Son of man, and explains Jesus' role in terms of service and suffering, not in terms of the militant Messiah (Mark 8:27 *ff.*).

Paul's use of the term "Christ" is instructive. He frequently used it in combination with Jesus, "Jesus Christ" or "Christ Jesus." In most cases it has ceased to mark a function but is instead a proper name. Paul can speak of being "in Christ," or "Christ in me," suggesting that the original messianic function has been lost. He has now accepted inwardly the concept of Christ, that is, he has identified the Christ with his experience of the risen Lord. This is, of course, a far cry from the political-military figure of the Jews. It is perhaps fair to say that this now widespread way of using the title, though not at all true to the developed Jewish concept, does justice to the basic hope that prompted it at the start, namely, that God will finally vindicate his people. (*see Christology, Historical Jesus, Name*) E.L.T.

METANOIA (*see Repentance*)

Metaphysics (meh-tah-*fiz*-iks) "*Metaphysics*" is the name of a book by the Greek thinker Aristotle. The book really concerned "*first causes*," that is, the most basic things. The Hebrews were also concerned about basic things, but they told stories and recalled events rather than using ideas and logic. Christians took reason from the Greek thinkers and stories of faith from the Hebrew people. Thomas Aquinas, who lived from 1225-74, said ideas were not as important as faith. A Christian can use ideas to understand more clearly what this faith means, however. Martin Luther, who lived from 1483 to 1546, said that only God's mercy could save man from his sin, and metaphysics was not important. Today Karl Barth is a thinker who follows Luther, but another Protestant thinker, Paul Tillich, has said Christian thought can still use metaphysics in an important way.

The word "metaphysics" was first used by librarians in the ancient city of Alexandria. They were cataloguing the collection of the writings of Aristotle (384-322 B.C.), the famous Greek thinker. They noticed a writing that was untitled by Aristotle and decided to give it a title. Since it appeared in Aristotle's work after his treatise on *Physics*, which he had titled himself, the librarians simply provided the writing a name that located it. They called it *Meta Physics*, which means, "The books which come after the books on physics." The name has been applied to this portion of Aristotle's writing ever since. And even though it was a word unused by Aristotle or the Greek thinkers before him, the word has been also connected with the subjects about which Aristotle wrote. And what were those subjects? The words of Aristotle tell us: ". . . all men suppose what is called Wisdom to deal with the first causes and the principles of things. . . ." Thus, "philosophy of first things" is a fair designation for metaphysics. Although they did not call it metaphysics, Plato (c. 427-347 B.C.) and some of the other philosophers prior to Aristotle had already wrestled with these problems. Their works are invaluable in considering this issue (see especially Plato's dialogues *Parmenides* and the *Sophist*). The ancient Greek philosophers were the first men on record to analyze reality by the use of reason and to try to record their thoughts in logical order.

Other ancient men in different cultures from Greece were surely no less aware of the importance of "the principles of things," but their thoughts took the form of myths and stories. The ancient Israelites, for example, had told wondrous stories of Yahweh's creating the world and of his controlling history. For them Yahweh was the source of everything.

When Christianity appeared in human history, it emerged within a world in which both Greek and Israelite patterns of thought were common. Although the Hebrew Bible (the Old Testament) was regarded as sacred, the language and culture of the earliest Christians were also colored by the Greek heritage. When Christianity began to think out its own theology it had Greek philosophy as well as the old Testament from which to draw. The Hebrew stories of Yahweh's dealing with his people and the philosopher's thoughts about God in their philosophies

191

of first things could be used wherever they were compatible with Christian faith.

As Christian theologians thought out their positions, they both used and criticized the Israelite and Greek resources. They *interpreted* the Bible and *reformulated* many Greek metaphysical assertions. As the centuries passed a great contest between theology and metaphysics was carried on. During the thirteenth century, the great theologian Thomas Aquinas (*c.* 1225-74) gained a greater familiarity with ancient metaphysics, especially Aristotle, than had any theologian before him. Aquinas then distinguished "sacred, or divine theology" from metaphysics. Aquinas well knew that any philosopher interested in metaphysics would consider the problem of God in the search for first causes. But rational thought about God, argued Aquinas, cannot be equated with revealed knowledge of God. By drawing such a distinction Aquinas made clear the tension between philosophers and theologians. Philosophers often think theologians are uncritical, and theologians often accuse philosophers of being too rational. For example, Martin Luther (1483-1546) argued that in the matter of man's relation to God, reason is unable to contribute anything of value. Only God's mercy is able to save man. Metaphysics, then, is not important for theology, according to Luther.

In the nineteenth century, theology became much more interested in the branch of philosophy known as ethics than in metaphysics. Even philosophers paid less attention to metaphysics. Roman Catholic theology did, however, retain a great commitment to the theology of Thomas Aquinas.

The most widely celebrated Protestant theologian of the first half of the twentieth century, Karl Barth (1886-   ), rejected *any* dependence of theology on philosophy. The Bible was greatly re-emphasized by Barth and those following his lead.

Some major theologians, however, have argued that metaphysics is much more intimately related to theology than Barth would admit. Paul Tillich (1886-1965), in his notable *Systematic Theology*, has attempted to construct a theology upon a metaphysical base.

Thus the issue today is not resolved. Whereas some philosophers still seek the "philosophy of first things," some theologians think that metaphysics offers a great resource for doing theology. Other theologians think the Bible is the basic—even the only—resource for doing theology. It seems that still the Bible must be *interpreted* and that metaphysics must be *reformulated* in order for theology to utilize either resource. (*see* Ontology, Reason, Theology) J.B.W.

Methodology (meth-oh-*dahl*-oh-jee) *This word means the study of methods used by any thinker to study the subjects in which he is interested. In theology, Paul Tillich uses the method of correla-*

tion. Man's reason (philosophy) asks the important questions about God and life. Man's faith (theology) gives the answers to these questions. Karl Barth uses a dialectical method. In dialectic, truth is discovered by holding on to two ideas that seem to be opposite one another. For example, Christ is both God and man. John Macquarrie proposes another method, with three parts: (1) describing the outside world through use of the senses; (2) interpreting God, the Bible, and the outside world by using various principles; and (3) applying the knowledge gained to the lives of Christians.

Methodology means the systematic organization and analysis of the principles and processes guiding a particular inquiry. For example, it is possible to state in straightforward propositions what is involved in the scientific method of any specific science. From these broad categories it is further possible to suggest the general characteristics of the methodology of science. By the same token, analysis may be offered of the method of education, history, etc. In other words, methodology is the self-conscious attempt to describe the process of any inquiry seeking knowledge.

The interest in methodology that has grown dramatically during the nineteenth and twentieth centuries has directly carried over into theological studies. Because the broad field of theology is composed of many particular disciplines, there is no single theological method any more than there is a general scientific method, apart from the methods of the particular sciences. Some illustrations of methods of particular theological disciplines follow.

For biblical theology the method widely accepted today is sometimes called the critical method. (see Biblical criticism)

The method used in systematic or philosophical theology determines the results. Paul Tillich (1886-1965) attempts to carry out a method of *correlation*. Philosophy asks the questions, and in parallel fashion, theology provides an ordered response. Karl Barth (1886-   ), follows a *dialectical* method. John Macquarrie (1919-   ), a British theologian recently teaching in America, has proposed a three-fold methodology. It includes these approaches: (1) *description* through phenomenology (reports of sense experience); (2) *interpretation* by giving special attention to recent theories of hermeneutics; and (3) *application* to the life of faith within the community.

From the foregoing examples it should be clear how specific methodologies for particular disciplines are developed. Finally, however, it should be mentioned that certain methodological principles have cut across many particular methods. Such a principle is *typology*. This has been used, for example, by biblical scholars on a wide scale and by some systematic theologians, such as Karl Barth. This method proceeds within any discipline by searching for events, men, and ideas, that will suggest the formation of types. A type is an ideal structure that can only be approached by concrete events or men, never attained. But the constructed type provides a point of reference by which to evaluate the specific. Some theologians, such as Tillich, go so far as to suggest that without typology to provide the frame of reference, it is impossible to evaluate and interpret the concrete and specific events with which the theologian is directly concerned. (*see Dialectic, Dogmatics, Hermeneutics, Theology, Typology*) J.B.W.

MIDDLE AXIOM (*see Principle*)

MILIEU (*see Contextual*)

MILLENNIUM (*see Apocalypse, End*)

MINISTER (*see Orders*)

MINUSCULE (*see Manuscript*)

Miracle A miracle may be defined as an event conflicting with the laws of nature and is therefore said to have been caused by a supernatural agency. In a society that has no well-developed concept of the orderliness of nature, unusual events may the more readily be given a supernatural origin. It has been pointed out that miracle in the Old Testament is generally subordinate to moral and religious purpose, although there are exceptions to this, as in the case of the Elisha cycle of stories; in that case the miracle is used to "enhance the skill and cunning of Elisha." (See Norman K. Gottwald, *A Light to the Nations*, pages 263 ff.)

The New Testament, of course, contains many illustrations of the miraculous. Sometimes these are mighty works attributed to Jesus; at other times they are performed by apostles. In general, it may be said that mighty works of Jesus are evidential; that is, they attest to his divine mission and person. An illustration of this is Mark 4:35-41, the story of Jesus stilling the storm by a command. The act causes the people to ask, " 'Who then is this, that even wind and sea obey him?' " This kind of miracle was not uncommon in the Hellenistic age. The performance of mighty deeds was characteristic of great or unusual persons, whether of emperors or of others. A good example of this is the account of the life of Apollonius of Tyana as reported by Philostratus (*c.* 170-245). In some ways the life of Apollonius is reminiscent of the life of Jesus of Nazareth. Some scholars feel that much of the miraculous element of the Gospels may be explained in terms of the Hellenistic miracle worker, the *theios anēr* (*theh*-ahs ah-*nair*), or divine man. For the Hellenistic age had its heroes, men who had by virtue of their greatness been raised to the level of the divine, or gods who had descended to the level of the human. The evidence of their divine character was shown by their works. That this element is a part of the New Testament miracle there can be no doubt, although it is doubtful that the Hellenistic *theios anēr* presents the only possible pattern for Jesus as a worker of miracles.

The mighty works of apostles are accomplished through the name of Jesus or by virtue of the power of the Spirit they possess. Thus Peter heals the lame man at the Beautiful gate of the Temple by the words, " 'In the name of Jesus Christ of Nazareth, walk.' " (Acts 3:6) The point here is that "the name" is identical with the person, so that the power of Jesus is invoked for the act of healing. Note, in this connection, Acts 9:34: " 'Aeneas, Jesus Christ heals you; rise and make your bed.' And immediately he rose."

The miracles of the Fourth Gospel might be understood merely as evidence of Jesus' divine nature. But though this element is undoubtedly present in the miracles there, they cannot be confined to this alone. For the miracles of John are called "signs" (John 2:11; 4:54); that is, they are "pointers" to something existing beyond themselves. Consequently, while the story of the raising of Lazarus (John 11:1-44), *is* evidence of Jesus' divine nature, it goes far beyond this simple fact and presents the fundamental teaching about Jesus as a life-giver, a teaching set forth in clear fashion in 11:25: " 'I am the resurrection and the life. . . .' "

The miraculous element contained in the biblical materials poses a problem for many persons in the modern world, because the present age accepts a scientific world view. The Bible, on the other hand, emerged from a prescientific age and took "mighty works" for granted (see World view). Indeed, it would be a miracle were there no miracles in the Bible. In the history of the church many attempts have been made to deal with the miraculous element. One approach in the nineteenth century was to rationalize the miraculous. That is, the stories were interpreted in such a way that the miracle could be explained in purely natural terms. The story of Jesus stilling the storm was explained with the claim that at the moment Jesus uttered his word of command, the boat came under the lee of the land and so into calm water. But all such attempts to deal with the miraculous element in the Gospels are futile. The miracle belongs to the time and must be allowed its full place in the material. In the last analysis, miracles demonstrate the basic biblical conviction that in the history of God's people, God's presence was a reality. (*see Power, Transcendent*) E.L.T.

Mission Though "mission" is included in the Revised Standard Version only five times (1 Samuel 15:18, 20; Acts 12:25; 2

195

Corinthians 11:12; Galatians 2:8), its meaning marks all that the Christian church does. Mission means "sent out" or "assigned task." The Great Commission, given by Jesus, was the springboard from which the early disciples moved into a program of missions: " 'Go therefore and make disciples of all nations, baptizing them in the name of the Father and of the Son and of the Holy Spirit. . . .' " (Matthew 28:19) Jesus' mission emphasis is marked by his frequent use of such words as "go," "do," "make," and "be."

The traditional understanding of mission is that the Christian proclaims the good news and converts persons "in the world" to his faith. According to this view, the apostles went out to preach Christ to a sinful world. Gradually they added numbers to the church, until by the third century, half the population of the Roman Empire were Christians. Later thinkers, such as Augustine (354-430), Luther (1483-1546), Calvin (1509-64), and Wesley (1703-91), sought to change the world, not by influencing legislation or writing constitutions, but by converting and influencing the individual, who then through his secular occupation would transform state and society. The Puritans picked up Calvin's notion of the "holy commonwealth" and sought to make part of the new world an entirely Christian state.

This view faced increasing criticism in the twentieth century, both from practical workers, like pastors and foreign missionaries, and from scholars. Liberal thinkers saw the mission of the church as that of transforming society by working on the structures themselves, rather than by converting individuals (see Social gospel). In 1934, Reinhold Niebuhr's *Moral Man and Immoral Society* pointed out that the individual Christian can be pious and virtuous without really affecting the social and economic injustice around him. Foreign missionaries found themselves in the position of spiritual imperialists, handing out Bibles to ignorant Africans and Asians, while their more realistic friends in business and politics took in the land and labor for profit.

Accordingly, the Bible and Christian thoughts were viewed in a different light: The Bible does not distinguish between sacred and secular. The whole life of man, rather than a split between body and soul, is emphasized. Heaven is a symbol of God's holiness, but God has made all of creation holy. The Incarnation means that God has entered history to stay. The early church saw God at work in the world. Augustine and the Reformers were trying to bring about God's justice and righteousness among men; they were not interested in setting up a spiritual sanctuary so that Christians could withdraw from the world. Wesley's social concern was a direct attempt to make the Kingdom of God real in human history.

In the 1960's, the phrase "church in the world" has come to mean the same thing as "mission." Some see the internal life of the Christian congregation (*koinonia*) as preparation for its real task of mission in the world (*ekklesia*). This mission is variously defined as transforming social structures, being present alongside the oppressed neighbor, and carrying out social services.

Harvey Cox's *The Secular City* (1965) called on the church to proclaim modern technology as good, rather than clinging to an irrelevant "religious" task. He depended partly on the thought of Arend T. van Leeuwen (1918-   ), whose *Christianity in History* outlined the revolutionary influence of Jewish and Christian symbols on man's stance toward the world. Because Christianity saw the world as creation, it did not fear to change nature. The result was a growing sense of man's power and of scientific achievement. Van Leeuwen sees the mission of the church, however it has been accomplished, as having the effect of releasing man from his religious fears. (*see Church*, EKKLESIA, KOINONIA, LAOS, *Secularization*) G.E.S.

MODALISM (*see Trinity*)

Moderation In Greek thought moderation or temperance was understood to be closely connected with many other virtues, particularly wisdom and prudence. Here the most significant virtue for man is wisdom. Knowledge or truth is life giving. It enables a man to distinguish between good and bad deeds. It lets him make the right choices. Prudence is the use of right judgment or wisdom in making decisions. The concept of temperance was developed in opposition to the hedonists, who taught that pleasure is the highest good. The hedonists encouraged man to indulge in his desires; thus, if man desired something he should pursue it wholeheartedly. Socrates (*c.* 470-399 B.C.) and Plato (*c.* 427-347 B.C.) insisted that man needs reproof. Man's desires should be checked. This is not to say that desires are bad, but man needs to use reason to control his desires. Man has "power over himself," and he should use this power.

Moderation is urged in the New Testament as self control (Acts 24:25; Titus 1:8), mastery over passions (1 Corinthians 7:5), temperance (Titus 2:2), and sobriety (1 Thessalonians 5:8). All of these call for a well-balanced life by means of self-control. Man should not become consumed by the wrong concerns. Man is to be more concerned about the neighbor than he is about food or drink.

Augustine (A.D. 354-430) sees moderation as essential to the Christian life. In his life man feels pulled to do many things, and if he allows these impulses to operate freely in his life, they will prevent him from giving himself completely to the meeting of the neighbor's needs. The Christian will not allow anything to keep him from loving the neighbor.

197

Thomas Aquinas (c. 1225-74) more specifically identified certain actions as being harmful to the Christian life. Many natural desires are viewed as dangerous and have to be kept in close check. The Christian life is the conquering of these bodily desires by the soul. Certain actions, like prayer and fasting, are of specific help in this task. The Christian life realizes its ideal perfection in the monastic life. Imitation of Christ refuses to have anything to do with the desires of the flesh.

John Wesley (1703-91) is influenced by Augustine and Aquinas. He wants to have nothing to do with drunkenness. He is convinced that man needs to restrain himself by developing holy habits. This enables the Christian to keep all desires under control. The purpose for this is to release the Christian for specific work in the world. One does not practice moderation for moderation's sake.

Following Wesley, Methodists have pushed "temperance." In fact, at times it appears that they have become almost intemperate in their commitment to temperance. This problem can best be understood by viewing the relation of the two words "abstinence" and "temperance." Abstinence means to refrain consistently from certain actions. Temperance suggests that excessive indulgence in anything may be harmful and therefore should not be allowed to happen. Temperance is not a complete withdrawal; it continues a relationship while setting limits.

Moderation is rooted in the realization that nothing is bad in and of itself. At the same time it recognizes that anything improperly used may be damaging to human life. Moderation suggests restraint, as opposed to withdrawal, as a more helpful way of relating to this world's goods. (see Ascetic) J.S.H.

MONARCHIANISM (see Christology)

Monism (moh-nism) From the Greek word mones, monism means the view that reality is a unity, that it is singular. With significant variations on the theme, the majority of Western thinkers have been advocates of monism. The ancient philosopher Parmenides (fifth century B.C.) was a defender of rigorous monism. For him reality is stable, fixed, absolute, and eternal; it is one. One of the perennial problems for monists lies in the relationship between appearance and reality. This, of course, raises the epistemological questions. What is the relationship between the knower and that which is known? For philosophers who follow Plato (c. 427-347 B.C.), the mind of man guarantees the connection. Knowledge results only when the appearance is pierced, and the real is grasped.

Christian theology was confronted early in its history by the problem of dualism. In response Christianity took its stand firmly upon its heritage of monotheism from Judaism. Obviously the faith in one God is quite related to the philosophical notion of the singularity of reality, monism. Confronted with the same epistemological problems, Christianity proposed revelation as the means by which the one God can be known. This was not generally held to be in contradiction with a respect for reason as the means of access to reality.

Some critics of the orthodox ways of speaking about the one God as a trinity claimed that Christian theology was in fact advocating polytheism. These rigorous rationalists, whether ancient or modern, have stood upon the premise that one does not equal three, nor does three equal one. Unitarianism is one modern form of what regards itself as true monotheism. It is also monism.

Apart from whether or not it is adequately formulated, however, it is clear that the vast majority of Christian theologians advocate monotheism. The affinity with philosophical monism underscores this. (*see* *Dualism, Epistemology, Trinity*) J.B.W.

MONOPHYSITISM (*see* *Christology*)

MONOTHEISM (*see* *Theism*)

MORAL ANXIETY (*see* *Anxiety*)

Morality Morality is a set of rules whose purpose it is to help individuals know how to relate to one another in society. Ethics or "moral philosophy" is distinguishable from morality in at least two respects. (1) Ethics is a branch of philosophy that examines morality as it relates to an understanding of man. Morality is a set of rules developed by society to shape human conduct. (2) Ethics concerns itself with general questions of right and good. It does not try to solve particular problems. Morality includes a specific set of rules intended to solve specific problems. "Amoral" means "without morals," in contrast to "immoral," which means "not moral." If the above distinction is made between morality and ethics, one can be "amoral" without being "unethical." One can refuse to follow the moral code of society, but at the same time reflect on the meaning of human actions.

Morality, like laws, conventions, and etiquette, is a social system. All are developed by society to guide human conduct. Laws are written down in the official documents of the society. A specific punishment is prescribed in these documents for breaking of the law. The courts determine the exact punishment to be given the breaker of the law. The law enforcement officers carry out this punishment. In matters of convention or etiquette there is a much less clearly-defined situation. There is broad disagreement in regard to some specific questions concerning what is etiquette. A breach of etiquette is usually punished by some form of mild rejection. Morality is somewhat different from either one of these. Moral rules are more clearly defined than etiquette but not as clearly defined as law. The breaking of a law draws the most clear-cut and severe response from society. Social rejection is, however, still quite distinctive in regard to those who break the moral code. Each society develops its own morality, decides what variations will be allowed, and decides how this morality will function.

A new school of ethical thought is developing in our own day. It is known as the "new morality." The "new morality" constitutes a movement away from the traditional understanding of morality. Morality has traditionally given man a set of rules that he should always obey. Armed with this set of rules man knows what his duty is in any given situation. He is to follow these rules regardless of the consequences. The new morality is concerned to help human beings do what needs to be done. Man is to make his decisions on the basis of what will be the most help to those involved in the situation. He does not have a set of rules that he is determined to follow at all times and in all places. Morality is an attempt to promote rational self-guidance. (see Ethics) J.S.H.

MORTAL SINS (see Sin)

MYSTERIUM TREMENDUM (see Holy)

Mystic A mystic is one who seeks to lose himself in God. Buddhism and Islam, as well as Christianity, have had many mystics. G. van der Leeuw (1890-1950) views mysticism as a form of religion in which active and passive, subject and object, God and man, lose themselves in each other. Man turns inward upon himself to find God and salvation. But similarly, God is everywhere, so that mysticism is close to naturalism. Van der Leeuw says that mystics usually disregard morality, since salvation lies within. At the same time, they follow rigid disciplines. They are like the ascetics because they practice fasting, prayer, and self control. Understandably, the monastic orders of the Middle Ages were centers of mysticism. Meister Eckhart (c. 1260-1327) was a Dominican mystic with views unacceptable to the church. He died at his trial for heresy. Ernst Troeltsch (1865-1923) says mysticism is close to the sect as a religious type, in that they both withdraw from human affairs. "Quietism" is the attitude of remaining passive before the state, work, and even sex. The Quakers are mystical in the sense that they wait, in worship, for the Spirit to move a person to speak. However, the Quakers are often active in human affairs. Paul Tillich (1886-1965) is sometimes called a mystic because he spoke of the "God beyond God," that is, the true God who lies out of the reach of human ideas and religion. Tillich also speaks of salvation as the reunion of being and non-being, which is similar to some mystical themes. (see Transcendent)

Myth   Popular thought often views myth as untrue. The student of literature, and certainly of the Bible, needs to view myth in entirely different terms. Though myth is admittedly a kind of language different from that of science, some consider it to be a highly effective means of communication. It may be ineffective on the purely rational level, but, since life is more than reason, other languages are needed to carry on communication beyond the purely rational. This is one reason why we have art, poetry, and music. It is not accidental that ancient man, in his response to the religious dimension of experience, expressed himself in terms of myth. Religion, from the nature of the case, deals with many questions that lie beyond the scope of scientific investigation. Myth is an attempt to state man's faith in the reality beyond experience and the meaning and value of that reality for life on the historical level. The language is poetic and symbolic, but the reality it seeks to express is taken as supremely important for man. Thus we have the myth of the beginning in the opening chapters of Genesis.

It is important to note that the characteristic Hebrew way of conveying truth was by story and symbol rather than by factual description. This same characteristic is evident in Jesus' use of the parable. The power of myth lies in large part in its appeal to the emotions. In this respect it has much in common with art.

A great deal has been said in recent times regarding the place of myth in the modern world. The controversy over myth has been prompted largely by the work of Rudolf Bultmann (1884-   ). Bultmann's view is that the three-story world of ancient times no longer means anything to modern man. The mythological structures in the biblical material, themselves based on that cosmology, are pre-scientific and therefore unintelligible. In order to make the biblical message understandable to modern man, it must be demythologized (dee-muh-*thah*-loh-jighzd). What Bultmann is doing is to interpret the New Testament in terms of modern existentialism. There is no guarantee that the outcome of this will be any more successful than the nineteenth and early twentieth century approach of liberal theology. Some have suggested that the *kerygma* (proclamation) of the New Testament needs *re*mythologizing rather than *de*mythologizing. Or, perhaps, what is really needed is a new appreciation of the language of myth together with a knowledge of the ancient mythology itself. It is doubtful that any culture, including the scientific, can operate apart from underlying mythological assumptions regarding the nature of things. Bultmann's great service in this respect has been to draw attention to the problem of communication.

The Enlightenment, characterized by rationalism, tended to make a sharp distinction between myth on the one hand and truth on the other, as if these were mutually exclusive. The progress of science has reinforced this distinction, so that for many "truth" means what can be scientifically

201

or empirically verified. But religious language, certainly the language of worship, attempts to communicate ideas and feelings that admittedly lie above and beyond the province of scientific language. One can be perfectly at home in the modern world and still be sensitive to the need for a different kind of idiom, the mythological, which can alone do justice to the reality that lies beyond science. The case for the abandonment of myth has not yet been made. (*see Experience, Language, Rationalism, Symbol, Truth, World view*) E.L.T.

NABI (*see Prophet*)

Name Perhaps the most important single thing to be said about "naming" in Hebrew thought is the identity of name and person. Because of this, the name of a child was full of meaning. Often the name was given because of special circumstances surrounding a child's birth (*e.g.*, 1 Samuel 4:21); sometimes it was connected with a prophetic message (*e.g.*, Hosea 1:4, 6); sometimes it had to do some hoped-for quality to be realized in the child (*e.g.*, Genesis 35:18; compare Matthew 1:21). But the relation between the name and the person is the all-important consideration.

This relationship between name and person had important implications. It meant, for one thing, that when one knows the name of a person he has the power to exercise control over that person (see Mark 5:9). To blot out the name of the people meant to destroy the nation (*e.g.*, 2 Kings 14:27). In the New Testament, to invoke the name of Jesus was to call upon the power in him. An example of this is to be found in 1 Corinthians 5:3-5, where Paul says that he has pronounced judgment on a man guilty of incest "in the name of the Lord Jesus. . . ." The invocation of the name makes his power effective in the church (see Collect). A good example of the power of the name of Jesus appears in an account of the activity of Jewish exorcists in Acts 19:13-17. ("Exorcise" means to drive an evil spirit out of a person.) One might compare this with Matthew 7:22. At other times, "the name" occurs in connection with persecution. In Matthew 10:22 Jesus tells his disciples that they will be " 'hated by all for my name's sake' " (compare Acts 5:41; 9:16). Perhaps the expression, "on behalf of the name" or "for the name" was a technical phrase, meaning to suffer as a Christian, as in 1 Peter 4:16. To suffer for the name is the same as to suffer for Christ. The "name" is practically equal to "person." Whether it was the exorcism of demons by the power of the name, the working of miracles in the name of Jesus (Acts 3:6), or baptizing in the name of Jesus (Acts 19:5), the close connection of name and person is fundamental (see Baptism).

An important feature of the "name" in Hebrew thought is found in the various names for god. The name Yahweh (yah-way) apparently was the name of the deity worshiped by the Kenites, the deity whom Moses found there and whom he embraced as his God (see Exodus 3:1 ff.). So sacred was his name—the tetragammaton YHWH—that after the Exile of 586 B.C. it ceased to be pronounced. And where the Scriptures read Yahweh (YHWH), it became customary to read Adonai (a-doh-nigh) (Lord). Other names for the deity were Elohim (a plural form for deity), and El Shaddai (usually translated "God Almighty"). The use of Yahweh and Elohim (el-oh-heem) coincides with the J and E documents respectively, and the names have played an important role in the identification of these sources. The sources seem to suggest that Elohim or El Shaddai were names given to God before the revelation of Yahweh to Moses. The connection of Yahweh with the sacred mountain, Sinai Horeb, is of great importance, since in the tradition this sacred mountain is the site of the giving of the law to Moses.

One of the interesting features of the New Testament is the variety of names given to Jesus. They are in fact the product of christology, the doctrine of Christ, which is largely what the New Testament is about. The name "Jesus" itself has significance, as Matthew shows (see 1:21). The name Jesus is the Greek form of the Hebrew "Joshua," which means "Yahweh is salvation." Other titles for Jesus in the New Testament are Christ, Son of man, Son of God, Lord, Logos (translated "Word"), Rabbi, Prophet, High Priest. Each of these titles has a history of its own. This means that the church had at its disposal patterns of thought by means of which it could express its faith in Jesus. (see Miracle, Source criticism) E.L.T.

Natural law   The traditional view of natural law stems from the work of Thomas Aquinas (c. 1225-74) and the Scholastics, who relied heavily on the thinking of Aristotle (384-322 B.C.). In this view, nature is an ordered unity in which each being has its place. Animals obey the laws of nature by instinct. Man, a rational soul, has the ability, however, to choose right and wrong. The final end of man is to see God—to understand His truth and find fulfillment in Him.

203

God's eternal law, his will, is the basis for the order of nature. Eternal law is clearly expressed in divine law, the Ten Commandments. When man uses his reason to understand eternal law, he shares in it, and this sharing is natural law. The general principle of natural law is "incline toward the good and avoid the evil."

Jacques Maritain (1882-   ) interprets Aquinas to mean that man is *inclined* toward the good, not that reason alone is the means for understanding natural law. In this way he hopes to meet the criticisms of those who say that man becomes moral through means other than reason, such as personal conscience. Maritain says that the law of nations (*jus gentium*) is, however, known through the use of conceptual reason. An example of the law of nations is the principle, "Do not condemn anyone without a hearing." Positive law (*jus civilis*) is even more specific; it is the legislation of a society, such as the law to stop at red traffic lights.

Some critics of natural law say that it is a concept native to Western civilization. Therefore, there is no absolute law of nature, but only the moral codes of particular cultures. Natural law thinkers are less absolute than they once were, though, and many concede that factors other than reason influence man's morality. Today natural law thinkers are not confined to Roman Catholicism. Paul Ramsey (1913-   ) is a Methodist with views very close to natural law morality.

Karl Barth (1886-   ), a Swiss theologian, de-emphasizes the value of natural law. He says that natural man is a sinner who has completely fallen away from what he should be. Natural man has no health in him. Therefore, natural man cannot have any direct knowledge of God or God's will.

Paul Tillich (1886-1965) sees Barth's position as too strong a rejection of natural law. The natural life of man has truth contained in it. Man can, by use of his reason, become aware of the difference between right and wrong. Right and wrong are a part of the created world. However, it is wrong to assume that the laws contained in human relationships are the same as the ones we see there. Man is capable of misreading the laws contained in nature. There is a difference between the truth contained in human life and man's understanding of that truth. (*see Natural theology*) J.S.H.

Natural theology   *Natural theology has a long history in Christian thought. It began in Greek philosophy, particularly in the work of Aristotle. In the Middle Ages, Thomas Aquinas distinguished between revealed and natural theology. By making such a division he opened the possibility that natural reason could criticize and even reject revelation. Such criticism was offered in the deism of the eighteenth century. Since then, many attempts have been made to revise the meaning* *of the term. In the many instances in which natural theology has been discussed, the key issues have remained: reason and revelation.*

Natural theology is a confusing term because there are at least two clear meanings for it in western intellectual history. (1) It refers to formulations about God based upon ideas said to be innate or natural to man. Every man is assumed to be religious by nature (*homo religiosus*). When some men reflect on this natural aspect of human existence, the result is "natural theology." (2) It refers to theological ideas attained by the use of natural, unaided reason. In this use, natural theology is often contrasted with revealed theology. Lack of clarity as to which of these meanings is being used has often resulted in criticism of natural theology.

The development of the ancient stoic philosophy, perhaps most notably in the work of Marcus Aurelius (A.D. 121-80), expressed natural theology in the first sense. Aurelius drew a contrast between the *particular theologies* of the many different religions then popular in the Roman Empire and what was regarded as a measure of theological belief common to all people. As Cicero put it in his treatise on the gods, "What the gods are is a matter of dispute, but that they are is denied by nobody." Only within such a context does the work of a group of second century Christian theologians known as the apologists make sense. They wrote defenses (*apologies*) of Christianity aimed at showing that the particular theological formulations of Christianity were the best expressions of "natural theology" to be found, because they were corroborated by God's revelation. Thus began the *apologetics*, which has had a close relationship with natural theology in Christian history. Apologetics is a fundamental effort to establish contact with and to defend Christianity within a given culture through forms of communication intelligible to that particular culture.

Plato (*c.* 427-347 B.C.) and Aristotle (384-322 B.C.) began and developed the second form of natural theology. Complex though their arguments were, they demonstrated what is a common dictionary definition of natural theology: "a theology based on human reason apart from revelation." Speculation by the unaided human reason establishes what can naturally be known of God, the soul, immortality, *etc.*

When Thomas Aquinas (A.D. *c.* 1225-74) wrote his famous theological studies, he made a distinction between natural theology and revealed theology that has troubled Christian theologians ever since. The former tells us that God is; the latter tells us the exact content of knowledge of God. The distinction is most clear in an illustration. It can be known by natural reason that God exists. It can only be known through revelation that God is a trinity. Aquinas expended great energy in attempting to demonstrate through five different arguments that God exists. He reviewed Scripture and the church tradition to set forth what revelation had made known.

The Protestant reformers, Martin Luther (1483-1546) and John Calvin (1509-64), were dissatisfied with Aquinas' distinction. They denied all validity to natural theology. But to make their case they had to agree that man's reason as God created it might have been able to reach God. Man had fallen into sin, however, and as a result of original sin, reason had become corrupt so that it no longer could lead to God, thus requiring revelation. Man by falling into sin was responsible for having given up reason's power to know God. This enabled the Reformers to further emphasize God's graciousness in coming to guilty man in revelation. In principle they accepted Aquinas' distinction but rejected the significance he had attached to natural theology. They argued that faith alone in God's revelation is enough for salvation. What is supremely important is the distinction between natural theology and revealed theology. As a result of this distinction, the rationalism of the seventeenth and eighteenth centuries discredited revelation as the giving of propositions of truth. As a result natural religion, as the sequel to natural theology, gained popularity in deism, and revealed religion was on the defensive.

Clearly between the thirteenth and eighteenth centuries a momentous shift had occured in the relationship between philosophy and theology. Philosophy had declared its freedom from theology and had become an independent field of human inquiry. Consequently philosophy insisted upon subjecting the claims of revelation to rational examination. Natural religion (deism) resulted when some philosophers concluded, from their examination of the claims of revelation, that Christianity was saying no more than a rational man would accept on the basis of reason and common sense. Lord Herbert of Cherbury (1583-1648) was one of the first Englishmen to argue this. Any part of Christian theology that did not meet the criteria of reason was rejected as excessive and unnecessary. Deism forced a radical rethinking of the meaning of revelation in some quarters. Orthodoxy was not abandoned by any means, since Roman Catholicism continued to propound the Thomistic position. But liberal Protestantism came to markedly different views on not only revelation but also natural theology.

Liberalism. This broad movement sought to bring Christianity into a more vital relationship with Western culture during the nineteenth and early twentieth centuries. It sought a more positive attitude toward the movements within culture than had Protestant Orthodoxy (see Dogmatics) or the defensive Christianity of the eighteenth century. In order to bring about this new attitude, liberalism acknowledged the vitality of the growing scientific movement and of the freedom of human reason.

Liberalism was more an attitude than a movement, and its followers were to be found throughout Europe, England, and America. Liberalism's major thrusts are sometimes summarized this way: (1) a broader liberal spirit, coupled with a belief in the authority of the Christian experience; (2) respect for science and the scientific method, particularly as applied to the study of the Bible; (3) care in proclaiming any truth to be "ultimate," coupled with the centrality of Jesus Christ in the lives of those who experienced Christian faith; (4) confidence in man and his future, a confidence often expressed in some form of social idealism. These attitudes expressed themselves as Protestants took the lead in such fields as biblical criticism (which see), especially in Europe, and in the movement known as the Social Gospel (which see), especially in America.

From this brief look at liberalism it is not surprising that liberals led the way in reformulating their views of revelation and reason. First, liberalism denied that God ever reveals propositional formulas about himself. Rather, they argued, God reveals himself in a concrete experience of a particular man. That man then may reflect upon his experience and formulate propositions from or about it. These theological formulations are of man's own making and are only more or less meaningful to other men. Of great significance in this view is that revelation is God's activity. But it follows naturally to ask, "Does God reveal himself to all men?" Is there a general revelation available to all men? Liberalism consistently would answer "yes" to these questions. This affirmation implied that whatever a man says about his experience of revelation must be meaningful to other men. But how? Reason was regarded as the most likely means. Thus, the role of reason had also to be reinterpreted. In this second thrust, liberals accepted to large extent the analysis of Immanuel Kant (1724-1804) that there are limits beyond which reason cannot reach. Reason can provide criteria for evaluating whether a given use of language is meaningful, etc. But it can neither prove nor disprove the existence of God, nor can it fully describe God. Liberalism, in effect, said that if the claims of revelation had been extravagant, so had the claims of reason, and both must be less proud of their claims. To large measure liberalism was denying the validity of the distinction between revealed and natural theology.

Its high regard for the value of experience made it natural for liberalism to support the Christian education movement, especially when Christian education was viewed as the moral nurture of the individual in the community of faith.

Neo-orthodoxy (see Dogmatics) strongly reacted against liberalism. Subsequently, Karl Barth (1886-   ) and Emil Brunner (1889-1967) engaged in a long debate over natural theology. Barth rejected natural theology and Brunner defended it.

Paul Tillich (1886-1965) has attempted to recast the whole issue in full knowledge of the long history of natural theology, apologetics, liberalism, and Barth's attacks. He argues that natural theology or philosophy of religion raises the human questions about God. The task of theology is to respond to these questions by offering theological symbols, which speak meaningfully to the issues. (see Methodology)

John Macquarrie (1919-   ) and Schubert Ogden (1928-   ) are two contemporary theologians who are vigorously pursuing their interest in the problem. (see Experience, Faith, Reason, Religion, Sin) J.B.W.

Naturalism Strictly speaking, naturalism holds that the universe of experience does not require any supernatural origin or control. Further, in its extreme forms, it denies any deity apart from nature. In modern times, naturalism has confined reality to what can be examined by natural science. It has been identified with materialism. One of the consequences of such a view has been the distinction between "revealed theology," which God discloses himself, and "natural theology," which is discoverable by examining nature. If one denies the reality of revealed theology and depends only upon natural theology, then natural religion results. This view was particularly influential during the eighteenth century. A few Protestant theologians during the twentieth century have attempted to revise the traditional view of naturalism and to make it more acceptable to Christianity. Henry Nelson Wieman (1884-   ) is the most noteworthy American example. Karl Barth (1886-   ) and the advocates of neo-orthodoxy have fully rejected any form of naturalism. (see Natural theology) J.B.W.

NAVE (see Sanctuary)

NECESSARY BEING (see Aseity)

NECESSITY (see Destiny)

Negation (neh-gay-shun) Negation means either nonexistence or falseness. Immanuel Kant uses the term "negation" to mean that a proposition is, rationally speaking, self-contradictory and thus false. Friedrich Nietzsche presents negation in terms of weakness. Psychologically, negation is most frequently understood as "hate," the death instinct, or destructiveness. Paul Tillich uses the negative term "non-being" to point to the fact that man can fail to be what he was created to be. Emil Brunner views negation in terms of man's experience of what he does not want. The undesirable experiences of life pose a problem for man. Will man accept and affirm all of life or only part of it? Any partial affirmation of life is actually a negative reaction to it.

Negation is a declaration that something either does not exist or that it is void of value. A man denies the truth of a given statement. A person gives a "no" answer to a question. Negation also takes place when a man treats another as being valueless (treats him as a thing). Negation is the opposite of affirmation. In ethics negation is considered a part of the decision-making process. In every choice that a man makes he says "yes" to some possibilities and "no" to others. Man as a creature of choice is faced with the obligation of saying "no" to the right things and "yes" to the right things.

Immanuel Kant (1724-1804) understood negation primarily in terms of contradiction. Man is to act on a basis of rules that he is willing for everyone to accept. Man should not do anything he would not want all men to do. (For Kant's concept of the categorical imperative, see Deontological.) Man rationally analyzes the situation and judges what course of action is the best possible course of action. If his decision is self-contradictory or self-defeating, then it is wrong. For a man to make a promise that he does not plan to keep is for him to live in a negative or contradictory fashion. The purpose of a promise is to build trust and stability and thus give to man something he can depend on. But a promise that is a lie does the opposite of this and is thus self-defeating. Truth is a universally valid proposition. Lying is always wrong because it is concerned about the wrong thing. If man lies to protect his reputation he acts in a self-defeating way. He is untrue to that which is universally valid and thus hurts his reputation, which he was originally trying to help. For Kant man affirms life when he uses his rational ability to live in a logical way. Man negates life when he lives in an illogical or contradictory way.

Friedrich Nietzsche (1844-1900) reacted against the rational emphasis of Kant and against romanticism. He located value in physical strength. Life's impulse to protect itself and to make itself stronger is a natural virtue. Weakness, softness, and martyrdom are all signs of sickness. In the real world power is the thing that is of value. Power is respected, and it accomplishes good for man. Nietzsche taught that Christianity itself was a negation of life, since it encouraged man to become weak or soft. To encourage someone to "turn the other cheek" rather than resist an offender is cowardly, the opposite of courage (which see). Rather than affirming and defending life, Christian teaching would have man roll over and play dead. Nietzsche also wrote that the Christian belief in immortality is itself a way of depriving this world of its value. The Christian teaching of immortality calls men to give up the good life in this world in order to have a good life forever in the world to come. Immortality assumes that the good life in this world really is not worth having. This world is a valueless hallway through which man passes. If man completely rejects life in this world he will then receive a life that is truly valuable. Nietzsche sees this as nothing but a negation of life. Man needs to turn from religion and God, which lead to death (negation of life) and sickness. Man needs to affirm his full humanity and develop his own personal power.

Psychologically, negation is identified as hate, the death instinct and in general, anything destructive of life. Karl Menninger (1893-   ), in *Man Against Himself* and, along with Jeanetta L. Menninger, *Love Against Hate*, explores man's ability to affirm or preserve life (which he identifies as love) and his ability to negate or destroy life (which he labels as hate). Man has within him a basic drive toward life. Man has a will to live. He wants to build up and continue life. Man also has within him a basic drive toward death—the death instinct. This death instinct may take the form of self-destruction. A man may steal something in order to get the community to arrest and punish him. A man may deliberately watch television and refuse to study for a test so that he will fail. Both of these acts are concrete forms of self-hate. The ultimate act of self-hate or self-negation is suicide. Menninger sees man as possessing both of these drives (the drive toward life and the drive toward death). Throughout the life of man these two drives are in constant conflict with one another. Man's future is secured when love prevails over hate. Man needs to overcome hate with love, negation with affirmation.

Paul Tillich (1886-1965) recognizes that man participates in being and non-being. "Being" here is used to mean man's attempt to realize his full humanity. A man participates in being when he freely chooses to accept his life as it comes to him and directs his life by means of free and responsible decision. A man participates in non-being (failure to be a man) when he lets others make decisions for him. A man is not "being" when he refuses to do something simply out of fear of what his neighbor might think. Negation is man's refusal to be a full human being. Life comes as a possibility for man if he will accept it. Man says "no" to life when he refuses to accept and live his own life. Ethical thought is thus an attempt to understand what it means to have the courage to live.

Emil Brunner (1889-1967) uses negation in still another sense. Life itself sometimes comes to man as a clear affirmation of his being. Life says a "yes" to man when everything seems to be going his way. He is a success in what he is doing and receives recognition. On other occasions life comes to man as a "no." Man sees his dreams and hopes crumble. He does not get what he wants out of life. Ethics tries to help man to see value in both the "yes" and "no" that come to him in life. The Christian is called upon to affirm all of life. Man affirms all of life when he accepts both the "yes" and "no," and reacts to both responsibly. Man negates life when he tries to accept only the "yes" and not the "no" of life. Man makes a mockery of life if he is willing to accept only a portion of life as it comes to him. Any and all partial acceptance of life is a negation of life.

Soren Kierkegaard (1813-55) recognized that man in the midst of life is brought before nothingness. Death is a symbol of nothingness, as are sin and meaninglessness. Meaninglessness, sin, and death are experienced by man as cutting himself off (alienating) from life. In the face of these three, man is full of dread because he is confronted by the absurd. Man's life is taking place while he is falling down a bottomless pit. All of his activities are thus being called into question or negated. Only by a leap of faith can man find meaning to his life. Man can, when brought face to face with nothingness, choose to live as if what he does makes a difference, but if he does this he will have to make this decision in faith, since there is no other basis for it. (*see Alienation, Theodicy*) J.S.H.

Neighbor In the Old Testament the word "neighbor" is used most frequently in reference to the Israelite's responsibility to a fellow Israelite (Exodus 20:17; Leviticus 19:18). Sometimes "neighbor" is used in a general way to mean simply another person (Jeremiah 22:8). In a nomadic society Israelites had frequent contacts and transactions with one another. Individual contact with non-Israelites was rare. In this context neighbors are relative equals who have the same basic rights and obligations. The law (which see) is an attempt to specify and regulate obligations between neighbors. The law is a servant of neighborliness in that it attempts to call Israelites to a sense of fair play and justice (Exodus 20:1-17). Throughout the Old Testament a man is regarded as responsible for his neighbors' well-being (Genesis 4:1-16). This responsibility for one's neighbor is expanded in the Old Testament to include the resident alien (Leviticus 19:33-34) and the stranger (Job 31:32). A neighbor may be a companion, a friend, or simply another person. The New Testament takes as central to the Old Testament understanding of neighborliness the statement in Leviticus 19:18 to love the neighbor as oneself. This takes seriously the Old Testament idea that when a man mistreats his neighbor God is offended. Man's obligation to his neighbor is rooted in and inseparable from his relation to God (Matthew 25:31-46). If the question, "Who is my neighbor?" means whom the man of faith is obligated to be concerned about, the Old and New Testaments give an expanding answer to that question. The concept "neighbor" grows in scope to include all mankind.

Perhaps the most significant passage of Scripture for understanding the biblical word "neighbor" is Luke 10:25-37. Jesus is here recorded as stating man's obligations in terms of the great commandment: " 'You shall love the Lord your God with all your heart, and with all your soul, and with all your strength, and with all your mind; and your neighbor

NEO-ORTHODOXY

as yourself.' " Then Jesus is asked, " 'And who is my neighbor?' " He
replies by telling the story of the Good Samaritan. The question would
seem to be asking: Who am I responsible for? If that question is the
one Jesus answers, then a neighbor would be defined as one who is in
need. Actually Jesus answers the question by telling what quality constitutes neighborliness. Man is a neighbor to another when he shows
mercy to the other. Neighborliness means showing unlimited mercy to
anyone in need. This is true apart from any question about what the
other deserves or how he has acted in the past (see Luke 6:27-36). A
Christian is called upon to help anyone who needs help, any time, any
place. The love of neighbor commandment has been understood by
some to mean that one loses all concern for himself. Matthew 5:38-42
and Romans 12:14-21 suggest that the Christian should not be interested in defending his own honor. If taken literally these passages suggest that a Christian has no right to protect himself or stand up in defense of himself. The Christian concern to help others, however, need
not be understood in terms of self-depreciation. Erich Fromm
(1900-   ) has suggested that man cannot love another unless he
loves himself. Mature love overcomes separation and hostility while
preserving the full humanity of the separate individuals involved. Helping build up the neighbor is not something that demands tearing down
one's own life. Rather, helping one's nighbor and building up one's own
life are necessary partners. Christian love of neighbor involves man in
a depth relationship of concern to help. This goes beyond "neighborliness," which is often misunderstood as being nice to or getting along
with those who happen to live in the same neighborhood. (see Love,
Works) J.S.H.

NEO-ORTHODOXY, NEO-REFORMED (see Dogmatics)

NEO-THOMISM (see Metaphysics, Natural law, Natural
theology, Reason, Revelation

NEPHESH (see Body)

NESTORIANISM (see Christology)

NEUROTIC ANXIETY (see Anxiety)

NEW CREATION (see Cosmogony, Freedom, Redemption)

NEW MORALITY (see Morality)

NICENE CREED (*see Christology, Creed*)

Nihilism (*nee*-huh-lism) This doctrine doubts that anything exists, or, if it exists, that it can be known, or if it is known, that such knowledge could be communicated to anyone else. The ancient Greek philosopher, Gorgias (483-375 B.C.), was the first to defend nihilism. Christianity holds that reality exists, that it is good because it is created by God, and that it is knowable because God reveals it. A Christian cannot easily be a nihilist. J.B.W.

Nominalism(*Nahm*-eh-nuhl-ism) To the question "What can I know?" nominalism answers, "only concrete individual things." Only by seeing specific objects that are alike in some ways would anyone ever conceive of "trees." If one examines particular trees, then one may classify other similar objects as trees. This process, however, is abstract. The name "tree" is only a word by which the mind organizes its experiences. In the Middle Ages, theologians had great debates over this issue. Some, called "realists," insisted that the idea of a "tree" is more real than any particular object that anyone calls a "tree." The theologian William of Ockam (*c.* 1300-*c.* 1349) was the most vigorous defender of nominalism in the history of Christian theology. One of the most important results of nominalism has been the modern attention given to the uniqueness of individual men. Religiously and philosophically, nominalism is related to existentialism. (*see Realism*) J.B.W.

NONES (*see Office*)

Normative (*nor*-muh-tiv) A norm is a standard or model of correctness. For a community to accept something as normative, it must regard it as established by a recognized authority. In Christian theology the question of what is normative often arises in connection with ethical behavior. Monogamy is, for example, the normative pattern of family life for most Christians. However, normative may have an even broader meaning. For many theologians the New Testament is normative. Any departure the theologian makes from the Scripture must be shown to be only apparent, not real. One must understand what any given theologian regards to be normative in order to evaluate his work fairly. (*see Authority*) J.B.W.

Noumena This Latin word means the awe that religious persons feel toward a place or a thing touched by the spirit of a god. The philosopher Immanuel Kant (1724-1804) defined noumena as the world beyond sense experience. Since no one could feel or touch that world, they could not really know about it. Instead, they could only know about the "phenomenal" world, the objects and beings that could be felt, touched, seen, or measured. If Kant is right, then it is hard for theology to say it knows very much about God and the world of the spiritual. For that world is beyond the senses and thus beyond human knowledge. In order to get around this problem, some theologians claim that while we cannot *know* about God, we can *believe* in him. They usually depend on a notion of revelation, rather than reason, for man's awareness of God. (*see Holy, Language, Phenomena*)

Number   The biblical use of numbers may be classified as (a) the ordinary use to which no symbolic or other significance is attached, and (b) the symbolic use, where certain numbers have in the course of time received special force. It is with the latter group that this article is concerned. It has been pointed out that in the ancient Orient there was a preference for round numbers in indefinite statements. There was also in the Near East a tendency to associate the use of numbers with religion. In the later period, that is to say, by the time the New Testament was written, many of the numbers in common use had undoubtedly lost their original meaning and become largely customary.

In late Judaism and in the New Testament the number *seven* is prominent. In non-biblical literature we read of seven heavens (Slavonic Enoch 3 *ff.*; Testament of Levi 2 *ff.*); also of seven high mountains, seven large rivers, and seven great islands (Ethiopic Enoch 77:4, 5, 8). Its occurrence in the New Testament is common: seven loaves and seven baskets (Matthew 15:34 *ff.*; Mark 8:5 *ff.*); the seventh hour (John 4:52); seven churches, seven candlesticks, seven stars, seven seals (Revelation 1:11-20; 2:1; 3:1; 5:1, 5). It may have been thought of as the perfect number, conveying the idea of completeness.

The number *twelve* stands out in both the Old and New Testaments. According to tradition the tribes of Israel numbered twelve. It was natural that this should be incorporated in ritual, symbolism, and history. Examples of this are found in Exodus 28:21; Leviticus 24:5; 1 Kings 7:25; Ezekiel 43:16. It is not surprising that the number figures prominently in New Testament as well. In many cases the disciples of Jesus are referred to simply as "the twelve," although a comparison of the various lists make it difficult to determine exactly twelve disciples. It is possible that "the twelve" is a Christian duplication of the twelve tribes, since early Christianity considered itself to be the true Israel.

The number *forty* appears in both Testaments in a more than literal way. The most notable reference is Jesus' forty days of temptation in the wilderness (Mark 1:13). Matthew and Luke have it that Jesus fasted for the forty day period (Matthew 4:2; Luke 4:2). This seems to be a reflection of the forty days spent by Moses on Sinai (Exodus 24:18; 34:28). The reference to the temptation reminds us of the repeated use by Old Testament writers of the number forty for times of testing. It is of note that the number forty appears in Acts 1:3 as the length of time between Jesus' death and the Ascension. In the Old Testament the rain fell forty days and forty nights at the time of the flood (Genesis 7:4, 17). These are but examples of a widespread use of the number, especially in the Old Testament.

Other numbers that seem to have possessed symbolic value are *three, three and a half* (the half of seven), *five, a hundred, seventy,* and *seventy times seven, ten thousand.* Undoubtedly there are others. The reasons for the symbolic use of these numbers are in some cases fairly clear; in other cases they are obscure. Undoubtedly the preference for the round number accounts for some of the usages. When one number is used as a round number, then multiples of that number also become important. The number seven with its multiples may be an example of this.

Special mention may be given the number *six hundred sixty-six* in the Johannine Apocalypse (Revelation 13:18). In some manuscripts the number reads *six hundred sixteen.* Obviously this number is a reference to some person in the historical situation that lies behind the Apocalypse. This is possible because Greek letters had a numerical value. Various guesses have been made about the meaning of the reference. The best possibility is that it refers to one of the emperors, either to Nero (37-68) or Domitian (51-96). This practice of adding up the numerical value of letters is called *gematria.* Other examples occur in early Christian literature. E.L.T.

NURTURE (*see* "*Liberalism,*" *under Natural theology*)

OBEDIENCE (*see Duty,* Kenosis)

Office   This word has several meanings. The quire offices, or hours, were devotionals followed by groups at intervals of three or four hours: nocturns (cock-crow), lauds (day break), terce (about nine A.M.), sext (about noon), nones (3 P.M.), vespers (sunset), prime and compline (intervals during the night). Monasteries during the Middle Ages followed these offices, but their use declined after the Reformation. "Office" also means the levels of ordination, such as deacon and elder. Finally, it is sometimes used to refer to certain rituals, such as "the office for the commissioning of missionaries." (*see Orders, Vesper*) G.E.S.

Omnipotence (ahm-*nip*-oh-tuhntz) Literally, omnipotence means "all powerful." Theologians have often used this term as one of God's attributes or qualities. Only God would be so described. It is a controversial idea because it is finally an unclear idea. For example, does omnipotence mean that God can do anything he wills? Can he create a God more powerful than himself? If so, he would no longer be omnipotent. If not, he would not be omnipotent to start with. This kind of problem has usually led theologians to conclude that omnipotence must mean, as Thomas Aquinas (*c.* 1225-74) has taught, that God can do "that which is genuinely possible." By so modifying the idea, omnipotence comes to mean perfect power rather than unlimited power. Paul Tillich (1886-1965) and Karl Barth (1886-   ) have both dealt significantly with this problem in contemporary Protestant theology. (*see Attributes*) J.B.W.

Omnipresence (ahm-neh-*preh*-zuhntz) Literally, omnipresence means "everywhere present at the same time." Like omnipotence and omniscience, this is one of the classical theological attributes of God. It has meant that God is never limited to being present only in some particular place or at some particular time. Further, it has meant that in all places and at all times God's creative power is at work. The opposite of omnipresence is "nowhere," the implication of nihilism or of some forms of naturalism. Gustav Aulen (1879-   ), a Swedish Protestant theologian, has written meaningfully on this topic. (*see Attributes, Naturalism, Nihilism, Omnipotence, Omniscience*) J.B.W.

Omniscience (ahm-*nis*-see-uhntz) Literally, omniscience means "all knowing." Along with omnipotence and omnipresence, omniscience is one of the attributes of God, according to many classical theologians. But, if it is claimed that God already knows everything including the past, the present, and future, this raises great problems. If God knew that evil and sin would come into the world, why did he not create it differently? If he knew evil would come and did nothing about it, in what sense is he all loving? Or, if he is all loving and could not avoid evil for his world, in what sense is he omnipotent? Many recent Protestant theologians say that such questions are irrelevant and assert that omniscience refers to God's perfect love. Some philosophers, *e.g.*, Charles

Hartshorne (1897-   ), have argued that omniscience means that God knows all that it is possible to know. But since the future is not yet, it cannot be known. When it is present or past, God will know it. Many theologians reject this view because they think it limits God. (*see Attributes*) J.B.W.

ONTIC ANXIETY (*see Anxiety*)

Ontology (ahn-*tah*-loh-jee)   *Derived from a combination of Greek words, the strict meaning of ontology is "discourse on being itself." As such it is a branch of the more inclusive field of metaphysics (which see). In the history of the Western philosophical tradition, metaphysics has been the most encompassing word to use when asking about what philosophy deals with.*

But in modern thought, metaphysics has become suspect in the eyes of many, philosophers as well as others. Since Immanuel Kant (1724-1804) not only distinguished between "pure reason" and "practical reason" but denied that metaphysics could be verified, it has declined in its influence (see Verification). But ontology has retained its interest for many philosophers. Especially under the impact of pragmatism in America and existentialism in Europe, great attention has been given to the reality of existence or being. Among the most important philosophers along this line is Martin Heidegger (1889-   ) the German existentialist, whose thought has profoundly influenced such Protestant theologians as Rudolf Bultmann (1886-   ) and Paul Tillich (1886-1965).

Because both the philosophical issues and theological implications of ontology have received such full attention in his writing, Paul Tillich's thought will provide the basis for the remainder of this article. He insists that the fundamental meaning of philosophy is the search for an answer to the age-old question, "Why is there something and not nothing?" Or, as Heidegger has put it, "Man is that being which asks what being is." Theology shares this basis with philosophy and to that extent, the task of both converge.

But theology also differs from philosophy. Theology is not primarily concerned to discover the *structures* of existing reality. Rather, it concerns itself primarily with the concrete and personal *meaning* of existing as a human in a particular time and place. In his concern with this meaning the theologian is also concerned with the commitment of men to this existential meaning. The supreme example of this is man's faith ("ultimate concern" in Tillich's words) in the "Ground of Being," perceived as God. In this commitment Tillich shows himself to be first and foremost a theologian. He clearly is of the opinion that philosophy must ask the right questions about the meaning of existence and equally insistent that theology, in its concern for concrete commitment to these questions, must answer the question.

Tillich very helpfully lays out what must be the four areas of concern in all thought about ontology. They are: (1) the basic ontological structure; (2) the "elements" constituting that structure; (3) the characteristics of being that are the conditions of existence; and (4) the categories of being and knowing. In other words, the structure of reality must always take into account both the essence (ontology) and the existence (science or technology) of reality. These questions seem to characterize the ontological enterprise, regardless of which particular thinker is being considered.

The religious significance of ontology is most evident in its relation to the theological doctrines of God (the structure of reality) and of man (existent beings) in the world. Whether recognized or not, all theological formulations of these doctrines, and many others as well, have ontological implications. Tillich, and other theologians, insist that theology must be fully self-conscious about its presuppositions and conclusions if it is to be meaningful to critical mankind. (*see Epistemology, Ontology, Reason, Revelation*) J.B.W.

Oral tradition The expression "oral tradition" applies to both Old and New Testament study. The Jews of the first century had their written law, the Torah. But by the first century of our era there had grown up a vast body of tradition that was not reduced to writing. This tradition had as its purpose the interpretation of the written law in order to make it relevant to new situations. It had to do with the regulations of certain matters, as, for example, the observance of the sabbath. In New Testament times this tradition was accepted by the Pharisees but not by the Sadducees. In theory, the oral law did not possess the authority of the written Scriptures, but in practice the distinction did not always hold.

Oral tradition lies behind much of the Gospel material. The Synoptic Gospels, in particular, are largely composed of units of tradition that circulated orally. Form criticism has as its concern the tradition in its oral form and the *Sitz im Leben* or setting in life, which each tradition reflects. (*see Form criticism*) E.L.T.

Orders Early in the Christian movement those chosen or appointed to special places of leadership in the church were given specific titles. The functions of these leaders were more definitely fixed as the church's organization became more complex. Those named to leadership in the religious community have usually been set apart for their particular function by a ceremony or rite known as "ordination," or "laying on of hands."

The apostles were the earliest ministers of the church (see Apostle). Ministers in the early church also included *prophets*, who had special gifts of interpreting revelations of the Holy Spirit to the church. They also traveled from one church to another. A third classification was *teachers*, given the task of instructing new converts. Another office was *pastor*, meaning "shepherd," a title which is used in the Bible for "ruler" of a congregation.

Bishop (*episcopos*) means "supervisor" and is the New Testament office given to those who have authority over others. This may be same as pastor and elder in biblical use (Titus 1:5-11). It did not assume the technical sense of bishop, as we know it today, until the second century. In the earliest histories, bishops were pastors of congregations, except in larger areas where they presided over several congregations.

Another biblical order is that of the *deacon*, which means "servant." This office arose at the request of the apostles (Acts 6:2-6), to release them from serving tables so that they could give more time to preaching and praying. The deacons order may have included dedicated women, who were "deaconesses" (1 Timothy 3:8-13).

Monasticism, whose influence in the church began to be strongly felt in the early fourth century, brought with it several orders. Among them were the Augustinians, the Benedictines, the Capuchians, the Carmelites, the Dominicans, and the Franciscans. The Mendicant Orders (Franciscans, Dominicans, Augustinians, and Carmelites) took vows of poverty and depended upon mendicancy, or begging, for their needs. Such begging was regarded as an act of humility, and provisions were obtained by their labors or the generosity of others.

In The United Methodist Church, there are two ministerial orders, deacons and elders. *Deacons* are ministers who have made enough progress in their preparation for eldership to receive a first order of the ministry. They have authority to conduct worship, to preach, to perform marriages where the laws of the state or province permit, and to assist in the administration of the sacraments. *Elders* are ministers who have completed their formal preparation for the ministry, and have been elected itinerant (traveling) members in full connection with an annual conference. Ordained elders in The United Methodist Church are authorized to preach and teach the Word of God, administer the sacraments of baptism and the Lord's Supper, and to give pastoral care to the congregation. The order of deacon precedes the order of elders in time, and each order has a status and validity of its own. A lay worker in The United Methodist Church is qualified for a chosen field but meets personal and professional "standards of excellence" in order to be consecrated by a bishop. He is seated in an annual conference with privilege to speak but not to vote. A deaconess is a woman lay worker who, unlike other lay workers, is appointed by a bishop.

A *bishop* is an elder of the church elected to serve as a bishop or administrator in the church for life. He is regarded as a shepherd over many flocks and pastors. He is administratively responsible to the Council of Bishops and the General Conference. His office is administrative and thus is not an actual order. Bishops in The United Methodist Church are "consecrated" and not "ordained." In some communions, an area served by a Bishop is called a "diocese." Churches other than The United Methodist Church in which the office of bishop is found, include Eastern Orthodox, Protestant Episcopal, Anglican, Roman Catholic, and Swedish and German Lutheran, among others. In some churches, the bishop is a separate order.

In some churches, notably the Anglican, Roman Catholic, Episcopal, and Orthodox, the ordained minister is known as a *priest*. Other denominations have questioned the use of this term for the minister of the congregation. They believe the priesthood of all believers means that each individual is his own priest before God, and that no person can exercise the priestly function for another. Priests are usually called "Father" while other pastors have been called "Reverend." The use of "Father" is universal in the Roman Catholic Church but is optional in the Anglican Church. The word "Brother" arose to distinguish ordained priests from lay-brothers. (*see Apostle, Cardinal, Conference, Diocese, Episcopal, Prophet*) G.E.S.

Orders of creation This term refers to the separate areas in which the Christian is called to obey God. The basic idea is rooted in the concept of the natural law. During the Middle Ages, all of life was viewed as coming from God and tending toward God. However, God had appointed the levels of society—serfdom, royalty, the clergy—as "natural." With the reformation, natural law continued as a force, but it was reinterpreted. Martin Luther (1483-1546) thought in terms of "two spheres"—the law of Christ and the law of the world. They were not totally separate. However, the church's duty was to teach the law of Christ, the law of love. By transforming individuals at the center from which moral action springs, society would be changed. Luther saw the state, the family, and economics as separate orders. More recently, Emil Brunner (1889-1967) has spoken of the "life of love," the I-Thou relationship of the Christian community, as one order. The "natural forms of community" are then family, labor, state, culture. Dietrich Bonhoeffer (1906-45) insists that life is one, but he speaks of "the four mandates" —labor, marriage, government, and the church. (*see Natural law, Vocation*)

Ordinance Literally, this is an authoritative rule, decree, or command. In church history the term has been applied in several ways.

In some cases the practices or ceremonies of the church have gained widespread acceptance and then are given the status of an ordinance. This is done either by an authoritative council or by an authoritative pronouncement by a bishop or pope. It was by this means that in Catholic liturgy seven sacraments became ordinances. Thus, ordinance may also refer to one of the specific sacraments. By analogy those acts or pronouncements the church believes to have come directly from God's authoritative action may be referred to as God's ordinances. (*see Authority, Doctrine, Dogma*) J.B.W.

ORIGINAL SIN (*see Sin*)

ORTHODOXY (*see Conservative, Dogmatics*)

P SOURCE (*see Source criticism*)

Pagan From the Latin word, *paganus*, which means "a countryman" or "country dweller," it refers to an irreligious person or a heathen. "Heathen" is the term usually used to indicate some one who is hostile toward religion, while a pagan is someone who simply refuses to become interested. The word grew in use because Christianity had its earliest and strongest appeal in the city rather than rural areas. Country dwellers came to be called pagans, and the use of the word has continued. (*see Apostasy, Heresy*) G.E.S.

PALEONTOLOGY (*see Archaeology*)

PANENTHEISM (*see Process*)

PANTHEISM (*see Immanent, Theism*)

PAPYRUS (*see Manuscript*)

Parable The parable is a literary form, common in rabbinical literature, and is found in both the Old and New Testaments. A good Old Testament example of the parable is found in 2 Samuel 12:1-4.

In the New Testament, the Synoptic Gospels contain numerous examples. These Gospels reflect Jesus' method of teaching by parable. It is of interest that the Gospel of John contains allegories but not a single parable. The parable is a story, usually brief, intended to illustrate a single point. The parable of the Prodigal Son in Luke 15, for instance, illustrates the love of God for his children, a love that is not dependent on their merit. The interpretation of the parable is often abused by confusing it with allegory, in which the various details of the story are intended to represent some idea or thing not in the material itself. In the parable, on the other hand, the details of the story are there simply to make it a good story. They should not be allegorized. (see Allegory, Form criticism) E.L.T.

Paraclete (pa-ruh-kleet) The Greek word paraklētos had as its original meaning "one who is called to somebody's aid." This accounts for the rendering "advocate," which is found in some translations. This legal idea is rare. The more usual meaning is the general idea of helper, mediator, intercessor. "Helper" seems to be about the best translation for the term as it appears in the New Testament.

The Paraclete appears in John's Gospel, which refers to the future Coming One, the Holy Spirit (14:16, 26; 15:26; 16:7). John's concept of the Paraclete is a part of the author's doctrine of the future, which differs radically from that of the Synoptics. The latter reflect the view that the two ages appear one after the other, whereas John presents two worlds one above the other in space. The synoptics and early Christianity generally look to the future, to the Parousia or the coming of Christ. John, on the other hand, sees Jesus as the abiding Presence, Spirit, and Paraclete at the same time. (see PAROUSIA, Spirit) E.L.T.

Paradigm (pair-uh-dighm) A paradigm is a pattern or an example that establishes the model for all similar events or analyses. The notion of a paradigm is valuable in several different kinds of study. In learning a language, for example, the study of verbs is done by using an example that exhibits all the usual changes for the tenses of verbs in that language. Or, in studying literature, an example will be taken as typical, such as one of Jesus' parables. By analyzing the paradigm the student will gain a technique for analyzing all the other parables. Although the term is not religious, it is invaluable for studying religion to establish paradigmatic examples. Some form critics, like Martin Dibelius (1883-1947), use paradigm in a narrow sense. They mean certain kinds of narrative stories found in the Gospels. The stories began in oral tradition, were closely related to the sermon in form, but existed by themselves as brief stories. Mark 2:1-12 is an example. (see Form criticism, Pronouncement story) J.B.W.

PARADISE (see Fall)

Paradox   In the original Greek, "paradox" meant literally "against current opinion." But in the history of thought it has been used in several different ways: (1) as something simply absurd; (2) as a wise saying; and (3) as something both true and false. In modern Protestant theology the word has come into great prominence, especially under the renewed influence of Soren Kierkegaard (1813-55). But its history is as old as Christianity itself. Blaise Pascal (1623-62) wrote: "there are reasons of the heart that the reason knows not of." Nicholas of Cusa (1401-64) wrote of the "coincidence of opposites." And Tertullian (*c.* 160-230), the father of Latin theology, wrote such radical things as, "I believe, because it is absurd." But already in the New Testament itself one reads that he who loses his life will find it.

Clearly, then, the theologians who use paradox in Christian discourse believe reason is limited. Some conclude that all discourse about God must be paradoxical. These thinkers are often charged with intellectual laziness or irresponsibility, or both. Thinkers who object to paradox view reasoning about God as formal logic. Whatever characterizes sound reasoning about anything applies equally to reasoning about God. These believers in the power of formal reasoning usually rely on some form of analogy.

The defenders of the use of paradox in "God-talk" generally side with Kierkegaard, who said the problem is not formal, but rather existential. As Kierkegaard put it: "It is the duty of the human understanding to understand that there are things which it cannot understand, and what those things are." God is not understandable.

Since Christianity affirms that the Eternal (God) has come into time (in Christ), it affirms a logical contradiction. Time and eternity are incompatible. To formal reason the affirmation is illogical and absurd. Christianity acknowledges this when it further affirms that God's activity in Christ can only be received in faith.

But why do such theologians believe reason to be limited in this way? The answer is also theological. Reason is limited not only because it is finite and imperfect, but most importantly because it is caught in sin, *i.e.*, it is separated from God. Try as he may to reach God through reason, man fails—he is unable to overcome his own sinfulness. And, if he were able to do so, there would be no need for God's activity in Christ. Man would claim to know God; yet he has scarcely understood the meaning of human love and hatred. To this "human predicament" God came in the paradox of the cross of Christ. In order to give man life, Christ died. That is the paradox.

Paradox is most important in the work of modern neo-orthodox theologians. Among them the names of Emil Brunner (1889-1967), H. Richard Niebuhr (1894-1962), and Reinhold Niebuhr (1892-   ) stand out. (*see Analogy, Christology, Dialectic, Existential, Faith*) J.B.W.

223

Parallelism Parallelism is a feature of Hebrew poetry in which two lines with different wordings are used to express the same thought. Its literary function is that of emphasis. A good Old Testament example of parallelism is found in Psalms 8:4:

what is man that thou art mindful
of him,
and the son of man that thou
dost care for him?

The second line of this example lends weight to the first. But the meaning is the same in both lines.

In the Gospels, examples are found in Matthew 21:5, a quotation from Zechariah 9:9; and in John 19:24, again an Old Testament quotation, this time from Psalms 22:18. In both instances the New Testament writers appear to have misunderstood the function of parallelism, and they interpreted the texts quite literally. E.L.T.

PARAMENTS (*see Sexton*)

Parish Traditionally, this is the geographical area under the charge of a pastor. Residents in the area of a particular church make up the parish. In the Roman Catholic Church, parish lines determine which church communicants should attend. (*see Curate, Rector*) G.E.S.

Parousia (pa-*roo*-zee-ah) The Greek term *parousia* means "presence," "coming," "advent." In early Christianity and in the New Testament it often has the technical meaning of the coming of Jesus as the Messiah. The function of the Messiah is the inauguration of the new age and the judgment of the world. The belief grows out of the Jewish doctrine of the two ages, the present evil age to be replaced by the new age or the Kingdom of God. According to late Jewish tradition, a tradition found in the Synoptic Gospels also, it is the Son of man who is to come on the clouds of heaven to inaugurate the new Kingdom. In the synoptics, and in early Christian tradition before the synoptics, the exalted Jesus is identified with this Son of man. Almost from the beginning the church looked forward to his coming, to the *parousia*. The belief in the *parousia* is sometimes called eschatology (doctrine of the last things), and the belief that Jesus will *soon* appear is described as imminent eschatology. (*see Eschatology*) E.L.T.

PASCHAL (*see Sacrifice*)

PASSION (*see Atonement, Character*)

PASSIVITY (*see Faith, Grace, KENOSIS*)

PASSOVER (see Communion, Sacrifice)

PASTOR (see Orders)

Patriarch The word "patriarch" comes from a composite Greek word meaning "father of a nation." Sometimes it is applied to the heads of families living in the period before Noah (Genesis 4:17-26; 5:3-31). It is also applied to the twelve sons of Jacob, the ancestors of the "twelve tribes of Israel" (Acts 7:8). But a more restricted use of the term is its application to Abraham, Isaac, and Jacob. Abraham stands out as the father of the race (Hebrews 7:4 ff.; 11:12). There is one New Testament reference to "the patriarch David" (Acts 2:29), but this use is unusual.

The expression "Patriarchal Period" is given to the time before Moses. During that period the ancestors of Israel were nomadic or semi-nomadic tribes located in the Syrian and Arabian deserts. The stories dealing with the Patriarchal Period, found in Genesis, are legends and traditions written down long after the events. It is with Moses that the birth of the nation becomes a reality. E.L.T.

PATRIPASSIANISM (see Impassible, Trinity)

PATRISTICS (see Church fathers)

Peace Peace is closely associated with the Judeo-Christian ethic of love. Killing and destruction, which occupy man's time when he is at war, are contrary to man's basic nature. The most famous "peace passage" in the Bible is Isaiah 2:4 (parallel in Micah 4:3-4). It refers to a future period when God will destroy all instruments of war and vanish war from the face of his earth. In the Old Testament, shalom (peace) means wholeness or completeness. This definition applies when the term is used to refer to military or economic matters as well as spiritual matters. The covenant God has given to man shows man the way to peace. This may be described as the removal of sickness or as a means to health. The same is true of society. The formula is a simple threefold one. (1) If a man has the right relationship to himself, to others, and to God he will have peace. (2) The covenant is the occasion for man assuming this right relationship. (3) If man is faithful to the covenant, then God rewards man with peace.

In the New Testament peace is used to include the Old Testament meaning, the classical Greek meaning and still more. The classical Greek meaning of the word "peace" was an absence of hostilities. In the epistles

225

peace is used quite frequently as a friendly greeting. Beyond this, peace has three basic meanings. (1) Peace is the opposite of war and thus indicates the absence of conflict or strife, *i.e.*, harmony and the proper orderliness necessary to harmony. (2) Peace is used to describe man's state of being or condition as restored to the right relationship to God through Jesus. (3) The word also is used to indicate serenity.

Peace is sometimes used as a psychological category to indicate that a person is sound of mind. Here peace means that a person is not psychotic. *The Power of Positive Thinking*, by Norman Vincent Peale (1898-   ), is an attempt to help man keep control of himself. Man looks on the brighter side and sells himself on the fact that he is able to do what needs to be done. Psychology itself raises serious questions about this approach. It tends to be unrealistic by refusing to take seriously the difficulties involved in life and thus does not offer a creative solution to the problems of life.

Paul Tillich (1886-1965), in *The Courage to Be*, refers to peace as something quite different from peace arrived at by positive thinking. Here peace is gained by risking oneself in the midst of life's uncertainties. Man sees correctly the life and death questions being faced in his history. To respond to these questions involves a person in certain risks. A person may be thrown into great turmoil and distress because he has decided to do the right thing. This peace comes only from doing what needs to be done. J.S.H.

PEACE OFFERING (*see Sacrifice*)

PELAGIANISM (*see Freedom*)

PENTATEUCH (*see Source criticism*)

Pentecost Known also as "Kingdomtide" or "Whitsunday," Pentecost literally means "fifty days" or "the fiftieth day." In the Jewish faith, it came exactly fifty days after the Passover and was the festival that celebrated the completion of the harvest. In the Christian community, it is the seventh Sunday after Easter and commemorates the coming of the Holy Spirit. Its observance may be traced to the third century. Some call it the birthday of the Christian church. (Acts 2:1-4) Pentecost is now observed as a festival of victory in the church, and members are sometimes received. "Whitsunday" comes from "White Sunday," when candidates were baptized and received into the church, usually in white robes. G.E.S.

PEOPLE (*see Elect*, Laos)

226

Perfection   The Old Testament concept of perfection indicates a state of being fully grown or fully-developed. In this rather strict sense the term is applicable only to God. When the term is used of men its meaning might better be rendered upright, blameless, or mature. God's claims on human life (the law) are to be taken seriously and obeyed. In the Old Testament no man has reached the full state of complete obedience.

Aristotle (384-322 B.C.) taught that perfection "lacks nothing in respect of goodness or excellence and cannot be surpassed in its kind." Perfection is an ideal state that man can know and identify with. In the New Testament perfection is used to indicate man's becoming fully committed to doing the will of God (Matthew 5:48; 19:21). Perfection is used in the New Testament to indicate the fulfilling of prophecy. It is also used to indicate God's work through Christ's suffering. God works through Christ's suffering to make Christ perfect and fully to accomplish his work (Hebrews 2:10).

John Wesley (1703-91) taught that a Christian must be disturbed by his mistakes. He must be concerned to stop "what he should not be doing" and start "what he should be doing." Man is to be "going on to perfection." Wesley understood scriptural perfection to be "pure love filling the heart and governing all the words and actions." Harald Lindström, in *Wesley and Sanctification*, points out that Wesley's use of "perfection" is governed by three primary meanings. (1) The word is used in connection with the Christian's obligation to be completely consumed by love of God and neighbor. (2) Perfection also is used to point out that the Christian's intentions are to be without blemish. This use is like that of Soren Kierkegaard (1813-55), who said purity of heart meant "to will one thing." Perfection includes the removal of all barriers in man's attitude toward the neighbor. (3) Wesley also uses perfection to indicate the Christian's responsibility in imitation of Christ.

Throughout the church's discussion of perfection two questions continue to be unsolved. (1) Is perfection a possibility for man in history? (2) Is perfection a state of sinlessness? Or does perfection only mean that the Christian does not mindfully or willfully "transgress the law"?

The question of man's perfection does not play a central role in present day theological circles. Neo-orthodoxy in its reaction to liberalism has caused a new emphasis to be placed on the fact that man is a sinner.

Present theological conversation is concerned about the word "perfection" as it applies to God. Is God perfect in the sense that he is whole or complete (lacking in nothing)? Or is God perfect in the sense that he is that being than which no other being could conceivably be greater, but who still has the potentiality to become greater? This latter idea leaves open the possibility that God is both perfect in his being and at the same time significantly related to the world. (*see Holy, Process, Sanctification*) J.S.H.

Pericope (peh-*rik*-uh-pee)   The term pericope is composite, being made up of two Greek words that together mean "to cut around," and so "to delimit." A pericope is a well-defined unit of tradition, which, however, may appear embedded in a document. By the application of critical method, the scholar is often able to isolate such a unit, which has the characteristic of being complete in itself. A pericope may extend all the way from a thoughtful saying to a story.

An example of the pericope as a story is the well-known *pericope adulterae*, found in our Gospel of John (7:53–8:11), but is also found in some manuscripts at the close of Luke's Gospel. The story is in all likelihood an ancient tradition that at one time circulated independently but found lodging in manuscripts of John and of Luke.

Form critics have identified many independent units of tradition embedded in our Gospels. Each of these had its own history (oral, and in some cases written). The setting of the pericope in its original modifying situation is called its *Sitz im Leben*, setting in life. (*see Form criticism, World view*) E.L.T.

Petition   In The United Methodist Church, any member of the church, lay or clergy, and any organization in the church, may send a request to the General Conference. Such requests might include proposed changes in church law or recommendations for a resolution. Petitions must follow a required form. At the General Conference each petition is handled by a committee, and if approved, is sent to the Conference for a vote.

Petition also means a request presented to God in prayer. (*see Prayer, Conference*) G.E.S.

PHARISEE (*see Priest, Resurrection*)

Phenomena   A "phenomenon" is an appearance that can be experienced. If Israel defeats an enemy in battle, we can be fairly certain it was a "phenomenon." However, if Israel claims it was God who helped them win the battle, then the claim is not phenomenal but "noumenal."

When used in religious thought, the idea of phenomena is helpful in distinguishing between the events and experiences that can be measured and proved and those that cannot. However, the problems are (1) what to do about borderline cases (such as the Resurrection and Transfiguration) and (2) what the importance is of the noumenal world. On the last point, most theologians have said that though God belongs to the noumenal world, we can believe in him through means other than sense experience. (*see Noumena, Revelation*)

PHILOSOPHICAL THEOLOGY (*see Theology*)

PHILOSOPHY (*see Epistemology, Metaphysics, Ontology, Reason*)

PHILOSOPHY OF RELIGION (*see Religion*)

Piety This term has been used for personal relation to God, especially one's devotional life. It is used in contrast with profane or secular. As a movement, Pietism, led by Philipp Jakob Spener (1635-1705), was a revolt against intellectualism in the seventeenth century and a return to evangelical Christianity. It stressed the feeling of conversion and not the knowledge of truth. In this sense, piety has taken on a negative connotation and is sometimes used in connection with false emotion. Such misuse should not deny the accurate use of the word, which really pertains to one's personal expression of final loyalty to God. G.E.S.

PISTIS (*see Faith*)

PLEROMA (*see Gnostic*)

Pluralism As the name implies, pluralism is the view that many interests, groups, and powers have rights in a society. The state, for example, is not the absolute ruler because it has to take into account the desires of many interests. Nor is law absolute, for it has to adapt itself to the needs and rights of conflicting groups, rather than standing on tradition.

The church is interested in the concept of pluralism because the idea also denies that religion is a final authority. In a pluralistic society, religious groups are only one kind of many kinds of groups. They are not necessarily the most important, and they have no more rights than non-religious groups.

Many Christian thinkers today call on the church to take seriously its role in a pluralistic society. They hold the church cannot expect favored treatment, nor can it expect to dominate. Churches have to be content with being a minority. They have to recognize that men may choose to operate through other groups to build up the whole society. In reply, critics of pluralism point out that some standard or value is always needed to help groups solve their conflicts. Whatever the standard is, it is, in effect, a sort of absolute for the whole society. Some Christians contend the church needs to build up its membership and its institution as much as possible, so that it can have the means to operate as a powerful force for religious purposes. Pluralism is to be distinguished from "functionalism" (see Functional) and "localism," the view that the local group is the final authority on what is best for its interests. (see Secularization)

PNEUMA (see Spirit)

Polity The way a church is organized is its "polity." For example, the polity of Methodists is basically episcopal and representative, that of Southern Baptists congregational and democratic.

POLYTHEISM (see Theism)

Pope Derived from the Latin word, *papas*, which means "Father," this word refers to the Roman Catholic Church's regard of their highest leader as the Holy Father. He is the sovereign of the Papal State, Vatican City, and is considered the Bishop of Saint Peter's, Rome. Popes are elected by the College of Cardinals at a special conclave that begins fifteen days after the death of the reigning Pope. The election takes place by secret ballot, of which one more than two-thirds of the votes cast assures election. The Pope-elect is then consecrated for his holy office in the Sistine Chapel in Vatican City and reigns until his death. (see Bishop, Cardinal) G.E.S.

Positivism (*pahz*-eh-tuh-vism) When something is believed to be fixed and definite, it is said to be positive. The French philosopher, Auguste Comte (1798-1857), proposed that a fruitful way of gaining knowledge would be to examine only those things that are positive. All matters of speculation, imagination, or wishing were to be excluded from consideration. This program has become one very popular stream of thought in the modern world. In England a school of thought developed early in the twentieth century was called "logical positivism." The aim was to achieve certain knowledge, even if about only a limited range of positive facts. Because of the severely restricted limits within which positivism operates, its value for theology is limited. J.B.W.

Possibility (see Potentiality)

Potentiality In ordinary use potentiality means something with the quality of being possible, as opposed to being actual. Thus, by extension, a potentiality is something capable of being or becoming.

In any discussion of a potentiality it is clear that a thing may as well not be or not become, as that it may.

Obviously connected with any concept of potentiality is actuality. In this contrast potentiality refers to the power a thing possesses simply because it is what it is. A dog, a man, and a tree—each contain certain potentialities that uniquely belong to their being what they are. A man simply has different potentialities from a dog's. Potentiality is different from actuality. Although a person may have certain potentialities, he may not make actual these potentialities. Potentiality is also strictly different from possibility, which is the merely conceivable or imaginable.

In medieval scholastic theology, deeply influenced as it often was by the thought of Aristotle (384-322 B.C.), any change observed was regarded as a movement from potentiality to actuality. All finite creatures were regarded as being made up of both potentiality and actuality. By contrast, the absolute, infinite, and perfect God was regarded as *actus purus*, pure actuality. This was held to be the only way to avoid some notion of changeability in God. A perfect God, according to this way of thinking, is unchanging.

Recent theology in liberalism and neo-liberalism has emphasized God's involvement with His creation. One of the consequences of this emphasis is that if God is involved, then he must be affected by events in the world. Such theologians have not been afraid to affirm that this must mean that God changes. Neo-orthodox theologians reject this view on the ground that it is guilty of the ancient heresy of patripassianism.

Potentiality and actuality in and of themselves are useful tools for rational analysis. It seems, however, that any real thing must be analyzed by both terms, rather than making one or the other absolute. (*see Idealism, Metaphysics, Ontology, Process, Realism, Reality, Theism, and Theology*) J.B.W.

Power　Power is the energy that causes things to happen. We may speak of the power of health, electrical power, political power, or a "powerful personality." The power of God refers to the fact that God cannot be either conquered or ultimately defeated.

In the Old Testament power is the ability to do something. Thus, it is the capacity that includes both moral and physical strength to do a job. When Moses questions his own right to be the one who leads Israel out of Egypt, God's presence is the guarantee of Moses' authority and power to do the job. Moses will be successful in the attempt because of the power of God, which supports him (Exodus 3:11-22). In the Old Testament all power is derived from God. Man, created in God's image (Genesis 1:26), is free to make decisions, and these decisions influence history (Joshua 24:14-15 and Deuteronomy 11:26-32). Therefore, man is a

231

creature with power. What he does makes a difference in this world. In the Old Testament power is understood in concrete terms. It is the ability to shape and direct the course of human events. Power is political and military (see the books of Joshua and Judges). God's power does not destroy man as a center of power. Yet, from time to time in the Old Testament good and evil spirits do enter into history and take control of man. In the New Testament the terms *dynamis* and *exousia* are used to refer to that which has control over a man (Luke 10:19; Matthew 7:22). Involved in the question of power is the question of authority (*exousia*) (Luke 20:1-8). Power in the New Testament is also associated with the Greek idea of angelic creatures who have an existence independent of man. The good and evil spirits are at war on the earth battling for control of man. Man's heart is the battleground (Mark 1:21-28). Evil spirits cause sickness to occur (Mark 5:1-13). Christ is the power of God that makes men whole (Romans 1:16; John 20:31; 1 Corinthians 1:18, 24). Man is able to stand against the powers of the world if he lives in faith and is guided by God's spirit (Ephesians 6:10-20).

Paul Tillich (1886-1965) defines power as the energy to resist non-being. God gives man his being. In fact, God is the power of being. If a man trusts in God he gains from this the ability to be a fully human person. Through this trust he is able to stop doing destructive acts. He gains the ability to build up life. Thus, power is basically good or constructive or life affirming. Power is to be distinguished from force or compulsion. Power moves and changes the world. Life would be an impossibility without power. Power uses force that is irresistible. Power is misused when a man is forced to do something that is not just or fair. Power, love, and justice supplement one another.

Power has to do with the movement of life. It is thus concerned with the state of the world. "State" here refers to the existing circumstances, politically and otherwise. Religion answers the question: In what direction should life move? Or for what purpose is life's energy to be used? Power comes to man as a good gift. Man can misuse power and destroy his life. The church has made two serious mistakes in relation to the question of power. On occasions the church has been so impressed with the danger present in power that it has tried to retreat from any contact with power. In effect, the church tries to cut itself off from life and thus not get involved in power struggles. On other occasions the church has tried to gain complete control of the world so as to use force to build up the church. Religion fulfills its function when it seeks to help man discover the meaning and purpose of his life so that he may properly use the energy that he has.

Reinhold Niebuhr (1892-   ) has proposed an alternative to the two mistakes of retreat and force. To begin with, man should recognize the fact that power is the product of spirit. To be without power would be to be dead. Thus, all of life includes power. Man's job is to try to combine power and justice. He is to use this world's energies in a manner that will be fair to all men. At the same time man is to face the fact that God alone is able to combine perfectly power and justice. All human structures that seek to control man's use of power end up being unfair to some. Man is to be involved in the tedious task of discovering what use of power will come closest to being fair to all persons concerned. (see *Authority, Negation*) J.S.H.

PRACTICAL THEOLOGY (see *Theology*)

PRAGMATISM (see *Experience, Truth*)

Prayer   The means by which man communicates with God is called prayer. It is that act in which the creature places himself in contact with the Creator in order to express his feelings and longings. Joy, thanksgiving, and requests for God's direction are expressed in such communion. The act of prayer is based on a relationship of faith in God and is not the mere use of pious words and phrases. Prayer is a two-way communication in which the one offering the prayer allows himself to listen and receive God's presence as well as to speak.

G. van der Leeuw (1890-1950) regards prayer as an exercise in power. When the person who prays is passive ("thy will be done," for example), he permits the divine to have power over him. When the person who prays is active (as in "give us this day our daily bread") he seeks power over the divine. When the believer is aware of caution in approaching divine power, he may call attention to his seeming presumption: "We are bold to pray, 'Our Father. . . .' " In this view, some forms of prayer are meant to insure greater success, but pure form without feeling is seen to be an empty religious ritual.

Jesus encouraged his disciples to pray when he said, " 'Whatever you ask in my name, I will do it. . . .' " (John 14:13) The example of prayer that he gave his disciples is the Lord's Prayer (Matthew 6:9-13; Luke 11:2-4). A famous biblical prayer is the one known as Jesus' high priestly prayer for the world (John 17).

There are several forms of prayer. *Invocation* is a prayer spoken at the opening of a service to seek the presence of God. The formula, "In the name of the Father, and of the Son, and of the Holy Ghost," sometimes used at the beginning of sermons and special occasions, is a traditional invocation. In Orthodox, Roman Catholic, and Anglican liturgies, the epiclesis is a form of the invocation. It is used to invoke the presence of the Holy Spirit in the Eucharist. *Benediction*, though frequently taking the form of prayer and often considered a closing prayer to a service of worship, is more accurately a blessing spoken by the officiating clergyman asking God's presence to be upon the people. *Intercessory* prayer is prayer to God on behalf of others. Reference to Christ's intercessory prayers may be found in Matthew 19:13; Luke 22:32; and John 17. A *petition* literally means "an asking" and constitutes a request that one places before God for direction and help. *Confession* is an admission of guilt and may be both individual and congregational. "Confession" is used in some traditions, however, for the admission of sins by a penitent to a priest before communion. *Supplication*, related to the word "beg," means earnestly and whole-heartedly making an entreaty to God asking his help. Prayers of *thanks-giving* are praises to God for his mercies and goodness. (*see Office*) G.E.S.

Predestination Although predestination is often equated with foreordination, technically it should be more restricted. In this restricted sense, theologians have meant that God has eternally willed a destiny for his intelligent creatures. In its starkest form it may be put thus: God saves whomever he wills to save. Some, like John Calvin (1509-64), have also held that in order to be consistent, one must also say that God wills to damn those whom he does not will to save. This strict interpretation is referred to as "double predestination." Most modern Protestant theologians have rejected the idea. Paul (in Romans) and Augustine (354-430) were two of the early theologians who gave considerable attention to the question. (*see Destiny, Election, Freedom, Providence*) J.B.W.

Pre-existence This is not a biblical expression. The idea of pre-existence, however, is fairly common in the biblical literature, especially in the New Testament. In the Old Testament, where Wisdom is personified, as it is in Proverbs 8, Hebrew religion has been influenced by Greek thought. In Proverbs, Wisdom is present at the creation of the universe. Though the book does not expressly say that Wisdom was the creator, the creative nature of Wisdom is suggested by calling Wisdom a "master workman" (8:30). In the Jewish Philo of Alexandria (first century B.C.-A.D.) the Greek Logos takes the place of Wisdom. In the Fourth Gospel the Logos is the creative agent and is pre-existent. To the extent that in the Christian tradition Jesus is identified with Wisdom or Logos, he is said to have been pre-existent. For the writer of John's Gospel the Logos was "in the beginning with God," and then at a point in time the "Logos became flesh and dwelt among us." This is John's statement of the incarnation. A doctrine of the incarnation presupposes (see Presupposition) pre-existence; that which already existed as divine being became man. A similar idea is expressed in the Book of Hebrews, although in that book the term Logos is not mentioned. But the idea of Logos is contained in 1:1-3. In Hebrews, the creative Logos appears in Jesus, who is described as the ideal High Priest. Hebrews is strongly influenced by Platonic ideas, so that the notion of an order of reality transcending this finite, changing world influences its view of Jesus. From the nature of the case, the Jesus of Hebrews is eternal. In addition to John and Hebrews, Colossians 1:15-16 contains the notion of pre-existence, the idea of the creative Logos being present there also.

Most of the titles for Jesus found in the New Testament do not contain in themselves the notion of pre-existence. The title "Logos" lent itself to this idea very readily. Along with Logos we might mention the title "Son of man." This expression is found in Ezekiel, where it probably means simply "man," in Daniel, and in non-biblical Jewish apocalypses, notably the Book of Enoch. The meaning of "Son of man" in Daniel and Enoch is extremely uncertain. However, it can safely be said that it refers not to a human being but to a heavenly being who will exercise judgment upon the world. This title appears in the New Testament, especially in the Synoptic Gospels. Scholars believe that Jesus used the title for the agent of God who would usher in the kingdom of God, as it was believed, in the near future. The early church identified Jesus with this heavenly Son of man. To the extent that he was fully accepted as Son of man in the sense of Daniel and Enoch, the idea of pre-existence was present in the early church.

The concept of pre-existence affirms that the life of Jesus was more than an isolated event in history—it was indeed the life of God made manifest in the world. The use of terms like Logos and Wisdom raised the values experienced in Jesus to cosmic proportions. The Christian affirmation is that the answer to the question, "What is God like?" is answered by the assertion, "He is like Christ." The idea of pre-existence points beyond the particular historical event of Jesus' life to the ground of its being in God. (*see* KENOSIS, PAROUSIA, *Word*) E.L.T.

Presbytery Technically meaning "a body of presbyters," it is derived from the Greek word, *presbuteros*, which means "elder," (used, for example, in 1 Timothy 5:17) and includes the ministers and elders (both teaching and ruling) within an area. (*see* Episcopal, Orders, Session, Synod) G.E.S.

PRESENCE (*see* Communion, Spirit)

Presupposition (pre-suh-poh-*zish*-uhn) In logic a presupposition is what must be assumed if a desired result is to follow from what is being solved or argued. In theology, it must be presupposed that God is good in order for his creation's goodness to follow. Without such a presupposition, it will be no more certain that the creation is good than that it is evil. In a somewhat more unusual sense, a presupposition may be not the assumption that leads to a conclusion, but the conclusion itself. If a conclusion is presupposed, it is in order to reason back to discover its causes. In this case one would presuppose that the world was created. Then one would reason that there must have been a creator of the world. J.B.W.

PREVENIENT GRACE (see Grace)

PRIDE (see HUBRIS)

Priest Religion is often divided into "priestly" and "prophetic." It is sometimes said that the prophet represents God to man, but the priest does exactly the opposite—represents man to God. Priestly religion is ritualistic and cultic. It may extend from primitive forms of expression to complex and sophisticated forms.

The Old Testament speaks of two orders of priests, the Aaronic and the Levitic. However, according to one line of tradition, the Levites were not priests, but rather were appointed to assist the priests (Numbers 3:9; 8:19; 18:1-6). A distinction between priests and Levites is made in the New Testament (Luke 10:30-35; John 1:19). In late Judaism the priests were responsible for religion centered in the Temple at Jerusalem. In this period the synagogue was perhaps more influential in the lives of the people than Temple religion. We may associate the Pharisees more with the synagogue and the Sadducees with the Temple. (see Prophet, Sacrifice) E.L.T.

PRIESTHOOD OF ALL BELIEVERS (see LAOS)

PRIESTLY SOURCE (see Source criticism)

PRIME (see Office)

Prime mover This term was made prominent in philosophy by the ancient Greek philosopher, Aristotle (384-322 B.C.), and in theology by Thomas Aquinas (A.D. c. 1225-74), who used Aristotle's philosophy. The term refers to what is absolutely basic. It is the source of all change—movement being the force behind all change. In itself, since it is first, or primary, it is unchangeable. This means that there is nothing more basic than the prime mover that may cause change. Thomas Aquinas constructed several arguments for the existence of God upon this presupposition. Aquinas took it as an article of faith that God and the prime mover were identical. J.B.W.

Principle A principle is the fundamental truth from which specific conclusions are drawn. In ethics a principle is a general rule from which specific sources of action are to be determined. The Greek word meaning principle also means beginning (*arche*). A principle is a beginning out of which other things proceed. Principles are the source or the original out of which the factual world has come. In Greek thought principles have mysterious life-giving and life-depriving power. A principle is the ultimate basis upon which something depends. In Greek ethical systems a principle is a fundamental rule that guides conduct. Socrates (*c.* 470-399 B.C.) was committed to the principle that the law and order of the state is good.

In the New Testament principles are the original material out of which everything evolves. Principles are supraterrestrial beings with great power in this world. Evil spirits or principles have the ability to wreck man's life. The messiah comes, setting men free from evil principles. The evil powers are overcome by the love of God in and through the messiah.

Roman Catholic ethical thought places considerable emphasis on the importance of principles. Following Aristotle (384-322 B.C.) and Thomas Aquinas (A.D. *c.* 1225-74) axioms or principles are seen as reason's grasp (man's understanding) of the natural. A principle is basic and actually more important than specific decisions, since a principle is that out of which the specific decision grows. A principle expresses the discovery of parts in nature and the order of these parts. Thus, the principle of justice takes into consideration the different factors and persons involved in human decisions and suggests the way these factors and persons are to be related. Principles, being basic truths, are necessary prerequisites for all learning. Principles will serve the purpose of bringing order out of chaos, and health out of sickness.

In Scholastic thought, "middle axioms" or "middle principles" were used to compare extremes and bring them together. Value is constituted out of the middle axioms. It is a pivotal or organizing principle in Scholastic thought. In recent years the term "middle axiom" is used in a quite different way. John Bennett (1902-) uses the term as a principle more specific than universal ethical principles, but more general than specific laws or legislation. An example of Bennett's use of "middle axiom" is that the national community, meaning labor and business, as well as government, is responsible for maintaining full employment. (*see Deontological, Natural law*) J.S.H.

Process A process is a continuous action, operation, or series of changes taking place in a definite manner. Thus, it is used as synonymous with becoming, action, existence by thinkers committed to a dynamic view of reality. From this basic commitment certain philosophers have created an encompassing metaphysics. In this country two

237

of the most notable are Alfred N. Whitehead (1861-1947) and Charles Hartshorne (1897-   ). Their writings represent one of the most important attempts in the twentieth century to revive metaphysical thought from the doldrums into which it passed in the nineteenth century.

Process philosophy is, first, a metaphysics closely related to the natural sciences. One of the major reasons for the defection from traditional speculative metaphysics was the influence of science. Second, unlike many other modern philosophers, Whitehead and Hartshorne have consistently shown a great respect for and interest in religion, and they have made significant contributions to the philosophy of religion. For example, Whitehead thinks that the religious vision has historically shown more capacity for expansion and revision than any other mode of human perception. This, he thinks, is a great cause for hope and optimism regarding the future in general. Hartshorne, a close follower of Whitehead, has written extensively regarding matters of central interest to theologians. In his *Man's Vision of God, Philosophers Speak of God,* and *The Divine Relativity,* one finds many of his most provocative analyses. Hartshorne has rigorously criticized traditional theism. He proposes a position like this: There is no Being in all respects absolutely perfect (as in classical theism); but there is a Being in some respects perfect, and in others not so. Further, it is not impossible that this Being can be relatively perfect in all the respects in which it is not absolutely perfect. He calls this position "panentheism" (to be distinguished from "pantheism").

A rather large and important group of theologians have been influenced to greater or lesser degree by this process philosophy. Two of the younger contemporary theologians of significance are John Cobb (1925-   ) and Schubert Ogden (1928-   ), whose books, *A Christian Natural Theology: Based on the Thought of Alfred North Whitehead,* and *The Reality of God,* respectively, are directly influenced by Hartshorne.

Process philosophy, and the theology that employs it, represent one of the two most significant metaphysical options today. So-called "neo-Thomism" is the other. (*see Metaphysics, Ontology, Theism, Theology*) J.B.W.

Procession   Augustine of Hippo (354-430) said the Holy Spirit "proceeded" from the Father and Son (see John 15:26), but the Son was "begotten" by the Father. He understood himself to be interpreting the recent Nicene Creed (which see). The importance of Augustine's view is that the Trinity's three persons are seen in *relation* to each other. Thus one does not have to explain how three beings can be one being, for God is One being, but the Father begets the Son, and the Spirit proceeds from both.

G. van der Leeuw (1890-1950) understands "procession," as used in the entry of a choir or other group into a service of worship, as a circling motion to limit or concentrate power. Joshua's circle around Jericho is one example. The procession is also a sort of dance showing that divine power extends over a region or a part of life. (*see* Trinity) G.E.S.

PROCLAMATION (*see* KERYGMA)

Prolegomena (*proh*-loh-*goh*-meh-nuh) From the Greek, "prolegomena" means literally "to say beforehand." Thus in theology, the prolegomena to the body of a man's theology is the introduction. In it, he attempts to state the presuppositions and limits within which he operates. In a theological prolegomena, for example, one often finds discussions about revelation and how it relates to man's reason. It must be observed, however, that the word itself is not a uniquely theological term. J.B.W.

Pronouncement story Form critics classify the units of tradition in the Gospels in various ways. One classification, for example, gives four categories: paradigms (examples), tales, legends, and exhortations. Another analysis of the tradition uses the term "apothegm" (pronounced *ap*-oh-them) instead of "paradigm." Still another employs the expression "pronouncement story" instead of paradigm or apothegm. This expression has the advantage of focusing attention of a pronouncement of Jesus that frequently appears in the form and is the real reason for its appearance. Thus in Mark 2:23-28, the point of the story is Jesus' pronouncement found in verses 27-28: " 'The sabbath was made for man, not man for the sabbath; so the Son of man is lord even of the sabbath.' " This way of listing the forms in the Gospels is based on the assumption that units of tradition existed by themselves before being included in Gospels. The pronouncement stories are considered by some to be, next to the Passion narrative, the oldest of the traditional forms. (*see* Form criticism, Paradigm, Saying) E.L.T.

PROOFS (for God's existence) (*see* Theism)

Property When one speaks of a property in theology, he refers to a characteristic or an attribute of what is being described. Although any particular property may not necessarily be present, it is characteristically to be found. Thus, theologians often talk about Jesus' concern for Mary, his mother, as one of Jesus' properties. Now, Jesus would still have been Jesus had he not demonstrated such a property, but since he did, it is worth noting. Or, if one discusses a person's characteristics, he does not mean that the person would be essentially different without this or that property. But, in an effort to fully describe this

239

person, attention should be given to his properties. (*see Attributes*)
J.B.W.

Prophet The English word "prophet" is derived from a compound Greek word meaning "to speak for" or "on behalf of" somebody. The Greek translation of the Old Testament (Septuagint) uses this term in its translation of the Hebrew *nabi* (nah-*vee*). In the history of Hebrew prophecy this word applies to a relatively late development in which the prophet is considered to be God's spokesman or mouthpiece. The earlier word *roeh* (roh-eh), *i.e.*, seer, comes from a root meaning "to see." Samuel and the early prophets were seers. Associated with this early prophecy was the experience of ecstasy. First Samuel 19:18-24 is a good example of this. The mystical and transforming character of the experience is indicated by 1 Samuel 10:6: " 'Then the spirit of the LORD will come mightily upon you, and you shall prophesy with them and be turned into another man.' " Religious ecstasy was an outstanding characteristic of early Hebrew prophecy.

Some scholars believe that prophecy of the *nabi* type did not come into being until the Philistine conquest (*c.* 1200 B.C.). This type of prophecy is political as well as religious in character—if, indeed, the two can be properly separated in Hebrew thought. In any case, the great prophets of Israel such as Amos, Isaiah, and Jeremiah were deeply involved in the social and political issues of the day. But when they pronounce judgment on the nation, they do so as spokesmen for God: "Thus says the Lord" is their watchword. They are therefore essentially "forthtellers" rather than "foretellers," although the predictive element is present. Predictions of the future are not made independently of the prophet's sensitivity to what is taking place in society. It must be remembered, moreover, that the prophets belonged to Hebrew life and thought, in which the myth of the beginning (creation) was paralleled by the myth of the end (*eschaton*). All of history was under the control of God. Violation of his will or of the covenantal relation existing between God and his people would result in dire consequences.

Scholars of a somewhat earlier period tended to view the prophetic movement in Israel as entirely separate and distinct from law. It is now almost universally accepted that this position was in error and that the proclamations of the prophets are indebted to earlier legal formulations both with respect to form and substance. This indebtedness is particularly clear in the Book of Deuteronomy. Once this idea was accepted it was easy to claim that the prophets were not innovators but simply revivers of the older Mosaic religion. But the fact that the prophets built on the law does not at all deny that they creatively shaped that religion.

The New Testament prophets seem to be more individualistic, perhaps more ecstatic, than the prophets of the eighth century B.C. and the centuries following. In 1 Corinthians 14, Paul exalts prophecy over "speaking in tongues" on the grounds that the former edifies while the latter does not. In his discussion of the "gifts of the Spirit," with which chapters 12–14 are concerned, he makes edification the norm. (*see Apocalypse*) E.L.T.

PROPITIATION (*see Atonement, Redemption, Sacrifice*)

Proposition In the strictest sense, a proposition is a statement in which something is affirmed or denied in such a way that henceforth it may be regarded as true or false. In theological use propositions often will be made, then discussed, and finally agreed upon. Such propositions then may become presuppositions for subsequent discussions. In formal logic a proposition may be regarded as the content of a declarative sentence. For example, "God is love" may be regarded as a proposition that invites reflection and investigation. J.B.W.

Protestant Protestant is a term originally applied to followers of Martin Luther (1483-1546) who objected to the results of the Diet of Speier (1529). The results of the diet were that in Catholic lands the Lutherans were not granted religious liberty, while in Lutheran lands the Catholics were. A group of evangelicals felt that they must *protest* (object to) this arrangement. The use of the term was later expanded to include followers of John Calvin (1509-64) and Ulrich Zwingli (1484-1531). Today the term is frequently misused to refer to all Christians who do not belong to the Greek or Roman Catholic churches. Some of the larger denominations who do consider themselves to be Protestants are: Methodist, Presbyterian, Disciples of Christ, American Lutheran, and Lutheran Church in America.

Friedrich Schleiermacher (1768-1834) emphasizes reformation as an ongoing process—the church must be reshaped anew in each generation. Paul Tillich (1886-1965) developed Schleiermacher's thought further in speaking of the "protestant principle." All social orders (including the church) are relative and should be subject to criticism. Tillich concludes that a protestant is concerned to constructively criticize everything that is. Thus he avoids placing an ultimate value on anything earthly. A protestant is able to do this because of his commitment to the God who continues to make himself known. For Tillich this means that God is not limited to some former understanding of God. Thus, the protestant is one who says both a "yes" and a "no" to his own tradition. He says a "yes" to his past in the sense that he takes it seriously and tries to learn from it. He says a "no" to his past in the sense that he is willing to differ from it. At the same time a protestant is aware that his present

241

understanding of the Christian faith is imperfect and will need correcting.

In some respects the protestant is one who illustrates the concern of John Wesley (1703-91) that Methodism not "keep the form of Godliness while losing the spirit of Godliness." Man encounters God. He shapes his religion, or his church, according to his own understanding of this experience. He is in danger of assuming that his understanding of God is the measure of all men's experience of God. He makes this mistake when he places the kind of ultimate significance on "his experience" that belongs only to the God he has experienced. Dialectical theology is an attempt to avoid this idolatry. It assumes that all men know only part of the truth about God. All men need to learn from the experiences of others. Protestantism assumes that the church represents the Kingdom of God but is not identical to it. The church is made up of men who make mistakes; thus, the church is not to be allowed a privileged position exempting it from criticism. Service to God includes criticism of the church as well as criticism of the culture. (*see Dogmatics*) J.S.H.

Providence *Providence comes from the Latin words* pro, *before, and* videre, *to see. It means "to see before," which is "fore-ordering" or "seeing to it." In its basic thrust the doctrine of providence affirms the constant creative relationship God maintains with his world and men in the world. The idea of providence is suggested by but not used widely in the Bible. It comes from the Stoics, ancient thinkers who believed that the way things happened was inevitable but still good. Christian thinkers used the idea to mean: (1) preservation as God's purpose for his creation (man and the world). Some Christians wanted to point to a certain event and say that it was God's purpose. However, preservation really means that despite what happens, God has a good purpose. (2) In popular thought, God was thought of as a king, leading to the idea of Him as* Governor. *(3) Divine cooperation means that God and man work together in making things happen. John Calvin believed that God's providence meant God knew and decided in advance what would happen. John Wesley disagreed; what God knows is that men will act with freedom, he said.*

Theology regards the relation of God, man, and the world in different ways. God is the creator of the world; he is the preserver-sustainer of the world; and he is the savior of the world. These concepts relate God as Trinity.

Providence is a doctrine that does not arise from a precise use in the Bible. Rather, it is a term taken over from Stoic philosophy. In philosophical use, divine providence was equal to divine foresight or foreknowledge. Although some of these suggestions remained in theology, generally the concept was broadened. It includes three clear themes: (1) divine preservation of creation, in which God sustains his creatures in their particular modes of being (from the Latin *conservatio*); (2) the divine governing of creation by God's intimate and constant guidance of it (*gubernatio*); and (3) divine concurrence or co-operation. In the last notion, God's preservation and government appear in the actions of his creatures in such a way that any explanation of why a man does this or that must include both the creature's and God's involvement in the action. All these concepts obviously have a great deal in common.

Since providence depends on the concept of God, certain aspects of the doctrine of God must be considered. In traditional Christian theology God is held to be both transcendent and immanent. He is beyond the world, but he achieves his purposes within the world. This paradoxical view underlies any view of providence. Since it is a paradox, a tension remains in a doctrine of providence. If the tension is not maintained, then events will break down faith in providence, and along with it faith in God. But such tension is difficult to maintain, and serious problems are connected with the idea of providence.

The idea that God preserves creation is useful. It assumes a purpose for the world and man because of its divine creation. The belief in a purpose for creation strengthened Christianity's appeal in the ancient world, in which meaningless fate or destiny seemed to control existence. Such an affirmation did not originally mean, however, that men would be able to point to a particular event and conclude that it was proof of God's preservation and purposes. Rather, the faith in providence affirmed a faith that would not be refuted by any empirical evidence. Such a view often involved emphasis on divine foreknowledge and foreordination. It also led to rationalistic interpretations of providence that tended to forget the *faith* source of providence.

The notion of God's preservation was fairly sophisticated. It was often expressed in popular piety in terms of God's governance of his creation. Since, the argument goes, God made the world with its orders and natural law, then he must be respected as its sovereign. This is the source of what is sometimes called in theology the "sovereignty of God." This analogy is a very old one deriving from ancient, oriental societies in which the king was truly sovereign. He held absolute power for his subjects and all the property within his jurisdiction; he was absolute maker and enforcer of laws; he was the source of mercy and justice or cruelty and injustice. It is easy to see why God might be conceived as sovereign. But, like preservation, the idea of God's governance of creation tempts men to look for proofs convincing to human reason. Finding none that are universally convincing to reason, faith in providence is placed in danger.

The third notion involved in providence, divine concurrence or co-operation, is most closely related to philosophy. Medieval scholastics, dependent on Aristotle's philosophy as they so often were, discussed the relationship between primary and secondary causes. The case of human action is most uncertain. If the idea of providence entails a view of divine-human cooperation, then what meaning is left for human freedom? The degree to which human freedom is defended decides the various shades of doctrines of providence. For the strictest defenders of providence, e.g., John Calvin (1509-64), human freedom is totally denied, and divine control totally affirmed. Double predestination is a natural corollary of this view, and Calvin fearlessly accepted it. The most determined defenders of human freedom, e.g., Luis de Molina (1535-1600), Jacob Arminius (1560-1609), and John Wesley (1703-91), insist that providence does not mean that God's foreknowledge settles beforehand what will happen. Rather, as the creator who loves his creation, God knows the events of the future in the sense that he knows that men will exercise their freedom in the future. Since he has created man with freedom, he allows this freedom to work itself out. A mediating position between these opposites is probably taken by most theological views of providence. To a very large extent, however, the problems just mentioned remain unresolved.

Any overly rationalistic explanation of the doctrine of providence may easily lead to logical pitfalls. Although all the theological attempts to deal with the issues involved must be appreciated and evaluated, it is still true that providence is a provocative symbol that cannot be easily expressed in logic. Ambiguity and paradox continue, and the dynamic power of the symbol is easily lost in various efforts to explain it. Perhaps the clearest insights came from the covenantal theology of some Puritan groups in the sixteenth and seventeenth centuries. These ideas have been revived in the twentieth century by some theologians, such as Paul Tillich (1886-1965), who has written: "Providence is a *quality* of every constellation of conditions . . ." (*Systematic Theology*, Volume I, page 267). (*see Analogy, Destiny, Freedom, Grace, Immanent, Symbol, Transcendent*) J.B.W.

PRUDENCE (see Calculation)

Pseudepigrapha (soo-deh-*pig*-rah-fa) Literally, the term "pseudepigrapha" means "false writings." In general, a pseudepigraphon is any literary work to which a pseudonym, or false name, is attached. It has come to be applied, however, to a certain group of writings that claim biblical characters as their authors. A well-known source for these writings is R. H. Charles, ed., *The Apocrypha and Pseudepigrapha of the Old Testament*. The literary fiction involved here, namely, the attributing of a given work to a well-known hero of the faith, was considered perfectly legitimate in ancient times and presented for the ancients no ethical problem. (*see Apocrypha, Canon*) E.L.T.

PSYCHE (*see Self, Spirit*)

PSYCHOLOGY (*see Epistemology, Freedom*)

PUNISHMENT (*see Predestination, Sanction*)

Purgatory The Roman Catholic church designates purgatory as an intermediate state for the soul, following the death of the body. During this time of punishment the soul is aided by special Masses and prayers for the deceased. It is a time of penance and satisfaction for sins from which the faithful may be released to enjoy the bliss of eternity after the purification of their soul. (*see Limbo*) G.E.S.

PURPOSE (*see Teleology*)

QODESH (*see Holy*)

QUELLE (*see Source criticism*)

QUIETISM (*see Mystic*)

RADICAL (*see Conservative*)

RANSOM THEORY (*see Atonement*)

Rationalism (*rash*-uh-nuhl-ism) The use of this term ranges from precise, tightly defined meanings to quite vague and careless

245

ones. In the first, precise use, rationalism means "the principle or habit of accepting reason as the supreme authority in matters of belief, opinion, or conduct." (Random House Dictionary, 1966). Such a use is generally confined to philosophy, where a careful distinction is often drawn between reason and other faculties, such as the imagination or the sense organs. So-called "pure reason" is seen in such a view to underlie any genuine rationalism. In much looser use, the term sometimes merely means those systems of thought in which logic and deductive reasoning dictate the order and arrangement of the parts of the whole. This is used even when, in the system so designated, reason is not regarded as the ultimate judge of truth. For example, many of the medieval Scholastic theologians held that the truth they organized logically was supernaturally revealed. They explicitly denied that reason could establish these truths. To call such systems rationalistic is an arbitrary and uncritical use of the term.

Already it is obvious that for theology the crucial considerations in connection with rationalism are reason and revelation. Until the eighteenth century, revelation was regarded as the supreme authority for Christian faith. Reason was variously evaluated, but even in the highest estimates of the power of reason, any apparent contradiction between revealed truth and the conclusions of reason was resolved in favor of revelation.

But in the eighteenth century reason emerged from its slavery to revelation. By the time of the Enlightenment, defenders of revelation had to demonstrate that the claims for truth made in behalf of revelation agreed with the conclusions of reason. The roles had been reversed, and reason was increasingly regarded as authoritative, even to the point that reason stood in judgment upon revelation. Naturally some thinkers came to regard revelation as entirely superfluous, since it could only make known what natural reason, if properly used, could discover for itself. Thus, what is sometimes referred to as "theological rationalism" flourished. As a result, deism replaced revealed theism for many, and natural religion displaced revealed religion. One of the conclusions widely shared by such theological rationalists was that religion had value chiefly because it contributed to ethical uprightness. Anything in religion that failed to make man more moral came to be regarded as superfluous and expendable. Further, anything in traditional religion that appealed primarily to emotion, rather than reason, was accused of "enthusiasm," a term of abuse.

The works of the philosophers David Hume (1711-76) and Immanuel Kant (1724-1804) added to a thorough rethinking of the power of reason. Many thinkers of the late seventeenth and eighteenth centuries had uncritically employed and accepted the notion of the unlimited power of reason. Kant turned reason upon itself. By careful reasoning, he showed

246

that reason has limits within which it may legitimately operate. Beyond those limits it can make no claims that can be proven.

Some theologians were shaken from their dogmatic stance regarding the character of revelation. They were attracted to a more limited view of the power of reason. Faith was re-emphasized as the appropriate and most basic form of response to experiences of revelation. But faith could then express its understanding of these experiences in rational terms, provided that the limits of reason be acknowledged. (*see Existential, Reason, Revelation, Theism*) J.B.W.

REACTIONARY (*see Conservative*)

REAL PRESENCE (*see Communion* [*Holy*])

Realism The meaning of realism has been almost exactly reversed since the Middle Ages, as will be demonstrated below. The problem arises out of the most basic attitudes toward reality. From that basic beginning point the problem of epistemology is derived. Thus, realism is not primarily a matter of logic or epistemology, but rather of a basic conviction about reality.

In ancient philosophy and medieval Scholasticism what is today called idealism was then called "realism." It was held that universal ideals were more real than any individual examples of them. For example, if one sees a beautiful redwood tree and is led to reflect not about its texture, color, and height, but rather thinks about the structure of "treeness," he is thinking "realistically," as it was then conceived. The height and color of the tree are regarded as its accidents, and its treeness is regarded as its substance or essence, the basic reality of the tree.

Contrasted with realism was "nominalism." Basically this view represented the conviction that individual, existing things are the basis of reality. Thus, nominalism denied that universal concepts or essences have any independent existence. Rather, the nominalists insist that ideas, such as "treeness," are only names given by the mind to organize its experiences into classes, *i.e.*, into a classification system. Today, most thinkers who use the word "realism" to describe their understanding of reality mean exactly what medieval thinkers meant by "nominalism." Only the concrete, particular, individual things encountered by man are real. In the late medieval debate, between realists (idealists as they would today be called) and nominalists (realists as they would be called now) significant results were achieved. For the ancient and medieval Christian mind, committed as it was to universals, there was always the great danger that individual man would be prevented from developing his potentialities as a self. One of the results of the nominalistic reactions against realism was the great emphasis upon the ideas of selfhood and personality that have developed during the last five centuries in Western thought. Psychology, psychoanalysis, and existentialism are but a few trends of thought that illustrate the point.

One of the most radical of the medieval nominalist was William of Ockham (*c.* 1300-*c.* 1349). He argued that only individuals exist. Universals can claim to exist only as vocal sounds. One of the great theological issues affected by the nominalist-realist debate was the doctrine of the Trinity.

Somehow, idealism and realism must be held in tension. This is hard to do, but its advantages make the effort well worthwhile. Perhaps the most notable efforts in this direction lie in the work of the process philosophers and theologians. (*see Idealism, Process, Reality*) J.B.W.

Reality   To a common sense observer, the word "reality" may appear to have a completely clear meaning. However, reflection on the use of "reality" makes one aware that the word is used in relation to more than one aspect of experience. One discovers that the word refers to the actual as opposed to the fictitious; to the essence or absoluteness against the accidental or concrete; to the concrete, objectively demonstrable as against the ideal, undemonstrable; and to the most important as contrasted with the less important. In the words of religious mystics, reality is the "isness of what is." A single definition is obviously impossible. Further, in the religious use cited, religious experience or faith is the means by which awareness of reality is attained by men. In the other uses mentioned, reality is reached through reason, however that may be understood.

The importance of the term "reality" for theology lies precisely in the basic conviction that God is, as Paul Tillich (1886-1965) has argued, "ultimate reality." In this conviction God, rather than some philosophical principle such as the first cause or prime mover, is that without which nothing else could possibly be. Creation is the action by which God imparts reality to his creation. To the perennial question "Why is there something and not nothing?" theologians answer "God." Philosophers, however, without appealing to revelation, which provides God as the answer, have speculated and experimented in efforts to discover the "really real." In either the theological, philosophical, or scientific efforts to discern reality, it becomes increasingly evident that what is there is not reality, but only the manifestations of reality. (*see Absolute, Analogy, Authority, Contingent, Dualism, Epistemology, Metaphysics, Monism, Ontology, Reason, Revelation*) J.B.W.

Reason   *Reason derives from the Latin word* ratio. *It is regarded by many thinkers as man's highest capacity. In such views it is* assumed that reason is the way man learns about reality. Of course, this also assumes that reality is reasonable. Logic is the branch of philosophy that has traditionally concerned itself with whether or not reason is working properly. The theological tradition of Christianity holds many views regarding reason. Thomas Aquinas valued it very highly. Martin Luther felt it to be totally inadequate for Christian faith. Immanuel Kant, as a philosopher, tried in the eighteenth century to establish the limits of reason. Many contemporaries, theological and others, continue the debates upon the topic.

The meanings attached to "reason" have varied in the long history of Western thought, but a fairly representative meaning is "the power or faculty of acquiring intellectual knowledge, either by direct understanding of first principles, or by argument." In its task, the acquiring of knowledge, reason is a part of the larger issue of theories of knowledge, or epistemology. Further, any discussion of reason must include reflection about what is there to be known, about the reality of being itself. This is formally called ontology. In the history of Western thought until very recently there has been an unswerving commitment to the idea that ontology (what is to be known) takes logical priority over epistemology (how to know what is to be known).

Classical philosophy from the fifth century B.C. to the nineteenth century held that reason is the structure of the mind that enables it to grasp and to transform reality. The effects of reason are held to function in knowledge, aesthetic judgments, ethical action, and technical control. As Plato (c. 427-347 B.C.) conceived this notion of reason, it is the most nearly perfect analogy between humans and God. To deny reason is finally both antihuman *and* antidivine. This is obviously a very comprehensive view of reason as the humanizing character of man as man. Within this broad view there is also often found a more limited notion of reason. Paul Tillich (1886-1965) calls it a "technical concept of reason." By this latter view, reason is reduced to a consideration of the knowing ability of man. It is aimed at discovering means to achieve specified ends. The most obvious example of technical reason is the technology of the past two centuries in which a goal is projected, and means to achieve it are sought. No problem arises so long as the ends (goals) sought are reasonable, as well as the means for achieving them. One of the shortcomings of contemporary philosophy is that it has accepted a technical view of reason as sufficient. A brief review of the history of rationalism will clarify this point.

Plato held that human reason can discern a system of truths that are eternal and necessary apart from sense experience. Man, as human, has within him the ability of reason to know these truths. Such a view is referred to as "idealism," since it is based on innate ideas.

René Descartes (1596-1650) symbolizes the development of this notion. Beginning with the abstract truths of mathematics, Descartes analyzed "innate ideas" to discover what universal and necessary truths will enable men to know the meaning of all sense experiences. By a complex and controversial argument, Descartes states the reality of God is necessary in order to insure that the objective world really corresponds to the necessary truths of reason.

Against the idealism of Plato and Descartes stands the rational empiricism of John Locke (1632-1704) and David Hume (1711-76). According to this view, the notion of innate ideas was rejected. In its place was proposed the idea of reason as a "clean slate" (*tabula rasa*) upon which sense experience leaves its impression. Knowledge is gained only as a result of concrete, empirical experience as reason orders and correlates these impressions. By such a view, there are no universal, necessary truths. Only experienced reality is knowable.

Both the idealistic and the empirical views distinguish between the known object and the knowing subject. The relationship between the object and the subject poses one of the chief problems for any philosophy based on reason. Theologians have apparently assumed some common ground between them. This common ground usually assumes that the rational structure of the mind corresponds to the rational structure of reality to which the mind responds. However, the danger is that the live, creative aspect of both the known object and also of the knowing subject may not be recognized. What one knows at one time may have to give way to what he knows reasonably another time. The great tendency in rationalism is to try to make static what in reality is dynamic.

In Christian history the issue of reason has played a dramatic role because of the vastly important question of the connection between reason as a natural capacity of man and revelation as God's self-disclosure. The Bible is not a speculative philosophical collection of writings. Rather, it is a continuous witness of the response of Hebrews and Christians to their experiences of God's revelation. Surprisingly little attention is given in the biblical literature to the questions of human knowledge raised by the classical philosophical tradition.

But Christian theologians have dealt with this question since ancient times. In general two tendencies seem to have prevailed. On the one hand, in the case of such men as Clement of Alexandria (*c.* 150-*c.* 215), Origen (*c.* 185-*c.* 254), and Bonaventura (*c.* 1221-74), revelation was viewed as God's disclosure that confirmed and made possible freedom of reason. On the other hand, in such men as Augustine (354-430) and Thomas Aquinas (*c.* 1225-74), God's revelation was posited as an absolute conclusion that sound reasoning had to reach. The church, in the first view, encourages men constantly to be open to the dynamic of God's revelation. In the second instance, the church is an authority insisting upon the fixed and static form of God's revelation.

The history of Protestant theology can be told in similar terms. Martin Luther (1483-1546) recovered, in principle, a dynamic view of man's knowledge of God. But with the emergence of Protestant orthodoxy the static notion regained the upper hand. Against both the Protestant and Roman Catholic orthodoxies, man in the Enlightenment insisted upon the freedom of human reason as the expense of and in the absence of any sound view of revelation offered by theologians. Secularity rapidly degenerated, however, into secularism (see Secularization). In the process, men reacted against the objective view of reason and turned to more subjective views.

This predicament forced a rethinking of the doctrine of revelation in modern theology. Nineteenth century liberalism exalted man's reason by virtually denying that there is any content in God's revelation. It was almost as if God's revelation meant only man's discovery of truth by his own experience and reason. Such relativism of revelation brought its own reaction, in the form of neo-orthodoxy (see Dogmatics), which reaffirmed the objective content of God's revelation at the expense of human reason, whose power to know God was radically denied. This debate still is going on in many quarters of theology.

One of the most careful students of this problem in modern theology has been Tillich. In his *Systematic Theology* he devoted a large number of pages to a careful analysis and consideration of the history of the problem and present prospects for coming to terms with it. Meanwhile, another group of theologians has arisen who believe the whole problem to have been falsely conceived, and who choose other possibilities. These younger theologians believe a new starting place must be found that will allow theology to follow some model other than that of classical philosophy. (*see Analogy, Epistemology, Revelation*) J.B.W.

RECEPTIONISM (*see Communion, Grace*)

Reconciliation To reconcile is to bring together two opposing parties or points of view. In the New Testament, man needs to be reconciled to God, not the reverse (2 Corinthians 5:18). Men are also to be reconciled to each other (Matthew 5:24) and the church has a ministry of reconciliation (2 Corinthians 5:18). Paul Tillich (1886-1965) spoke of the reunion of being and non-being, of the Creator and the creation. Thus he emphasized the concept of reconciliation.

One question about reconciliation is whether it should be an immediate or long-range goal of the church. For example, it may seem evident that within the church, love for neighbor means harmony in human relations. However, if peace and quiet mean that men cannot express their doubts and disagreements, reconciliation is reduced to surface harmony and to support of the present order of things. If the church seeks to accomplish an important goal, such as the goal of bringing about justice among men, conflicts are inevitable. Men in the church will disagree with each other, and the church will be in conflict with many powers in the community. The church may claim that justice among men is more worthy than reconcilation, or it may claim that justice is actually a means to real reconcilation. The question, then, is when (a matter of timing) and how (a matter of means) the church works for reconcilation. (*see Atonement, Forgiveness, Redemption, Soteriology*)

Rector From the Latin word, *regere*, which means "to direct," a rector is the clergyman who directs a particular parish. In the Anglican Church, it is the same as pastor, while in the Roman Catholic Church, a rector is a priest directing a church that is without a pastor. The administrator of a university school is sometimes referred to as "rector." (*see Orders, Parish*) G.E.S.

Redactor (ree-*dak*-tohr) A redactor is one who edits or revises a document for a given purpose. In some cases the editorial work may be slight. In other cases it may be considerable. It may be simply "improvement" in grammar and style, or it may involve the insertion of new concepts. In ancient times redaction was a rather common practice. Sources were gathered together, and the editor would unite his source according to some plan, providing the proper connectives. The Gospel of Mark is an example of this kind of editorial work. In that Gospel we see the original units of tradition given continuity by editorial connectives such as the phrase, "and it came to pass," which occurs frequently throughout the Gospel. Perhaps a clearer instance of redaction occurs when a book, as such, has been revised. Many scholars see an instance of this in the Gospel of John. It has long been believed that Chapter 21 of John is later than the original Gospel. Some feel that the author of that chapter is a redactor, and that his hand is to be seen at several points in the book. An example of this type of redaction is John 19:35. (*see Manuscript*) E.L.T.

Redemption Redemption means to "buy back." Traditionally Christians have held that man was cut off from his Creator God. In order to reclaim mankind, God provided payment (or propitiation). Through the offering of Jesus Christ on the cross, God accomplished the process by which man comes to him, namely through belief in Jesus Christ. God's grace provides for man's salvation through the purchase accomplished on the cross.

Redemption is a major theme of the Old Testament as well as the New Testament. In the Revised Standard Version "redeem" and the words stemming from it occur 130 times in the Old Testament and 17 times in the New Testament; the term translated "ransom" occurs 20 times in the Old Testament and 5 times in the New Testament. The Hebrew concept involves payment for a life that has been released, which would otherwise have been condemned to death. The ancient Israelites believed that the first-born offspring of man's beasts belonged to God. If the owner chose not to sacrifice it, he could provide an acceptable substitute sacrifice. Such deliverance, obtained by a ransom payment, was familiar in Hebrew thought and is used with regard to the redemption of the nation from sin (Deuteronomy 7:8), and to individuals (Job 33:28).

The Bible uses "sacrifice" to accent the cost to God (Ephesians 5:2; Colossians 1:14). Jesus interpreted his own ministry to include that of laying down his life for the world, "For the Son of man also came not to be served but to serve, and to give his life as a ransom for many." (Mark 10:45) Paul refers to the sacrifice of Jesus Christ as man's having been "bought with a price." (1 Corinthians 6:20)

Several points of view have been taken by Christians in regard to redemption:

1. The biblical language about "ransom" and "sacrifice" means that God repaid the devil in order to buy back man from sin. Jesus is the sacrifice, replacing the Old Testament sacrifice of animals.

2. Creation is good and redemption is the nurture of man's spiritual, moral, and intellectual life. God the Father intends that his children (that is, all men) should grow to love one another and to have faith in Him. He shows his concern through Christ's death on the cross. The new life possible for man is seen in the Resurrection.

3. The biblical language is a symbol of man's sense of slavery to the powers of evil. This evil is sensed in a split within man (his alienation from himself) and between men. Evil is real and man can only heal the breach by accepting God's offer of grace in Jesus Christ. This view itself includes two interpretations:

a. The Neo-reformed thinkers like Karl Barth (1886-) see God's grace as finally including all men. Before "universal salvation," however, the power of sin and death can overwhelm man. One must take seriously the symbol of sacrifice, for God's grace issues from his agony over man and creation. In Barth's view, God does for man what man cannot do for himself.

b. Existentialist thinkers like Rudolf Bultmann (1884-) see the real act of salvation in man's self-understanding. When man comes to see that he is himself responsible for his alienation, then he can grasp the gift of new life opened up by Jesus Christ. This view is very close to that of Paul Tillich (1886-1965), whose favorite term for the redeemed life was the "new creation."

(see Alienation, Faith, Grace, Perfection, Sacrifice, Santification, Soteriology) G.E.S.

REIGN OF GOD (see Kingdom of God)

RELATIONALITY (see Relativity)

Relativity In philosophical terms, a theory of relativity holds that the values and claims to knowledge of any person varies according to the factors within himself and his environment that influence him. It is the opposite of absolutism. Relativity is an idea applied in anthropology and sociology. In these disciplines the awareness of the different values and attitudes of peoples throughout the world has often led to a full-blown relativism. This development is ironic, because the unswerving allegiance to relativism is in fact only a form of absolutism, a concept vehemently denied in the systems of study themselves.

The issue of relativity becomes serious in the comparative study of religious traditions. Many religions have consistently proclaimed their doctrines to be absolutely true. This can be plainly observed by studying orthodox Christianity. In viewing the dogmas of orthodoxy to be eternal revelations, orthodoxy opposes any form of Christian theology that seeks to give a place to the dynamic or relativistic view of revelation. Such a posture has been called by Paul Tillich (1886-1965) an "absolutism of tradition." This example points at once to the strength of relativity and to its limits.

When defenders or relativity insist within Christianity that God is a living God constantly revealing himself to men, there are surely notable supports for such a view to be found within the Bible. But this strength is somewhat negated by the fact that many relativists would deny the desirability and certainly the necessity of seeking support from the Bible, or anywhere else. Generally the only test to which a relativist will submit his claim is the pragmatic one—does such a view work or function effectively? According to this general view, truth is relative to a particular person or group within a particular situation or predicament. All forms of absolutism are rejected.

Critics of relativity insist that there is yet another problem of relativism. When relativity is raised to the level of self-consciousness and encounters representatives of rationality, it is often forced into denying the absolute principles upon which traditional rationalism is built. A consistent relativist will neither appeal to revelation to overcome its own doubts and skepticism, nor will it simply retire from the arena of thought and action. Tillich called this "cynical relativism" and charged that it "uses reason only for the sake of denying reason—a self-contradiction which is 'cynically' accepted." (*Systematic Theology*, Volume I, page 88)

Closely connected with relativity is what may be called "relationality." The philosophers A. N. Whitehead (1861-1947) and Charles Hartshorne (1897-   ) and the theologians John Cobb (1925-   ) and Schubert Ogden (1928-   ) propose this view. The relationists insist upon the intimate connection between the knower and all his relationships as they explain how and what men may know. A relationist need not be also a relativist.

Relativity is also important in ethics. According to ethical relativists, the rightness of any act or goodness of an object depend upon or consist in only the attitude taken by an individual or a group. It was at this level of differences in behavior that anthropologists, and subsequently psychologists, became convinced of the accuracy of the description called "relativity." (see *Absolute, Contextual, Epistemology, Ethics, Reason, Revelation*) J.B.W.

Religion *Religion usually means the acts of men toward powers beyond the world of nature and history. Almost all cultures have religions in some form. "Comparative religions" is the study of the world's religions. By the 1800's some Christian thinkers were saying that true religion led to true morality. Friedrich Schleiermacher was a German thinker who did not agree. Religion to him was based on man's "feeling of absolute dependence" on God, and it affected not only morality but every area of life. Still, Christianity was seen as the highest religion, and comparative religion seemed to treat Christianity as one religion alongside others. Karl Barth said Christianity was not a religion. Instead God's revelation in Christ judged religion to be like the law—man's way of trying to save himself. Paul Tillich argued that all men experience revelation, but to worship church, Bible, or religion is evil. Faith in God is the worship of God alone.*

The Latin word *religio* means "to tie" or "to bind." Scholars have traced over seventy different meanings of religion. Further, many different methods have been used to study religion. Philosophy of religion, psychology of religion, sociology of religion, mythology in religion, and history of religions are but some of the highly developed methods.

One of the few widely accepted theories about religion is that man is a *homo religiosus*, a religious animal. It is now evident that all cultures have religion in some form. So the issue is not really whether or not man should be religious. He is! Rather, the issue is the relation of religion to all the functions of individuals, societies, and cultures.

For Christianity the issue of religion has been acute. Some scholars, emphasizing the connection of Christianity with other religions, have examined the similarities and differences between Christianity and other religions. This study has often been called "comparative religions." Other scholars have felt that only the unique features of Christianity should be emphasized. This course has sometimes led to the conviction that Christianity is different from other religions so that it should not even

255

be considered a religion at all. If this last view is followed to its conclusion, it leads to a definition of all religion as being "a futile human attempt to reach God," as Paul Tillich (1886-1965) said. This view means that Christians are unique just because they are free from being religious animals. Tillich did not accept this conclusion.

The history of Christian thinkers dealing with the issue of religion indicates the course of the debate. In Acts the story is told that Paul once visited Athens. He preached a sermon there which began, " 'Men of Athens, I perceive that in every way you are very religious.' " He had observed the statues of the gods in the Areopagus and among them he had seen one honoring "the unknown god." Paul told his hearers that he wished to tell them about that god—the only true God. Except for polite interest, the men of Athens did not seem to be moved by Paul's attempt at apologetics. Henceforth, Paul decided to preach only that gospel that had been revealed to him.

Augustine of Hippo (354-430) wrote a treatise entitled "On True Religion," in which he defended Christianity for having the qualities that make a religion genuine. Thomas Aquinas (c. 1225-74) discussed those things that can be known about God by the use of reason and those things that can only be known by revelation. In so distinguishing between "revealed theology" and "natural theology," Aquinas provided the basis for discussions in the seventeenth and eighteenth century about "revealed religion" and "natural religion."

By the beginning of the nineteenth century it was commonly assumed that religion must be evaluated by the level of morality that it produces in its followers. This view, however, made religion only a way to achieve the higher purposes of moral actions. Friedrich Schleiermacher (1768-1834), the most influential Protestant theologian of the nineteenth century, firmly rejected such a view of religion. He insisted from 1799 onward that religion, as a "feeling of absolute dependence," is basic to human existence. Religion affects morality, but it also affects everything else in which men engage. To be a man is to be religious. Beginning there, then, one may describe what it means to be a Christian man. And the effects of being Christian show in everything that a Christian does. Other religions are not untrue, but rather are less adequate, said Schleiermacher.

By the middle of the nineteenth century Western scholars were becoming more aware of the Scriptures, ways of worship, and patterns of culture of other religious traditions. They began to develop a means by which religion could be studied scientifically. This method has come to be called "history of religions," although some scholars would prefer to call it "science of religion." The result of such an approach seemed to some Christians to be destructive, because it appeared that Christianity would be treated as only one religion alongside other religions. And if this were done, what would happen to the traditional Christian belief that Christianity is the one, perfect, and complete way of faith?

The reaction was vigorous. One aspect of the work of the great Karl Barth (1886-   ) has been to reject any and all claims that Christianity can in any manner be thought of as a religion. Barth thinks that when men are confronted by God's revelation in Christ they are demanded to give up any human attempt to evaluate or compare God's claim with anything else. The Christian sees the world through eyes opened by revelation and no longer through the eyes of men seeking to discover God. Human ideas and needs cannot limit or modify God's revelation.

Paul Tillich, however, is perhaps the best known contemporary Protestant theologian to affirm the connection between Christianity and religion. He did not fight the battle on the grounds of distinguishing between natural theology (or natural religion) and revealed religion. Rather, he insisted that all men experience revelation. These experiences are the ground of all the concrete expressions of religion. Tillich has observed that men begin to trust the forms of worship, the scriptures, the creeds, and the theologies of their religion instead of the revelations that give rise to these expressions. Tillich thinks of this as a demonic distortion of true religion. In this sense, Tillich agrees that Christianity is not essentially a religion. When Christians trust the church, the Bible, or theology more than the God who gives rise to them, they commit idolatry.

After all these remarks, we now can say that religion is characterized by faith in God who reveals himself. Religion then expresses itself in the life of those men who have faith in God, however the divine may be conceived. In this sense religion always expresses itself in the personal life of men. Further, religious traditions are concerned with institutions such as the church. Worship, theology, religious education are part of the Christian church. So long as religious life and religious institutions do not become ends in themselves, they are the means by which Christians celebrate God's revelation in Christ.

Philosophers, aware of religion everywhere, have created the philosophy of religion. Since, however, some philosophers are also religious, they sometimes become theologians and produce philosophical theology.

One of the most comprehensive and provocative descriptions of religion was written by Alfred North Whitehead (1861-1947):

Religion is the vision of something which stands beyond, behind, and within, the passing flux of immediate things; something which is real, and yet waiting to be realised; something which is a remote possibility, and yet the greatest of present facts; something that gives meaning to all that passes, and yet eludes apprehension; something whose possession is the final good, and yet is beyond all reach; something which is the ultimate ideal, and the hopeless

quest. (From *Science and the Modern World*. The Macmillan Co., 1925, page 275. Used with permission.)
(*see Biblical criticism, Myth, Natural theology, Theology*) J.B.W.

Religionless In *Prisoner for God*, Dietrich Bonhoeffer (1906-45) spoke of "religionless Christianity." He also wondered if modern men could do without God. Bonhoeffer had apparently come to feel that men could understand truth and live a moral life without religion. The problem is what "Christianity" would mean if it does not mean a religion. Some thinkers today view Christianity as a faith in man's possibilities and a hope that history will turn out for man's good. Thus it is not church, ritual, moral law, nor any of the other outward signs usually suggested by "religion." Thomas Luckmann, a sociologist, writes of "invisible religion." He points out that even where people do not attend church or follow religious activities, their values and world views become a religion of their own. (*see Atheism, Secularization*)

RELIGIOUS EXPERIENCE (*see Experience*)

RELIGIOUS LIBERTY (*see Protestant*)

Repentance Derived from the Greek word, *metanoia*, repentance literally means "a change of mind" or "a change of direction." In contrast with remorse, which is merely being sorry for one's actions, repentance means acknowledging one's errors and seeking a new orientation and direction. The French word for "thinking" is *pensé* and comes close to the idea involved in repentance (re-pensé). It is a re-thinking of one's situation and determination to chart a different course.

Christians have found a variety of ways to express repentance. The ideal for the early Christians was obedience to God. Yet they recognized that sin was everywhere present, even among the church members. The problem was what should be done with members of the Christian community who sinned. Tertullian (*c.* 160-230) listed seven such sins—idolatry, blasphemy, murder, adultery, fornication, false witness, and fraud. *The Shepherd of Hermas* indicated that following baptism one repentance was allowed, but no more than one could be permitted. Clement of Alexandria (*c.* 150-*c.* 215) insisted that if more repentance were permitted, there would be no difference between Christians and others.

Over against rigorous attempts to make the early Christians morally and spiritually obedient were such obvious teachings of Jesus as the Lord's Prayer and the matter of genuine repentance for forgiveness no matter how many times a person had sinned. Job is remembered for

258

his repentance clothed in sack cloth and sitting in ashes. Other penitents fasted, eating only very plain food, wept, and dressed in mourning garb. Later, penitents bowed before the elders of the church asking mercy and begging their pardon.

At the Council of Nicaea (325), it became necessary to define conditions for readmission into the church because penance was not provided for certain sins. Some sinners were kept waiting for periods of time, as long as ten years, without being permitted to receive the Eucharist. Penance was placed under the direction of a bishop, who later gave this responsibility to the priests. They heard confessions of the faithful and provided absolution (the forgiveness of sins) to them. Thus evolved the sacrament of penance that continues to be one of the sacraments in the Roman Catholic Church. (see Absolution, Forgiveness, Sacraments, Sin) G.E.S.

Representation A concept entering religious thought from sociology, especially the sociology of religion, identified with Émile Durkheim (1858-1917). To him, representation means a real or imagined artifact such as language, story, image, or sacred object, by which the mind conceives and grasps reality, especially social reality. Social reality is made accessible by its representation; it is available in no other way. As the source of the representations that are the social base for all communication, religion is the foundation of thought. "Religion has not confined itself to enriching the human intellect, formed beforehand, with a certain number of ideas; it has contributed to forming the intellect itself." Émile Durkheim, The Elementary Forms of Religious Life, trans. by Joseph Ward Swain (London: George Allen and Unwin, 1915, page 9.) (see Myth, Religion, Symbol)

Reredos (rehr-dahs) The screen or partitioned wall behind a church altar is the reredos. It usually contains religious symbols and is often ornamental. Usually made of wood, it is sometimes constructed of stone or metal and should not be confused with the dossal, which is the ornamental cloth hung behind the altar. G.E.S.

Resurrection Belief in the resurrection of the dead plays little part in the Old Testament, although existence in Sheol after death is a part of Hebrew religion. Passages that reflect belief in a resurrection of the dead are found in Isaiah 26:19 and especially in Daniel 12:2. The Daniel passage is considered important, for it reflects the beliefs of the Hasidim, who were in all probability the predecessors of the Pharisees. The latter developed the view of the general resurrection of the dead, and their views are reflected in the New Testament. They differed in

259

this respect from the Sadducees, who, on the basis of the Scriptures, denied the doctrine.

In the New Testament, the idea of resurrection is paramount. But it adds to the doctrine of a general resurrection, the special resurrection of Christ. The resurrection of Christ is for New Testament writers of cardinal importance. The entire New Testament, in fact, is written in the light of the resurrection faith. But a distinction must be made between the proclamation of the event and the narratives depicting the Easter story. The event itself is lost to history; stories such as those of the empty tomb are secondary to the faith itself. Rationalistic attempts to explain the resurrection of Christ began early, but have nothing in common with the earliest view that Christ's resurrection was a mighty act of God. (A rationalistic attempt is one that tries to give reasons to explain a miracle or supernatural event; see Rationalism).

From the Christian point of view, the resurrection of believers is always related to the resurrection of Christ. This relationship is described sometimes as a relationship of "faith," as in Paul, or as "belief," as in the Gospel of John. Both the sense of new life in the present and resurrection in the future are viewed as dependent on that relationship.

The doctrine of the resurrection of the dead appears late in Hebrew religion. For the most part, Old Testament writers think of the after life as a shadowy existence in Sheol, the underworld and the adobe of the dead. Sometimes the state of the dead is denoted as "sleep" (1 Kings 2:10; Psalms 13:3; Daniel 12:2), probably the best description of the inactive status of the dead in Sheol. In almost all such instances (Daniel 12:2 is an exception), there is no hint of release or resurrection from Sheol. In fact, some writers, notably Ecclesiastes, absolutely deny the possibility of life after death. This lack of a clear view of the resurrection of the dead probably holds true of the Book of Job as well, although one section, 19:23-27, reflects the conviction of some kind of ultimate vindication for the righteous, perhaps extending into death itself. But the passage is full of textual difficulties.

There are in fact but two clear references to the resurrection of the dead in the Old Testament. The first is in Isaiah 26:19, a passage that is dated by some scholars not in the time of Isaiah of Jerusalem (eighth century B.C.) but as late as the fourth or third century B.C. The second reference, Daniel 12:2, is more important. This reference is notable, not only because it advances a view of resurrection, but also because it includes among those to be resurrected the wicked as well as the righteous and their treatment in terms of their respective deserts.

The doctine of the resurrection as reflected in Daniel seems to have originated among the Hasidim. The Book of Daniel came out of the persecution of the Jews by Antiochus Epiphanes (168-165 B.C.). During that persecution, the pious Jews (Hasidim) refused to submit to sacrifice to pagan gods and chose martyrdom instead. Behind their stand was the conviction that God would not abandon his people, that they would be vindicated even in death. Thus the doctrine of resurrection has its roots both in a historical situation and in Hasidic theology. It is with the apparent successors of the Hasidim, the Pharisees, that the doctrine of the resurrection had its real development. This is the group we meet frequently in the New Testament. It is of interest to note the difference that emerges there between the Pharisees and the priestly group, the Sadducees, with reference to the resurrection of the dead. For the latter rejected the doctrine as unscriptural (*i.e.*, as lacking in the Pentateuch). In Acts, where Paul is before the Sanhedrin, a division arises among Pharisee and Sadducee members of the council over his proclamation of the doctrine of resurrection. Then the writer of Acts adds, "For the Sad'ducees say that there is no resurrection, nor angel, nor spirit; but the Pharisees acknowledge them all." (Acts 23:6-8) This acceptance and rejection of the resurrection of the dead on the part of Pharisees and Sadducees, respectively, is the situation found among Jews in New Testament times.

In the New Testament, the doctrine of the resurrection of the dead is of paramount importance. Jesus seems to have accepted it (Mark 12: 18-27). But in the New Testament, primary stress is placed on the resurrection of *Jesus* from the dead, the nature of the general resurrection being determined by the relation of the individual to him. This emphasis introduces a new element into the history of the doctrine of the resurrection.

The resurrection of Jesus is a cardinal tenet of New Testament religion. Its importance is indicated not only by the fact that it is found throughout all of the major documents of the New Testament (the Book of Hebrews being the great exception, although it is not entirely absent even there), but also because the entire New Testament is written in the light of the resurrection faith of the Christian church. Perhaps the earliest witness to the resurrection in Christian tradition is found in 1 Corinthians 15:3 ff. This is generally understood by scholars to be a pre-Pauline tradition, and, as such, gives us a very early statement regarding the "appearances," however they may be understood, of the risen Jesus. We cannot say, in fact, much more than the tradition says about "what happened." The Gospel stories about the resurrection (Mark 16 and parallels) are not precisely accounts of the resurrection but rather empty tomb stories. Compared with 1 Corinthians 15, they are distinctly secondary, and give objective evidence to faith in the resurrection. Even Paul, whose writings are fairly extensive, fails to detail his experience of the risen Lord. In Galatians 1:15-16 he says, "But when he who had set me apart before I was born, and had called me through his grace, was pleased to reveal his Son to me, in order that I might preach him among the Gentiles, I did not confer with flesh and blood. . . ." This is undoubtedly a reference to Paul's conversion but also a reference to his initial experience of the risen Jesus. Yet he shuns any details of the experience, except to say that it was a divine revelation. Scholars are in wide agreement that the experience of the risen Jesus came first to Peter. This conclusion is reached largely on the grounds of the tradition in 1 Corinthians 15, but also on the dominant role of Peter in other materials related to the resurrection (notably Mark 14:28; 16:7; Luke 22:31).

First Corinthians 15, in addition to the early tradition contained in the first verses, gives us some indication of how Paul felt about both the resurrection of Jesus and the resurrection of believers. His discussion of the resurrection is prompted by its denial in the Corinthian church (verse 12). He begins by saying that a denial of the general resurrection means also a denial of the resurrection of Christ, and a denial of the latter nullifies the gospel. Paul, of course, rejects this possibility and affirms instead the resurrection of Christ, the "first fruits," and then, at the end, the resurrection of those who belong to Christ. Just as all men share in the death of Adam, the corporate nature of humanity being stressed, so those who are "in Christ" share in the life of Christ. Paul, however, goes a step further in his discussion of resurrection, when he raises the question, " 'With what kind of body do they [the dead] come?' " (verse 35) In effect his answer is that the "body" can be both physical and spiritual or, to put it another way, there is both body of flesh and body of spirit. The body of flesh dies, but the body of spirit is resurrected. This apparently was as true of the body of Jesus as of the body of believers. This idea of a spiritual body does not mean that Paul conceived of the resurrection of Jesus or of believers in some vague "spiritual" sense. The risen Jesus was still Jesus, for the term "body" denoted for him the continuation of the person's individuality.

Views of the resurrection, such as the "swoon theory," or the notion that the body of Jesus was stolen from the tomb, may be discarded as rationalistic attempts to explain a difficulty. The best of modern scholarship admits that the event of the resurrection is not available to critical investigation. But it does stress the historical character of the Easter faith of the disciples and goes on to acknowledge that that faith is the basis of the existence of the church itself. This is not to say that the Easter faith is for scholarship the creation of the disciples, but rather to admit what the evidence permits, namely, the existence of that faith, and not to go beyond the evidence to some theoretical reconstruction of events. The Easter stories in the Gospels are themselves to be viewed as evidence of the resurrection faith and not as records of the event. While the resurrection may for many modern Christians be viewed simply as symbolic of new life, it is clear that this was not the case for the early

Christians. They believed that the resurrection of Christ was a mighty act of God. While the narratives concerning the event itself might vary, as they certainly do, the proclamation of the resurrection is still consistent: God raised Jesus from the dead. This is not to deny the value of resurrection as symbol of new life, but rather to put the Christian belief in Christ's resurrection in historical perspective. The thoughtful Christian today must make a distinction, then, between rationalistic attempts to explain the resurrection of Christ, which began as early as the first century, and the event itself, which the New Testament writers proclaim, but do not chronicle.

Christ's resurrection, from the Christian point of view, does not stand as an isolated event in history. As an act of God, it is viewed in relation to the believer. In 1 Corinthians 15:20-23, Paul assumes the Pharisaic notion of the general resurrection of the last day, but now it depends on the resurrection of Christ. Whether by faith, as in Paul, or by belief, as in John, the person who relates himself to the living Christ (the Christ who conquered death) shares in the victory over death. The resurrection of Christ, therefore, has social consequences. A real continuity exists between the resurrection event and the origin and character of the Christian church: "Blessed be the God and Father of our Lord Jesus Christ! By his great mercy we have been born anew to a living hope through the resurrection of Jesus Christ from the dead." (1 Peter 1:3) The concept of "life" emerges as perhaps the dominant characteristic of the Christian community. This is notably present in the Gospel of John, where "eternal life" is equivalent to salvation (John 17:3). But eternal life in John is more than an existence of unending time; it is mainly a quality of life, a sharing in the divine life that Jesus has made possible. Life as both present and future is stressed, but in any case its possession is due to the believer's relation to Christ. (*see Body, Eschatology, Eternal, Immortality, Kerygma, Life, Time*) E.L.T.

Revelation *Revelation is the word for man's knowledge of God. It is a crucial issue for Christianity because Jesus Christ is regarded as God's supreme revelation. Theology must include revelation because the Christian view of God regards Him as One beyond man's understanding. In order to know such a God at all, He must make himself knowable, and revelation is the means by which this is done.*

Revelation may refer either (1) to the act of God's self-disclosure or (2) to the content of that act. In (1), thinkers almost always take certain ideas for granted (that is, they presuppose certain things). First, they presuppose that someone or something is hidden that may be made known. Second, they presuppose that when the hidden becomes known, it is not because it has been discovered, but rather because it has made

263

itself known, i.e., it is disclosed. These presuppositions indicate that revelation is not a uniquely Christian term, in spite of its widespread use by Christian theologians. Thinkers in other religious traditions and philosophers have often used the concept.

In the Bible the concept of revelation in the precise sense discussed above is scarcely to be found at all. Neither the Old nor the New Testament contains any fully-developed concept of revelation. Rather, the Christian concept of revelation has been developed in order to provide a way of understanding what is contained in the Bible. Thus, often when it is said that the Bible is a witness (indeed, the most crucial witness) to God's revelation, what is meant is that unless the Bible is seen as a witness to God's self-disclosure, Scripture will not be understood at all. The proper subject of revelation is God, and were there no such revelation, the Bible clearly asserts that God would not be known. "No one has ever seen God; the only Son, who is in the bosom of the Father, he has made him known." (John 1:18)

Crucial to any discussion of revelation is the question of how God reveals himself to man. Christianity is distinct in insisting that God acts in history. Thus, history is the medium of revelation and concrete, specific events are regarded as revelatory. These acts, however, do not in and of themselves necessarily convince men of their revelatory character. Thus, a group of chosen men, the prophets and above all Jesus Christ, are regarded as sent by God to interpret His revelatory acts. The words of men proclaiming the Word and work of God are thus viewed as the witnesses to God's revelation. Also, in the unique case of Jesus Christ, not just his words but also his life, death, and resurrection are taken by Christians as the highest instance of God's dialogue with man. Revelation after Jesus is generally said to be of the Holy Spirit. But in the mainstream of Christian theology the Spirit does not bring "new" revelations. Rather, the Holy Spirit makes known in each successive revelation the content of the supreme revelation in Christ. Thus, the issue of the content of revelation is really the heart of the matter.

Two dramatically different views of that content are found within the history of Christian theology. First, revelation is regarded as the disclosure of supernatural truths. Second, revelation is regarded as a disclosure of God himself, not of propositions. Analysis of these two theories will show both the complexities and problems included in any idea of revelation.

Christian orthodoxy or dogmatics usually thinks of revelation as the passage of supernatural truths to man. One of the problems in such a view is that two quite different kinds of language may be regarded as appropriate. Either language that discusses the essence and nature of God, or language of personal symbols, may be appropriate. In the first instance it will be claimed that revelation brings knowledge about God that is unattainable through the use of natural reason. For example, Thomas Aquinas (*c.* 1225-74) insisted that natural reason could know that God exists. Revelation is required, however, to know that God is a trinity. This truth is preserved in dogma. Since faith is regarded as the appropriate human response to revelation, faith must mean the giving of intellectual assent to the dogmas of the church. Martin Luther (1483-1546) took the route of personal symbols to express his view of revelation. He argued that God reveals his mercy, grace, and righteous disposition, not his metaphysical essence, toward man. This is indeed something that can be known, but the requirement of faith is not simply to give intellectual assent to the proposition "God saves men by his grace." Rather, faith means *fiducia, i.e.,* confidence and trust in what God has revealed. For Luther, the biblical statement, "I believe; help my unbelief," means faith in the sense of confidence. But Luther still operated to a large extent within orthodoxy, even though re-interpreted in the sense described.

In the nineteenth and twentieth centuries, the impact of rationalism and new science brought about a widespread revision of ideas among Protestant theologians. The thrust of this revision was a rejection of revelation viewed as propositions and an acceptance of revelation understood as God's disclosure of himself. Within this alternative there are also two possible interpretations. First, the Holy may have such an awesome effect that no language is adequate. Mystical silence or irrational speech may result. Although few Christians accept this possibility, it is clear that such a view of revelation would be in keeping with the general framework (see Mystic). The divine-human encounter creates a situation of dialogue or conversation between God and particular men. This point must be underscored. When revelation is viewed within this general framework, it can *only* occur between God and a specific man. It is never a general, *i.e.,* public event. Many modern Protestant theologians have defended this view of revelation, particularly those connected with the neo-orthodox development. Rudolf Bultmann (1884-   ) is a representative of this perspective. One of the great challenges to these respective views of revelation is whether they can be reconciled in any way.

Does revelation still occur? This question divides theologians. Those with orthodox sympathies generally concede that it does, but they insist that such events must be measured against the biblical witness. Such theologians practically imply that present revelation serves only to confirm the once-and-for-all revelation of God in Christ. Those theologians with less sympathy for orthodoxy often insist that the living God is free to disclose himself in ever new ways. They often grant considerable authority to Scripture but insist that what is witnessed to in the Bible is the freedom of God. Thus, they refuse to be tied to a rigid inspirational theory of the authorship of the books in the Bible. Further, such thinkers are often inclined to look for revelation in contemporary events and words (see *e.g.*, Robert Short: *The Gospel According to Peanuts*). However understood, revelation stands at the center of the Christian view of reality. (*see Dogmatics, Faith, Rationalism, Reason*) J.B.W.

REVEREND (*see Orders*)

REWARD (*see Sanction*)

RIGHT (*see Conservative, Deontological, Righteousness*)

Righteousness The word "righteousness" is used in the Old Testament in a variety of ways. It is used to indicate the correct social relationships. Man has responsibility for the community in which he lives. Laws specify some of these obligations. A righteous man is one who upholds these laws. A wicked man is one who breaks them. The significance of these laws lies in their importance for the community, because one who breaks the law tends to destroy the community. Righteousness is also used in the Old Testament in a judicial sense (as in a court of law) to mean that a man is innocent of wrong deeds. Righteousness sometimes refers to the covenant made by Yahweh with the Jews; thus, righteousness stands for Israel's doing what Yahweh demands of her. But Israel's doing is held up and strengthened by God's grace in the sense that God keeps his relationship to Israel even when Israel is disobedient.

Aristotle (384-322 B.C.) uses the term in a twofold sense: (1) to show what is legal and fair and (2) to indicate that God is a just judge. Plato (*c.* 427-347 B.C.) uses the term to describe the citizen who believes correctly and does his duty. Jewish literature of 200 B.C. uses the term "righteousness" as being closely connected to mercy. In the New Testament the term is used to indicate the proper relation of man to God. Man needs to have a better relationship to other men, and if he is to do this, he must rely on God as the source of his right relation to others. He must be faithful to the demands God makes on him in his relationship to others. The term is also used in the sense of man getting what he deserves. If he is destructive he will receive the appropriate reward.

Paul uses the term "righteousness" in a relational way. Man has a wrong relation to God, self, and others. God in Christ gives man the opportunity to have that relationship corrected. Man, if he trusts in God as revealed through Jesus Christ, will be brought into the right relationship to God, self and others. Thus, man is justified (made righteous) by faith (see Romans, Chapter 5). Man is made righteous here and now; through faith he has this right relationship. Though man continues to sin, now he is set free from wrong relationships and can live freely.

John Wesley (1703-91) strongly contrasts "the righteousness which is of the law" and "the righteousness which is of faith" (see sermon, "The Righteousness of Faith"). The righteousness of faith assumes that man is a sinner and that God through Jesus Christ works out for man his salvation (righteousness); hence, righteousness cannot be earned. The man of faith is concerned to grow to perfection, but this is the result of *being* a righteous man and not an attempt to *become* one. The Puritan movement understood righteousness quite differently. The man who is faithful is the one who associates with good things and good people. Such faithfulness aims at character and moral goodness. The end result of clean living is that God declares man to be acceptable. (*see Justice*) J.S.H.

Ritual From the Latin *ritus*, ritual is a worship form using various symbols and traditions. Such rites as baptism, marriage, ordination, church membership reception, confirmation, burial of the dead, dedication of churches, commission of missionaries, ground-breakings, and the like are found in church books of ritual. The words and forms, formal or informal, used to guide the experience of worshippers provide ritual. In some churches, notably among the Quakers, there is an absence of ritual while other communions, such as Anglicans, use ancient hymns and follow established patterns for prayers, Scripture, and other elements in worship. (*see Liturgy*) G.E.S.

ROEH (*see Prophet*)

ROMAN CATHOLIC (*see Catholic*)

ROMAN CREED (*see Creed, Symbol*)

RUAH (*see Spirit*)

RULE (*see Canon, Doctrine, Normative, Principle*)

RULE-DEONTOLOGICAL (*see Deontological*)

Sabbath This word comes from a Hebrew word meaning "to rest." God rested on the seventh day of creation. The Hebrews set apart one day in seven to show honor to God. The basic idea is that holy time consecrates the rest of time. The Sabbath is a symbol that all of creation is holy. The idea that observing the Sabbath separates holy and profane time is not typically biblical. Christians changed the Sabbath from the seventh day of the week to the first day, in honor of the Resurrection. For Christians, every Sunday is a celebration of the Resurrection.

SABELLIANISM (*see Christology*)

Sacrament From the Latin word, *sacramentum*, which means "an oath of allegiance or an obligation," sacraments have been variously defined as means of grace, memorials to Jesus Christ, sacred signs or symbols, and ordinances. The sacraments of baptism and the Lord's Supper are observed by all Christian churches, though some, like Baptists, prefer not to use the word sacrament and speak of them as "ordinances." The Society of Friends speaks of all of life as sacramental and refuses to call any of the sacraments special. The Roman Catholic Church and Eastern Orthodox Church recognize seven valid sacraments.

The Anglican Cathechism defines a sacrament as "an outward and visible sign of an inward and spiritual grace given unto us, ordained by Christ himself; as a means whereby we receive this grace, and a pledge to assure us thereof." The two aspects of all sacraments are the external or outward act, which can be seen, and the inward or internal change, which is unseen. The basis for sacraments is found in the life and ministry of Jesus. Protestants generally restrict their sacraments to those two in which Jesus participated—baptism and the Lord's Supper. Baptism has historically been the rite through which one is initiated into the Christian church. Both adults and infants are baptized. Communion stood at the center of worship in the early church and is based upon the final meal that Christ ate with his disciples before his crucifixion.

The five additional sacraments observed in the Roman Catholic Church include confirmation, penance, holy orders, holy matrimony, and extreme unction (last rites). Confirmation is really the completion of baptism and is usually administered by the bishop. In the Eastern Orthodox Church, however, a priest may serve in his place. Penance includes contrition, or sorrow for sin, the confession of sins to a priest, and a statement by the priest of God's forgiveness, thus absolving the sinner in God's name. Holy orders are given by the bishop and confer the privileges of the ministry. Holy matrimony is both a legal and ecclesiastical contract in marriage, the minister serving as the witness to the parties who contract with each other in a lifelong union. Requirements with regard to the marriage ceremony have been altered in recent years to allow the participation of Protestant clergymen in Roman Catholic weddings. Also, the requirement of a written contract insisting that children of the union be reared as Roman Catholics has been dropped. Extreme unction is to anoint a dying person with oil to confer grace upon him. (*see* Absolution, Baptism, Communion, Grace, Lord's Supper, Orders) G.E.S.

Sacrifice A sacrifice is an offering made to God. The value and usefulness of sacrifice is important. Offering something without value destroys the idea of sacrifice. Christian concepts of sacrifice usually do not mean the purchase of forgiveness, nor the appeasement of God's wrath, but an expression of sorrow for sins that have been committed and an approach to God expressing faith and seeking pardon. Also, Christian sacrifice may be an act of worship, thanksgiving, and praise.

The Bible records sacrifices in both the Jewish and Christian traditions. Leviticus provides the best Old Testament study of the Hebrew sacrificial system. Old Testament sacrifices centered around animals; the word *zebah* (slaughter) was used for sacrifice. Among Old Testament sacrifices are: (1) The *burnt offering*: Usually a public sacrifice offered for the entire community (Exodus 29:38-42), these were unblemished male lambs entirely consumed by fire. The poor were permitted to sacrifice doves or young pigeons (Leviticus 1). (2) The *peace offering*: Female and male animals were acceptable and those not perfect in every detail might be used. Certain parts of the animal were eaten, following the sacrifice, by the one making the offering and his friends. This act introduced the eating of the common meal still symbolically practiced in the communion. The peace offering was intended to aid in the promotion of peace between man and God (Leviticus 3). (3) The *sin offering*: This offering did not come into prominence until the period following the Exile and could be offered for an individual, for someone in authority, or for the entire community. Described in Leviticus 4, it is restricted to sins committed unwittingly, or without prior knowledge, then later discovered. The sacrifice consisted of a young bullock, whose blood was taken into the sanctuary ("tent of meeting") by the high priest. (4)

269

The *guilt offering:* Described in Leviticus 5:14 ff., this offering had much in common with the sin offering and was also not practiced until after the Exile. It seems to have been used by those persons who stole from their neighbor, and who returned the amount taken, then offered a lamb as a sacrifice to help cleanse themselves of the guilt. (5) The *meal* (or *cereal*) *offering:* Described in Leviticus 2, it early included both animal and vegetable offerings but was later restricted to offerings other than animal. Flour and olive oil were offered, the significance being that since men eat more than flesh at a meal, it is only right that God should be offered more than flesh. (6) The *paschal lamb:* This was the sacrifice of a lamb, whose blood was sprinkled on the doorposts to protect a house from evil (Exodus 12:5-8). Other offerings used were drink offerings (Numbers 15:5), heave offerings and wave offerings (see Leviticus 7:34 in the King James Version). The sacrifices were normally made at the altar of the Temple and the blood taken by the high priest into the Holy of Holies (the inner sanctuary or holy place).

The early Christians saw the death of Jesus as a sacrifice. The fact that the Crucifixion took place at the Passover made such a comparison obvious. The *kerygma* does not refer to Jesus' death as a sacrifice, even though forgiveness of sins is proclaimed (see Acts 2:22-36; 3:12-16; 13:26-47, RSV). In fact, part of the failure of Hebrew religion is seen as its use of sacrifice (Acts 7:42-51).

The Book of Hebrews takes the idea of sacrifice and explains in detail the way Jesus has succeeded in a sacrifice, whereas the Hebrew use of sacrifices failed (Hebrews 7:26-28; 10:4). Still, Hebrews sees Jesus making the sacrifice; the man of faith can only accept it and hold on to faith (10:14, 23).

Paul, in contrast, saw the man of faith as one who himself had to make the sacrifice, just as Jesus did. The Christian sacrifices himself (Romans 12:1), not only once, but daily (2 Corinthians 4:7-12). The Christian, then, shares in the sufferings of Christ (Philippians 3:10) and actively strives toward the call of Christ (3:13; 2:12-13).

Reinhold Niebuhr (1892-   ) defines *agape* as the sacrificial love of Christ. Paul Ramsey (1913-   ) questions this view, since for the sake of the neighbor a Christian may sometimes have to "sacrifice the sacrifice" and live on in the agony of compromise. (*see* Atonement, KERYGMA) G.E.S.

SADDUCEE (*see* Priest, Resurrection)

Saga (*sah*-guh)   In their analysis of the traditions found in the Old Testament traditions, scholars have been able to identify various literary forms, such as myths, sagas, legends, tales, and proverbs. The myth, the saga, and the legend tell of extraordinary happenings of the past. The saga represents a particularly rich element in the Old Testament. Scholars distinguish between several types of sagas in the Old Testament, but those dealing with the tribe and the people are most characteristic. These look to the past, to an ancestor whose actions influenced the on-going history of the people, and who, in some sense, lives on in history. The tribe is often represented by an individual. In Israel the idea of representation was exceedingly strong. So the story of an individual is often in fact the story of a tribe. This type of tribal or national saga is characteristic of the Book of Genesis. The hero sagas have Moses as their beginning point. Examples are Exodus 32:15 ff.; Joshua 1:11; Judges 3:7 ff. The Hebrew concept of group solidarity gave contemporary meaning to ancient acts of the group and individual acts of valor. The saga was, therefore, a constant reminder of the mighty acts of God in the history of the people. (see *Form criticism, Legend, Myth*) E.L.T.

Saint From the Latin word, *sanctus,* which means "holy," saint is used by Christians in two ways. It is used with regard to all persons who belong to God and who believe in Christ. In the New Testament, Paul addressed letters to saints in various places (Romans 1:7; Philippians 1:1). By this he meant those who received baptism and were members of the church. Church membership and discipleship are used synonymously in the New Testament; thus the word "saints" refers to all Christians.

It also means those whom the church has regarded as especially holy. During the first century, sainthood was given to martyrs who were killed because of their faith. November 1, "All Saints Day," honors these persons. The church later established standards by which persons could be recognized as saints, and their names were taken by many churches and individuals. This concept was opposed at the Reformation, and many Protestants now recognize as saints only biblical persons. A "hagiographa" is a book or collection of saints and their lives. (see *Holy*) G.E.S.

SALVATION (see *Redemption, Soteriology*)

Sanctification Sanctification presupposes justification and indicates what takes place in the Christian life between justification and death. More specifically, it is used to describe God's work of making the believer a "holy man." In Methodism it has been viewed as God's action that finds its completion in "Christian perfection."

In the New Testament a Christian is not a perfect man. He still has problems and struggles. Difficulties continue in his life after he professes faith in Jesus as the Christ. The Christian is in process of being made whole.

In Roman Catholic theology justification and sanctification are understood as being closely connected. Justification takes place through sacramental grace. Man repents of his sin. God, through the sacraments, makes man acceptable to Himself, but since man continues to sin after being justified, he continues to need to repent and receive more grace. The work of being made fully acceptable to God is sanctification.

Martin Luther (1483-1546) understood sanctification as the end result of the work of God's grace, begun in justification. Faith is followed by good works. Ascetic exercises are of value in that they help us to keep our minds on the right things. The Christian does not want to continue to practice evil deeds because they would hinder his serving the neighbor. He is concerned to have nothing to do with anything that would keep him from this work.

John Wesley (1703-91) stressed sanctification or "Christian perfection" or "growing in grace." He recognized the fact that man does make wrong choices after justification. The Christian must repent and turn again to performing "good works" if he hopes to be made perfect in the Christian life. These "good works" are of two kinds. (1) Man has certain disciplines that, by God's grace, help to make him fit instruments in the hand of God. (2) Man must do works of mercy (or charity). This second type of "good works" is the specific meeting of the needs of the neighbor.

Should a man be concerned to develop the right habits or should he simply serve man? Wesley says that we should be concerned about both. The Christian is to continue to grow in his commitment to God. When a man becomes a Christian he begins a journey that requires of him his all. At the same time man may fall away from this task. When he does he has "fallen from grace." He needs to admit what he has done and then begin anew the work of becoming perfect. (*see Holy, Perfection*) J.S.H.

Sanction　The basic purpose of a sanction, especially in ethics, is to motivate men for moral actions. At the back of every system of ethics is an authority—faith in God, the idea of the good, or the belief that human life is a value in itself. When a person makes judgments, he always appeals to these authorities. For example, Christians have often claimed that men should love one another simply because neighbor love is a command of God.

But in between the authority and the individual's judgment to take an action lies the sanction. The church, the state, a parent, or a philosophy wants to show its approval of particular acts it considers worthy. Therefore, it recommends certain actions and deplores others, so that men may receive approval or disapproval for their actions.

Natural law thinkers have often spoken of conscience itself—its approval or remorse—as a sanction.

Close to the concept of sanction is the concept of rewards and punishments. Christians have often referred to the delights of heaven or the miseries of hell as a motivation for action.

Psychologically, however, rewards and punishments seem to do as much harm as good. Theologically, they are questionable because they seem to depend on self interest as the most basic motivation.

Today, these concepts of sanctions are often used by ethical thinkers:

(1) individual conscience as the final referee of right and wrong;

(2) the goodness of human life as an end in itself;

(3) avoidance of pain or evil;

(4) love of neighbor as an end in itself;

(5) duty to God or to an abstract idea of the right. (*see Authority*) J.S.H.

Sanctuary From the root word, *sanctus* (holy), it means "a place set apart for religious purposes and consecrated to worship." In common usage, church goers speak of entering the sanctuary to worship. Technically, the sanctuary is the area of the altar within the chancel and should be distinguished from the nave, or place where the congregation is seated. The classical use of sanctuary is the place of the altar. G.E.S.

Sanctus (*sahnk*-toos) Literally translated "holy," this is the last part of the preface in the Anglican Communion service or the Roman Catholic ritual beginning with the words "Holy." At this point in the service, a bell (the sanctus bell) is rung by the server. Its use comes from the hymn sung by the angels in Isaiah 6:3, " 'Holy, holy, holy. . . .' " Protestants also use the sanctus in the service of communion, just before the prayer of consecration. It may be said or sung by the congregation, or sung by a choir. Sometimes it is called the "trisagion" (thrice holy). G.E.S.

SARX (*see Body, Flesh*)

SATISFACTION (*see Atonement, Sacrifice*)

SAVIOR (*see Name, Soteriology*)

Saying In historical criticism, or more precisely in form criticism, the term "saying" refers to individual units of tradition that embody "sayings," usually "sayings of Jesus." These sayings appear embedded in our Gospels, but it seems clear that they originally stood alone, not related to their present context. Examples are the sayings in Matthew 11:25-30. But illustrations of this category of traditional form are numer-

273

ous in the Gospels. It seems that the early church placed great emphasis on "sayings" or "words" of Jesus. It is quite possible that the church gathered many of these sayings together at a very early period. (*see Literary criticism, Pronouncement story*) E.L.T.

Scandal (of the cross) The Greek word *skandalon* has a variety of meanings, but when it relates to the cross, it means that which gives offense, causes revulsion and opposition. In 1 Corinthians 1:23 the crucified Christ is a scandal to the Jews. In Galatians 5:11 the preaching of the cross is the cause of opposition.

In the light of the nature of crucifixion, it is easy to understand why the Christian gospel, with its stress on the cross, should have raised questions on the part of both Jews and Gentiles. The idea that a crucified Jew could be the Messiah was not easily acceptable. Crucifixion itself was a form of punishment reserved for the lowest of criminals. This in itself would cause serious problems. Moreover, ideas associated with the Messiah, such as the belief that the Messiah would not suffer, would add to the problem. It is no wonder, when it is viewed from the point of view of the time, that the cross was, as Paul said, a stumblingblock to Jews and foolishness to Greeks. (*see* KERYGMA) E.L.T.

Schism (*ski*-zim) From the Greek word, *schizein*, which means "to split," schism is used in the New Testament as a division or separation (1 Corinthians 11:18). A later and a more technical meaning is an opposition to the teachings of the established church. The most pronounced schism in ecclesiastical history occurred in 1054 when the Eastern church and Roman church separated, and each established its own seat of authority. This split is known as the "Great Schism." Other splits over doctrine or church polity have resulted in the establishment of various sects and the rejection of some communicants on the grounds of heresy. (*see Heresy, Sect*) G.E.S.

SCHOLASTICISM (*see Essence, Reason, Substance*)

SCRIPTURE (*see Canon, Inspiration, Word*)

SCROLL (*see Manuscript*)

SECOND COMING (*see Ascension, Eschatology, Kingdom of God,* PAROUSIA)

Sect Used in contrast to denominations, a sect is marked by independence and does not have a national or regional organization as denominations do. Sects are not concerned with tradition and usually require a particular religious experience for membership, reject an official clergy, are exclusive and individualistic, and sometimes arise because of a special emphasis (like healing or speaking in tongues). Holiness groups and Pentecostals are examples of sects. Lutherans, Presbyterians, and United Methodists are examples of denominations. (*see Denominations*) G.E.S.

Secularization (*sek*-yew-luh-ruh-*zay*-shuhn) The Latin term *saeculum* gave rise to our word "secularization." It was first used to refer to a division of powers in the Treaty of Westphalia (1648), which ended the Thirty Years War. Some of the lands formerly administered by the church were handed over to some of the principalities involved. The treaty used diplomatic language to keep from offending the church any more than was necessary. Thus the term *saeculum* was used for the lands transferred from the spiritual to the purely political authorities. It could be used because at the time it was a neutral word. Though it meant "worldly" it did not imply "materialism" or any of the negative meanings it suggests today.

After 1648, the term "secular" came to mean "worldly." During the growth of Pietism and Puritanism, Christians saw the church over against the world. The road to faith lay through the church. The result of this division was an emphasis on the parts of the Bible, such as 2 Corinthians 6:14–7:1, dealing with the difference between the holy and the profane. Not until nineteenth century critics pointed out that both Hebrews and the early Christians viewed the world as one, was this mistake corrected.

Contemporary thinkers like Arend T. van Leeuwen (1918-) Cornelius van Peursen, and Friedrich Gogarten (1887-) have shown that Christianity itself is responsible for secularization. In contrast to the animism and magic of many primitive religions, the Hebrews believed creation was man's domain. The creature ruled the creation. Since nature was "desacralized," that is, freed from its power of the holy, man could fashion and control it. When God became incarnate in Jesus Christ, God entered the world and is still at work in the world. Especially during the Reformation did secularization increase. Once man became convinced that only the authority of individual conscience really mattered, he was free to control both nature and history.

Some thinkers, like Gibson Winter (1916-), distinguish between secularism and secularization. The former is the attitude that only the material and the worldly matter. It is a new form of idolatry, in contrast with the view that man is responsible for himself, his neighbors, and the whole creation. Secularization, then, involves a morality.

Does it also involve a faith? Paul Tillich (1886-1965) contended that man is naturally religious. If he does not worship God, he will worship self, race, nation, or some other false god. Yet many modern men seem to live responsibly without faith in God, or in any supernatural reality.

Another question raised by secularization is the stance of the church. Exactly what "in the world" is good? Many secular thinkers argue the church should be in the world and that the worldly is basically good. Yet automation, nuclear weapons, and the wastes of industry bring many evils to man. The church faces the task of knowing what in the culture surrounding it is worth fighting for and what should be fought. (*see Church, Mission, Reason*) G.E.S.

Self *A self is a human being. Socrates understood man's ability to "guide" or control his life as the key to the self. Aristotle explored the varying natural attributes of man in order to present a clear picture of the self. In the Old Testament it is assumed that man is able to decide what course his life will take. The self is capable of obeying God's demands. The New Testament builds on the Old Testament concept of the self and further develops this concept along the lines of man's ability to sacrifice his own wishes in order to be of help to his neighbor. The self may be conscious, mentally aware, and sensitive to the feelings of others and itself. Man's self-awareness poses several questions for him. How shall he deal with his own desires to grow as a person? What is man to do when his own drive for growth conflicts with the duties that either he himself or the community or both place on him? Psyche means the spiritual essence of man or the soul.*

The word "self" may be defined simply as a person. "Self" includes all the attributes of a person—physical, mental, moral, and social. The self cannot be understood apart from its own past experiences and the impact of the environment has on the self. To be a self is to be able to make decisions and therefore in some sense to influence one's own future as well as the future of others. Self is sometimes used as equivalent with the ego, "I." This is to interpret the self as the natural physical man. Man is a self when his life is not determined by any outside force.

Socrates (*c.* 470-399 B.C.) understood the self chiefly in terms of man's ability to guide or determine his own life. The call for a moral life is a call for the use of reason and the exercise of autonomy. Autonomy here means the right of self control or self shaping. A genuine self is one who uses reason to discover the ideal man (including how one should act) and then *decides* to pattern his life after this ideal. He is an agent in that he acts to determine his own future. Aristotle (384-322 B.C.) examined the different bodily desires and bodily hungers included in man. Man realizes his full potential (the happy life) when he uses his reason to control these desires. The self is able to hold in check these desires and hungers and follow a moderate path (self-control). Following these two fathers of philosophy, Western thought has recognized the fact that morality is a social institution. Men could not live together without some

276

rules by which men pattern their behavior. At the same time morality is a call for self-guidance or self-realization. A self is one who holds his own life in his own hands and has the power to destroy it or build it up.

In the Old Testament a self is capable of controlling its own behavior. Man is capable of practicing moderation. Thus, in the Old Testament the self is called upon to discipline itself (self-discipline). A self is one who has the possibility of living sensibly. A self has the ability to secure and use wisdom in deciding what he will do so that selfhood includes the quality of prudence.

The New Testament includes the Greek idea that the self is able to perfect itself through the use of self-control. The important New Testament concept of self-denial means saying no to one's own desires in order to do something more important (the will of God). The Christian is one who can discover what his relation to his neighbor should be by observing his own love for himself. He is to have this kind of love for the neighbor. The Christian is to love the neighbor for his own sake. The New Testament teaches that rejection (denial) of oneself is required of anyone who would follow Christ (Mark 8:34; Matthew 16:24; Luke 9:23). This may be called an ethics of sacrifice; a giving up one's selfish desires in order to do what needs to be done.

The self is capable of consciousness. It can perceive mentally what passes in its own mind. It can be aware of moods, attitudes, and feelings. It can be aware of abstract judgments and participate in decisions about values. A self exercises all of these abilities not only in relation to others but also in relation to the self. A self not only thinks, acts, and decides to do certain things but is at the same time aware of these actions and of itself (self-conscious). This self-consciousness is something that a self cannot get rid of. Therefore, a self's concern to participate in the world cannot be separated from his concern for himself (his status or position in the world). Man may allow his self-consciousness to become a problem in his relation to the world, however. If man uses conversation with others as an opportunity to brag about himself or make himself look good, his awareness of himself has become a problem for him. The same would be true if man used conversation as an opportunity to degrade himself (self-subjection, abasement, or self-depreciation). Man needs to discover a means of dealing with his own awareness of himself so as to properly appropriate this knowledge.

F. H. Bradley (1846-1924) taught a morality of self-realization. It is a moral duty for each self to become the best possible self. The self does this by discovering its duties to itself, some of which are social duties. The self becomes the ideal self by always being willing to do one's duties. Paul Ramsey (1913-   ) points out that Christian love calls the self to concern itself with the neighbor and not simply with realizing oneself. Present day discussion about the self is concerned with many questions:

How does self-love differ from selfishness? Is there ever an occasion when self-love and love of neighbor are in contradiction with one another? Can you love anyone else if you do not love yourself?

Paul Tillich (1886-1965) has pointed out that the self is a whole and should be treated as such. It is wrong to divide the self into parts (mind, body, and spirit) and analyze them as if the parts are separate and unrelated. His notion is sometimes referred to as the "wholistic view" of the self. The interrelated parts and their close working connection one with another in the self has been broadly recognized in the fields of education, psychology, and religion.

Man's awareness of himself includes the awareness that he will die. Man is also aware that he does that which he should not do. Finally, man can be aware of the fact that he has lost sight of any meaning for his life. Martin Buber (1878-1965) points out that the genuine self comes to fullness of life, and helps others to come to fullness of life, when the individual self dares to accept himself as who he is and allows others to accept themselves as who they are. (*see Body, Heart, Image of God, Love, Spirit*) J.S.H.

SELF-ACCEPTANCE (*see Acceptance*)

SELF-CONSCIOUSNESS (*see Consciousness, Self*)

SELF-IDENTITY (*see Identity*)

SELF-REALIZATION (*see Freedom, Self*)

Self-understanding This is a term that has been most used in psychological and existentialist philosophical discussions. It refers to the image a person has of himself. Thus, it is obvious that one may have an accurate or an inaccurate self-understanding. Some theologians have found this a highly useful way of discussing sin and salvation. Typically, such theologians will argue that an accurate—a true—self-understanding requires an awareness of the full range of realities that affect the self. To become aware that one's selfhood ultimately depends on one's relationship with God is to be saved. Thus, an authentic self-understanding is equated with salvation. Inauthentic self-understanding is taken to be equal to continuing to dwell in sin. Rudolf Bultmann (1884-   ) and John Macquarrie (1919-   ) are two theologians who have written extensively in this vein. (*see Existential, Soteriology*) J.B.W.

SEMI-PELAGIANISM (*see Freedom*)

SENSUAL (*see Appetite*)

278

Septuagint (sep-*too*-ah-jint) The Septuagint is the Greek translation of the Old Testament. The common symbol for the Septuagint is LXX. This grows from the tradition that the translation was made by seventy (or seventy-two) Jewish elders living in the city of Alexandria in Egypt. The tradition is found in the Letter of Aristeas. The story is that Ptolemy Philadelphus was advised by his librarian, Demetrius, to secure copies of the Hebrew Scriptures from Jerusalem and to have them translated. The translators, working independently, produced perfect copies, much to the delight of king and people.

The tradition is not historically trustworthy in many of its details. It is doubtful that the translation occurred at the directive of the king. It is more likely that the Septuagint was a religious educational enterprise. The Jews living in Alexandria were numerous, and, since Hebrew was becoming lost to them in favor of the vernacular, Greek, it was urgent that they have the Scriptures in that language. There is no doubt that the tradition is correct on the score that the translation was made in Alexandria. It is noteworthy that the Septuagint was the Bible of the early church, and the New Testament reflects that fact. (*see Apocrypha*) E.L.T.

SERMON (*see Homiletics,* KERYGMA)

Session In the presbyterian form of church government, the session is the ruling body of a local congregation, composed of the active elders. It includes those ordained as ruling elders (lay leaders) and teaching elders (clergymen). The session of the Presbyterian Church is equivalent to the charge conference of The United Methodist Church. (*see Episcopal, Presbyter*) G.E.S.

SEVEN (*see Number*)

SEXT (*see Office*)

Sexton Historically, the sexton was an officer of the church who rang the bell, placed the paraments (altar cloths), dug graves in the churchyard, and generally cared for the church property and buildings. Today he is a caretaker of church property. G.E.S.

SHALOM (*see Peace*)

SHEKINAH (*see Glory*)

Shema (*she*-mah) The Shema has been called "Judaism's confession of faith." The name comes from the first word of Deu-

279

teronomy 6:4-5: " 'Hear, O Israel: The LORD our God is one LORD; and you shall love the LORD your God with all your heart, and with all your soul, and with all your might.' " In late Judaism this formula was recited as a part of the religion of the synagogue. The service consisted of prayer, the reading of Scripture, and a homily or sermon. The Shema preceded the prayer in the order of service, introducing the worship in a most fitting manner. Few passages are more representative of the heart of Judaism than this. It affirms one of the great central themes of the religion—monotheism. It is of interest that Jesus, when asked to identify the greatest of the commandments, answered by reciting the Shema (Mark 12:29). E.L.T.

SHEOL (see Cosmology)

Shrove Tuesday "Shrovetide" is the period immediately before Lent, including the Monday and Tuesday prior to Ash Wednesday. Shrove Tuesday is the day immediately preceding Ash Wednesday and takes its name from Shrive, which means "to confess one's sins" and "to minister the sacrament of penance." Shrovetide has also been referred to as "Carnival," which comes from the Latin term, carnem levare, which means "to take away the meat," and has been used as a time of festival and rejoicing just before confession on Shrove Tuesday and the fast period that begins on Ash Wednesday. (see Ash Wednesday, Lent) G.E.S.

Simul Justus et Peccator (si-muhl yews-tuhs et pek-ah-tohr) Simul justus et peccator is a Latin phrase that literally means "simultaneously justified and sinner." This phrase is used to express the Reformers' point of view that man comes to have the right relation to God through faith and not through any accomplishments of his own. Man is to accept in faith the fact that even though man is a sinner God forgives and accepts him. (see Acceptance, Justification by faith, Sin) J.S.H.

Sin Sin is man's failure to be what he was created to be. In the Old Testament sin is man's failure to be true to the covenant God has made with him. The prodigal son illustrates sin as the son (man) rebelling against the loving father. According to some forms of Christian theology every man has been affected by "original sin" and thus stands in the wrong relationship to God, self, and neighbor. Such sin may be overcome only through faith in the love of God. Sin may also mean man's refusal to trust in God's love. Some Christian thinkers have understood sin to mean moral uncleanness. In Plato sin is understood as equal to wrongness. Sin in twentieth century theology has been primarily understood as meaning that man has the wrong relationship to self, neighbor, and God. Thus, "sin" is a singular concept and not plural, "sins." Sin is man's attempt to place himself in the center of life, in disobedience to God. In this view, man has certain responsibilities to God, neighbor, and self but fails to accept these responsibilities as his own. He defies the value of obedience and lives a life shaped by pride and selfishness. Sin as disobedience may be a moral concept, or it may include the concept of health: man is sick and in need of help. Religion then becomes the means by which God heals sickness. Several different words with many shades of meaning have been used to say what sin is and what it is not.

In the Old Testament the assumption in the background is that man cannot achieve a full life apart from the law. Man is estranged or at odds with self, others, and God. His relation to God is strained, if not hostile. Six words used in the Old Testament indicate different aspects of what sin means. (1) One word interprets man's condition as being that of missing the mark. Perhaps through ignorance or folly he has simply not turned out to be what he should have been. (2) A second aspect of sin refers to man's guilt. (3) Sin is a willful transgression, or breaking, of the law. This transgression is a rebellious attempt to defy God. (4) Sin has a bad result in that it cripples human life and distorts human relationships. (5) Sin is also seen as conscious evil or wickedness. Man is aware of what he is doing. He is aware of the results his action will have. He intellectually decides to go on with his unfortunate acts. (6) Sin is also used to indicate that a man is bad or wicked in the sense that he breaks the moral law of the day. In brief, the Old Testament pictures man as both free and responsible. Man misuses his freedom and is in trouble (Genesis 3). He is and will be punished for his misuse of his freedom. God alone can set things right in the present situation. God has made a covenant with his people for this purpose. If Israel is true to the covenant then sin will be overcome (see Atonement).

The New Testament makes a significantly different emphasis in regard to sin. In the Old Testament both the individual and the group are held responsible for sin. In the New Testament both strands are still present, but individual responsibility is emphasized. Jesus' understanding of sin is one of the son leaving the father's house. Man is unhappy and restless in his relation to God. He tries to separate himself from God. Jesus' life and teaching emphasizes the fact that God is willing to forgive man. If man will accept this forgiveness he can come back and have fellowship with God. For Paul sin is man's desire to go it alone. Man thinks that he does not need help from anyone. He asserts himself. He tries to build up his own life. This is most obvious in the religious life of man. Man thinks that he can take the law and follow it, in this way building up his own righteousness and showing himself to be a good man. However

281

all the requirements of the law cannot be met. Wholeness comes only if man trusts in God and gives of himself in doing the will of God.

In the Christian understanding of sin the doctrine of "original sin" has played a predominant role. Man is born into a community of sin. All men have sinned. Man by nature has a tendency toward sin. Man is corrupt in that he has become totally bad. Everything he does is corrupted; he is in a state of total depravity. At the same time, all men are created free. They have the ability to make choices.

In the Middle Ages sin was understood as moral uncleanliness. The Roman Catholic Church classified sins by the degree of seriousness of each. A proper cost of repentance in regard to particular sins was devised. A mortal sin is a deliberate sin in some weighty matter bringing spiritual death. A venial sin is a mistake made in a slight matter and not deliberate. In either case, man has misused his freedom. He can be made morally clean only through the sacraments administered by the church. In the Middle Ages the grace of the sacraments freed man from the punishment he would otherwise have received.

What this Middle Ages view meant was that failure to obey the laws of the church was a sin. Martin Luther (1483-1546) revolted against this idea of sin. Sin is not the breaking of a law. Sin is misplaced loyalty—having one's heart set on the wrong things. Thus it leads to idolatry, for the sinner is one who refuses to let God be God.

Plato (c. 427-347 B.C.) had said that sin is wrongness. To say that a man is a sinner is simply to say that he does the wrong things. Philosophy had also talked of sin as man's ignorance. Man is unreasonable in that he knows what his reason tells him he ought to do, and yet he does not do it. Man needs to be more reasonable. Liberal theology is built on this understanding of sin. Man can learn how to use his freedom. If man will just give of himself to the task he can figure out an answer to all of the problems confronting man. Men can solve these problems if they work together in a spirit of cooperation using their natural abilities.

Existential philosophy says that man is not as rational as the above philosophy would assume. Man is more than reason. Reason is never able to solve man's problem. Man is an irrational creature. Man's problem lies more in misplaced values than in misusing reason. Paul Ramsey (1913-   ) interprets sin in this same vein. Sin is the opposite of all that Christian love means. Man cannot get past his own self-centeredness. To be locked in sin is to be trapped in a desire to exalt oneself. Therefore the sinner fails to be concerned about the neighbor. Reinhold Niebuhr (1892-   ) agrees with the existentialists that evil is irrational. Man does not have control of himself. If man is to have a healthy life it must come because of service to the One who transcends man's life. Man's life is properly structured when it is centered in the claim that goes beyond man. Paul Tillich (1886-1965) understands sin to be man's estrangement from himself, from others, and from God. Man's life is healthy only when it is properly grounded in God. Man is a value-assigning creature. He decides what will be important to him. He decides what he will be concerned about. This decision places ultimate concern in something. Man is aware that he may fail to have as his ultimate concern that which he should. In his freedom is the possibility that his entire life will turn out to be meaningless. This possibility is the ground of man's anxiety. Tillich's understanding of sin faces in a sharp way the question: What is the relation of sin to mental illness? (*see Alienation, Negation, Theodicy*) J.S.H.

SIN OFFERING (*see Sacrifice*)

SITZ IM LEBEN (*see Form criticism, Oral tradition, Pericope*)

Skeptic Often quite negative connotations are associated with this word when it refers to religion, especially to Christianity. In this context a skeptic is regarded as someone who doubts parts of or all Christian claims of truth. It should be noted, however, that the word really refers to a mental attitude. As such it amounts to systematic doubting. Such a person when confronted by a proposition will typically ask such questions as, "Why do you take it to be true?" or "What are the bases for such judgment?" Thus, the asking of such questions in itself may be of greater service to Christianity than the unquestioning and uncritical attitude that simply accepts propositions about God, man, and the world. Paul Tillich (1886-1965) was one theologian who tried to see the contributions of skepticism. He often exhibited the "faith to doubt." (*see Agnostic, Cynic*) J.B.W.

Social Gospel "Social Gospel" is a term used to describe the message a small group of Christians proclaimed in the late nineteenth and early twentieth centuries. Walter Rauschenbusch (1861-1918) is considered the outstanding spokesman for this group. The Social Gospel begins by applying Christian brotherliness or love to human behavior. This leads to an interest in developing a "good society." Society may be so structured as to be destructive of human life. The Social Gospel tries to reshape society in order to make of it a constructive force.

The basic concern of the Social Gospel is that the Christian gospel should be relevant and helpful to man. This concern has to some extent been present throughout the life of the Christian church. But a movement arose in the nineteenth century with an emphasis unique enough to distinguish itself. In the 1700's and early 1800's in America, Christian preaching was generally concerned to deliver the individual from his sin by helping him to have an emotional religious experience. During that period issues such as slavery, economic questions, prison reforms, and war and peace seem to have been considered outside of the church's concern. The church assumed its task was to help people have a "religious experience."

In 1848 the Christian Socialist movement began. This group tried to arouse in Christians a sense of guilt for the damage brought to human life by certain social practices. This movement was concerned that all human beings get their fair share of the physical products necessary to sustain life. It dealt with such questions as: "Are our business practices fair to all who are involved?"

A *Theology for the Social Gospel*, by Walter Rauschenbusch, is an attempt to show that the gospel demands that the Christian be concerned about society. Here society means the laws, customs, and actual way people relate to one another in a public group. The community in which a man lives deeply affects his individual life. The Christian is one who is working to bring about the kingdom of God in this world. One means is to criticize injustice wherever it occurs. Man can do away with evil (unfair) institutions; and when he completes this task the kingdom of God will be established on this earth.

Careful examination of Jesus' teaching of the kingdom of God uncovers a different interpretation of how God's rule on earth is to be established. Jesus taught that a catastrophic interruption will occur in history. Man's use of his freedom will lead to almost complete destruction of human life on earth. God will somehow miraculously intervene in history to prevent man from completely destroying himself. Although Rauschenbusch was aware of this element in Jesus' teaching, he also detected clearly the belief that God works in and through man to establish his kingdom. Both of these strands of Jesus' teaching are in the New Testament. In this century Christian theology has been seeking a way to take both sides of Jesus' teaching seriously.

Liberal theology built on the ideas of Rauschenbusch in order to develop a specific understanding of what man can do in order to bring about the kingdom of God. It sought to give an accurate word picture of Jesus' actual life and a list of Jesus' teachings. Once this was done man could follow Jesus' example and teaching and in so doing build the kingdom of God on earth.

Serious criticisms have been raised about the liberal school of thought. World wars I and II have brought man to a less optimistic picture of what man can accomplish. The assumption that man will completely eliminate injustice from society seems unrealistic. The Social Gospel has made the point that the Christian cannot afford to be indifferent to injustice in society. It led to the adoption, in 1908, of a social creed by the Methodist Episcopal Church, the first American denomination to draw up such a creed. (*see Kingdom of God, Natural theology*) J.S.H.

SOLA SCRIPTURA (*see* Authority, Church)

SOMA (*see* Body)

SON OF GOD (*see* Christology, Name, Virgin birth)

SON OF MAN (*see* Christology, Eschatology, Messiah, Name, Pre-existence)

SORGE (*see* Anxiety)

Soteriology (soh-*tir*-ee-*ahl*-oh-jee) Soteriology is the study of salvation. The word came into use in the nineteenth century and has its roots in the Greek words, *sozein*, meaning "to save," and *logos*, which is a "study" or a "discourse." Christology is concerned with the person of Jesus Christ, and in soteriology his saving work is studied. The sin of man, atonement, redemption, and the grace of God are among matters considered.

In the Old Testament, salvation meant "made wide," "set in an open place," or "freedom in spacious places." It became definitely related to victory and deliverance from oppression. In the New Testament it came to mean release from the captivity of sin to the freedom of a new life.

Some of the questions raised with relation to salvation and that form the basis for some differences among denominations and sects are: (1) What is the role of man in salvation? Is faith an "act" or only a passive acceptance of grace? (2) What is God's role in salvation? Does he choose to save men against their will? (3) Who will be saved? Will God determine a definite number of persons to be saved and others to be lost? (4) Is salvation immediate or gradual? (5) How does man believe? Is belief possible only through the gospel proclaimed by the church, or is belief possible outside the church? (6) Is man's salvation final, or can it be lost?

Some views of salvation that have been a part of the church's history are: (1) The doctrine of election attributed to Augustine (354-430) and held by Calvinists. It holds that God chooses some to salvation and not others. (2) The Arminian view believes that God makes salvation available to all and that some respond in faith and love though others reject it. Arminians insist on the free will of man in the exercise of his faith. (3) Universalism teaches that God does not intend that any souls should be lost and that eventually he will redeem all men. The view that all souls will finally be restored to God began with Origen (*c.* 185-*c.* 254) and is sometimes referred to as "apocatastasis."

The meaning of salvation depends on the meaning of sin. If sin is death, salvation is life. If sin is guilt, salvation is freedom. If sin is sickness, salvation is health.

During the Reformation, guilt for disobedience to God's commands was an overriding emphasis. Man was saved by God's grace, which man received through his faith. Justification by faith was the way man was "set upright," so to speak.

In the centuries after the Reformation, the church developed into a spiritual avenue of salvation. Revivalists in America emphasized the punishment that would befall a sinner in the afterlife. By contrast, salvation meant the reward of living with God forever.

But in Europe, Friedrich Schleiermacher (1768-1834) was raising a question about salvation that would undercut many attempts to gain eternal life. What is sin? asked Schleiermacher. Simply man's consciousness that he was incomplete. What then was salvation (or as he preferred to call it, "redemption")? Man's consciousness of God. And what of heaven and hell? These could only be human ways of expressing the perfection or imperfection of man's life. Following Kant, Schleiermacher did not ask about things it was impossible to know about, such as supernatural life after death.

Karl Barth (1886-   ) rejected Schleiermacher's approach, saying it made salvation depend on man instead of God. Only God's grace can save, insisted Barth. He reveals himself in Jesus Christ. Man's faith is necessary, but it does not compete with God's grace. Barth tried to restate the traditional view of salvation in a way that would make it hold up in the face of criticisms that it was meaningless to modern man.

Today many thinkers admit that modern man does not feel guilty. He does not often feel he needs to be saved from anything. Yet some, such as Gerhard Ebeling (1912-   ) insist that man "needs" salvation. Ebeling sees man as basically a responding being. However, he is unable to provide himself with a healing response. God has spoken in Jesus Christ a healing Word, and the Word leads to man's salvation.

Existentialist thinkers follow Schleiermacher in viewing salvation as a human experience. Rudolf Bultmann (1884-   ) understands salvation as man's understanding of himself—his realization that he is separated from himself, coupled with the assurance that new life is possible for him.

In the history of Christian thought, salvation has been understood on two levels: (1) personal, and (2) historical. In the first sense the question is whether individuals can be saved in isolation from the rest of society. In the second sense the question is the fate of all history, or of all humanity. (see *Election, Faith, Flesh, Grace, History, Judgment, Predestination, Redemption, Sin*) G.E.S.

Soul   The ancient Greeks used *anima* as a term including what we would call both "mind" and "soul." The Greeks, however, thought of the *anima* of the universe, in which the individual shared. In Plato's thought, especially, the *anima* became more important than matter or desire.

In the New Testament, Paul used *soma* to mean "body," in the sense that man has a relation to himself. (First Corinthians 9:27 is an example.) He used the Greek word *psyche* (*sigh*-kee) sparingly. Where the Old Testament used *nephesh* (the Hebrew word for "life"), Paul seems to use *psyche*, which comes close to meaning "self." Second Corinthians 1:23 is an example.

During the Middle Ages, thinkers like Thomas Aquinas (*c.* 1225-74) returned to the Greek concept and thought of man as divided into body and soul. The body is animal flesh; the soul is the rational spirit with which man sees God.

Today "soul" is used (1) by conservative thinkers to mean the spirit of man; (2) by liberal thinkers to mean man's self. (*see Self, Spirit*) G.E.S.

Source criticism   Source criticism is usually classified as higher criticism, as distinct from lower or textual criticism. The purpose of source criticism is to identify sources embedded in a given document. It is part of literary criticism, itself a subdivision of higher criticism.

Perhaps the most famous example of the application of source criticism to the Old Testament is found in the identification of four sources for the Pentateuch (the first five books of the Old Testament), sources that have been given the labels J, E, D, and P. This identification disposed of the traditional notion that the Pentateuch was written by Moses. That elements of the tradition do indeed go back very early is not denied by source criticism. But the Pentateuch is a combination of at least these four sources that have been brought together for religious purposes by an editor. J is a product of the southern kingdom and is noteworthy for its use of the name Yahweh for the deity. E, on the other hand, comes from the north, and it uses Elohim as its title for God. D is found in the book of Deuteronomy. P is a priestly document. Each of these sources can be dated: J by the ninth century B.C., E by the eighth century, D by the seventh century, and P by the fifth century. The Pentateuch or Torah was in existence by 400 B.C.

The most important application of source criticism to the New Testament has been to the Synoptic Gospels, Matthew, Mark, and Luke. It had long been noted that these Gospels have a great deal of material in common, but at the same time there are wide areas of difference. It is obvious that some kind of relation exists between them. The question was the nature of this relationship. This question has been given the name "the Synoptic Problem." Various solutions have been offered. By far the most important is the one that views Mark as the earliest Gospel and as a source for Matthew and Luke. Yet it is clear that the Marcan source does not account for all the material in the first and third Gospels. Some of the material left over is common to Matthew and Luke. This material has been given the symbol Q (from the German Quelle, meaning "source"). Again, when the material from Mark and the material from Q has been assessed, it is noted that there is still material peculiar to Matthew and material peculiar to Luke. One scholar, B. H. Streeter (1874-1937), has labelled these M and L, respectively. This gives us a four-source hypothesis. Attempts have been made to name the places where these sources originated, although the attempts have not proved too successful.

The Gospel of John presents its own set of problems. John seems to be less a compilation and more a composition than the Synoptics. Yet some scholars feel that a source lies behind the "signs section" (John 2–12) and perhaps behind the "discourses" (John 13–17). There is the strong possibility, moreover, that John was using the Synoptic Gospels as a source, since some elements of the synoptic tradition appear in that Gospel. The famous Prologue to the Gospel (John 1:1-18) may be a Christianized version of a Hymn to the Logos. In general, however, John is more highly personal than the Synoptics, in the sense that its author is truly a composer.

Two other examples of the use of sources in the New Testament may be noted. The first is the obvious dependence of 2 Peter on the Letter of Jude. The second is the use of Colossians by the writer to the Ephesians. But these examples do not by any means exhaust the possibilities; they are illustrative only. Source criticism is an important tool in biblical investigation. But it still remains, after the possible sources have been investigated and the authors' adaptations noted, to study the document for its own sake and for its own contribution. (see Biblical criticism, Literary criticism) E.L.T.

SOVEREIGNTY OF GOD (see Providence)

Spirit *Spirit has two meanings—the Holy Spirit or third person of the Trinity and the spirit of man. The doctrine of the Holy Spirit has been neglected in theology, and the early church was slow to develop a systematic view of the doctrine. In the early centuries of the church, christology was important, and the human and divine natures of Christ were disputed. When councils discussed the Holy Spirit, they referred to the Bible but did not speak of the "nature" of the Holy Spirit. Though the Gospel of John makes much of the Spirit, it was not until about the fourth century that the creeds of the church emphasized the Holy Spirit. Not only is God Spirit, but so is man. The Bible speaks of* *man's being made in the image of God (Genesis 1:26-27), and says the breath of life was breathed into him by God (Genesis 2:7).*

The Old Testament uses the Hebrew word *ruah* (breath) for the Holy Spirit. In the Old Testament, the Holy Spirit was present at creation and continued to guide the course of Israel's history as God's presence and power was felt in the world. God's spirit directed the Patriarchs in their journeyings, provided wisdom to the judges, courage to the prophets, and divine presence to the priests. The Psalmist writes of the presence of God, and the Hebrews sensed that it was his hand and breath that guided them. The word *ruah* also refers to the "spirit" or "breath of man," which came from God's spirit. Since Hebrew thought did not divide man into parts (as the Greeks did—into body, soul, and mind), the spirit included such concepts as soul, heart, and mind.

The person and presence of the Holy Spirit is decidedly seen in the New Testament. Prior to his ascension, Jesus promised to send the Holy Spirit to his followers (Acts 1:5, 8). At Pentecost the Holy Spirit revealed himself. Some New Testament writers relate the power of the Holy Spirit to the Resurrection. Miracles, the gifts of prophecy, speaking in tongues, and other special gifts are also products of the Holy Spirit's work. The Greek word *pneuma* (*new*-mah) is the New Testament word for both Holy Spirit and spirit of man. It differs from the Hebrew use of *ruah* in that *pneuma* refers primarily to the will or soul, while the word, *psyche* (root of our term "psychology") relates to human activity of the mind or personality. The Latin word, *Spiritus*, which means "breath," is used for the intelligence or impulse.

The "self" or "person" of man's spirit finally depends upon God rather than upon man himself. At Pentecost, the Holy Spirit was not a gift to particular individuals but to the entire community of Christians; thus the church is a community empowered by the dynamic of God's Holy Spirit. *(see Church, Heart, Pentecost, Trinity)* G.E.S.

SPIRITUAL ANXIETY *(see Anxiety)*

STATE *(see Power, Theocracy)*

STEADFAST LOVE *(see Love)*

Stewardship In the Bible, a steward supervises a household or manages someone's affairs for him (Luke 12:42). The idea carried over into the church, where a bishop was a spiritual supervisor. The church has usually applied stewardship to the use of money. Sometimes stewardship of time and talents is included. There are two opposing views of good stewardship: (1) Religious stewardship is an offering to God of a share of the gifts granted to man. Usually a standard decides whether one is a good steward. This idea is closely connected to "holy habits." To be truly religious, a person worships and prays at regular times. He may observe the Sabbath as a special day. Similarly, he gives a portion of his income "to God," that is, to the church. This viewpoint encourages discipline, but it tends to separate religion and everyday life. (2) If all of creation is created by God, then man owes his life, not merely a share of it, to God. The only true sense in which man can be a steward is by being faithful and obedient to God. This idea is much like the concept of thanksgiving. Worship and giving may be only symbols, or giving may be emphasized for its purely practical help, rather than for its religious meaning. What really decides whether a man is a good steward is whether he loves his neighbor and is faithful to God. In this view, spending money on education, taking time for recreation, and using talents for enjoyment may be seen as good stewardship. This view makes life into a whole but may easily slide into irresponsibility toward institutions and toward the neighbor in need. (*see Sacrifice, Tithe*)

STOIC (*see Destiny, Natural theology*)

STRANGER (*see Alienation, Neighbor*)

Structure Structure refers to the way in which things are arranged. In biology the structure of the body is discovered by determining the way the different organs in the body are arranged in relation to one another. Contemporary sociology uses the term "structure" to refer to the way people are related to one another in society. In small personal groups there may be no formal structure to the group. The group has no written laws or clearly stated ways of acting; yet, the group does develop a certain structure. It has ways of acting, and certain persons assume leadership roles in the group. Structure, a means of relating to people, is a part of every human relationship.

Structure is more frequently used to refer to the formal structures of society. In a city, state, or federal government people are related in ways that are more easily observable than that of a small personal friendship group. Here there are laws, customs, and moral teachings that are usually stated in relatively clear fashion. Different interest groups in the society have specific purposes and power to accomplish these purposes. The form or structure of society can either help or hurt man's attempts to develop his full humanity. But how is man going to change society if it needs changing? Society is shaped by power groups in society. Laws and customs do not just happen—they are brought into existence by applied pressure.

In the nineteenth century Walter Rauschenbusch (1861-1918) became convinced that man's problems are due to the ills of society, not individual failure. If society were shaped properly then man's problems would be solved. The Christian needs to work at the task of redesigning society. Laws are to be revised and customs changed in order to bring them into accordance with the will of God. When this is done the kingdom of God will be established on earth. Reinhold Niebuhr (1892-) agreed with the fact that Christians need to be active in trying to reshape society. His teachings call man to recognize that any and all forms of government (democracy included) are only partially just. Every form of government ends up being unfair (or unjust) to some. The Christian is to be one who is constantly examining society in order to discover and correct the injustice occurring from the structure of the society in which he lives. (*see Justice, Social Gospel*) J.S.H.

Style Some thinkers in Christian ethics refer to a "Christian style of life." A style is a form of action, or a way of doing things, rather than the content of action. Some thinkers call it a "quality" of moral action, such as joy and courage. Style may involve the attitude or basic position a Christian takes toward decisions and issues. For instance, if a Christian were ready to change laws and customs when they interfered with human welfare, such openness would be part of his style. The term remains vague, however, and raises questions about how to tell good style from bad. (*see Aesthetics*)

SUBCONSCIOUS (*see Consciousness*)

SUBORDINATION (*see Christology, Trinity*)

Substance In Scholasticism, the theology of the Middle Ages, the concept *substantia* (substance) gained a widespread currency. Substance came to mean the independent reality that underlies all things. The characteristics of a thing, e.g., a tree—its height, coloring, age, bark disease—are said to be its accidents. Underlying those particular accidents, however, is the substance we may call "treeness." Thus even if the accidents change—if the tree grows higher, changes color, gets older —the substance does not change. The idea of substance was very important for the development of the idea of Christian sacraments by Scholasticism. When the concept of tran*substan*tiation was put forward, it meant that the accidents of bread and wine remain, but miraculously, their substance is changed to the body and blood of Christ. (*see Essence, Transubstantiation*) J.B.W.

Succession (Apostolic) Roman Catholics consider Peter to have had special authority, which he transmitted through the apostles and popes, to the present time. They believe this authority has been transmitted in a line of unbroken succession. The Anglican Church claims a similar succession, which is not recognized by authorities in the Roman Church. (*see Apostle, Pope*) G.E.S.

Supererogation (soo-*pehr*-oh-*gay*-shuhn) Works of supererogation are acts beyond the normal requirement. In Roman Catholic theology works of supererogation are the good deeds performed by the saints over and above the requirements for salvation. This idea was developed by Gregory the Great (*c.* 540-604 A.D.). God's grace corrects us by means of the commandments. Man can either cooperate or not cooperate in this work. If man cooperates the gift from God becomes man's merit in that man does what is expected of him. In fact, by the grace of God man can do more than God commands him to do. The works of supererogation done by one member of the church can be transferred or given to the credit of another member of the church. J.S.H.

SUPERNATURAL (*see Transcendence*)

SUPPLICATION (*see Prayer*)

Sursum Corda Translated from the Latin, *circum* (upward) and *corda* (hearts), it means "lift up your hearts." The *sursum corda* is a versicle that invites the congregation to join in thanksgiving to God. Used in the communion and mass, it is a hymn of joy found in the ancient liturgies. (*see Liturgy, Versicle*) G.E.S.

Symbol Derived from the Greek *symbollein*, meaning "to throw together," symbol is an object, an image, a concept, or a combination of these that awakens awareness of a real but otherwise unknown relationship. Further, a symbol participates in that to which it calls attention.

Symbols arise from vision, intuition, or imagination rather than by means of rational thought. This is clear in such biblical instances as the vision of the "valley of dry bones" (Ezekiel 37) and the Apocalypse of John (Revelation). By virtue of their participation in the reality to which they call attention, symbols have a life of their own. They function for man by laying a claim upon him, not by his thinking his way to them. Some psychologists, following the lead of C. G. Jung (1875-   ), have even gone so far as to suggest that symbols arise from man's unconscious dimension and in this deepest sense reveal the unity of man. In any case symbols seem to be a uniquely human means of communication. The contemporary German philosopher, Ernst Cassirer (1874-1945), has written persuasively of man as the "symbol making animal."

Evidence from ancient times and primitive peoples shows that symbols and religion were inseparable. Given this connection, it should be no

292

surprise that many symbols taken over by Christianity have long histories in other religious traditions. Examples are light—"Jesus is the light of the world"; water—the basic element of baptism; dove—symbol of the Holy Spirit, along with fire. From such a brief list another aspect of symbolism becomes apparent. Any particular interpretation given a symbol by a religious community operates in that way for only a more or less restricted group of people. Common experience and shared presuppositions are as necessary for symbolic functioning as for any other form of communication. There would seem to be, therefore, neither universal nor private symbols.

Although visual images are often connected with the notion of symbols, no such restriction can be fully maintained. Action and spoken language may also be cited as two other media of symbolism. The most persuasive illustration of this unity of act and word is to be found in the fact that what is today called the "Apostles' Creed" was originally referred to as the "Apostles' Symbol." Spoken at the time of the reception of baptism, the Apostles' Symbol opened "the entrance into life everlasting," which gave "great protection" (Bishop Ambrose, fifth century). Such language leaves no doubt that the function of the symbol was thought to be very real. An extension of this analysis would reveal the symbolic function of other aspects of the liturgy of the church—its language, colors, objects, and priestly actions and garments.

In a time when increasing numbers of men are sensitive to symbolic function, it is becoming clear how little the traditional symbols of Christianity function in our secularized world. That the phrase "the death of God" receives as much circulation as it has suggests that even the symbols of the ultimate, of God himself, are no longer functioning for large numbers of modern men. One must suppose that the continued life of Christianity depends largely upon the degree of success in interpreting its symbolism. Two modern theologians who have attempted directly to speak to this issue are Paul Tillich (1886-1965) and Rudolf Bultmann (1884-   ). (see Attributes, Creed, Truth) J.B.W.

SYNAGOGUE (see Diaspora, Priest)

Synod The Presbyterian, Lutheran, and Episcopal churches use synod to mean governing body of the church. In the early church, it was synonymous with "council," and was used to designate any church meeting called for a particular area. In the Presbyterian Church, it ranks between the Presbytery and the General Assembly. In the Lutheran and Episcopal churches, it is a regional organization of congregations. (see Conference, Presbytery) G.E.S.

Synoptics (sin-op-tiks) The New Testament presents us with four Gospels, the first three of which are customarily called the

"Synoptic Gospels" or simply, "the Synoptics." In its application to the Gospels, "Synoptics" suggests the fact that a common view of these books is possible; they may be "viewed together."

The Gospel of John is ordinarily classified separately. This is recognition that it belongs to a different literary strain, although Synoptic-type material appears in it also. In general, however, the Fourth Gospel represents true composition, while the Synoptics are built on traditions already in existence in the church. While the distinction should not be overstressed, the Synoptic writers worked more as compilers of tradition, while the author of the Fourth Gospel was a composer. (*see Literary criticism, Source criticism*) E.L.T.

SYNTHESIS (*see Dialectic*)

TABULA RASA (*see Reason*)

TASTE (*see Aesthetics*)

Te Deum (tay *day*-oom) Meaning "Thou God," it is an ancient Christian hymn of unknown authorship, sometimes incorrectly ascribed to Saint Ambrose. The words, "We praise thee, O God," are a part of the daily matins of the Roman Catholic Church and are sung on all Sundays except Advent and Lent. The Protestants also sing this chant, especially on occasions of thanksgiving and rejoicing. (*see Prayer*) G.E.S.

TEACHER (*see* Kerygma, *Orders*)

Teleology (tee-lee-*ahl*-oh-jee) From the Greek words *telos*, meaning the end, and *logos*, meaning discourse, teleology means discourse about the end. It is a word that in this specific form was probably coined in the eighteenth century by a German philosopher. It is the doctrine that the universe has a final purpose or goal toward which it is moving. By extension of the argument, everything within the universe would have its own end or purpose contributing to the larger design or purpose of the universe. Though they did not call it teleology, Plato (*c.* 427-347 B.C.) and Aristotle (384-322 B.C.) taught that there is a first cause from which the world originated and a final end toward which it moves.

Christian theology has made a great deal of teleology. By identifying God as the first cause and final end, it has appropriated the Greek heritage quite directly. Moving from sense experiences of objects and living things, theologians and philosophers developed an argument for the existence of God. Thomas Aquinas (A.D. *c.* 1225-74) argued this way: Objects without self-motivation or intelligence nonetheless act so that they achieve the best possible results. Obviously the purpose fulfilled in such objects would not occur by chance with nearly the frequency that in fact occurs. Therefore they must be directed by something that guides them with intelligence and motivation. Some intelligent being, therefore, must exist. This we call God. For Aquinas, this was a conclusion unaided, human reason could naturally reach. It was one of the bases for his "natural theology."

Later thinkers were often very attracted to this argument. It has been called many things—"the argument from design" and "the psychic-theological argument," in addition to the "teleological argument." One of its most eloquent defenders was William Paley (1743-1805), in his *Evidences of Christianity*, his remarkable defense of natural religion and its compatibility with Christianity. Other thinkers have severely criticized the argument. B. Spinoza (1632-77) and David Hume (1711-76) attacked it vigorously. Hume's argument was typical of his critique of all the proposed arguments for the existence of God. No man ever experiences, he argued, more than a minute fraction of the universe in which he lives. It is illegitimate and unreasonable to jump from such limited experience to theories about the entire universe. Further, even if the logical jump were justified (which it is not, according to Hume), there would still be no reason to identify the first cause with the Christian understanding of God.

Such philosophical attacks were given great support by the developments in physical sciences in the late eighteenth and nineteenth centuries. The growth of awareness of the waste of life, the innumerable species that had not survived, was one aspect of the development of biology. To a very large extent the combination of attacks from philosophy and science caused theologians to abandon the traditional formulations of the theological argument.

But the Hebrew-Christian view is that time and space had a beginning (creation) and are moving to an end (the kingdom of God). Perhaps no argument can prove the truth of this view if the argument is based empirically, that is, by using only the knowledge of sense-experience.

But by the same token, the view cannot be disproven empirically. Christian teleology then becomes a matter of faith, whatever form of discourse is adopted. (*see End, Natural theology, Theism*) J.B.W.

TEMPERANCE (*see Moderation*)

TEMPLE (*see Priest*)

Temptation In both the Old and New Testaments, God may test man but not vice-versa. One of the most serious sins, from the biblical view, is for man to test God (Deuteronomy 6:16; 1 Corinthians 10:9). God tests man by trying his faith, as in the stories of Abraham (Genesis 22) and Job. The phrase, "lead us not into temptation," from the Lord's Prayer, puzzles many. However, in the background is the belief that God does indeed tempt (or test) men of faith. Dietrich Bonhoeffer (1906-45) says that man is too sure of himself if he feels he can ward off every temptation. Instead, the man of faith knows that it is all too easy to reject God. For temptation to make any sense, sin must be clearly defined and powerful. Where there is no sin, there is no temptation.

TEN COMMANDMENTS (*see Decalogue*)

TERCE (*see Office*)

TETRAGRAMMATON (*see Name*)

TEXT CRITICISM (*see Literary criticism, Manuscript*)

THANKS (*see Prayer*)

THEANTHROPISM (*see Christology*)

THEIOS ANER (*see Miracle*)

Theism Derived from the Greek word *theos*, theism is a conception of God. In ordinary use it refers to a specific concept—that God is an existent, unified, and perfect Being who created the cosmos. Though distinct from it, he guides the cosmos by providential care. As such, theism is one form theology takes. Other concepts of God with which theism most typically is contrasted are pantheism, deism, and polytheism. Each of these sheds light on the content of theism.

Pantheism is an older and widely shared concept of the divinity in which God is co-extensive with the cosmos. Pantheism holds, then, that

God is really just another name for the cosmos. A perception of the workings of the cosmos is at the same time a discovery of how God works, according to a thorough-going pantheism. God is wholly immanent in this view.

Deism is the view, particularly widespread in the eighteenth century Enlightenment, that holds God to have been the creator of the cosmos. Having completed the task, he allows it to run its natural course. In other words, deists typically deny that God is providentially involved in the on-going processes of the cosmos. God is wholly transcendent in this view.

Monotheism and polytheism are contrasted in a different way. Most theistic positions, in order to be fully developed, are monotheistic, that is, they hold to the oneness or unity of divinity. Polytheism holds that there are many gods. Henotheism is faith in one God, who is, nevertheless, only one god among many. This may have been the view of the early Hebrews.

Theism is the concept of God that has been most typically held in the history of Christian theology. The combination of the immanence of God (seen in creation and sovereignty) and transcendence (seen in revelation and judgment) are typically found in Christian thought. This concept was available to early Christian theologians in the metaphysical speculations of classical Greek philosophers. Christians were attracted toward this view because it leaves room for the basic transcendence of God to intervene in time and space.

Theism is not without its critics. Nor have theologians generally used the concept without qualifying and clarifying it in some respects. Thus, a really precise description of theism is not possible apart from a careful analysis of a total theology.

Among contemporary thinkers, Charles Hartshorne (1897-   ), a process philosopher, and the theologians Paul Tillich (1886-1965) and Schubert Ogden (1928-   ) are the most helpful. (*see Dualism, Monism, Ontology, Reality*) J.B.W.

Theocracy (the-*ah*-kroh-see)   A theocracy is any human organization ruled directly by God. God appoints his own representatives, who then rule the church or state. Theocracy assumes that authority to rule people is derived directly from God. Democracy assumes that authority to rule people is derived from consent of the people. In John Calvin's thought the whole people of God (the church) are the appointed representatives of God in this world. However, most frequently it is assumed that special groups of priests or political leaders are the appointed representatives of God. Theocracy teaches that no man has the right to question the authority of a man whom God has appointed. (*see Pluralism*) J.S.H.

Theodicy (the-*ah*-doh-see) Literally, this word is derived from the Greek words meaning "deity" and "justice." As the word has been used, it means the theological attempt to justify faith in God's goodness in spite of the abundant evidence of evil in the world. In ordinary use the term has often come to refer to theological affirmations about the problem of evil. The problem is especially acute for Christian theology, since the primary revelation of the goodness of God is proclaimed through the cruel and evil crucifixion of Jesus. There have been several different kinds of attempts to deal with theodicy in the history of Christian theology. One alternative, however, seems to have been often used. According to this view, God created the world in such a way that men have real freedom and in such a way that there is relative stability in the world. Evil is real because men, in order to be free, must be free to misuse the creation. There are abiding difficulties in every attempt to treat such a problem, however. (*see Dualism, Monism, Providence*) J.B.W.

Theology *Theology is the study of God. A theologian is a person who studies God. Theologians try to make as clear as possible what it means to use language about God. Theology does not have to be Christian. A Christian theology studies God as He is known through Christ. Since the church witnesses to Christ, the theologian is (1) a person who has faith in God through Christ, and (2) one who takes part in the church.*

Philosophy of religion is another kind of study. It uses reason to study God and religion. Theologians also use reason, but they usually use knowledge revealed by God as well. Some theologians use philosophy, and since there are many philosophies, there are many different kinds of theology. Some theologians believe only the Bible and creeds should be used. Besides "philosophical theology" (or apologetics) and "biblical theology," there is "historical theology" (which studies the different ways the church has thought of God in the past) and "practical theology" (which studies worship, preaching, teaching, counseling, and church organization).

In following the strict literal meaning of the two Greek words for "deity" and "discourse," theology is sometimes said to be only concerned with discourse about the existence and nature of the divine. That this is a severely limited view is obvious. If it were rigidly adhered to, the vast bulk of what passes as theology would have to be disqualified. Broadly conceived, theology is a discourse about the whole range of problems that arise in considering the relation of man to the divine. It is obvious that neither of these positions requires limiting theological discourse to Christianity, but Western thinkers have often used "theology" to mean only "Christian theology."

Theology can be defined as that form of language that arises from participating in and thinking about religious faith. Further, theology seeks the clearest statement of this faith that the language available makes possible. Christian theology, then, is that form of clear language that attempts to express the content of the experience of Christ as the origin of one's faith. Since the church is the historical community that witnesses to Christ as the foundation of its faith, the Christian theologian is one who participates in that witnessing community. Further, by this definition, the theologian himself is one who has experienced religious faith through Christ. Participation, therefore, means sharing in a community and personally experiencing faith. The classical definition of theology as "faith seeking understanding" meant this kind of participation.

Clearly, theology is quite similar to, yet very different from, philosophy of religion. The philosopher of religion seeks to examine religion, not by participating in faith, but by using criteria that have been developed in the philosophical discipline. For example, whereas the theologian speaks about the knowledge given in revelation, the philosopher of religion will measure such knowledge by the philosophical study of how men "know." Or, whereas the theologian speaks of Christian ethics, the philosopher of religion will evaluate such statements in light of philosophical reflections upon the "moral." Thus, as traditionally conceived, theology differs from philosophy of religion because the theologian begins from his participation in faith, whereas the philosopher of religion begins from some philosophical commitment.

Yet the connection between theology and philosophy is extremely complicated. By the definition of theology offered above, the effort is made by the theologian to express *as clearly as possible* the content and meaning of his faith. But by what standards is clarity to be measured? Very often, in the history of theology the answer has been that clarity is to be insured by meeting the tests of logical consistency and coherency. And these, of course, are philosophical tests! In the second century, Christian theology was attacked by philosophers. Some theologians responded by trying to make theology at least philosophically respectable, if not acceptable. Since those earliest instances theologians have continued to turn to philosophical categories. And what in an older day would have been called apologetic theology is often today called philosophical theology.

Not all theologians, however, are convinced that the alliance between theology and philosophy is as valuable as some think it to be. For in the second century, when Christianity was under attack, and where efforts were first made on philosophical grounds to defend it, certain aspects of Christianity's heritage from Israelite religion and history would not yield to philosophical expression. Loyalty to the Hebrew heritage has created a tradition of theologians who resist the alliance between theology and philosophy.

In the modern era, philosophers have declared their independence from the ancient Greek philosophical tradition and have formulated new philosophies. For theologians attracted to philosophy this has raised the serious question: "Is there a 'right philosophy' to use in doing theology?" Many theologians agree that this is a most important question, but they do not all agree that there is one answer. Thus, there are philosophical theologians who choose existentialist philosophy, others who choose language analysis, and others choose process philosophy. These are but a few of the possibilities. In such a situation the resulting theologies are going to be very different from each other, thus creating many theologies.

Other theologians believe the many differences among philosophical theologians betray a fundamental error. And the error is in the starting place. Theology is doomed to fragmentation so long as many different philosophical measurements are used. Rather, argues someone like Karl Barth (1886-   ), theology should begin with the Bible, and let whatever is found there serve as the only ground for measuring theology. When the Bible and the creeds of Christianity are regarded as authorities, rather than this or that philosophy, dogmatic theology results.

Theology, therefore, is classified by its starting place. If philosophy is most highly esteemed, philosophical or apologetic theology results. If the Bible and creeds are primary, then dogmatic or biblical theology results.

One other note must be added. Theology has traditionally understood itself to be in service to the church. Where it has given attention to specific aspects of the church, special titles have often been adopted. If, for example, the systematic theologies of other periods are the primary focus of study, this discipline is called "historical theology." If the Bible is the more specialized center, this is called "biblical theology." If the church in its practice is the center of attention, this is called "practical theology." (see Dogmatics, Faith, Natural theology, Reason, Revelation) J.B.W.

Theonomy (the-ah-noh-mee) Theonomy assumes that man's natural rational abilities become fully developed only when reason is united with God, who created man. God is the ground out of which man's reason grows. God is the law of the universe; therefore it is wrong to set the natural world or natural reason over against divinity or revelation. The natural is rooted in the divine. Man's becoming fully human is not opposed to the will of God. Rather, man can become fully human only in union with God, who is the ground out of which human life comes. This word can best be understood as an answer to the problem arising out of the conflict between heteronomy and autonomy. (*see Heteronomy*) J.S.H.

Theophany (the-*ah*-fo-nee)   Literally, the word is derived from the Greek words meaning "deity" and "appearance," hence appearances or manifestations of God to man. As such, it is one aspect of the broader concept of "revelation." Theophanies are said to occur in many religious traditions. Several stories are often referred to as theophanies in the Old Testament. Two of the best known such stories are those of Yahweh's appearance to Moses in the burning bush (Exodus 3) and to Job in the whirlwind (Job 38:1). The Christian view of the incarnation of God in Christ would seem to be the classical instance of a theophany. Some theologians, however, in their concern to preserve the uniqueness of God's revelation in Christ, have denied that it had the character of a theophany. (*see Epiphany*) J.B.W.

THESIS (*see Dialectic*)

THOMISM (*see Metaphysics, Natural law, Natural theology, Reason, Revelation*)

Time   Along with space, time makes up one of the simplest necessary conditions for existence. There is no conceivable existent reality apart from its involvement in time and space. But what is time? The remarkable range of suggested answers to that question to be found in the history of thought suggests that there is far from universal agreement. Quite arbitrarily, then, two common concepts, both of which play important roles in the Christian theological tradition, will be examined. They are *chronos*, hence the English word "chronology," and *kairos*, a more complex notion.

Western philosophy has usually viewed time as chronology. The common sense notion is that time can be accurately measured by clocks and calendars. One may speak of a short duration of time—"five minutes" —or a longer period—"a century of time." By this view time is the medium within which all events occur, apparently in succession. One may describe a day's activities by presenting them in the order of time. By extending the argument, one can say the small periods of time are parts—past, present, future—of a larger whole. One of the great arguments between Parmenides and Heraclitus (*c.* 500 B.C.) was over the movement of change implied by this concept of time. Parmenides said change is illusory and that reality is fixed, eternal, and absolute. Heraclitus denied permanence and insisted that change is a characteristic of everything, without exception. Heraclitus' influence in ideas about time in Western thought is obvious.

The Bible, too, speaks of time in this chronological sense. But it contributes almost nothing to any theory of time. Rather its contribution lies in its use of *kairos*. The best translation of *kairos* may be "the time of opportunity or fulfillment." This theme is found often in the Old Testament. Although aware of time in the sense of a series of events, the biblical writers—particularly the prophets—sought to demonstrate that time comes laden with God-given possibilities. And he who really has understood time will dwell upon interpreting its possibilities, not upon the quality of orderliness. Jesus is depicted as one who came in the "fullness of time" (*kairos*). His preaching, life, death, and resurrection are presented as having proclaimed the true importance of life in time. (Romans 5:6; Galatians 4:4; Ephesians 1:10)

The debate referred to earlier between Parmenides and Heraclitus points to a fundamental issue in considering the issue of time. Some see time negatively, as the destroyer of everything that exists. Others see it positively, as offering the possibilities for new creativity. But, of course, neither view can exclude the other and remain faithful to men's experience of time. How one finally values time is not possible by an analysis of time, for it leads to a logical contradiction.

Theology derived from the biblical testimony about time has traditionally seen it positively because it is one aspect of God's good creation. There is, to be sure, a great problem in connection with the evaluation of time and eternity. But, even so, from the standpoint of faith in God, time must finally be seen as good. In order to see it as good, every moment in time must be seen as a potential time of doing and being the will of God. Recent theologians under the influence of existential philosophy have argued the present is the crucial moment in time. It demands a decision to be faithful or not. And if the decision is "no," then this moment, as soon as it is past, is lost. But part of the meaning of God's graciousness in this view is that another moment succeeds this one. God comes from the future and demands a "yes" or a "no" in each present. Time is the heart of the matter, in such a view. (*see Eternal, Existential, History*) J.B.W.

TIMELESS (*see Eternal*)

Tithe Tithing, the giving of one's possessions to the Lord, was a custom among the early Hebrews. It was essentially a practice belonging to a rural, agricultural society in that it recognized God as Lord of the land, and, at the same time, expressed thankfulness for his bounty. In Numbers 18:21 all tithes in Israel are given to the Levites " 'for an inheritance, in return for their service which they serve

. . . in the tent of meeting.'" Since the Levites possessed no land, the tithe was their main source of support. On their part, the Levites were to give a tenth of what they received to the priests. A somewhat different practice is suggested in Deuteronomy 14:22-29. According to that passage, every third year a tithe of the produce of the fields was to be paid to the poor.

The New Testament mentions the tithe in two places only: in Matthew 23:23 (compare Luke 11:42) and in Hebrews 7:5 ff. The former passage presents Jesus as criticizing the Pharisees, who have tithed "'mint and dill and cummin, and have neglected the weightier matters of the law, justice and mercy and faith. . . .'" The passage in Hebrews in no way suggests tithing as a Christian practice but is merely a part of the writer's argument that the priest-king Melchizedek is a type of Christ. There is in fact no basis in the New Testament for the practice of tithing. The New Testament view is that all of life is to be presented to God (see Romans 12:1). (see Stewardship) E.L.T.

TORAH (see Law)

Transcendent The word derives from a combination of Latin words, which together mean "to go beyond" or "to surpass," as in, "God transcends our conceptions of him." The word suggests an image of space. Its opposite is "immanent." It is important to observe this contrast alongside other images. For example, God may be called "eternal," meaning he is not bound by time. The problem of how to speak of God's location vis-a-vis space is common to many religious traditions.

Primitive religions seem to have regarded the presence of the divine in nature. Since they viewed the divine as located, they held an immanent view of the gods. As cultures and civilizations developed, the notions of divinity as immanent remained, as in Greece and Rome, to a large extent. Natural religion is a corollary of such a view.

Other religious traditions, such as Judaism and Islam, along with Christianity, have regarded God as above man and the world. Some ancient philosophers, such as Plato (c. 427-347 b.c.), held that view also. Neoplatonists kept this philosophical tradition alive in Western culture. Some religious sects within Judaism, Islam, and Christianity have maintained along with neoplatonists that this transcendent God is to be experienced only by mystical visions. They argue that the world of matter and the senses is an illusion, i.e., not real. In more extreme cases the material world is even regarded as evil.

The mainstream in these three religions, however, has traditionally held God to be both immanent (knowable within and through the world) and at the same time transcendent. This paradox is crucial, especially within Christian theology. It raises particularly the necessity for revelation—for God to disclose himself to man. Some parts of the Bible seem to support such a view. One of the clearest places where this paradox appears is in the doctrine of creation. The world, because it was created by God, is good. But because it is a creation, and not the creator, it is not the supreme good. This paradox has enabled Christianity to avoid the temptation to make an idol out of a doctrine. The transcendent-immanent God is not exhausted by his creation. Idolatry means taking the world or some portion of it as God. The problem, however, is how to avoid a view that the world is evil by overemphasizing the transcendence of God, and how to avoid idolatry by overemphasizing the immanence of God. Christianity has tended to err more in the former direction than the latter.

Certain neo-orthodox theologians have tended to overemphasize transcendence. Karl Barth (1886-   ) stressed, in his early theology, the notion of Soren Kierkegaard that there is an "infinite, qualitative difference between God and man." This makes God "wholly other" and tends to devalue the goodness of the world. Barth was over-reacting to Protestant liberalism, in which the immanence of God in the world was stressed. Liberalism stressed reason, as did science, and sought to harmonize theology and science. Neo-orthodoxy has sought to recover a biblical view of revelation that cannot be discovered by scientific methods.

Transcendence is not the same as supernatural. Some theologians have used it in a way that implied that it was. Supernatural means something other than natural and may be meaningfully connected with transcendence or immanence. Supernatural often refers to those experiences that apparently cannot be explained by natural causes. Science, for example, cannot deal within its own methodology with supernatural events. (see Attributes, Dogmatics, Holy, Immanent, Natural theology, Providence, Revelation) J.B.W.

Transubstantiation From the Latin words, trans, meaning "across" or "over," and substantia, meaning "substance," it is the traditional Roman Catholic view that the bread and wine of the sacrament are changed into the body and blood of Christ. It holds that the accidents (the taste, appearance, etc.) of the bread and the wine remain the same, but that the essential substance actually becomes the body and blood of our Lord. (see Communion [Holy], Substance). G.E.S.

TRESPASS (see Sin)

Trinity This word comes from the two words tri-unity, which mean "three united" or "three in one," and has to do with the being or essential nature of God the Father, Jesus Christ the Son, and the Holy Spirit. The doctrine of the Trinity teaches that God is one in substance or being, but that there are three essential distinctions in his person. This does not mean that there are three Gods, but that one God reveals or unfolds himself to man through the Logos (or divine Word) in his Son, Jesus Christ, and in the comforter, the Holy Spirit. The word "person," as used in discussions of the Trinity, is the Greek word *hypostases* (hy-poh-*stay*-sees), which means "under the essence."

Though the word "Trinity" is not contained in the New Testament as such, there is evidence that this idea is implied by the biblical writers. See Matthew 28:19; 2 Corinthians 13:14; and Hebrews 6:1-8.

In the first centuries of Christianity, *subordinationism* held that both the second and third persons of the Trinity were in a secondary relationship to God the Father. *Modalism* (*moh*-dah-lism), on the other hand, tended toward the denial of any distinction between God and Christ and taught that there was one absolute God, and that Father, Son, and Holy Spirit were merely modes ("forms") of God. In this view God showed himself under three names just as an actor might wear three different masks to play three different roles (*persona*) in a play. Another view held that the Father had died leaving his work to the Son (*Patripassianism*). The Cappadocian Fathers (Basil, Gregory of Nyssa, and Gregory Nazianzus) seemed to be the first of the Fathers to give their attention to the doctrine of the Trinity. The Councils of Nicaea (325) and Constantinople (381) affirmed the belief that God's nature is not divided, but that God is the Creator, the Son is the Redeemer, and the Holy Spirit is God's continuing presence in the world. Tertullian (*c.* 160-230) is credited with having used the formula, "one substance, three persons." Augustine (354-430) set forth the position that has become traditional and was of greatest consequence in the early church. He conceived of God as a personal Father and as one divine reality, with three co-eternal and co-equal distinctions, which he called "persons." God's divine nature is fully in each person and though they are self-subsistent, the presence of each is sensed by the others. Augustine's analogy was one of self-consciousness, in which the Son or Word came as the intellect or mind of God, and the Holy Spirit as the will with a bond of unity existing between them.

Augustine's idea of the Trinity was expanded by Thomas Aquinas (*c.* 1225-74) in his *Summa Theologica*. The Reformers seem not to have doubted the doctrine of the Trinity and did not dispute it. In more recent times, major attention has been given this doctrine by Karl Barth (1886-   ). Barth defines the Trinity in terms of God's unity as Revealer (Father), Revelation (Son), and Revealedness (Holy Spirit).

Barth further rejects the use of the word "person," since its meaning has changed so much since its first use. Emil Brunner (1889-1967) sees the Trinity doctrine as secondary and is primarily concerned about the *kerygma* of the church. (*see Christology*, KERYGMA, *Spirit*)

TRISAGION (*see Sanctus*)

Truth *Truth is derived from an old English word, troew, which means loyal or honest. At this level it means conformity with what is real or actual. Any assertion that claims to be true is immediately confronted with the question, "How can this be verified?" (see Verification) The word or concept of truth plays a significant role in religion, and the problem of verification is acute, because religion proceeds mainly from faith or intuition. Yet the truth of faith is not always subject to the kind of proofs reason often demands. Of course, it is equally difficult to deny such truth claims, and this often raises the issue of authority to settle disputed truth claims within a particular religious tradition.*

Is truth an absolute, fixed reality that awaits discovery, as the idealistic rationalist would have it? Or is truth a functional or operational assumption, which is tested by its pragmatic effectiveness, as the pragmatist or relativist would have it? Is truth a way of knowing or a way of doing? Some of these issues must be rooted out to gain real insight into the issue of truth.

The Bible preserves several interesting and significant attitudes toward truth. In the Old Testament truth is presented as an attribute that properly belongs to God (Psalms 25:5; 86:11; 145:18). In such usage it is clear that truth refers to faithfulness in the sense of reliability or trustworthiness. By analogy, wherever truth is used in reference to men in the Old Testament, it generally suggests that such persons are dependable or consistent.

In the New Testament the shift in language to Greek produces a subtle and highly significant shift in connotation. In Greek the word for truth is *alētheia*. Literally the word means "unveiling" or "unveiled." In this sense it is clear that truth refers to the actual state of things rather than to inaccurate reports of them. Further, according to Plato (*c.* 427-347 B.C.) thinking is the human activity by which man gains access to truth. Armed with such truth, a person is expected to behave in a manner consistent with the truth. Put the other way around, wrong action is due to ignorance of the truth. In such a view the role of reason is obvious. During the Greek era, philosophers and others commonly assumed that revelation rather than reason was the means for attaining truth.

The fusion of the Hebrew and Greek concepts of truth led to some important nuances in the New Testament. Aside from the extensive use of the concept "truth" in the writings of John, it is important to note that other uses imply that Christian revelation has displaced all other ways of apprehending the truth for Christians. This is the meaning of: "In him [Christ] you also, who have heard the word of truth, the gospel of your salvation. . . ." (Ephesians 1:13) Such usage carries a strong connotation of truth as something intellectually apprehended. ‍

In the Gospel of John the idea of truth receives its fullest biblical explanation. Truth is equated with revelation and refers explicitly to the divine-human encounter. Truth is the self-manifestation of God to man. It is not a general idea, as in typical English usage, but refers strictly to God's self-disclosure in Christ. Truth is not a matter for rational speculation but rather is an awakener of conscience, a call to be obeyed or disobeyed. Truth is to be done: "But he who does what is true comes to the light, that it may be clearly seen that his deeds have been wrought in God." (John 3:21)

The options are basically two-fold, with a large number of variations on the themes. On the one hand, truth is connected with ways of knowing, and in this regard reason and revelation are the crucial concerns. On the other hand, truth is connected with a mode of existence that is mainly concerned, not with how truth is known, but rather with the life that results from it. In the long history of Christian theology the concern for truth hinges upon these attitudes toward the nature of truth.

By now it must be clear that truth is a complex of issues. One must take into account both the *nature* of truth, which is a universal kind of concern, and the *criteria* for evaluating truth claims in any given context, which is a very particular concern. In the recent philosophical movement known as language analysis, Stephen Toulmin, a philosopher of ordinary language, has offered some helpful suggestions in dealing with these two questions. Regarding the *nature* of truth, Toulmin proposes that we think of truth as equal with "whatever is worthy of belief." Toulmin argues that the criteria for evaluating truth claims in any given category will vary from case to case. For example, in physical science a hypothesis may achieve the status of "truth" (*i.e.*, be worthy of belief) if it can be verified under experimental conditions. But it would be a "category mistake" to impose this kind of empirical verification upon a theological proposition. In the case of theology other criteria have to be evoked. Clearly, then, by making such distinctions it is possible to remove many of the false conflicts between science and theology. The basic requirement is to avoid the misleading and mistaken path of category mistakes.

Such distinctions lead to several implications in the theological concern for truth. First, theologians have to be very careful in what they say can be known from revelation. If one enters the realm of how men know what they claim to know, one must be willing to accept the criteria (tests) for establishing truth appropriate to epistemology (the study of knowledge). In order to gain an audience among epistemologists, theologians have to fight the battle again and again for the knowledge value of analogy, symbols, and myths, which are the language forms of theological discourse. Second, the connection between truth claims and morality must be continually examined. The theological danger is that the things that Christian men do will be used as measurements for whether or not they have really "heard" the truth of Christian revelation. For example, when Christian truth gets connected with ethics, it often gets said that no Christian can possibly do this or that. Or, it is said that a Christian *must* do this or that—*e. g.*, he must be a pacifist. But such attitudes too often reflect a failure to recognize the complex connection between intellect and will. Further, such a view of truth borders too often on a "works righteousness" view requiring a Christian to earn his salvation rather than receiving it as God's gift. (*see Analogy, Epistemology, Experience, Language, Revelation, Verification*) J.B.W.

TWELVE (*see Number*)

TYPOLOGY (*see Fall, Methodology*)

ULTIMATE CONCERN (*see Faith, Religion*)

UNCIAL (*see Manuscript*)

Unconditional In relation to certain theological views of the nature of God, this term is closely connected to, if not identical with, the idea of the absolute. The literal meaning of unconditional is "without conditions" and means, in reference to God, that he is unchangeable. As such it would refer to the aseity and impossibility of God. In other contexts it may refer to God in relation to his creation; *e.g.*, God's justice toward his creatures may be said to be unconditional. It is a less widely used concept by theologians today than at other periods in Christian history, although Paul Tillich (1886-1965) made very suggestive use of the concept. (*see Absolute, Aseity, Contingent*) J.B.W.

UNCONSCIOUS (*see Consciousness*)

UNDERSTANDING (*see Epistemology, Self-understanding*)

UNITY (of Church—*see Catholic, Ecumenical*; of God —*see Shema, Theism, Trinity*)

UNIVERSE (*see Cosmogony, Cosmology, World view*)

UTILITARIAN (*see Hedonism*)

Value Values have been considered in four different ways. (1) A thing is considered to be of value if it is useful or helpful. (2) Value is considered in relation to what it accomplishes, as a means to an end. (3) Value may also be viewed as contained in the object. (4) Something may be considered as of value in and of itself. The opposite of value is "evil" or "worthlessness." A thing is frequently labeled as valuable if it satisfies human need.

In philosophical thought the term "value" has been primarily used in two basic ways. There are moral values; for example, it is good for man to be honest. Man has certain obligations that he should carry out faithfully. A moral value is something that man should do or an obligation that man should fulfill. In philosophical thought value is also used to indicate that something is good separate and apart from any obligation. Health, wine, and knowledge may be called good or labeled as having value. Value in this second sense is an answer to what might be called a pre-moral question. Man is faced with this basic question: What is the good life? Or what is worth having in life? To answer this question is to declare certain things to be of value.

In the thought of Plato (*c.* 427-347 B.C.) certain "objective ideas" are considered to have a real and eternal existence. These ideals are the really valuable things in life. Man's life is of value to the extent that he participates in these ideal forms.

H. Richard Niebuhr (1894-1962), and Christian theology in general, has considered value in terms of relationships. Man is of value because he is of value to God. Man's neighbor is of value because of his value to God. Value is derived or bestowed. Situation ethics affirm that nothing is of value in itself. Value is relative to the circumstances of a particular situation. This way of talking about value is based on three assumptions. (1) No set of facts proves something to be a value. (2) A value is always relative to the persons involved. (3) The practical question, "Does it work?" (or, "What are the results of this particular choice?") is central for the Christian concept of value. If something does not benefit man then it is of no value. (*see Idealism, Relativity, Social Gospel*) J.S.H.

VATICAN II (*see Aggiornamento, Ecumenical*)

VELLUM (*see Manuscript*)

Verification (veh-ruh-fuh-*kay*-shuhn) *This word means to judge whether a sentence is true or not. Ancient philosophy thought of truth as fixed and unchanging. Later Christian thinkers agreed. Both Christians and others thought of reason and faith as ways to find truth. With the rise of science in the eighteenth century, a new standard was set for deciding on truth: Could an idea or a sentence be tested by the senses? If you could not see, hear, taste, feel, or touch the things to which a sentence pointed, how could you tell if it was true? Christian thinkers took various positions toward this new standard: (1) Some agreed with it. Since "God" is an idea that cannot be tested by the senses, the idea meant nothing. (2) Some disagreed and went on talking about God, love, and eternal life as they had before. (3) Some said faith verified itself. If God reveals his truth to man, the truth is tested by the person who believes, not by using tests of science.*

From the Latin, this term literally means the process of establishing the truth of an assertion. Only where there are challenges to the claims made for any truth assertion is verification an issue. Any consideration of verification procedures hinges upon the question of truth itself. Since theology makes claim to be a witness to the truth, it must attend to the characteristics of revealed truth, and the relation between its witness to truth and other witnesses.

For the classical philosophical tradition all considerations of truth presupposed that it was fixed, eternal, and absolute. It was thought to be rational and accessible through the use of right reason. The classical theology of Christianity found the philosophical assumption quite compatible with its own views of revelation. According to such a view, revelation brought to man truth that could be accepted by faith. For many such theologians, truth was thought to be the same whether received in faith or discerned by reason: God is one; God is truth; truth must be one. Experience of revelation that gave rise to faith and reasonable reflection that gave rise to certainty were thought to verify truth claims. But such a unifying view of truth and verification was not destined to go unchallenged.

As reason gained its independence from revelation in philosophy and science after the seventeenth century, the means of verification were altered. On the one hand, to judge the truth of assertions of pure reason, the laws of logic assumed the role of verifying principles. Since reason was assumed to conform directly with reality and its laws, then a demonstration that any assertion conformed to the laws of right reason was taken as self-evident verification of its truth. On the other hand, advocates of empiricism insisted that only assertions that could be empirically demonstrated were verifiable, such as scientific experiments. Gradually, under the impact of the remarkable advances made in scientific investigations, and under the effects of the demonstrated limits of pure reason, the empirical view gained ascendancy.

Meanwhile, theological truth claims were subjected to rigorously critical examination. The older views of revelation, like those of reason, fell prey to the mind-set of an increasingly secular world. As a result theology, along with philosophy, tried to reconceive its task. Classical metaphysics ceased to be the major function of philosophy. Also, systematic theology became a less typical style for theology.

In the changing intellectual milieu the means of verification were also reconsidered. One popular device in philosophy was that "true" was restricted only to those assertions that are empirically verifiable. Although the criteria (tests) for verification on so limited a basis were soon refuted, the effect of the episode lingers among contemporary philosophers. In such a situation, theology generally took recourse to one of three options. (1) It accepted this principle of verification by empirical means only, and by and large gave up the central affirmations of traditional theology. For example, it is impossible to demonstrate empirically even the very reality of God. If this is necessary to verify God's reality, then the assertion of its truth can no longer be made. Of course, it is equally impossible to disprove God's reality. So theological agnosticism resulted. (2) It ignored the recent developments in philosophy, or denied the validity of such limits and continued to discuss theological truth assertions as if they were made within a context in which traditional principles of verification were viable. (3) It claimed that faith needed no other verification than the experience of it. As it is sometimes put, revelation is self authenticating. It evokes faith in the person who experiences revelation. None of these seem to be universally persuasive in the second half of the twentieth century. Many theologians have been forced to demand that all serious thinkers re-examine the issue of truth and consequently the means of verification. For without such rethinking, not only theology, but also many of the most basic human realities would seem to be unverifiable. (*see Language, Truth*) J.B.W.

Versicle (*ver*-seh-kuhl) A versicle may occur at any point in the service of worship and is the recitation of a small verse by the priest or minister, followed by a congregational response. Example: "The Lord be with you . . . and with thy Spirit." G.E.S.

VERSIONS (of Bible—*see Canon, Septuagint*)

Vesper Originally used for office at the early evening hour, the word vesper now designates a service of worship that occurs in late afternoon or early evening. It is also known by the name "evensong," which is the English name for vespers and has been called "eventide." (*see Office*) G.E.S.

Via negativa (*vee*-ah neh-guh-*tee*-vah) From the Latin, meaning the "negative way," this term has a long history in Christian theology. For those theologians who have used the concept it has been applied to man's ability to know God. Since God is limitless and every ability man possesses is limited, then it is more fitting to say what God is not than to try to say what he is. For example, because all human experiences are limited by time and in space, God must be eternal (timeless and spaceless). Perhaps the most notable advocate of such a position was a medieval theologian, Nicholas of Cusa (1401-64). Also, in general the mystical tradition has used the term. When one has said all that he knows God is not, that is, when one has gone all the way on the *via negativa*, then one may learn what God is, but such intuition is beyond knowledge. (*see Faith, Methodology*) J.B.W.

Vicar In the Anglican or Episcopal Church, a minister who has charge of a mission or a dependent parish of which the bishop is the rector is a vicar. He may also be a priest in charge of a chapel within a parish. In England, the vicar is a priest of an Anglican parish whose tithes are owned by a bishop, a spiritual business corporation, or a layman. (*see Curate, Rector*) G.E.S.

Virgin birth   The birth narratives in Matthew and Luke say that Jesus was conceived in Mary by the action of the Holy Spirit. Matthew quotes Isaiah 7:14, where, however, the Hebrew word may mean only "young woman," instead of "virgin." The Scriptures seem to speak of a "virgin conception" more nearly than a "virgin birth."

Sometime in the second century, when the earliest part of the Apostles' Creed was shaped (see Creed), the phrase, "born of the Virgin Mary," was used, referring to Jesus. At this time the purpose of such a phrase was probably to affirm that Jesus was truly a historical person. "Was there really a person named Jesus?" people may have asked. "If so, who was his mother?" His mother, the church replied, was Mary—the Mary called the Virgin.

The doctrine of the Virgin Mary remained in the background, accepted by Christians, but not usually an important doctrine, until the nineteenth century. In 1835 David Friedrich Strauss (1808-74) published *The Life of Jesus Critically Examined*, in which he called attention to many of the inconsistencies in the Bible itself. For example, the genealogies (Matthew 1:2-16; Luke 3:23-38) are not the same. About the same time, Friedrich Schleiermacher (1768-1834) wrote that the doctrine of the virgin birth is superfluous, since Christ can be considered the Redeemer without it.

Fundamentalism (which see) rose in opposition to the criticisms of men like Strauss and Schleiermacher. It considered virgin birth to be literally true, and that Jesus could not be considered the Son of God without it.

In recent years, the doctrine has been accepted by many as an expression of truth, rather than as a literal fact. James Smart, for example, interprets it to mean, in combination with the phrase, "conceived by the Holy Spirit," the "completeness and unbrokenness" of Jesus' relation with God. (*see Legend*)

Virtue   Virtue in its most basic sense refers to the internal power that leads one to habitually perform good deeds. Virtue is the opposite of vice. A virtuous man decides consciously to do his duty because of who he is. He is altruistic in that he has moved beyond self-centeredness to concern for others. Virtue includes more than a warm feeling or affection for others—it involves a concern to do the right. In classical Greek thought virtue is the ease or speed with which one acted justly. A course of action that is always right may also be called a virtue. Four cardinal virtues were listed in Greek thought: prudence, temperance, fortitude, and justice. Man consciously seeks these virtues, since reason exercises control over the passions.

In order to help man in this basic task of "self-development" the four cardinal virtues were expanded into rather long lists of things to do (virtues) and not to do (vices). The New Testament writers borrowed some of these lists of virtues and vices and included them in their writings (see Galatians 5:19-23; Colossians 3:12-14; Romans 1:28-32). The Christian, it is assumed, will do good and avoid evil. The Christian has been freed from the evil powers that cause a man to do bad deeds. He is a slave to God and thus uses his life in doing good deeds. First Corinthians, Chapter 13, places a special emphasis on the virtues of love, faith, and hope.

Augustine (354-430) emphasizes the unity of virtue. When he talks of the "four cardinal virtues" he talks of them as the fourfold division of virtue. They are not in competition with one another. Man does not need to try to structure virtues in the order of their importance. They belong together and should be viewed as a whole. All Christian virtues have one common basis: they arise out of Christian love.

Roman Catholic theology assumes that natural man cannot be educated to do the right things. God inserts his grace into man. This happens through the seven sacraments of the church. God's grace once infused in man takes man out of the natural order. Man is no longer concerned with the development of his natural abilities for their own sake. He now sees all of his natural abilities as serving a supernatural end. The three Christian virtues, faith, hope, and love, are referred to as the theological virtues. Once these three virtues are properly understood, then the four cardinal virtues (prudence, temperance, fortitude, and justice) take on a new significance. They now represent opportunities to be used in service to God. They can be learned and cultivated. But in the past man used these virtues for the wrong reason. He used them to build up his own pride in himself. The Christian is to use these natural virtues in service of the supernatural virtues.

The Protestant understanding of virtue is built on the idea that God has done more for man than man can ever repay. Man is grateful for the forgiveness he has received. This gratitude shows itself in man's attempt to do the will of God.

Present day thought is recognizing more and more the fact that any list of good deeds will sometimes need to be violated. Thus, for a man to follow always a certain list of virtues may be a bad thing. There may be occasions when love demands that a man tell a lie. Thus, Christian thinkers assume that love is the only virtue that should always be followed. (see Character, Habit, Natural law) J.S.H.

VISION (see End, Teleology)

VITALISM (see Life)

Vocation The Latin word *vocatio* means literally "to call out." The Old Testament understanding of "vocation" is based on God's call of Israel to be his people. The Hebrew word for vocation is ordinarily used in the sense "to call" or "cry out" (Judges 9:7; Isaiah 6:4). God summons Israel to be his people, and that is their life's work (Isaiah 43:1; 49:1; Hosea 11:1-2). In Second Isaiah the term "vocation" is closely related to the term "election." God has "elected" or "chosen" Israel, and in this election God's people find the purpose of their lives. In the Old Testament vocation may also be used to indicate the trade in which a man is working. In the New Testament the Greek word *kaleo*, which means "to call," is used to refer to the fact that the Christian is called to follow Christ. The Christian is "summoned," "invited," or "called" to participate in the work of God. Jesus of Nazareth worked in this task and showed what the Christian is to do. Thus, his life has become for the Christian a summons to participate in the same work.

In the Middle Ages there was a marked tendency to distinguish between sacred and secular work. God can best be served by man working in sacred, that is, church-related, jobs. Secular jobs (such as medicine, the law, agriculture) are of value. They serve a purpose and are needed. However, in the Middle Ages these jobs were viewed as being of less service to God than were church jobs. The monastic life is the highest calling, since it is the farthest removed from any contact with the secular world. The Reformation reacted against this understanding of what a Christian is called to do. The Reformers concluded that the cloistered life is not necessarily a good thing. Martin Luther (1483-1546) tried to eliminate the distinction between religious and sacred jobs. He saw all obligations as religious. There are no special religious obligations. The love flowing from faith takes the form of specific and concrete service to the neighbor.

Work is sometimes understood as a curse or punishment placed on man because of his sinfulness (Genesis 3:17-19). Traditionally the Christian church has rejected this understanding of work. Rather, work is a part of man's natural life. Man's life is enriched and extended by his work. Work is also viewed as man's duty or obligation as in the view that if a man will not work he should not eat.

Vocation can be further understood by contrasting it with four words. (1) The word "occupation" means "taking possession." A man's occupation is the job that he takes as his own. He takes this as his own, and it occupies his time and attention. (2) "Work" is more specifically something a man does, such as teaching or farming. (3) The word "career" refers to the course of life, or profession, a person is following. (4) The term "calling" is used to describe the state of being divinely called. God summons man to do a specific job. This is sometimes understood as meaning that man hears a voice speak to him. Others use the term "calling" to mean that they "feel" that God wants them to be a missionary or a teacher, for example. However, the New Testament seems to say that God "calls" man to the life of faith (see Romans 8:28; 1 Corinthians 1:26; 1 Peter 2:21) rather than to a specific task. It is clear that every Christian is "called" in the sense that he has received the Holy Spirit, which accompanies baptism. (see Baptism, Spirit)

The term "vocation" implies that man has both a responsibility and an opportunity to make a constructive contribution in this world. Man responds, then, to his calling by means of work, occupation, or career; but vocation remains something more than the specific means. (*see Holy, Works*) J.S.H.

VOLUNTARISM (*see Freedom*)

WELTANSCHAUUNG (*see World view*)

WHITSUNDAY (*see Pentecost*)

WHOLE (*see Monism, Perfection*)

WILL (*see Freedom*)

WISDOM (*see Courage, Epistemology, Pre-existence*)

Witness The idea of witness appears in both Old and New Testaments. It is used in connection with the taking of an oath (Genesis 21:30). In some cases God is said to be witness (1 Samuel 12:5; Romans 1:9). Witnesses are necessary in legal matters (Numbers 35:30; Jeremiah 32:10). In the Fourth Gospel the legal witness idea is used in connection with Jesus' person and claims (John 5:31 *ff*.; 8:13 *ff*.). The same Gospel presents John the Baptist as a witness to Jesus. In fact, witness to Jesus as the Son of God is John the Baptist's sole function in the Fourth Gospel. The term is applied to one who testifies to God

(Isaiah 43:9-12) and to the work of Christ (Luke 24:48). It is applied, further, to the men of faith listed in Hebrews 11:4–12:1. An important expression of "witness" is the death of the martyr. The martyr witnesses through his death (Revelation 17:6). In Revelation 1:5, Jesus is called "the faithful witness." But the word "martyr" in the Greek is the same as that for "witness." It is easy to see how the idea of martyrdom passes over into the concept of witness. Jesus himself was the proto-martyr. Stephen, Polycarp, and the long line of the martyrs whose blood became the "seed of the church" testified to the Lordship of Christ, and so became witnesses to the faith.

In addition to the witness of the martyrs, and in fact the more normal method, was the witness made through preaching. The word *euangelion* means "good news," and for the Christians the good news, "the gospel," was the redemption God had wrought through the event of Jesus: his life, death, and resurrection. The importance of early Christian preaching in this regard is plainly stated by Paul in his Letter to the Romans: "But how are men to call upon him in whom they have not believed? And how are they to believe in him of whom they have never heard? And how are they to hear without a preacher?" (10:14) One might say that the career of Paul, with its stress on preaching, was one of witness to the gospel as he understood it.

As time passed the message of the Christian church needed consolidation. In the second century, the church was faced with the threat of heretical movements. We see in the Pastoral Epistles (1 and 2 Timothy and Titus), attributed to Paul but not written by him, an attempt to state the "true faith" in the face of heretical threats. In the latter part of the second century there was an increasing attempt to state the faith in terms of the apostolic norm. (see Normative) The true faith was thought to be apostolic faith. In that period the witness of the church was a witness in terms of what was considered to be early and apostolic proclamation.

Changing conditions call for new approaches to the Christian witness. But the instinct of second-century Christians in looking to the classical or New Testament period for the normative gospel was true enough. Departure from it represents a perversion of Christian witness. Yet the New Testament proclamation must be communicated in relevant ways to modern man if it is to be vital and meaningful. The task of relevant witness is one that perennially faces the Christian church. (*see Apostle, Authority, Evangelism*, KERYGMA) E.L.T.

Word   The term "word" is important in both the Old and New Testaments. In the Old Testament God is represented as speaking to various persons: he makes a covenant with Abraham (Genesis 17:15-21); he gives the Ten Commandments on Sinai (Exodus

20:1 *ff*.); he speaks through the utterance of the prophet (Amos 7:15-16; 1:3*a*; Ezekiel 3:16). In Genesis 1 creation takes place through the utterance of God. These passages are only illustrations of a characteristic and pervasive feature of Hebrew religious thought. Behind the word, of course, lies the powerful and creative thought that is in the mind of God.

When we come to the New Testament, we find that in certain cases the term becomes a title for Jesus. The best example of this is in the Prologue of John's Gospel (1:1-18). It is of interest to note that Word as a title for Jesus is not found elsewhere in the Gospel, although many others are found there. Perhaps John was using a "hymn to the Word" as a source and adapted it to serve as an introduction to his story of Jesus.

The term "Word" (*Logos*) had several meanings in New Testament times. The Stoics, popular philosophers of the day, thought of it as divine Reason. According to them, every man possesses a spark of the divine, and it is his duty to fan that spark into a blaze. The term is used by others of the time, such as Philo, an outstanding Jewish thinker of Alexandria in Egypt. But in Philo the Word is not identified with a person as it is in John. The Gnostics used it in their systems of thought, which attempted to bridge the gulf between Spirit and the material world.

As used in John, the Word is Jesus. The Word, who was with God in the beginning, came to dwell among men. As John puts it, "And the Word became flesh and dwelt among us. . . ." (John 1:14) In coming into the world, the Word reveals God. Those who respond to God's revelation in the Word find salvation, which John's Gospel characteristically calls eternal life.

A note should be added regarding other uses of the term "word" in the New Testament. Sometimes the term is applied to the message as a whole (John 8:31), or to the Christian gospel (Romans 10:8). In popular usage it has come to mean the Scriptures. This last use is no doubt an extension of the importance attached to God's speaking. But the idea of the Word as Scripture is not particularly biblical. (*see* Gnostic, Incarnation, Revelation, Stoic) E.L.T.

Works Work in its most general sense includes everything man does, accomplishes, or causes to happen. In the Old Testament work is man's lot in creation. God gives the command and man responds. Man's work is faithful service to God. Paul understands God's work to be the reconciling of the whole world to himself through Christ. Man through faith may accept this work and thus be placed in the right relationship to God, neighbor, and self. The Christian man is thus not working to earn God's love. He accepts God's love in faith and responds in faithful service. James points out that faith shows itself in the work that the Christian does (2:18-26).

Early Christian leaders were impressed with the necessity of Christians doing "good works." Tertullian (*c.* 160-230) understood the role of man's works in relation to a legalistic background. To satisfy God, whom he has offended by sin, man is called on to perform good works. The church sets forth the kind of works believed to be acceptable. Furthermore, it offers the sacraments to strengthen man for his work.

Martin Luther (1483-1546) rebelled against the idea that man can and should do good work in order to earn merit for himself. The special works that the church calls man to do, such as the disciplines of monastic life, are self-chosen and represent false holiness. Genuine service to God is man's faithful response to the claim of God, whom the Christian meets in the neighbor. Further, man's good works can play a role reconciling the neighbor to God. If man relates to the neighbor in order to "work out his own righteousness" he is using him for a selfish purpose.

The term "doing" is sometimes used to describe continual acts of love or service, regardless of whether such acts can be measured or not. A cup of cold water is a "deed," and one cannot measure the amount of good that it does.

"Making" refers to constructive acts that obtain results or produce effects. An engineer who helps construct a highway and a governor who helps establish a just society are both making something. Such acts are works that can be measured.

Traditionally, Christian love has been viewed as a deed and not a product. The Christian "does" good deeds, and they do not "make" character or produce rewards. In popular thought this distinction sometimes breaks down. Then a Christian is viewed as one who does good works, that is, who produces an effect you can see.

Some contemporary thinkers argue that "making" does contribute to "doing." This debate relates somewhat to the question of love of self versus love of neighbor. If I love myself, I value the good works that I "make." If I love my neighbor, I love the good works that I "do." Some thinkers argue that one must love himself before he can love the neighbor. You must be able to "make" something before you can "do" something. Others argue the Christian should love the neighbor and forget about the self. They believe "doing" is all and "making" is nothing. This last view is basically self-depreciating; the first view is basically self-realizing. (*see Neighbor, Self, Vocation*) J.S.H.

WORLD (*see Cosmogony, Cosmology, Secularization*)

World view The historian has to take into account the commonly accepted outlook of the age he is considering. This "outlook" embraces social, anthropological, religious, cosmological, philosophical, and scientific assumptions of the time. Sometimes the term "world view" is applied. Some scholars, however, prefer the German term *Weltanschauung* (*velt*-ahn-show-unk) ("conception of the world," "world philosophy") as being more expressive of the idea. For example, in ancient times, many people believed the universe was three-storied, with heaven above, earth in the middle, and the underworld beneath. This was part of the "world view" of men of the Bible. Today our "world view" is different. Most people today would think of the universe as an enormous expanse, moving out or in, with earth and man a mere speck in relation to the rest.

As applied to biblical history, it is the task of the interpreter to understand the world views lying behind the literature produced by the long and varied history of Hebrews and Christians. If he does not, the product of his work will undoubtedly be a modern view of the material, reflecting not the ancient world view but his own modern *Weltanschauung*. (*see* Hermeneutics, Miracle, Myth) E.L.T.

WORSHIP (*see* Liturgy)

YAHWEH (*see* Name, Source criticism)

YOM KIPPUR (*see* Atonement)

ZEBAH (*see* Sacrifice)